Red Nations offers an illuminating and informative overview of how the non-Russian republics of the Soviet Union experienced communist rule. It surveys the series of historical events that contributed to the break-up of the Soviet Union and evaluates their continuing resonance across post-Soviet states today.

Drawing from the latest research, Professor Smith offers comprehensive coverage of the revolutionary years, the early Soviet policies of developing nations, Stalin's purges and deportations of entire nationalities, and the rise of independence movements.

Through a single, unified narrative, this book illustrates how, in the post-Stalin period, many of the features of the modern nation-state emerged. Both scholars and students will find this an indispensable contribution to the history of the dissolution of the USSR, the reconstruction of post-Soviet society, and understanding the lives of non-Russian citizens from the years of the Russian Revolution through to the present day.

JEREMY SMITH is Professor of Russian History and Politics at the Karelian Institute, University of Eastern Finland. He has written extensively on the non-Russian nationalities of the Soviet Union, including two books: *The Bolsheviks and the National Question, 1917–1923* and *The Fall of Soviet Communism, 1985–1991*.

DISCARDED BY
CSU-PUEBLO LIBRARY

D1157464

RED NATIONS

The Nationalities Experience in and after the USSR

JEREMY SMITH

Professor of Russian History and Politics at the Karelian Institute,
University of Eastern Finland

CAMBRIDGE
UNIVERSITY PRESS

University Printing House, Cambridge CB2 8BS, United Kingdom

Published in the United States of America by Cambridge University Press, New York

Cambridge University Press is part of the University of Cambridge.

It furthers the University's mission by disseminating knowledge in the pursuit of education, learning, and research at the highest international levels of excellence.

www.cambridge.org
Information on this title: www.cambridge.org/9780521128704

© Jeremy Smith 2013

This publication is in copyright. Subject to statutory exception and to the provisions of relevant collective licensing agreements, no reproduction of any part may take place without the written permission of Cambridge University Press.

First published 2013

Printed in the United Kingdom by Clays, St Ives plc

A catalogue record for this publication is available from the British Library

Library of Congress Cataloguing in Publication data
Smith, Jeremy, 1964–
Red nations : the nationalities experience in and after the USSR / Jeremy Smith, Professor of Russian History and Politics at the Karelian Institute, University of Eastern Finland.
pages   cm
Includes bibliographical references and index.
ISBN 978-0-521-12870-4 (pbk.) – ISBN 978-0-521-11131-7
1. Federal government – Soviet Union.   2. Nationalism – Soviet Union – Republics – History.   3. Nationalism – Former Soviet republics – History – 20th century.   4. Minorities – Government policy – Soviet Union.   5. Former Soviet republics – History – 20th century.   I. Title.
JN6520.S8S59   2013
323.14709'04–dc23
2013006196

ISBN 978-0-521-11131-7 Hardback
ISBN 978-0-521-12870-4 Paperback

Cambridge University Press has no responsibility for the persistence or accuracy of URLs for external or third-party internet websites referred to in this publication, and does not guarantee that any content on such websites is, or will remain, accurate or appropriate.

In memory of my father, Christopher Smith,
and to my mother, Tessa Smith

Contents

Tables

Preface

In a perceptive article published in 1981, Radio Free Europe's Jaan Pennar wrote: 'It would seem, on the basis of the evidence on hand, that the Soviet Union is currently somewhat short on nationality policy.'[1] What Pennar understood more clearly than many of his contemporaries was that the national federal structure of the USSR, while ultimately derived from early Soviet policies, had for a long time ceased to provide the framework for implementing any coherent approach to the reconciliation of national differences with the Marxist-Leninist ideology of the Soviet state. Equally inadequate was a characterisation of the Soviet Union as a russifying regime intent on destroying those national differences – the survival and flourishing of national languages and cultures under the official patronage of the union republics in the late Soviet period provided sufficient evidence against such a characterisation, even if this was not always apparent to outside observers in the early 1980s. In reality, the last meaningful debates on Soviet nationality policy took place in 1924. What followed over the next sixty-seven years was a series of individual pronouncements and actions, ranging from the banal to the brutal, which at some times followed identifiable patterns or trends, but at other times were purely *ad hoc* and improvised responses to particular pressures. This 'shortage of nationality policy' is one of the considerations that has led me to write a book about the Soviet nationalities experience, rather than

[1] Jaan Pennar, 'Current Soviet Nationality Policy', *Journal of Baltic Studies*, 12, 1 (1981), 13.

Soviet nationalities policies, which has been the focus of much of my earlier work. The policies of the Soviet government, both broad ones and specific ones, undoubtedly impacted on the lives of non-Russians and are a part of this narrative, but I have tried to recount something more than that. Leaders in the Soviet republics and post-Soviet states, cultural figures and, at key moments, the broad population have also shaped the way the nationalities have developed and how they experienced Soviet and post-Soviet rule. In describing the nationalities experience I hope to have captured in general brushstrokes some of the cumulative effects of a combination of factors.

The story of the non-Russian nationalities of the USSR is, then, best presented as a more or less straightforward narrative, which this book aims to do. This is now possible thanks only to the determined efforts of a group of scholars who have been engaged in the study of the Soviet nationalities since the opening up of archives in Russia and elsewhere from the late 1980s. With the exception of a few sections, where I had recourse to my own archival research or one of the several excellent collections of published archival documents, I have drawn on the products of these scholars' research as published in books, journals and doctoral dissertations, or presented as conference papers. As soon as I started writing, it became obvious that in a single volume I could scarcely do justice to the rich and complex stories and cultures that these secondary works present. In particular, I was forced to narrow the focus of this account to the biggest nationalities of the USSR – specifically, the fourteen nationalities that, by the late 1940s, had their own union republics which, alongside the Russian Soviet Federative Socialist Republic, constituted the federal Union of Soviet Socialist Republics. The numerous smaller nationalities – Chechens, Tatars, Abkhaz, Jews and others, who either were granted autonomous status or were recognised as nationalities but with no territorial status – are dealt with only when their experience was of particular importance in the overall picture of the Soviet Union, as for example with the mass deportations of the 1940s. This is in no way to belittle the history and culture of these smaller peoples, many of whom are fully deserving of individual treatment. Not only was it impractical to cover the more than one hundred official nationalities of the USSR, but also a focus on the union republics allowed me to develop a number of the main themes of this book in a more coherent and comprehensible manner. Even when it comes to the larger nationalities, I have had to be selective as to which events or developments I have covered, and no doubt many readers will be disappointed at the neglect of particular episodes or the lack of application of particular themes to certain nationalities. In offering advance apologies to such readers, I also hope that the wide-ranging narrative presented here, however sketchy it may be, will increase understanding of the broader context in which particular nationalities experiences were played out.

I have also had to be selective in my use of secondary sources. No doubt there are important works that I have neglected, given the huge volume of literature on the peoples under consideration. There are numerous exceptions, but I have generally followed two rules of thumb – first, I have generally assumed that more recent works of scholarship are more reliable than earlier works. It is (or should be) generally the case in historical studies that later works build on and incorporate the findings of earlier scholarship. But in the case of the study of the Soviet Union there is a more specific reason for favouring later writings, namely the earlier inaccessibility of the archival sources which have been at the core of the most significant post-1990 studies, and which have considerably revised our appreciation of the experience of non-Russians throughout the Soviet period. The second rule of thumb is perhaps more controversial: I have preferred recent scholarship from outside the former Soviet Union, most of it in the English language, and have largely passed over the numerous works produced by scholars from Russia or from the nationalities which are treated in this book. Access to secondary sources was one factor, but an equally important consideration has been the high level of politicisation of history in the states that emerged from the rubble of the Soviet Union, including Russia. As a discipline, history has been neglected in many of the post-Soviet states, providing poor career opportunities and often subjected to the designs of political authorities and pursuing a functional nationalist agenda. In seeking to avoid works which are too biased or unreliable in terms of accuracy, I regret to have painted most scholars with the same brush, and to have neglected the contributions of those scholars who have succeeded in carrying out serious and objective research in the most trying of circumstances. As international contacts increase and opportunities for serious historical work develop, I look forward to the future acquaintance with and publications of those historians whose work deserves more attention than I have been able to afford them here.

An up-to-date account of the Soviet nationalities experience is long overdue – the last works that provided similarly broad coverage, Gerhard Simon's *Nationalism and Policy toward the Nationalities in the Soviet Union* and Bohdan Nahaylo and Victor Swoboda's *Soviet Disunion*, both appeared towards the end of the Soviet period.[2] Both are outstanding accounts for their time, and I have

[2] Gerhard Simon, *Nationalism and Policy toward the Nationalities in the Soviet Union: From Totalitarian Dictatorship to Post-Stalinist Society* (Boulder, CO: Westview Press, 1991); Bohdan Nahaylo and Victor Swoboda, *Soviet Disunion: A History of the Nationalities Problem in the USSR* (New York: Free Press, 1990).

drawn freely on them where there are gaps in later historiography. But neither was able to benefit from the fruits of archival research or to link the nationalities question in the USSR to its eventual collapse and the subsequent development of independent states. Since 1994, Yuri Slezkine's groundbreaking article, 'The USSR as a Communal Apartment, or How a Socialist State Promoted Ethnic Particularism',[3] has become the most commonly cited secondary work for an overview of Soviet nationalities questions. While Slezkine's conceptualization of the nationalities experience has deservedly informed subsequent understandings, the article's limited aims and coverage renders it insufficient as an overall account. Likewise, Ronald Suny's *The Revenge of the Past: Nationalism, Revolution, and the Collapse of the Soviet Union*[4] has inspired this book, among many other works, and established a clear framework for exploring the Soviet nationalities, but its focus is on the beginning and the end of the Soviet period and does not seek to provide an overall historical survey of the entire Soviet era.

This book draws on the work of the preceding twenty years of research to provide, in however sketchy a form, an overview of the Soviet nationalities experience. It is aimed at a broad audience – while some basic knowledge of the history of the USSR and its leading events and personalities is assumed, I have included a brief presentation of its main nationalities in Chapter 1 and have endeavoured to situate the nationalities experience within the overall development of the Soviet Union. Specialists on particular nationalities will be familiar with much of the content, but I hope will enjoy some benefit from seeing the subjects of their research

---

[3] Yuri Slezkine, 'The USSR as a Communal Apartment, or How a Socialist State Promoted Ethnic Particularism', *Slavic Review*, 53, 2 (Summer 1994), 414–52.

[4] Ronald Grigor Suny, *The Revenge of the Past: Nationalism, Revolution, and the Collapse of the Soviet Union* (Stanford University Press, 1993).

presented in a wider context. Researchers interested in other aspects of Soviet history, or of nations and nationalism in general, scholars of contemporary post-Soviet states looking for broad historical background, and students from a variety of disciplines looking for an introduction to the general topic or to the history of specific nationalities will, I hope, get some use from this book. I have also tried to write in a style that is accessible for the general reader, anyone who is just interested in the topic. Given the extent to which characterisations and understandings of the Soviet nationalities promulgated during the Cold War still persist not only in the popular imagination, but also among a large number of scholars from disciplines other than history, my purpose in synthesizing the products of recent research is to present as clear a picture as possible, albeit inevitably in a simplified form. In promoting understanding of the Soviet and post-Soviet nationalities experience, my book is only a starting point – there is plenty of excellent literature in circulation which goes into particular issues in much more detail, and there remains a good deal of work to be done.

As a historian, I have endeavoured to show how one set of circumstances and experiences derives from earlier ones. In particular I have attempted to link the post-Soviet experience to that of Soviet rule, and a central idea of this book is that the nation-building efforts which some approaches view as beginning in 1991 had in many respects been completed or embarked upon much earlier. For the most part, then, the book is chronologically structured, although there are exceptions. Most notably, I have gone back into the pre-Second World War history of the Baltic and other nationalities only at the point at which they entered the Soviet Union after 1945. Likewise, I have followed the story of the nationalities deported during the war through to their later Soviet experience in the same chapter. The book largely consists of narrative, and I have eschewed discursive theoretical or comparative discussion, while hoping that other scholars will find this book of use in such explorations of their own. I have, however, gone beyond pure narrative in analysing reasons and impacts of particular episodes. In doing so I have drawn extensively on analyses presented by other authors but, where such analysis is contested or unclear, I have drawn my own conclusions and it is exclusively my understanding that is presented in the text.

Rather than interrupt the narrative and analysis with historiographical discussion, for the most part I have indicated the sources of my own ideas or have presented alternative understandings in the footnotes. The main exception to this approach concerns the treatment of the great famine that caused horrific hardship and loss of life in Ukraine and elsewhere in 1932–1933. Here two considerations led me to include discussion of competing historiographies in the main text. First, western scholarship has become so polarised over the interpretation of the causes of the famine that I have so far found it hard to reach a conclusive opinion as to which is correct, or if the truth lies somewhere in between. Secondly, the debate among mostly western historians has become part of the history of Ukraine itself, especially when the *Holodomor* became a major part of the Ukrainian national self-narrative in the 1990s. Elsewhere, I hope that the notes, references and bibliography will provide sufficient guidance to those readers wishing to pursue in detail alternative interpretations of events.

The difficulty of standardising names and place names is a familiar one to writers dealing with sources and cultures which use different alphabets from that employed by the writer. This becomes especially problematic where changing states and regimes have resorted to wholesale policies of rewriting and renaming. As a rule, where there are widely accepted English-language versions of names and place names, I have used those rather than seeking to apply systematically any standard system of transliteration from Cyrillic or other alphabets. For many less well-known, or less-standardised, spellings, I have benefitted from the insistence of the post-Soviet states themselves in providing standard Latin forms of place names. Where place names have been deliberately changed, I have employed the name in use at the time which is being written about – so Petrograd, Leningrad and St Petersburg are all used for the same city. In a handful of cases, there is something of a grey area as to whether spellings have changed or a new name is in use. The most important of these is the country now almost universally known as Belarus, at the insistence of the independent state's political leaders in the early 1990s. At the time of the adoption of this official state name, there was extensive discussion as to the etymological link with the Russian name 'Belorussia'. The difference is in any case sufficiently great to consider there was never a Soviet Socialist Republic of Belarus, but a Belorussian SSR. Hence I use the name Belorussia for the Soviet republic, but Belarus for the post-Soviet state (and Belorussians up to 1991 but Belarusans afterwards).

I first embraced the idea of writing this book far too long ago, in 2000. I was only able to start serious work on it thanks to a generous Leverhulme Trust Study Abroad Fellowship awarded for 2005–2006, and I am extremely grateful to the Trust for its support, and to the Aleksanteri Institute in Helsinki which hosted my fellowship. I am greatly appreciative of my numerous friends and colleagues at the University of Birmingham's Centre for Russian and East European Studies, who were a constant support and inspiration when I worked there from 1999 to 2010, and whose efforts have kept the reputation of this renowned centre afloat during the most trying of times. I spent five months in 2010 at the Department of

History of the University of Michigan, where I learnt much from the acquaintance of several colleagues and was able to use the excellent university library in drafting a number of the chapters. Since the summer of 2010, I have enjoyed the outstanding atmosphere of the Karelian Research Institute at the University of Eastern Finland in Joensuu, and would especially like to thank my colleagues Ilkka Liikanen, Pekka Suutari, Paul Fryer and others there.

My most direct debt for this volume goes to the numerous scholars of Soviet nationalities whose works have formed the basis of this book, many of whom I have got to know personally and from whom I have profited from reading and hearing their understanding of Soviet nationalities. First and foremost among these is Ronald Grigor Suny, whose 1993 book *The Revenge of the Past: Nationalism, Revolution and the Collapse of the Soviet Union* inspired a whole generation of Soviet nationality scholars, myself included. His groundbreaking ideas run right through this book, and I apologise if I have not acknowledged his influence on every occasion I have drawn on it. Ron and his wife, Armena, became highly valued personal friends, inspirational in many ways. Armena's passing in November 2012 was a devastating loss to all of us.

Over the years I have benefitted greatly from discussions with many other scholars with whom I have shared interests, including Levan Avalishvili, Mark Bassin, Peter Blitstein, David Brandenberger, Juliette Cadiot, Robert Davies, Adrienne Edgar, the late Neil Edmunds, Yoram Gorlizky, Francine Hirsch, Geoffrey Hosking, Melanie Ilic, Kamala Imranli, Salavat Iskhakov, Oleg Khlevniuk, Nataliya Kibita, Giorgi Kldiashvili, Gerard Libaridian, Terry Martin, Mikko Palonkorpi, the late Brian Pearce, Hilary Pilkington, Michaela Pohl, Arsene Saparov, Robert Service, Alexander Titov, Valery Vasiliev, Stephen Wheatcroft and Galina Yemelianova, to name just a few. I have drawn freely on their ideas and hope I have provided suitable acknowledgement of most of them in the footnotes. Any omissions and errors are entirely my responsibility. Last but by no means least, I owe the deepest gratitude to my immediate family – to my wife Hanna, from whom I derive most of my understanding of international relations in the post-Soviet region as well as the love and support that has kept me going. I owe my children Saga, Max and Taika, for bringing me so much pleasure, for keeping me sane and for their patience at my frequent absences (both physical and mental).

I am extremely grateful to Michael Watson at Cambridge University Press, not least for his inexhaustible patience as agreed deadline after agreed deadline have passed. The usual regrets for taking much longer than intended over a manuscript are especially poignant and deep-felt in this case. In the course of 2010, when much of this work was drafted, three of the people whose opinions of the final version I would have valued as highly as anyone's left us. Soviet historical studies lost two of its greatest figures in the course of that year, Moshe Lewin and Richard Stites. I never got to know Moshe Lewin beyond a couple of email exchanges, but he was an early pioneer of the approach to Soviet history which has informed so many later historians, myself included, and his little book *Lenin's Last Struggle* first stimulated my interest in Soviet nationalities many years ago. No less a figure in the study of Soviet history was Richard Stites, who I became well acquainted with through his regular sojourns in Helsinki. His great passion was for Russians and their culture and he had less interest in non-Russians, but he always provided stimulating insights into whatever topic was at hand. He is irreplaceable both as a colleague and a great entertainer. A few days after Richard passed away, my father, Christopher Smith, followed him. I had regularly used him as a reader to provide the 'layman's view' on my earlier writings, and the absence of his input has no doubt left this book poorer than it would have been. He was a wonderful father, an unassuming man but hugely successful in all his endeavours, much loved and greatly missed. It is to his memory, and to my mother, Tessa Smith, whose lifelong support and love has made me what I am, that this book is dedicated.

CHAPTER ONE

Introduction: the prison-house
of nations

In January 1881, Russian soldiers led by General Mikhail
Dmitrievich Skobelev stormed the fortress of Gök-Tepe, close to
the eastern coastline of the Caspian Sea. Eight thousand Turkmen
tribesmen, who had defeated a Russian force two years earlier, lost
their lives in the assault, against only 300 Russians. Over the next
three years, troops were able to use the fortress as a base to
subjugate the oasis of Merv and the town of Kushka. This represented the apogee of the Russian Empire. It was by now the third
largest empire in history, surpassed in size only by the Mongol and
British empires. It stretched from Poland in the west to the Pacific in
the east, and from Finland and the Arctic Sea in the north to the
borders of Turkey, Afghanistan and China in the south. The
process had begun in the fourteenth century with the 'gathering
of the lands of the Rus' under the leadership of Muscovy. Ivan III's
conquest of Novgorod in 1478 brought a number of Finno-Ugric
people – Votiaks and Cheremis – under Muscovy's control. When
Ivan the Terrible conquered and annexed the Khanate of Kazan in
1552, Muscovy became truly a multi-ethnic empire which held sway
over a large number of Muslims as well as Christians and pagans.
The Khanate of Astrakhan fell to Ivan four years later, after which
he turned his attention to the north, briefly occupying parts of
Livonia and Lithuania before defeat at the hands of Sweden
and the Polish–Lithuanian Commonwealth forced a retreat. In

1579–1582 a Cossack adventurer, Ermak Timofeevich, accepted a commission from the Stroganovs and, with the backing of the tsar, defeated the khan of the Sibir tribe and began a 300-year expansion of Russia across the Ural mountains and over the vast, sparsely populated expanses of Siberia.[1]

From this point on the Russian Empire expanded inexorably. During the eighteenth and nineteenth centuries, this expansion averaged thousands of square miles a day. While the westward expansion was completed with the third partition of Poland in 1795, the northwestern border was consolidated with the acquisition of Finland from Poland in 1809. Growth to the south was very much a nineteenth-century affair. The Russian Empire crossed over the Caucasus mountains and acquired the Eastern Kingdom of Georgia by agreement of the Georgian king in 1801, before the mountains themselves had been brought under control. The subjugation of the North Caucasus mountains was the most prolonged and bloodiest episode in the creation of the Russian Empire. From 1817 to 1864 the highlanders of the North Caucasus held off Russian rule and inflicted heavy losses on the Russian army. The resistance imparted a special aura to the region, which attracted the attention of literary writers, artists and even circus entrepreneurs from Russia to North America.[2] More importantly, it provided the peoples of the North Caucasus who had fought in the rebellion – Chechens, Ingush and others – with a narrative of resistance, with the memory of a hero, Imam Shamil, of almost mythical status and with extra reason to resent Russian rule given the brutality with which the revolt was finally suppressed. Apart from a brief occupation of

---

[1] The whole of this section is based largely on Andreas Kappeler's detailed history: Andreas Kappeler, *The Russian Empire: A Multiethnic History* (London: Longman, 2001).

[2] Charles King, *The Ghost of Freedom: A History of the Caucasus* (Oxford University Press, 2008), 100–41.

Turkish territory in the course of the First World War, the Russian advance in the Caucasus was completed with the end of the Russo-Turkish War of 1877–1878.

The conquest of Central Asia was also initiated and completed in the course of the nineteenth century. The eastward expansion lasted longest of all, and did not end once it reached the Pacific Ocean. Russians colonised Alaska from 1784 until it was sold to the USA in 1867. Profit from the fur trade drove this expansion across Siberia and beyond.[3] Russia occupied the island of Sakhalin, in the sea of Japan, in 1853, and it was formally ceded to Russia in 1875. By the 1860 Treaty of Peking, Russia consolidated its hold on the territory around the Amur river, including a coastal strip reaching as far as the Korean border to the south, where a Russian harbour town was built and given the name Vladivostok – Ruler of the East.

METHODS OF RULE

Most of the Russian Empire was acquired by military conquest, or by diplomacy backed up by the force of arms. Pacification of a conquered territory could be brutal. But once control was established, the approach was different. After subjugating Kazan, Ivan IV gave to the Kazan nobles the opportunity to join the Russian nobility, to continue to enjoy many of their privileges and to make up an important part of the administration of Kazan and the surrounding area. This set the pattern for much of colonial rule, which relied on the co-optation of local elites into the ruling Russian class. In the nineteenth century Georgian and Armenian nobles in particular played leading roles in the army and the civilian

---

[3] Alan Wood, *Russia's Frozen Frontier: A History of Siberia and the Russian Far East, 1851–1991* (London: Bloomsbury, 2011).

administration. Alexander I initially antagonised the Georgian nobility by abolishing its Bagratid monarchy. And yet, after a number of early revolts, by the 1860s the Georgian nobles were a fully integrated part of the Russian noble system. Ukrainians and Belorussians were generally treated as though they were Russians, which made it difficult for culture to flourish, but elsewhere national life for the few non-Russian intellectuals was lively, while local customs, religions and traditions were generally allowed to continue unhindered. While missionaries from the Russian Orthodox Church were active in Muslim areas, especially along the Volga, they had no special powers and only half-hearted support from the Russian state. Less-developed tribes, especially the numerous small ones scattered in Siberia and the North, were more subject to missionary activity than other peoples and, unlike other nationalities, were not invited to participate in Catherine the Great's Legal Commission in 1767. Nomads in particular were treated with suspicion, but as the empire formally assumed control of the Kazakh lands in 1822, Alexander I's chief reformer and prime minister, Mikhail Speransky, issued an administrative code for these '*inorodtsy*', which granted even them a certain amount of self-administration and safeguarded the privileges of their elites.

Even after the emancipation of the Russian peasantry in 1861, and in spite of the severe overpopulation of central Russia, migration was tightly controlled. Peasants were still tied to their land through the powers of the communes and obligations to pay redemptions on land granted them under the Emancipation. Meanwhile the state kept a tight check on population movements. Most migration into the non-Russian lands was, then, illegal – peasants escaping poverty or redemption payments, or fleeing justice. Much of this flight at the time was towards the newly conquered lands of Central Asia. The illegal status of these migrants encouraged them to engage in friendly relations with the local population. The generals who led the Russian conquest also reached a series of accords with local Muslim leaders, regulating relations between the imperial forces and the local population, and leaving cultural and other forms of self-government in local hands. As a result, ethnic relations between Russians and Muslims remained fairly calm until the 1880s.[4]

Decrees of 1871 and 1881 allowed for regulated peasant migration, and a special decree of 1886 allowed for Russian rural settlement in Turkestan, but permission was still difficult to obtain. Illegal migration accounted for between 60 and 85 per cent of all migration in the late nineteenth century,[5] and in Turkestan Russian settlers flocked to the main towns in spite of official agreements to keep them away. A mass wave of migration in the 1880s transformed Tashkent not just in its demography but also in its infrastructure, with a ramshackle Russian quarter arising on the outskirts of the city against the wishes of planners who had hoped to use the city as a beacon of ordered Europeanness to enlighten the Muslim population. Legal migration, however small a part of the overall numbers it may have represented, also ensured that the army and governing institutions now had a care to protect the Russian population, a shift in attitude which was to further antagonise locals. Competition for land, the collapse of urban infrastructure, and insufficient water, medical and hygiene resources all contributed to both ethnic tensions and illness. The two came together in 1892 when inter-ethnic rioting broke out in the wake of a cholera

---

[4] Jeff Sahadeo, 'Epidemic and Empire: Ethnicity, Class and "Civilization" in the 1892 Tashkent Cholera Riot', *Slavic Review*, 64, 1 (2005), 123–4.

[5] Charles Steinwedel, 'Resettling People, Unsettling the Empire: Migration and the Challenge of Governance, 1861–1917', in Nicholas B. Breyfogle, Abby Schrader and Willard Sunderland (eds.), *Peopling the Russian Periphery: Borderland and Colonization in Eurasian History* (London: Routledge, 2007), 130.

epidemic that swept through Tashkent.[6] Throughout the Russian Empire, cities expanded rapidly with the industrialisation drive of the last two decades of the nineteenth century, with managers, foremen, white-collar and skilled workers, tradesmen, technicians and entrepreneurs creating a large chain of legal migration alongside the less controlled migration of unskilled labour.[7]

NATIONAL INTELLECTUALS

In the nineteenth century, nationalism was mostly the concern of an intellectual elite that had little contact with or influence over the peasantry who made up most of the population of all the non-Russian groups. The main exceptions were Finland and Poland, the former because there was a system of universal education sponsored by the Lutheran Church, meaning one of the highest literacy levels in the world; 'Fennomania' was tolerated so long as its main targets were the Swedish language and nobility. In response to the tsar's manifesto of 1899 restricting Finland's autonomy, however, the Finnish national movement turned against the Russian tsar, albeit peacefully at this stage. In Poland the national movement was led by the aristocracy and had some support from urban and rural Poles. But it could not command the loyalty of most Polish peasants. In spite of fierce resistance, the two great Polish rebellions of 1830–1831 and 1863–1864 were put down by the Russian army as the rebels ran out of supporters.

But for the other nationalities the nineteenth century, especially the second half, was an important period for the development of small national movements based on intellectual circles which were

---

[6] Sahadeo, 'Epidemic and Empire'.

[7] Eric Lohr, *Nationalizing the Russian Empire: The Campaign against Enemy Aliens during World War I* (Cambridge, MA: Harvard University Press, 2003), 4.

able to win mass support in the revolutionary years of the early twentieth century. A Ukrainian national group developed around the Society of Saints Cyril and Methodius, but was forced underground by tsarist persecution and had to operate in an environment where Ukrainian-language publications were effectively banned. The Georgian national movement which grew up around Ilia Chavchavadze in the 1860s was mostly concerned with the gathering of all the historic Georgian lands under one roof. Hence they were able to side with the Russian Empire and celebrate the tsar's victories against Turkey in 1878–1879, while some Georgian academics also began to turn their attention to the competing territorial claims of the Abkhaz people.

While it is difficult to talk about any kind of national movement among the Muslims of the Russian Empire, an important intellectual trend, Jadidism, emerged from Crimea and spread, especially to Kazan in the Volga Tatar region, but to some extent also in Central Asia. The aims of Jadidism focussed on modernising education, and it provided a secular vision of Islamic culture which combined progressive European ideas with Islamic customs. Jadidist circles in Crimea and Kazan were influential in organising around national demands in the twentieth century. Jadidism also had some influence in Azerbaijan, but there a national movement was more in evidence from the middle of the nineteenth century onwards. By the twentieth century, ideas of distinct nationhood were beginning to emerge among Kazakh and Turkmen intellectuals, but their numbers remained small and their ideas unclear.

It was an Armenian political party which first made the link between national and revolutionary politics. The Dashnaktsutiun (Revolutionary Armenian Federation) or Dashnak party was founded in Tbilisi in 1890. Its members adopted socialist ideas and were able to work together with the revolutionary Russian parties, but their main concern was for the Armenians across the border under the rule of the Ottoman Empire. Hence they did not initially oppose the Russian Empire, but when the tsar ordered the confiscation of Armenian church property in 1903 the Dashnaks already had in place an organisation that was capable of responding. They were able both to lead large demonstrations and to organise assassinations of tsarist officials, successfully combining social and national demands in their mobilisation of Armenians.

By then the Russian Empire was about to erupt into revolution. Although the beginning of the revolutionary movement in the capital St Petersburg is marked by the event of Bloody Sunday in January 1905, in some areas the revolution had already started. While Armenians were demonstrating in Tbilisi, Georgian peasants had responded to economic pressures by taking control of a large part of western Georgia in 1904 and establishing the Free Republic of Guria, which lasted for almost two years. With extraordinary rapidity, the Georgian branch of the Mensheviks – a branch of the Russian Social Democratic Labour Party – found themselves at the head of a peasant socialist movement which had no precedent in world history. The coincidence of class and national demands under Menshevik leadership made nationalism especially powerful in Georgia.

In the oilfields around Baku, an industry-wide strike in December 1904 secured the first general collective wage agreement in the Russian Empire. Muslim, Armenian and European workers co-operated in the strike movement, but two months later, playing on the growing rivalry between Muslim and Armenian traders in the streets of Baku itself, Russian authorities including the army were complicit in fuelling ethnic violence which continued for days and left hundreds dead. If the aim was to divide the oil-industry workforce it was perhaps overachieved. When conflict erupted again in

September 1905, this time it spread to the oilfields, but as well as fighting each other, Muslims and Armenians set fire to oil wells and destroyed company buildings.[8]

The reverberations of Bloody Sunday were clearly felt by Latvians, Lithuanians and Estonians, who responded much as their Russian counterparts did. But the revolutionary wave also produced a mass audience for national ideas among the non-Russians, and those ideas were gratefully received among those such as the Latvians who were well organised in the cities and were strongly pulled towards socialist ideas.

The turn towards russification in the reigns of the last three Russian tsars had one more important impact. Relations between local peasants and Russian settlers in the Fergana valley and Semirech'e region of Central Asia had continued to deteriorate in the wake of the later nineteenth-century migrations. In 1916, the government decided to subject Central Asian Muslims to a general call-up for the first time. Although this call-up was not to the army, but to work behind the lines in place of those who were at the front line, it was either misunderstood as a military draft or was in any case sufficient cause for the Muslims to rebel. As the rebellion spread from the cities to the countryside more than 3,000 Russians were killed and 10,000 settler farms destroyed. Muslim deaths probably exceeded 100,000, and hundreds of thousands more fled over the border into China. Government reprisals included confiscation of more land, which was handed over to Russian settlers, providing an additional grievance shortly before the whole empire was engulfed again in revolution.

---

[8] For a fascinating contemporary account, see J. D. Henry, *Baku: An Eventful History*, reprint edn (London: Ayer, 1977).

ETHNIC STRUCTURE OF THE RUSSIAN EMPIRE
ON THE EVE OF REVOLUTION

The peoples of the Russian Empire differed not only in obvious outward markers such as language and religion, but also in terms of levels of economic development and the social position of most of the members of each nationality as well as the degree of social stratification within the nationality. Most non-Russians were peasants, as were most Russians, but there were important distinctions in terms of the urban population and in the nationality of the nobles who ruled over the peasants. As this is essential to the background of events in 1917–1920 and beyond, a brief tour of the major nationalities of the Russian Empire on the eve of the Russian Revolution follows.[9]

The Belorussians and Lithuanians of the northwest of the Empire shared a common history in the Polish–Lithuanian Commonwealth in the sixteenth and seventeenth centuries, were mostly peasants and had little sense of national identity. Both continued to be subject mostly to Polish landlords. The Belorussians shared the Orthodox religion and were linguistically close to the Russians, whereas Lithuanians were more distinct through their Catholic religion, although this was also a factor further strengthening the dominance of Polish culture. A Belorussian socialist party, Hramada, had been in existence since 1902, but it could barely compete with the Russian socialist organisations. Estonians were also mostly peasants, ruled over by German landowners. The incipient Estonian national movement was strongly influenced by ties to Finland, which shared a similar language and religion. Latvians were the most urbanised of

---

[9] This section is based largely on the 'typology of nations' given in Ronald Grigor Suny, *Revenge of the Past*, 30–76.

Table 1.1 *Population of the Russian Empire, excluding the Grand Duchy of Finland, by nationality, according to the 1897 census*

Nationality	Total number
Russians	55,667,500
Ukrainians	22,380,600
Belorussians	5,885,500
Poles	7,931,300
Moldavians	1,121,700
Germans	1,790,500
Jews	5,063,200
Czechs and Slovaks	50,400
Serbs and Bulgarians	174,500
Greeks	186,900
Roma	44,600
Other Indo-Europeans	44,000
Lithuanians	1,658,500
Latvians	1,435,900
Estonians	1,002,700
Finns	143,100
Votiaks	421,000
Karelians	208,100
Izhoras	13,800
Chude (Veps)	25,800
Komi	153,600
Permiaks	104,700
Mordvinians	1,023,800
Mari	375,400
Voguls	7,600
Ostiaks	19,700
Georgians	1,352,500
Armenians	1,173,100
Kabardins	98,600
Cherkess	46,300
Abkhaz	72,100
Chechens	226,500
Ingush	47,800
Dagestan group	600,500
Ossetians	171,700
Turco-Tatar group (including Tatars of the Volga and Crimea as well as Azerbaijanis)	3,767,500

Table 1.1 (*cont.*)

Nationality	Total number
Arabs	7,000
Bashkirs	1,493,000
Karachaevs, Kumyks, Nogais	174,700
Other Turkic peoples	440,400
Uzbeks, Sarts, Kuramas	3,250,000
Taranchi, Kashgars, Uighurs	71,400
Kara-Kalpaks	104,300
Kazakhs, Kyrgyz	4,285,800
Turkmen	619,900
Chuvash	843,800
Yakuts	227,400
Kalmyks	190,600
Buryats	289,500
Iranians	31,700
Tajiks	954,100
Talysh	35,300
Tats	95,100
Kurds	99,900
Chukchi	11,800
Chinese, Dungans	57,400
Koreans	26,000
Others	355,800
Total	128,162,900

Source: Richard Pipes, *The Formation of the Soviet Union: Communism and Nationalism, 1917–1923*, revised edn (Cambridge, MA: Harvard University Press, 1997), 300–1.

Note: Non-Russian nationalities are listed, roughly speaking, by geographical location, starting in the west and moving east.

the Baltic nationalities, and there was a strong working class, especially in Riga. Latvian workers, and to some extent peasants, were solidly socialist and provided some of the most consistent support for the Bolsheviks.

Most Jews were settled in the western – Ukrainian and Belorussian – parts of the empire, where their movements were restricted by law. Although there were a number of Jewish bankers and merchants, most Jews in these areas were peasants and lived in their own villages. Their landlords were predominantly Polish, as they were for the rest of the population. Ukrainians were by far the largest non-Russian nationality in the Russian Empire. They were overwhelmingly peasants, while the Ukrainian towns were populated more by Russians and Jews. On the eve of the First World War, a large Ukrainian population dwelt across the border in the Austro-Hungarian Empire, but had lived under much freer conditions and consequently boasted a developed national culture. The links between these two distinct Ukrainian populations were to exercise Ukrainian nationalists until the point at which Stalin unified them in 1939.

The Georgian socialist movement was the most unified and most powerful. Since 1905, the Mensheviks had been able to retain their leadership over the Georgian peasant movement. The Georgian national movement, although it assumed this Marxist form, also looked back to Georgian history and culture and hoped to replicate in some ways the structures of the ancient Georgian state. Most Georgians were peasants, but there was a strong Georgian intellectual tradition and a small Georgian working class as well.

The Armenians were geographically divided and faced threats from various directions. Most Armenians had been living across the border in the Ottoman Empire. But when the wartime Turkish leadership became afraid of the possibility of an Armenian rising in 1915, a state-sponsored massacre of Armenians, mostly through starvation, almost destroyed the nation there. Those who could escaped to Russia, and took with them a hatred and distrust of Turkey that was never to be overcome. The concentration of

Armenians around Yerevan stems from this time and was therefore relatively recent. Armenians were scattered around Russia, and had a strong presence in Moscow and St Petersburg. Although most were peasants, many Armenians dwelt in cities and held important jobs in commerce and trade. As well as the problems with Turkey, Armenians had a difficult relationship with Azerbaijani Muslims going back to the 1905 events.

Azerbaijan was another peasant nation, and many Azerbaijanis were nomadic or semi-nomadic sheep herders, but a small elite was active in celebrating national culture from the middle of the nineteenth century. Although the term Azerbaijani was not widely adopted with reference to the Muslim population of this region until after the revolution, a nationalism of sorts was inspired largely by the existence of similar Turkic peoples across the border in Iran. This, and ethnic relations with Armenians, dominated Muslim national politics before the revolution. After the 1905 conflicts in Baku, the main centre for national antagonism became the region of Karabakh, especially its mountainous section, where the population was mixed and became predominantly Muslim only in the summer months when the nomadic shepherds took their flocks up into the mountains. A Muslim socialist party, the Hummet, was influential in Azerbaijan but was not as large as the nationalist Musavats.

The remaining Muslims of the Russian Empire could be distinguished by language, geography and occupation more than by nationality, which for most Muslims was only vaguely if at all understood. Nationality was more developed among the biggest peoples of the Volga region, the Bashkirs and Tatars. But even here there was some confusion as to any difference between the two groups. Bashkirs were mostly nomads and as a result had a reputation as excellent horsemen. Tatars were settled and predominated in the towns. A large Tatar intelligentsia eventually came to dominate the Russian Muslim movement. In Central Asia the nomadic Kazakhs, Turkmen and Kyrgyz and the sedentary Uzbeks and Tajiks alike saw themselves primarily in village, clan, Turkic or Islamic rather than national terms. Major towns such as Tashkent did have a large Muslim quarter, but this was closely linked to the Muslim countryside while being cut off from the Russian quarters. A clerical elite still held sway over much of the Muslim population of Central Asia, but they were challenged by a radical secular Jadidist intelligentsia.

Aside from the Georgians, Poles and Finns had the clearest sense of national identity, and both escaped direct Russian rule for good in 1917. They were among the most 'European' peoples of the Russian Empire, but were equally divided along social lines and experienced their own civil wars after independence. One factor which facilitated Poland's and Finland's withdrawal was the fact that they existed as distinct parts of the empire with clearly demarcated borders. This is not to say that they were ethnically homogeneous – in Poland's case far from it. But in the rest of the empire, it made no sense to think of ethnic groups as nations before 1917 for a number of reasons: first, while some, such as the Georgians, could look back to an earlier period of statehood for their historical borders, for most peoples this was not the case. While most villages could be identified as being inhabited by one or another ethnic group, different villages in the same regions, particularly peripheral ones, could belong to different groups. Most cities, meanwhile, were of mixed ethnicity, typically with a large Russian population settled in separate quarters from members of the nationality which also populated the surrounding countryside. Nationalists who had begun to emerge and organise in the late nineteenth and early twentieth centuries therefore had to contend with each other as well as with a peasant population that was largely illiterate and (in national terms) indifferent. With a few exceptions, such nationalist groupings appeared marginal to the people they claimed to represent at the turn of the century, although they were certainly gaining in influence in the years leading up to the First World War.

It was therefore something as a surprise, certainly to the major Russian political parties, that across much of the vast empire the revolutionary wave of 1917 should express itself in national terms, even more so than in 1905. But the war itself and the devastation it caused, not just on the front line but also in towns and villages far from it, led people to question who they were fighting for and, in turn, who they themselves were.[10] The russifying policies of Alexander III and Nicholas II contributed to the growth of ideas of separate national identity. They were not just abstract policies, but ones that attacked languages and religions, even modes of agriculture, which were at the heart of day-to-day existence and belief for the non-Russians. The revolt in Central Asia in 1916 was a response to such policies, and provided a foretaste of what was to come, but few anticipated that the national question would erupt as such a force during and after 1917.

[10] Lohr, *Nationalizing the Russian Empire*, 6–7.

CHAPTER TWO

Dispersal and reunion: revolution and civil war in the borderlands

The immediate course of the Russian Revolutions of 1917 was decided in the capital cities of Moscow and Petrograd and, indirectly, on the front line between Russian and German armies. But even away from the front lines, in cities around the periphery of the empire the struggle that determined the fate of the Provisional Government was also in evidence. Soviet power was declared in Tashkent before Petrograd. Here the soviet (workers' council) was almost exclusively Russian, and the Red forces remained isolated from the surrounding, Muslim-populated countryside. The Latvian city of Riga presented an unusual case of a working class dominated ethnically by non-Russians. Latvian workers were solidly pro-Bolshevik, and their influence on the struggle in the capital was reinforced by geographical proximity to Petrograd.

In the cases of both Riga and Tashkent, the overlap of social and ethnic backgrounds shaped the nature of events there already in 1917. As the Revolution developed into civil war the significance of the convergence of nationality and class became ever more apparent, and was one of the key factors behind the eventual victory of the Reds.[1] In Baku, as the Russian authorities were forced out, the stratification of the local workforce along national lines determined

---

[1] For further discussion on this, see Suny, *Revenge of the Past.*

the development of the conflict into one between Armenians and Muslims. National parties grew in importance and were the dominant forces in between the fall of the Bolshevik-led Baku Commune in 1918 and the Red Army's conquest in 1920.

Elsewhere in the Russian Empire, however, the nationality question was predominantly a peasant one. The speed at which national movements developed in non-Russian areas as well as their scale took many by surprise, including most of Russia's Marxists. Peasants, it was supposed, were unable to think beyond narrow local interests; least of all were they capable of constituting the kind of base for nationalism which in west European nation-states had depended on the spread of urbanisation and education. It was precisely the convergence of social and national factors in the Russian Empire, however, which underlay the growth of national movements. Bashkir peasants and soldiers may have been preoccupied above all with the acquisition of land and water, but as long as political power lay with the Russian- and Tatar-dominated cities their frustrations were bound to be expressed in a national form. To a greater or lesser extent this was the pattern that dominated across Russia. As national movements coalesced around intellectuals and politicians who shared a strong antagonism towards Bolshevism, independence developed as a key demand. Where such national movements developed, where the population was less mixed and the territory was not host to foreign or White armies, the consolidation of independence and the establishment of national governments proceeded full tilt. These conditions only really held in the South Caucasus (Transcaucasia or Zakavkaz in the parlance of the time), and even there local national antagonisms made for a far-from-straightforward picture. In sum, no two nationalities underwent the same experience of the Russian Revolution and Civil War.

1917

While the Provisional Government dithered over proposals for the status of the non-Russian regions of the empire, national movements were able to spread their influence from a small base of intellectuals to win significant support from peasants and other social groups. The breakdown of central authority gave locally elected soviets and equivalent bodies the ability to exert their control. These national governments were then able to negotiate their position with the central authorities from a position of some strength. The most important of these was the Ukrainian Central Rada (Council), which was organised on 17 March 1917. An All-Ukrainian National Congress held in Kiev from 19 to 21 April mandated the Rada 'to prepare plans for Ukrainian autonomy, and to take steps for its realisation'.[2] While this was effectively a unilateral declaration of autonomy, the Rada expected to be able to work co-operatively with the Provisional Government. The Rada passed radical social legislation, but it was over the political relationship with Petrograd that a split with the Provisional Government occurred.[3] The First Universal issued by the Rada on 23 June listed the Ukrainian demands for political autonomy, the establishment of separate Ukrainian military units and a series of measures in the spheres of culture and education. Given the Provisional Government's rejection of these, the First Universal declared that 'From this day forth we shall direct our own lives.'[4] An attempt in July to patch up the differences between the Rada and

---

[2] Wolodymyr Stojko, 'Ukrainian National Aspirations and the Russian Provisional Government', in Taras Hunczak (ed.), *The Ukraine, 1917–1921: A Study in Revolution* (Cambridge, MA: Harvard University Press, 1977), 6.

[3] John S. Reshetar, *The Ukrainian Revolution, 1917–1920* (Princeton University Press, 1952), 54.

[4] *Ibid.*, 61.

the leaders of the Provisional Government failed to overcome fundamental disagreements, so that on the eve of the October Revolution the Rada's leader, Volodymyr Vinnichenko, shifted from a position of supporting Ukrainian autonomy to declaring a federation of free republics.[5]

In Tashkent, the heady days following the February Revolution reflected the general optimism that the tsar's abdication would allow the people of Russia to rally around a united cause regardless not just of class, but also of ethnic differences. At a parade on 10 March, Russian workers were joined by thousands of Muslims. Muslim and Russian orators from all walks of life were joined on the platform by the tsar-appointed governor-general of Turkestan, Alexei Kuropatkin. By the end of the month, however, Kuropatkin was under arrest by order of the city soviet, and food was running out. With the food crisis mounting, the soviet took over Tashkent through a fourteen-member Revolutionary Committee on 12 September. Following the October Revolution in Petrograd, forces of the Tashkent Soviet fought off Provisional Government troops and further consolidated the soviet's power. A number of attempts to include the local Muslim population in this process failed, and the Tashkent Soviet consisted entirely of Europeans. This exclusion was justified on the basis that 'among the native population there are no class proletarian organisations'. In reality, Russian workers and soldiers were unwilling to give up the privileged position that colonialism had conferred on them. The revolution in Tashkent and elsewhere in Central Asia, then, was a Russian, urban and military one, which excluded not only most of the peasantry but also the Muslim population of Tashkent.[6]

---

[5] *Ibid.*, 65–82.

[6] Jeff Sahadeo, *Russian Colonial Society in Tashkent, 1865–1923* (Bloomington: Indiana University Press, 2007), 191–200.

Once the Bolsheviks had begun to emerge as the leaders of the discontented radical wing of the revolution in Petrograd, it took some time for this influence to spread to the rest of the country. In spite of offering the promise of national self-determination to the non-Russian peoples, support outside Central and Northwestern Russia was confined to the cities, and mostly to Russians. On the whole the national parties were in a better position to put themselves at the head of the increasingly radicalised movement in the border-lands. By negotiating with the Provisional Government from a position of strength, rather than agitating for a complete overthrow of the system, national parties appeared more attractive in terms of their ability to satisfy the national and social demands that increasingly preoccupied both the rural and the urban populations. In some regions, other revolutionary socialist parties had more success in attracting the support of the national movement. In Georgia, the Mensheviks maintained the monopoly of influence over the revolutionary movement which they had first acquired at the beginning of the century. As the Russian Mensheviks became increasingly compromised through their participation in the unpopular and impotent Provisional Government, however, the Georgian Mensheviks began to distance themselves from the rest of the party, to the extent that, by the time the Bolsheviks came to power in Russia, they could be considered more or less as a separate, national, socialist party.[7] In Ukraine, the Socialist Revolutionaries (SRs) expanded their influence in the countryside among peasants of all nationalities. While they continued to maintain links with the Russian SRs, as the latter split into distinct Left and Right factions, the majority of Ukrainian SRs became clearly aligned with the Left.

---

[7] Stephen F. Jones., *Socialism in Georgian Colors: The European Road to Social Democracy, 1883–1917* (Cambridge, MA: Harvard University Press, 2005), 236–81.

By championing the social and economic demands of the peasantry, the SRs were able to make more headway than the Ukrainian nationalist parties, but at the same time were forced to take a clear position on the national question.

In spite of the opportunities for nationalist parties to extend their influence, their collusion with the Provisional Government and their failure to decisively address social questions, in particular the land question, led in many cases to a drift in their support. In some cases the national movement began to subdivide, splitting along attitudes to the major questions that were facing the entire population of Russia – land and war. Anarchists and others were able to benefit from this atomisation but, by the time elections to the all-Russian Constituent Assembly were held in November 1917, it was the main socialist parties that picked up the overwhelming majority of votes.

For most of 1917, the borders between national and social interests remained fuzzy. Just as with central politics on the all-Russia scale, support for national parties inevitably declined as soon as they had grown in influence to the extent that they shouldered responsibility for the insoluble problems of the time. The Bolshevik takeover of October 1917 upped the stakes for national governments. Soon after, the Ukrainian Rada declared an independent Ukrainian state, Georgia, Armenia and Azerbaijan followed suit, and national governments claimed power in Estonia, Latvia and Lithuania. These acts created the conditions for civil war in the borderlands before the conflict between Reds and Whites broke out. Support for nationalist parties now meant secession, something to which all of the socialist parties, with the exception of the Georgian branch of the Mensheviks, were opposed to. In Ukraine and other borderlands, the question of independence split the population along ethnic lines as well as along lines of support for one or other party.

Table 2.1 *Votes for the Constituent Assembly, November 1917 (totals by region)*

Region	Socialist Revolutionaries	Bolsheviks	Mensheviks	Other Socialist parties	Constitutional Democrats (Kadets)	Other non-Socialist parties	Ukrainian parties	Muslim parties	Other nationality parties	Unclassified	Total
Northern	532,862	89,429	134,162	8,071	34,998	—	—	—	—	4,902	804,424
Northwestern	609,693	573,046	16,988	24,637	115,365	15,301	—	—	—	35,123	1,390,153
Estonia	3,200	119,863	—	—	—	—	—	—	176,781	—	299,844
Livonia	—	97,781	7,046	—	—	—	—	—	31,253	—	136,080
Belorussia	582,086	1,227,250	36,649	5,809	48,130	35,407	—	—	200,042	645	2,136,018
Central	1,929,991	1,997,659	121,900	38,012	297,934	125,101	—	—	—	40,810	4,551,407
Central Black Earth	3,401,838	710,519	50,670	26,454	170,119	29,143	11,871	36,043	—	9,250	4,445,907
Southeastern-Volga	1,700,273	526,490	22,390	54,919	94,362	54,874	5,240	261,839	121,111	52,912	2,894,410
North Caucasus/Black Sea	1,070,446	238,569	17,445	2,620	84,147	640,000	61,559	60,858	—	83,642	2,259,286
Kama-Ural	1,657,834	607,415	46,436	79,652	206,066	69,616	—	596,053	226,496	770,798	4,260,366
Siberia	2,094,785	273,982	48,230	97,668	87,465	22,397	—	25,830	23,512	92,320	2,766,189
Ukraine	1,597,363	859,330	108,933	81,174	247,500	203,376	4,354,325	—	541,104	207,858	8,200,963
Transcaucasia	105,265	86,935	569,362	—	24,551	—	—	—	350,000	751,340	1,887,453
Petrograd	152,230	424,027	29,167	30,728	246,506	55,456	4,219	—	—	—	942,333

Table 2.1 (*cont.*)

Region	Socialist Revolutionaries	Bolsheviks	Mensheviks	Other Socialist parties	Constitutional Democrats (Kadets)	Other non-Socialist parties	Ukrainian parties	Muslim parties	Other nationality parties	Unclassified	Total
Moscow	62,260	366,148	21,597	37,813	263,859	8,664	–	–	4,422	–	764,763
Army	1,512,815	1,592,370	131,908	8,297	65,599	3,055	522,948	15,133	3,510	96,999	3,952,634
Fleet	38,198	53,824	1,943	9,736	–	28	12,895	–	–	4,769	121,393
Total	17,051,139	9,844,637	1,364,826	505,590	1,986,601	1,262,418	4,973,057	995,756	1,678,231	2,151,368	41,813,623

Source: Adapted from Oliver H. Radkey, *The Election to the Russian Constituent Assembly of 1917* (Cambridge, MA: Harvard University Press, 1950), 76–78.
Note: In Olonets province in the Northern district, voters were allowed two votes each for the two places that were to be filled. The figures here and in the totals count both sets of votes, so reflect the number of votes cast rather than the number of voters. In Saratov province of the Southeastern Volga region, 53,000 votes were recorded for a combination of Ukrainian and Muslim parties without differentiation. In this table, these votes are recorded under the Muslim parties only.

CIVIL WAR IN CENTRAL RUSSIA

While the main military engagements of the Russian Civil War of 1918–1920 were fought on the peripheries of the former Russian Empire, more often than not in the non-Russian lands, it was the Bolsheviks' control of the Russian heartland that provided them with the munitions, soldiers, food and communications which eventually allowed the Reds to prevail over the Whites. In spite of the ethnically mixed nature of the industrial workforce in the main centres, the core of Bolshevik support was overwhelmingly ethnic Russian. Non-Russians did, however, comprise a significant proportion of the population in the Volga region and the Far East. These two regions were soon at the centre of the Civil War, as the remnants of the dispersed Constituent Assembly set up a rival government (the Komuch) in Saratov, while Admiral Alexander Kolchak raised the first substantial White army in the East. Kolchak himself did little to endear himself to non-Russians by making clear his affinity to the overthrown Russian Empire.[8] All the same, his short-lived alliance with the democratic Komuch and some tactical concessions over land gave him control over a number of non-Russian military formations. Foremost among these were the Bashkir cavalrymen, who were a major military force in the Volga region. Disillusioned with Kolchak's policies, however, their leader, Zeki Validov, did a deal with the Bolsheviks in February 1919. In return for the defection of the Bashkir cavalry, a Bashkir Revolutionary Committee (Bashrevkom) was granted authority over the Bashkir lands in the first experiment with Soviet national autonomy. This agreement was reached over the

---

[8] Jonathan D. Smele, *Civil War in Siberia: The Anti-Bolshevik Government of Admiral Kolchak, 1918–1920* (Cambridge University Press, 1997), 289–301.

head of local Bolshevik organisations, which controlled the towns of Ufa and Sterlitamak, where the Bashrevkom set up headquarters. The mostly Russian soviets were reluctant to surrender their power in the towns or to abandon the claims of Russian settlers to scarce land and water resources. The Bolshevik leaders Stalin, Trotsky and Lenin all intervened successively in an effort to maintain unity, but could only go so far in their support of the Bashrevkom. Eventually a series of disputes escalated into armed clashes. Validov fled to Central Asia in June 1920, where he was active in the Basmachi movement for a while before moving off to an academic career in Turkey. In the countryside, chaos ensued as Russians seized more land and thousands of Bashkir families were forced to abandon their farms.[9]

Throughout 1917 and the Civil War, several organisations competed to lead the Muslim population of Central Russia. The secular leaders of these movements came mostly from among the Tatars of the Volga region and were centred on Kazan. An All-Russian Muslim Congress met in Moscow in early May 1917, and following a heated discussion on the position of women it became clear that the progressive, secular Muslims were dominant. At its second Congress, in Kazan in July 1917, extra-territorial cultural autonomy was adopted as the preferred solution to the national question in revolutionary Russia. Iosif Stalin, then commissar of nationality affairs for Russia, tried to win this movement over to the Bolshevik side not long after the October 1917 Revolution. When this approach was rebuffed, the Soviet government instead formed a Muslim Commissariat headed by Mulla Nur Vakhitov until his

[9] E. H. Carr, 'Some Notes on Soviet Bashkiria', *Soviet Studies*, 8, 3 (1957), 225. For an account that differs somewhat from Carr's, see Richard Pipes, 'The First Experiment in Soviet National Policy: The Bashkir Republic, 1917–1920', *Russian Review* (1950), 9, 4, 303–19. The Basmachi movement is discussed further in Ch. 4.

death in August 1918. Meanwhile, however, Muslims had responded to the breakdown of central authority over the course of 1917 by organising their own secular administrations in the Volga region, and it took time for these to be brought under Bolshevik control. The key struggle took place between an independent pan-Muslim Russian Army Council or Harbi Shura, and the Muslim Socialist Committee of Kazan in March 1918. The defeat and flight of the Harbi Shura secured Kazan for the Soviets, and by mid April all independent Muslim organisations in the region were disbanded. Kazan briefly fell to the Whites in August 1918, but after it was recaptured in September Soviet-sponsored Muslim organisations were put firmly in control, secured by the promise of territorial autonomy in a Tatar Autonomous Republic.[10]

UKRAINE

Over the course of the Civil War, the main Ukrainian city of Kiev was overrun by no fewer than seven different armies. Following the October Revolution the Rada, now led by moderate Social Democrats, did not break immediately with Vladimir Lenin's government. Although the Third Universal of 19 November 1917 proclaimed a Ukrainian People's Republic, it stressed its pledge to a federal relationship with Russia. Lenin rapidly lost patience, however, with both the Rada and the Ukrainian Bolsheviks who failed to make any headway in Soviet and Constituent Assembly elections in Ukraine, and ordered the Red Army into Ukraine for the first time towards the end of December. The Red Army took Kiev on

[10] Alexandre A. Bennigsen and S. Enders Wimbush, *Muslim National Communism in the Soviet Union* (University of Chicago Press, 1980), 138–44; Azade-Ayşe Rorlich, *The Volga Tatars: A Profile in National Resilience* (Stanford: Hoover Institution Press, 1986), 126–41.

9 February 1918, the very day that the Austrian and German governments agreed a separate peace deal with the Rada, whose members had now fled west to Zhitomir. As the first peace talks between the Bolsheviks and German representatives broke down, German armies overran more Ukrainian territory and reinstalled the Rada in Kiev on 1 March.

Conflicts between the Rada and the German authorities over land policy led the Germans to replace the Rada on 29 April 1918 with a puppet government under General Pavlo Skoropadsky, who assumed the old Cossack title of Hetman. Although Skoropadsky adopted the trappings of Cossack tradition and promised to serve the Ukrainian nation, he was allowed to hold power only under a set of stringent conditions imposed by the Germans. These conditions included giving the Germans a monopoly over military forces and field courts, the lifting of any restrictions on free trade and the restoration of private land, a ban on strikes, and introducing the death penalty for vandalism on the railways.[11] At this point, the recently born Ukrainian national movement split along social lines, but also over attitudes to union with Russia and the stance taken towards the Germans. Ukrainian peasants continued for the most part to support the Left Socialist Revolutionaries, while a more popular national army fought in opposition to the Hetman, led by Simon Petliura. Among the Russian peasants of eastern Ukraine as well as in the major cities and coalfields the Bolsheviks were able to make headway, and established an alternative Soviet Ukrainian government in Kharkiv in November 1918. Not long afterward, the withdrawal of German forces from Kiev allowed nationalist forces, backed by Petliura's army, to overthrow Skoropadsky and

[11] Mark von Hagen, *War in a European Borderland: Occupations and Occupation Plans in Galicia and Ukraine, 1914–1918* (Seattle: University of Washington Press, 2007), 93–5.

establish a new government, the Directory, under Volodymyr Vinnichenko on 14 December.

These political and military developments took place against the background of social upheaval which, in Ukraine in 1918, went far beyond the widespread peasant seizures of land in 1917. Between April and June 1918, a series of peasant rebellions cost the lives of 19,000 German soldiers.[12] Acting independently of political leadership and without any clear programme or ideology, the peasants of Ukraine were fighting for land, against the iniquities of Skoropadsky and against German occupation. While these forces were able to rally for a while around Petliura and the Directory, the illusion of a unified national movement was unmasked when these same peasants flocked to the side of the Red Army following its second incursion at the start of 1919. Petliura's forces numbered nearly 100,000 in December 1918, but dwindled to 21,000 by February 1919.[13] As peasants rallied to the Bolsheviks, the Red Army was able to advance rapidly from its base in Kharkiv and captured Kiev in February 1919. Support for the Reds dwindled quickly to disillusionment as the Bolsheviks, under pressure to deliver grain to the army and Central Russia, appointed their own peasant soviets and committees, introduced communal agriculture and sent armed brigades to seize grain.[14]

None of the successive governments in Ukraine was ever able to establish control over the peasant movement. Another, mostly peasant, army formed around the young anarchist Nestor Makhno. Although an anarchist from an early age and lacking

[12] Arthur E. Adams, 'The Great Ukrainian Jacquerie', in Hunczak (ed.), *The Ukraine*, 253.

[13] *Ibid.*, 255–60. See also Arthur E. Adams, *Bolsheviks in the Ukraine: The Second Campaign, 1918–1919* (New Haven: Yale University Press, 1963).

[14] Adams, 'Ukrainian Jacquerie', 264–8.

credentials as a nationalist – having spent twelve years in Russian prisons, he spoke Russian as his first language – the charismatic Makhno managed to put himself at the head of a ragtag army combining Ukrainian peasants, army deserters and a handful of anarchist intellectuals. In line with his anarchist ideas, Makhno established local self-rule over the territories he controlled, but in this respect differed little from a number of local peasant governments that were cropping up across the former Russian Empire at this time. Makhno's biggest appeal lay in the granting of land to the peasants and his hostility to all landowners. At the height of the movement he controlled upwards of 20,000 men, providing an important force in Ukraine's civil war. In February 1919 Makhno joined forces with the Bolsheviks against the Whites, and in September acted in concert with Petliura against Anton Denikin, severely weakening the White general's supply lines at a time when he presented the greatest threat to Bolshevik rule.

Throughout 1919 and 1920, peasant armies played a largely independent role in the three-way contest for Ukrainian territory between General Denikin's White Army, the Bolsheviks' Red Army and Petliura's nationalists. Following the defeat of the Whites, the Bolsheviks turned against both the nationalist and the anarchist forces in Ukraine; they were able to establish their control by the very end of 1920, relinquishing it for a short period only as the Red Army retreated from the disastrous Polish campaign later that year.

All through the Civil War, the Jewish population of Ukraine was subjected to regular assaults or pogroms. Initially, Jewish organisations actively supported the Rada and opposed the Red Army invasion of January 1918. Petliura's anti-Hetmanate forces were responsible for many of the atrocities against Jews in the course of 1918, and they increased their anti-Semitic violence as the Germans withdrew and the Reds advanced again. Even worse pogroms – at least 213 separate ones in total – were committed by the White forces under General Denikin. Murder, rape and torture devastated about 700 Jewish communities. Between 1918 and early 1921 an estimated 50,000–60,000 Jews were killed. A few pogroms were carried out by Red Army units, but they were quickly disbanded and, for the most part, Jewish civilians saw the Reds as their best chance of protection. On one occasion, the 4,000 Jewish inhabitants of a town followed the Red Army *en masse* away from their homes rather than be left to the mercy of the Whites. The atrocities of Ukrainian nationalists and Whites alike did more than anything to ensure Jewish support for the Reds and, eventually, the merger of the main Jewish socialist party, the Bund, with the Bolsheviks.[15]

Control of Ukraine was vital not just to the Red victory in the Civil War, but also to the Bolsheviks' ability to regain most of the territory of the former empire and then rebuild the shattered economy. The remarkable growth of the Ukrainian national movement in 1917 promised to lay the basis for a strong independent state. Ukrainian national parties dominated the vote for the Constituent Assembly and, until the first months of 1919, Ukrainian nationalist agitators were able to operate with some success in the villages. But they were never able to broaden their appeal beyond support for economic demands, and so failed to consolidate the Ukrainian nation.[16] Even without the presence of German and White armies on Ukrainian soil, the very newness of

[15] Nora Levin, *The Jews in the Soviet Union since 1917: Paradox of Survival*, 2 vols. (London: I. B. Tauris, 1990), vol. I, 38–44.

[16] Andrew Wilson, *The Ukrainians: Unexpected Nation* (New Haven: Yale University Press, 2002), 125–6.

the national movement contributed to its failure.[17] Led by intellectuals who had no hands-on experience of politics, the movement
split along social and geographic lines and failed to come to terms
with the complex ethnic make-up of the region. The more organised
Bolsheviks had a solid base in the eastern cities and coalfields,
and were able to take advantage of nationalist weaknesses to win
peasant support at key moments. Ultimately their hold on Ukraine
was cemented by military might, but their ability to present a
coherent social programme as well as a solution to the national
question was just as important to their victory.

THE NORTHWEST

Finland's exit from the Russian orbit was secured with relative ease.
The Finnish parliament voted for independence on 6 December
1917, and secured recognition from the Soviet government at the
end of the month. Lenin chose to use the former grand duchy to
display to the world the sincerity of his policy of the Right of
Nations to Self-Determination. This decision was encouraged in
part by the weakness at that moment of the Russian communists but,
as the non-socialist majority in the Finnish parliament turned down
demands for radical social reform and froze the moderate Social
Democrats out of politics, the latter were driven to join forces with
the Finnish Reds and to seize power in Helsinki at the end of
January 1918. This set off Finland's own civil war, at three months
much shorter than Russia's, but equally brutal. Workers and tenant
farmers from the south flew the red flag against smallholders from
the north led by professional military men for the Whites. With

---

[17] For more on this interpretation of the failings of Ukrainian nationalism, see
Richard Pipes, *The Formation of the Soviet Union: Communism and Nationalism 1917–
1923*, revised edn (Cambridge, MA: Harvard University Press, 1997), 148–50.

support from the Germans, the Finnish Whites emerged victorious from this struggle.[18] The Bolsheviks did little to aid the Finnish Reds and, excepting half-hearted attempts to win Finland back to socialism through the establishment of Soviet Karelia across the border, did not interfere in Finnish affairs until 1939.[19]

The weakness of the nationalist parties in Belorussia meant it was relatively easy for the Bolsheviks to disband the Belorussian National Congress there in December 1917. The population of Belorussia proved the most solidly pro-Bolshevik anywhere in the Empire in the elections to the Constituent Assembly. The region was occupied by German troops for most of 1918, but as they withdrew in November the Bolsheviks were able to regain control of the region and proclaim the first effective non-Russian Soviet republic in December. In February 1919 the Bolsheviks merged the communist parties of Belorussia and Lithuania and declared a joint Lithuanian–Belorussian Republic (Litbel), redolent of the medieval Commonwealth of Poland and Lithuania. In this way the Bolsheviks hoped to overcome the complex ethnic divisions in this part of the northwest by combining solidly pro-Bolshevik Belorussia with more ambivalent Lithuania, and to have a basis for future attempts to extend their reach into Poland. In ethnic terms, they could rely on the support of Belorussian, Russian and Jewish peasants and workers, as well as parts of the Lithuanian population, and exploit the hostility to the expropriated Polish landowners. In spite of their weak position, Belorussian nationalists were involved in this government, but they soon left it. The Litbel

---

[18] David Kirby, *The Baltic World, 1772–1993: Europe's Northern Periphery in an Age of Change* (London: Longman, 1995), 260–1.
[19] Markku Kangaspuro, 'Russian Patriots and Red Fennomans', in Antti Laine and Mikko Ylikangas (eds.) *The Rise and Fall of Soviet Karelia* (Helsinki: Kikimora Publications, 2002), 24–48.

collapsed less than three months after it was established, when Polish armies occupied the territory in April 1919. The Polish occupying forces reinstated the old landowners and enacted other measures that were contrary to the radical mood of the time, and the return of the Reds in the course of the Polish–Soviet war was welcomed. A Belorussian Soviet Republic was created anew on 1 August 1920 but, under the terms of the March 1921 treaty of Riga which ended the Polish–Soviet conflict, almost half of the lands settled by Belorussians went to Poland, while Lithuania was recognised as an independent state.

In the Baltic region, the situation unfolded in an altogether more complex manner. Votes for the Constituent Assembly confirmed the support of a majority of the Latvian population for the Bolsheviks. Having seen off the German landowners, Latvians provided a valuable source of administrative and military manpower for the Bolsheviks, including the Latvian Rifle Regiment which in effect acted as a bodyguard for Lenin and other leaders. But Latvia, along with Estonia and Lithuania, became swept up in the Civil War. Following the initial breakdown of the peace talks at Brest-Litovsk, German armies completed their occupation of the region in February 1918. A Latvian provisional national council declared Latvia's independence on 15 January 1918. On 24 February, a day before the Germans entered Tallinn, a Committee of Elders declared Estonia independent and sent representatives to the major powers. A German-sponsored Lithuanian government had already declared its separation on 11 December 1917. These declarations had little meaning as long as the Germans occupied the region, but set the scene for the struggles that followed the collapse of Germany in the autumn. The Estonian provisional government contended for power with the Tallinn Soviet for a brief period before the Red Army advanced on 22 November. Latvian

Bolsheviks set up a Soviet government, which welcomed the Red Army into Riga in early January 1919. A Soviet government was also set up in Lithuania in December 1918, but controlled only a part of Lithuanian territory. With Allied agreement, German armies remained in the Baltic region and, together with Finnish and Russian White support, the pro-independence forces were able to drive the Bolsheviks out by August 1919. By early 1920, concerned that the independent states would join forces again with the Whites, the Bolsheviks agreed to recognise independence. Estonia was recognised by the Bolsheviks in February 1920, Lithuania in July and Latvia in August. Allied recognition followed in 1921 and 1922.[20]

CENTRAL ASIA

Weak ties between the peoples of Turkestan and a barely developed sense of national identity hindered the development of political parties and stable political formations in the chaos of the Russian Civil War. In the northern part of Central Asia, the Kazakh Alash Orda was founded in July 1917 and established itself as the main Kazakh national party, demanding territorial autonomy from the Provisional Government. Returning refugees who had fled to China after the 1916 revolt fuelled a brutal conflict between Kazakhs and Russian colonists. As a means of self-defence as much as anything, the Alash Orda allied first with the Orenburg Cossacks, and then with the Russian Whites, until the summer of 1919, when they went over to the Bolsheviks and formed an important part of the leadership of the autonomous Kyrgyz

---

[20] Kevin O'Connor, *The History of the Baltic States* (Westport, CT: Greenwood Press, 1967), 77–83; Kirby, *The Baltic World*, 276–90.

Republic, established in 1920. In the Semirech'e region, however, disorganised requisitions of food led to armed rebellion against Soviet power, first on the part of the Cossack communities, but then also among local peasants, leading to the beginnings of the Basmachi movement.[21]

Politics among the Muslims of Turkestan was divided between a conservative clerical tendency and a modernising secular one. After the October Revolution, the immediate struggle was between the Russian-dominated Tashkent Soviet and the secular, liberal Muslims organised under the Turkestan Muslim Central Council lead by Mustafa Chokaev. When a Congress of the Council declared an autonomous government in Kokand in November 1917, this threw it into direct competition with the Tashkent Soviet. Conflict broke out between the Kokand government and the local soviet in February 1918. When the soviet was reinforced by troops arriving from Tashkent, an easy victory was followed by a massacre and the destruction of the Muslim quarter of the city. After a failed attempt by the Tashkent forces to overthrow the emir of Bukhara, they were brought under the control of the Bolsheviks and the soviet was rebuked for its handling of the national question. Although Soviet control barely existed in the countryside, autonomy for Turkestan was proclaimed on 30 April 1918.[22] Throughout the Russian Civil War, in spite of the conciliatory attitude of the Bolsheviks, conflict raged between the Muslim countryside and the Russian towns as well as between Reds and Whites, and included two brief interventions by British forces. The Civil War and a succession of food crises led to a drastic decline in

---

[21] Marco Buttino, 'Study of the Economic Crisis and Depopulation in Turkestan, 1917–1920', *Central Asian Survey*, 9, 4 (1990), 60–2.

[22] Sh. B. Batirov *et al.*, *Pobeda sovetskoi vlasti v Srednei Azii i Kazakhstane* (Tashkent: FAN, 1966), 612–13.

the population of Central Asia. Overall, the number of Russians in the towns fell by more than half. The whole of Turkestan experienced a loss of more than 1.5 million of its population between 1915 and 1920.[23]

Paradoxically, the ethnically divided population of the North Caucasus managed to maintain a greater unity of purpose throughout the Russian Civil War than was the case almost anywhere else in the Russian Empire. Self-rule was a reality rather than a proclamation across much of the region, with neither Reds nor Whites able to either exert control or draw on the region for support. There was little social stratification in the mountains, most of the population shared a common marker of adherence to Islam, and the struggles against Russian colonisation in the middle of the nineteenth century provided a narrative of coherence and resistance. Russians and Cossack colonists lived in distinct communities, and it was they rather than the Reds and Whites who bore the brunt of the struggle for independence.

A Congress of Mountaineers held in Vladikavkaz in September 1917 formed a Union of Mountain Peoples and drew up plans for autonomy within the Russian Empire. On 20 October, they entered into an alliance with the Terek Cossacks and formed a Terek–Dagestan government. This arrangement soon broke down, however, over incompatible claims to land, and the highland Chechens and Ingush launched an all-out assault on Russian and Cossack villages in reclaiming the land that had been taken away from them by the tsars. The Bolsheviks were, with the help of retreating

---

[23] Buttino, 'Economic Crisis', 65–9.

soldiers, able to take control of the Vladikavkaz and Grozny Soviets, and proclaimed a Terek People's Soviet Socialist Republic in March 1918 under Noi Buachidze. The Soviet government's writ never extended much beyond the cities, however, and rivalries between Cossacks and other Russian settlers over land led to splits in the government before the Ingush and Chechens renewed their attacks in the early summer. The association of the Cossacks with the Whites led a number of Muslim leaders to turn to the Bolsheviks, encouraged by their promises of self-rule. A change of tactic by the Bolsheviks allowed them to re-establish themselves, relying on the one hand on the backing of the Chechen and Ingush forces, and on the other hand on the widespread use of terror against the Cossacks.[24]

This shift was of great significance. In most of the empire, the Bolsheviks could rely on a core of Russian workers for support, but now for the first time they were able to ally directly with non-Russian peasants. The Caucasus highlanders who backed the Reds were neither Marxist Bolsheviks nor nationalists. Their organisation and position were determined by clan structures, a shortage of land and general poverty, and hatred of the Russian and Cossack settlers whose presence denied them land and was a constant reminder of the bloody suppressions of the nineteenth century. While it took until the end of the Civil War for the Bolsheviks to establish any real control, they were eventually able to do so through a combined policy of co-opting local leaders and promising broad cultural and language rights as well as limited self-rule through autonomous government.

---

[24] Galina Yemelianova, *Russia and Islam: A Historical Survey* (Basingstoke: Palgrave, 2002), 108–9; Pipes, *The Formation of the Soviet Union*, 195–9.

The Gorskaya (Mountain) Autonomous Republic was established in late 1918 covering the Chechen, Ingush, Ossetian, Kabardin, Balkar and Karachai lands as well as parts of Krasnodar and Stavropol districts. In November 1919, the Dagestan Autonomous Republic was formed. This was essentially a tactical military alliance of convenience in the first place, but the form it took coincided with the principles on which the Bolsheviks were beginning to develop a national structure for the Soviet lands, in which autonomy, federalism and national-cultural development formed the centrepiece. In time, in line with the nation-building aims which were developed, the Gorskaya republic was divided into separate national republics. But the fact that Soviet power in the Caucasus lacked any genuine support base among either the local population or the Russian city-dwellers, such as the Bolsheviks enjoyed in most other areas, meant that when it came to implementing a new social order resistance was particularly strong and effective. Hence parts of the North Caucasus remained a thorn in the side for the remainder of the Soviet period and beyond.

In the short term, the Bolsheviks already had to compete for power in the region. A North Caucasian Emirate led by the ninety-year-old Naqshbandi Uzun Haji and modelled on the Islamic imamate of Imam Shamil in the nineteenth century, was created in September 1919 in Chechnya and western Dagestan. The emirate wielded considerable authority in the mountain regions even after the end of the Civil War and the death of Uzun Haji, when leadership passed into the hands of Shamil's grandson Said Bek. It took over a year to fully remove the emirate, and the region remained a centre of sporadic revolt up until 1925.[25]

---

[25] Yemelianova, *Russia and Islam*, 109.

THE BAKU COMMUNE AND AZERBAIJAN

Soon after the October Revolution, the South Caucasus became cut off from the rest of Russia. In spite of the importance of Baku's oil reserves, the violence in the North Caucasus mountains and the White armies' attention being focussed on the north meant that local forces were to decide the short-term fate of the region. Oil and the geographical situation of the South Caucasus meant that it was Turkish and British, rather than Russian, forces which carried out incursions into the region, while other international actors, especially the United States, intervened in the diplomatic sphere. The three national governments that formed a short-lived Transcaucasian Federation in 1918 were of very different characters, and a series of border disputes and ethnic conflicts doomed the effort at unity to failure. The Transcaucasian government (Sejm) was formed on 23 January 1918, and declared independence from Russia on 22 April. But, under pressure from Turkish armies in the south, the Menshevik Georgian leaders responded to German offers of assistance by declaring Georgia's independence on 26 May, bringing the federation to an end.[26]

In Baku, the political crisis that followed the October Revolution coincided with an acute food crisis, as the city was cut off from the supplies that it normally depended on from the North Caucasus. Soldiers carried out arbitrary seizures of food and goods, and theft became endemic. In response to the breakdown in law and order, thousands of Muslims took to the streets on 13 December 1917 and began to form their own self-defence organisations.[27] Thus the

---

[26] Ronald Grigor Suny, *The Making of the Georgian Nation*, 2nd edn (Bloomington: Indiana University Press, 1994), 191–2.

[27] Ronald Grigor Suny, *The Baku Commune, 1917–1918: Class and Nationality in the Russian Revolution* (Princeton University Press, 1972), 187–8.

revolution was born with a sharp division between the Muslim and European populations. Efforts by the Muslim Musavat, Armenian Dashnak, Menshevik and Socialist Revolutionary parties to form a coalition government soon fell apart. As news came to the city of ethnic conflict between Muslims and Armenians elsewhere, the Musavat and Dashnaks moved ever further apart. Violence flared up regularly because of both the partition of the city into Muslim and Armenian quarters and the long-standing rivalries stemming from the recent growth of the city and the ethnic division of employment in the oil industry. The Bolsheviks increased their influence in the city through the formation of Red Guard units in January 1918, but by then their alliance with the Musavat had fallen apart. Following the peace agreement between Soviet Russia and Germany, most Russian soldiers (who could have formed the backbone of a local Red Army force) went home. Now the Bolsheviks had to rely, militarily as well as politically, on the Dashnaks. A rising in the Muslim quarters was put down by armed Armenians, who then proceeded to massacre thousands of Muslims over 1–2 April. With thousands more Muslims fleeing the city, the Armenians were in full control. The City Duma was also discredited, and Soviet power was proclaimed under the leadership of commissars coming from the Bolsheviks, Left Socialist Revolutionaries and the Hummet leader Nariman Narimanov. The Dashnaks refused to take posts in the government but supported it nevertheless. Over the next three months, the 'Baku Commune' introduced a socialist programme to the municipality, which included nationalisation of the oil industry.[28] As a Turkish army approached Baku, the Bolshevik commissars resigned on 26 July over the soviet's invitation to the British to send forces to

[28] *Ibid.*, 227–58.

help defend the city.[29] Twenty-six of the twenty-seven Bolshevik commissars, led by Stepan Shaumian, were allowed to leave the city by ship but were murdered on the far coast of the Caspian Sea in circumstances which have not been fully explained.[30]

Meanwhile an alternative Muslim government under Fatali Khan Khoiskii had been formed in Ganja on 28 May 1918. Having survived an attack by the Baku forces in June, this government entered a military alliance with Ottoman Turkey and extended its control over the rest of the country. On 16 September an Army of Islam, composed of Azerbaijani government soldiers and Turkish units, entered Baku and conducted a retaliatory massacre of Armenians, leaving some 15,000 Armenians dead.[31] Under the 9 October armistice between the Turkish government and the Entente, the Ottoman forces withdrew from the South Caucasus and their place was taken by British troops, who remained until August 1919. The British encouraged multi-party politics, allowing the Bolsheviks to reorganise and enabling the socialist Muslim party, the Hummet, to gain some ground against the Musavat.[32] The government maintained democratic standards, took steps to consolidate Azerbaijani Turkish as the main language of the republic and built up an army of some 30,000 men. But in political terms the Musavat struggled to control a series of coalition governments.

Throughout the period of independence, tensions between Armenians and Muslims continued to rage, with the main focus of conflict being the ethnically mixed region of Nagorno Karabakh.

---

[29] Brian Pearce, 'Dunsterforce and the Defence of Baku, August–September 1918', *Revolutionary Russia* (1997), 10, 1, 55–71.

[30] Most likely, they were executed on the orders of the Socialist Revolutionary-dominated Ashkhabad Soviet. The surviving commissar was Anastas Mikoyan.

[31] Tadeusz Swietochowski, *Russian Azerbaijan, 1905–1920: The Shaping of National Identity in a Muslim Community* (Cambridge University Press, 1985), 138–9.

[32] Audrey L. Altstadt, *The Azerbaijani Turks: Power and Identity under Russian Rule* (Stanford: Hoover Institution Press, 1992), 90–6; Pearce, 'Dunsterforce', 56–66.

This became an object of international attention at the Versailles peace negotiations, where strenuous lobbying on the part of the Armenian population of Nagorno Karabakh and the government of independent Armenia failed to secure diplomatic recognition.[33] An Armenian-dominated assembly elected a People's Government of Karabakh in August 1918, and declared itself independent of Azerbaijan. Following Turkish military incursions in October, the British army brokered a deal under which Nagorno Karabakh would become part of the Azerbaijan state.[34] For most of 1919 and 1920, in spite of a further agreement reached between the Karabakh Armenians and the Musavat government in August 1919, the region was beset by ethnic conflict and open warfare between Armenia and Azerbaijan. A rising of Armenians in March 1920 sufficiently distracted the army of Azerbaijan to allow the Red Army, fresh from defeating the White General Denikin and securing Dagestan, to cross the border into Azerbaijan. With the Bolsheviks' Caspian fleet also sailing towards Baku, and Turkey unwilling to commit any further to the cause of Azerbaijan, the parliament in Baku voted on the night of 20 April 1920 to accept Bolshevik demands and effectively agreed to the sovietisation of the country.

ARMENIA

Armenians had one of the most highly developed senses of national identity in the Russian Empire and a well-organised political party – the Dashnaks – to fight for their cause. Conversely, they were in the least secure position. Pressed by Azerbaijan to the east and Turkey to the south, not to mention Russia, their population was still

---

[33] Gerard J. Libaridian (ed.), *The Karabagh File* (Cambridge, MA: Zoryan Institute, 1988), 13–21.
[34] Swietochowski, *Russian Azerbaijan*, 143.

scattered across Asia Minor, and the core Armenian territory around Yerevan was economically weak. With Russian forces in possession of substantial areas of Turkish Armenia at the time of the February 1917 Revolution, Armenian hopes initially rested on a Russian victory in the war, and all of the Armenian parties supported the idea of federation or autonomy within a united Russia. The Bolshevik victory in October, however, changed these calculations since not only were Armenian nationalists hostile to Bolshevism, but they also suspected that the new regime would abandon territory won from Turkey in the course of the war. These fears were realised when the Bolsheviks signed the Treaty of Brest-Litovsk in March 1918, ceding the territory back to Turkey.

With Turkish forces moving into the South Caucasus and news of the bloodletting in Baku reaching Armenia, inter-ethnic conflict swept through both the towns and the countryside. Although part of the Transcaucasian Federation, Armenians had to rely on their own forces to repel the Turkish army from Yerevan, which they did after a bitter fight. The dissolution of the federation in May 1918, just as Soviet Russia became embroiled in full-scale civil war, left Armenia completely isolated, and with no alternative but to declare an independent state. A peace treaty with Turkey gave Armenia the breathing space to build up a new government in a devastated land, until the defeat of the Central Powers in November 1918 led to a full Turkish withdrawal. The new government had to deal with poverty and disease resulting from war and revolution, so severe that as much as 20 per cent of the entire population had died by the middle of 1919. Border disputes with Georgia and Azerbaijan led to frequent clashes,[35] and with the threat from nationalist Kemalist

---

[35] Kamala Imranli, *Sozdanie Armyanskogo gosudarstva na Kavkaze: istoki i posledstviya* (Moscow: Ladomir, 2006), 102–34.

Turkey which had replaced the collapsed Ottoman Empire ever present, the Armenian government depended entirely on foreign support. The British were the first on the scene and offered limited assistance. Although there was extensive goodwill towards the Armenians at the Paris Peace Conference, the more powerful countries were unwilling to make a long-term commitment to such an insecure area. The US mandate over Armenia that was agreed at Paris was hamstrung by the American Senate's refusal to endorse it. Although supplies that were delivered by the United States were crucial to Armenia's survival until 1920, this was not enough to protect it once Turkey and Soviet Russia had revived.

Kemalist and Soviet forces approached Armenia at the same time, in the summer of 1920. As Turkish forces advanced in September to November, capturing Kars and Alexandropol, the Dashnak-led government was forced to choose between two evils. Since the Bolsheviks at least held out the promise of an Armenian political formation surviving under Soviet rule, it was to them that the government reluctantly turned. Treaties were signed with both Turkey and Soviet Russia in late November, and on 2 December the new state of Soviet Armenia was proclaimed in Yerevan.[36]

GEORGIA

The new government of Georgia formed in June 1918 was a national government headed by the Menshevik Noe Zhordania, which worked independently of the soviets. Under pressure from the peasantry who formed the bulk of their support, the government eventually turned almost all land over to the private ownership of

[36] Ronald Grigor Suny, *Looking toward Ararat: Armenia in Modern History* (Hoboken, NJ: John Wiley & Sons, 1993), 119–30.

peasants by a law of January 1919. In external relations, Georgia
faced a period of uncertainty once the Germans had withdrawn, and
disputes with Armenia over the border between the two countries
flared into a brief war in December 1918. But the Georgian government reached an accommodation with the British forces that were
now deployed in the South Caucasus and who brokered an end to
the conflict with Armenia. International recognition of Georgia's
and Armenia's independence was eventually forthcoming on
12 January 1920. Relations with Soviet Russia remained tense, but
a peace treaty was signed on 7 May 1920. Among European socialists,
Georgia under the Mensheviks became a model for how a more
moderate, non-Bolshevik socialist country might look. Grandees of
the European Left such as the German Karl Kautsky visited the
country and published enthusiastic portraits of independent
Georgia.[37] In reality, however, the Mensheviks had reacted to the
cross-class support they enjoyed and the overwhelming enthusiasm
for independence by posing as a national government, and it
appeared to enact social reform only in response to pressure from
below. This transformation antagonised the Russian Mensheviks as
well as Armenian and Azerbaijani parties. While the government was
popular and could call on the inner strength of the country, the
departure of first German and then British forces left it isolated and
unable to resist a hostile Soviet Russia.[38]

Georgian nationalism inexorably led to confrontations between
the government and the country's national minorities. Throughout
the period of independence, the Georgian government faced ethnic
unrest on its northern borders. Ethnic Ossetians staged three major
rebellions between 1918 and 1920. An Ossetian national council,

---

[37] Karl Kautsky, *Georgia: A Social-Democratic Peasant Republic*, transl. by H. J. Stenning
(London: International Bookshops Limited, 1921).
[38] Suny, *Making of the Georgian Nation*, 195–208.

formed in December 1917 and allied with the Bolsheviks, welded the social grievances of Ossetian peasants with nationalist demands. The brutal actions of the Georgian National Guard in putting down these revolts seemed to confirm fears that Georgia was hell-bent on destroying the Ossetian nation. Ossetian political leaders considered a range of options for the region's future – unification with Russia, direct subordination to the victorious western Allies or participation in a separate North Caucasus state – but none of them involved remaining in Georgia. In retaliation for the last rebellion in May 1920, the Georgian government expelled all Ossetians from the Gori region and resettled their villages with Georgians.[39] In the northwest, an Abkhaz assembly voted in favour of joining the Gorskaya republic in Soviet Russia.[40]

Unlike in Azerbaijan and Armenia, the Bolsheviks remained weak in Georgia and, their support for the Ossetian risings apart, were unable to exploit internal divisions there. The treaty of May 1920, when the Red Army was already in Azerbaijan, was part of a wait-and-see strategy under which an internal collapse of the Menshevik regime was expected.[41] When this did not materialise, however, the political leader of the Bolshevik organisations in the Caucasus Sergo Ordzhonikidze, himself a Georgian, grew increasingly impatient and made his own preparations for a takeover. On at least four occasions between April 1920 and January 1921 the leaders of the Russian Communist Party forbade Ordzhonikidze from 'self-determining Georgia' (in other words, staging a pretext to establish Soviet rule by force),[42] but by starting a rising in the

---

[39] Arseny Saparov, 'From Conflict to Autonomy: The Making of the South Ossetian Autonomous Region 1918–1922', *Europe-Asia Studies*, 62, 1 (2010), 101–9.

[40] Stanislav Lakoba, *Abkhaziya posle dvukh imperii, XX–XXIvv.* (Moscow: Materik, 2004), 59–81.

[41] Isaac Deutscher, *The Prophet Armed, 1879–1921* (Oxford University Press, 1970), 474.

[42] RGASPI, f. 17, op. 3, d. 74, l. 3.

Lori district on 11 February Ordzhonikidze forced the hand of the leading body of the Russian Communist Party, the Politburo. On 14 February the Politburo endorsed the decision to launch an all-out invasion of Georgia, much to the annoyance of the absent leader of the Red Army, Leon Trotsky, and the leading Bolshevik in Georgia, Fillip Makharadze.[43] The Eleventh Red Army crossed the border from Azerbaijan on 15 February and reached Tbilisi on the 25th.[44] It took three weeks to subdue the rest of the country. In the end sovietisation was relatively easy but, unlike the rest of the territory of the future USSR, it was achieved purely through military force. This fact, as well as the unusual strength of Georgian nationalism, meant that not only was Georgia to continue to pose problems for the Soviets, but its fate also provoked one of the most serious crises in the Communist Party leadership in 1922.

NATIONAL AUTONOMY

In spite of the failure of the experiment of local national autonomy with the Bashrevkom in 1919–1920, this became established as the basic model for governing the non-Russian regions of Soviet Russia. The principle of national-territorial autonomy was mentioned in Iosif Stalin's 1913 article on the national question and was also embodied in the Bolshevik Party programme, but little had been said or written about what this meant in practice. In March 1918, a plan was advanced for the creation of a Tatar–Bashkir Soviet Republic, which never materialised because of the Russian Civil

---

[43] Jeremy Smith, 'The Georgian Affair of 1922: Policy Failure, Personality Clash or Power Struggle?', *Europe-Asia Studies* 50, 3 (1998), 523–24.
[44] Suny, *Making of the Georgian Nation*, 207–9.

War. Nonetheless the principle had become established and was heralded as a breakthrough in nationality relations.[45] Soon after this plan was drawn up, on 30 April 1918, the formation of a Turkestan Soviet Autonomous Republic (SAR) was declared, covering the large area of tsarist Turkestan. Although in practice the writ of the Soviet government there was weak as long as the Civil War lasted, a full constitution for the autonomous republic was adopted in October.[46] A separate Tatar Autonomous Soviet Socialist Republic (ASSR) was created soon after the Turkestan SAR Autonomous Republic, in May 1920. While the Turkestan SAR gave the appearance of appearing as a result of local initiative, the Tatar ASSR came out of a decree of the all-Russian Council of People's Commissars (Sovnarkom).[47]

These regions, unlike the main Soviet republics, which remained formally independent up until 1923, were clearly in a position of subordination to Moscow. But they were given considerable authority in local government, ran the education system and cultural institutions, had some responsibility for the administration of justice (including the incorporation of local traditions such as forms of sharia law in the North Caucasus) and for health care, social welfare and agriculture.[48] A lesser form of autonomy was granted to 'autonomous regions', which did not form their own commissariats.[49] But in both types of autonomy, the local language was given full rein and, importantly, members of the local population were actively recruited into the regional government. National autonomy was seen as a way of overcoming the mistrust of small non-Russian peoples towards Russians and Russian

---

[45] *Zhizn' natsional'nostei*, no. 62, 8 February 1920, 2.
[46] Batirov et al., *Pobeda sovetskoi vlasti*, 612–13.
[47] W. R. Batsell, *Soviet Rule in Russia* (New York: Macmillan, 1929), 143.
[48] *Ibid.*, 142–8. [49] *Ibid.*, 165–72.

authorities. By enticing non-Russians into the administration in this way, the Bolsheviks hoped to compensate for the low level of Party membership in these areas. But autonomy went deeper than that. Autonomous government was accompanied by development of national cultures, literacy programmes and publishing in the local languages. The Russian term used by the Bolsheviks for these processes – *korenizatsiia* – literally means 'enrooting'. The autonomous territories became the means by which Soviet power was to become rooted in the non-Russian nationalities, a process which was to be developed on a grander scale in the first half of the 1920s.

By November 1922, national autonomous units had been set up for the Karelians, Chuvash, Kyrgyz (Kazakhs), Votiaks, Kalmyks, Mari, Buryats, Komi, Crimean Muslims and, in the North Caucasus, Kabardins, Balkars, Karachais, Cherkess, and Chechens. These all took territory away from the Gorskaya Autonomous Republic, which was finally dissolved in July 1924 with the formation of the Ingush and North Ossetian autonomous regions. The subdivision of the Gorskaya republic was particularly controversial. Because of the geographical and ethnic complexity of parts of the North Caucasus, joint-nationality autonomous regions were formed for the Kabardins and Balkars, and the Karachais and Cherkess. While there may have been an element of divide-and-rule involved in an effort to avoid the sort of united resistance that had plagued imperial Russia and was again evident in the Civil War, the major national groups of the North Caucasus were clearly distinguished by ethnicity, language and location, and the way in which autonomous territories were created was consistent with principles established elsewhere. At Party discussions concerning these institutions, it was emphasised that, as well as providing a basis of support for Soviet rule, the separation of nationalities into distinct units was seen as a way of reducing tensions between competing national groups and between them and Russians.[50]

Outside Russia, a South Ossetian Autonomous Region, an Ajarian Autonomous Republic and an Abkhaz Autonomous Republic were formed in Georgia. Originally, the Abkhaz Republic was conceived as entirely separate, but in March 1921 was to be linked to Georgia by a 'special agreement'. The vague nature of this agreement allowed Abkhazia essentially to operate as a separate republic with the same level of self-rule (or more) as the other main republics until its status was clarified as subordinate to Georgia in the 1930s.[51] Nagorno Karabakh remained a subject of controversy for some years. In 1918–1920 both Armenia and Azerbaijan had laid claim to the region, which had a majority Armenian population but was surrounded by Azerbaijani territory. After Azerbaijan was sovietised, the new government led by Nariman Narimanov continued to claim the region, but immediately after Armenia became Soviet the Azerbaijan SSR reversed its position and recognised Nagorno Karabakh as part of Armenia on 1 December 1920, together with the other disputed territories of Zangezur and Nakhichevan. At a meeting of the Caucasian Bureau of the Russian Communist Party – the Kavburo – on 3–5 July this position was reversed, however, and in July 1923 the Autonomous Region of Karabakh was formed as part of Azerbaijan, a status that was confirmed by the USSR Constitution, adopted in January 1924. Nakhichevan, although it did not share any border with Azerbaijan, was also constituted as an autonomous region of the Azerbaijan SSR.

---

[50] *Dvenadtsatyi s'ezd RKP (b), 17–25 aprelya goda 1923: stenograficheskii otchet* (Moscow: Institut Marksizma-Leninizma, 1968), 500.
[51] For more on the creation of autonomous republics, see Jeremy Smith, 'The Origins of Soviet National Autonomy', *Revolutionary Russia* (1997), 10, 2, 62–84.

Nations of the Soviet Union were born at a time of intense class struggle. The February Revolution in Petrograd provided the opportunity for nationalists in the borderlands to put themselves at the head of the peasant movement but, as the crisis deepened and the Bolsheviks came to power in Russia, nationalists had to face the competing demands of class and nation. In many areas – Ukraine, the Volga region, Azerbaijan and Central Asia – national differences intensified conflicts between town and country, although at times conflict took on a purely national character. The Bolsheviks deployed the support they enjoyed in many towns to back the establishment of Soviet power, but in most cases had to rely mainly on the force of the largely Russian Red Army. The task, then, was to integrate reluctant and largely peasant non-Russians into the Soviet system, without alienating the urban Russian core support base. This challenge lay behind often fractious disputes within the Bolshevik Party and the uncomfortable road to the formation of the Union of Soviet Socialist Republics.

CHAPTER THREE

Bolshevik nationality policies and the formation of the USSR: the Bolsheviks dispute national policy

In the chaotic conditions of the Civil War, the gap between central Bolshevik policies and local implementation was most often played out in the form of undisciplined Russian soviets and Red Army bodies acting in ways that antagonised the local population. But as Soviet power became more secure, it emerged that there were real differences, based on a mixture of prejudice and ideology, which divided the Party both in the regions and at the centre. It was rarely the case that competing positions were associated exclusively with Bolsheviks of different ethnic backgrounds: the groupings that became known as the 'National Lefts' and the 'National Rights' could, in places like Crimea, both be associated with leaders from the same national group. Disagreements over policy locally were reflected in ideological divisions which went to the top of the Party leadership. Although their positions were not so far apart, subtle differences between the two Bolsheviks who had the greatest influence over nationality policy – Lenin and Stalin – had important consequences for the future of the nationalities experience in the USSR.[1]

The different positions that had been adopted by the European Marxist movement over the national question before the First

---

[1] The account that follows is based on chapters of my first book: Jeremy Smith, *The Bolsheviks and the National Question, 1917–1923* (London: Macmillan, 1999).

World War continued to divide the Bolsheviks during and after the Civil War. The internationalists were represented by the leading Bolsheviks Yuri Pyatakov and Nikolai Bukharin, while the right to national self-determination was defended by Lenin with the support of the commissar for nationality affairs, Iosif Stalin. Although much of the debate remained abstract, the experience of the revolution and the task of putting back together the parts of the Russian Empire that had dispersed lent these arguments a concrete urgency. At the discussion of the new Party programme in March 1919, Pyatakov argued that 'the slogan "the right of nations to self-determination" ... has shown itself in practice, when it comes to the question of the socialist revolution, to be a slogan which is the rallying point for all counter-revolutionary forces'.[2] The programme eventually adopted a compromise position which stated that the question of who exactly should express the right to self-determination would be decided from 'a historical-class point of view, taking into consideration the level of historical development of any given nation'.[3] Given that the Bolsheviks, especially Stalin, depicted practically all of the nationalities of the former empire as 'backward', this policy effectively meant that in formal terms the question of self-determination could be settled by city soviets and the communists who ran them, even though they represented only a minority of the population.

While the principle of national self-determination was of little practical consequence during and after the Civil War as a result of this reformulation, its spirit was frequently invoked at the local level when it seemed that national rights were being violated by Soviet authorities. Internationalists continued to object to the more

---

[2] *Vos'moi s'ezd RKP (b)* (Moscow: Gosizdat, 1959), 78.
[3] *KPSS v rezoliutsiiakh* (Moscow: Gosizdat, 1963), 45.

detailed development of a new nationality policy. At the Tenth Party Congress in March 1921 Stalin framed this policy, the key to which was national-territorial autonomy, in terms of the need to eliminate 'backwardness' among the non-Russians: 'the Party's task is to help the labouring masses of the non-Great Russian peoples to catch up with central Russia, which has forged ahead'.[4] This was the same congress that introduced the New Economic Policy (NEP) to Russia in an effort to prevent the rift between the Russian peasantry and Soviet power which had become apparent in a series of peasant risings and the Kronstadt sailors' rebellion. In the same spirit as the NEP, the new nationality policy accepted the difficulties that were faced in building socialism and sought a way to eventually over-come them by giving some leeway for essentially non-socialist forces to develop. While the NEP was temporary, however, national autonomy and, a bit later, Soviet federalism were to be more lasting. Not all Bolsheviks accepted this but, when asked in 1923 how long he expected the national-territorial structure of the Soviet lands to last, Lenin answered 'for a long time yet'. The preservation of separate national identities, which had never appeared as a desirable aim in pre-revolutionary Bolshevik writings and which appeared to contradict Marx's famous slogan 'the work-ers have no country', was now embedded in Bolshevik policy.

While Lenin and Stalin were able to claim victory in the major debates at Party congresses and conferences on the national ques-tion, the fact that they faced so much opposition and had to swallow the occasional compromise did not bode well when it came to the situation on the ground. At the height of the Bashkir crisis in 1920 Yuri Lutovinov, a senior figure in the Russian government and

---

[4] *Desiatyi s'ezd RKP (b), mart 1921 goda: stenograficheskyi otchet* (Moscow: Gosizdat, 1963), 252.

sympathiser towards the Workers' Opposition, bluntly told a Bashkir delegate 'That whole autonomous republic, which you take so seriously, is only a game to keep you people busy.'[5] While Lutovinov was quickly reprimanded for this remark, it expressed an attitude that was common among rank-and-file communists, and was especially prevalent among Russian Bolsheviks who were active in regions of mixed nationality. Thus, it not only undermined attempts to institute autonomy and encourage participation in Soviet power by non-Russians in places such as Bashkiria, but also affected efforts to win nationalities to the Red side during the Civil War and threatened to provoke further conflicts along national lines after it.

These local Russian Bolsheviks were mostly newcomers to the Party with little grounding in Marxism, and it is unlikely that there were many cases in which their behaviour was motivated by an ideological adherence to internationalism, as was the case with Bukharin, Pyatakov and Lutovinov. Nor was it as straightforward as a case of racist attitudes, although this element (Great Russian chauvinism, as the Bolsheviks referred to it) was important. In Central Asia and the Volga region in particular, the legacy of Russian colonialism meant there were real issues at stake. Newly confiscated lands had to be redistributed and the righting of past wrongs was one of the principles that the local population referred to in their appeals. The introduction of the NEP in 1921 redefined the relationship between the towns and the countryside, but the exact redefinition of that relationship had to be worked out at the local level. Where predominantly Russian towns were surrounded by predominantly non-Russian villages, it took on a national character.

---

[5] Quoted in Pipes, 'The First Experiment', 313.

It was characteristically acute of Lenin that he understood this. He may have had a natural sympathy for the empire's non-Russians from an early age,[6] but he was also a realist whose priority was the preservation and strengthening of Soviet power. While not rejecting in principle the aspiration to a single, multi-national state, the realities created by the Russian Empire were that, should non-Russians be part of the socialist project, their confidence needed to be earned. As he wrote to Stepan Shaumian some years before the Russian Revolution: 'Why will you not understand the psychology that is so important in the national question and which, if the slightest coercion is applied, besmirches, soils and nullifies the undoubtedly progressive impor- tance of centralised states and a uniform language?'[7] The other side of this coin was the Great Russian chauvinism of many Russians including local communists, reinforced by the deployment of large numbers of tsarist administrators who, in Lenin's analysis, continued to hold the colonial attitudes of the old regime. Not only did these attitudes threaten to alienate the non-Russians, they were also a barrier to the full emancipation of the Russian workers. Hence Lenin was ready to concede a whole range of issues to non-Russian national sentiment, with the aim of simultaneously attracting non- Russians to the Soviet project and countering the prejudices inherited from the old regime.

NATIONAL COMMUNISM

How far the Bolshevik leaders were prepared to go in this direction is illustrated by a comment Stalin was claimed to have made to the

---

[6] Isabelle Kreindler, 'A Neglected Source of Lenin's Nationality Policy', *Slavic Review* (1977), no. 1, 86–100.

[7] V. I. Lenin, *Polnoe sobranie sochinenii*, 55 vols., 5th edn (Moscow: Gosudarstvo İzdatel'stvo politicheskoi literatury, 1964), XLVIII, 234.

Bashkir leader Zeki Validov and the Kazakh nationalist Akhmet Baitursynov, which stands in contrast to Lutovinov's statement above: 'although both of you are nationalists, we know you as people who will be able to accept the idea of worldwide revolution ... In your lands today begins the life of the party. We want to see you inside this work. Those who choose to be outside the organization, life leaves behind. You are not communists, but I want to see you as members of the party and to work with us.'[8] The Bolsheviks were serious about attracting nationalists to their movement, as they demonstrated in a number of regions. This policy could be justified ideologically through the analysis that nationalism among oppressed nationalities was objectively revolutionary.

In more practical terms, the Bolsheviks were short of reliable cadres among their own ranks in most of the borderlands, while many nationalists stood not far from the main social programme of the Russian revolutionaries. In Ukraine, the Bolsheviks took the opportunity of a split in the Socialist Revolutionary Party in May 1918 to woo the left wing of the party, who now called themselves the 'Borotbists' after their newspaper *Borotba*, meaning 'Struggle'. Although socialist, the Borotbists were also nationalist to the extent that they disagreed with the Bolsheviks on the relationship between Ukraine and Russia and on Ukrainian culture. But they shared the Bolshevik policies on Soviet power and the redistribution of land, which was sufficient for them to propose merging with the Communist Party of Ukraine. Although this advance was initially rejected by the Ukrainian communists, they were overruled by the Politburo of the Russian Communist Party, and in April 1919 the

---

[8] Steven Sabol, *Russian Colonization and the Genesis of Kazak National Consciousness* (Basingstoke: Palgrave, 2003), 149. The quote is sourced from Validov's memoirs: Zaki Validov Togan, *Vospominaniia: Bor'ba musul'man Turkestana i drugikh vostochnykh Tiurok za natsional'noe sushchestvovanie i kul'turu* (Moscow, 1997), 224.

merger went ahead. As part of this deal, the leading Borotbist, Oleksander Shumskyi, was admitted to the Ukrainian Soviet government as commissar of enlightenment, with responsibility for education and culture.[9]

Thousands of Jewish socialists, members of the Bund party, joined the Bolsheviks during the Civil War, many of them having been rescued from pogroms by the Red Army. In the middle of 1920, having already taken over its Belorussian branch, the Bolsheviks merged what was left of the Bund into the Communist Party.[10] The Azerbaijani socialist party the Hummet had already co-operated with the Bolsheviks in the Baku Commune of 1918 and merged with the Communist Party of Azerbaijan in 1920, providing most of the leadership of the new Soviet republic. These organisations were essentially socialist in orientation before linking up with the Bolsheviks, but the Kazakh Alash Orda, which had previously opposed the Soviets and made no secret of its nationalism, split at the end of 1919, with most of its leaders joining the Communists, while other members fled to join the Basmachi rebellion.[11] In the course of the Civil War, the Reds engaged in joint operations against the Whites with a number of radical Muslim organisations – the Kazakh Ush-Zhuz, the Crimean Tatar Milli Firqa, the Young Bukharans and the Young Khivans, and the Kazan Socialist Committee. While these organisations did not formally merge, many of their members ended up joining the Bolsheviks.[12]

This strategy of embracing non-Russian nationalists and giving them positions of responsibility was not without risk. The

[9] James E. Mace, *Communism and the Dilemmas of National Liberation: National Communism in Soviet Ukraine* (Cambridge, MA: Harvard University Press, 1983), 55–8.
[10] Zvi Y. Gitelman, *Jewish Nationality and Soviet Politics* (Princeton University Press, 1972), 161–74.
[11] Sabol, *Russian Colonization*, 148–9.
[12] Bennigsen and Wimbush, *Muslim National Communism*, pp. 26–223.

consequences of the alliance with the Borotbists in Ukraine became apparent a few years later and are dealt with in the next chapter. In the short term it was the Muslim 'national communists' who posed the greater problem. At the beginning of 1918, a Muslim Commissariat (Muskom) was formed under the People's Commissariat for Nationality Affairs (Narkomnats), initially headed by Mulla Nur Vakhitov, and then by Mirsaid Sultangaliev after Vakhitov's death in August 1918. Vakhitov, Sultangaliev and other members of the Muskom came out of the progressive Jadidist movement and, like other national communists, shared many of the social aims of the Bolsheviks. But they also adhered to notions of pan-Islamic and pan-Turkic unity which were at odds with the direction of Bolshevik nationality policy, and the Muskom frequently came into conflict with the other sections of Narkomnats and with Soviet organisations in the Muslim parts of Russia. Sultangaliev espoused a doctrine of 'proletarian nations' which asserted that, due to the relative lack of class differentiation in underdeveloped Muslim regions, the whole Muslim population should be treated as equivalent to the working class elsewhere. He called for the formation of a separate Muslim Communist Party and dreamed of a broad, pan-Turkic socialist state. Stalin generally backed the Muskom in these conflicts without giving in to their unorthodox programmes, and Sultangaliev became an especial protégé. But on 4 May 1923 Sultangaliev was arrested and charged with anti-Soviet activities which included forming a secret organisation and dealing with leaders of the Basmachi and Turkish communists.[13]

Sultangaliev's life was spared for the moment, and he was reassigned to work in the Caucasus. His was an extreme case, but a

[13] Jeremy Smith, *The Bolsheviks*, 228–32.

special meeting convened on 6 June to discuss the Sultangaliev Affair revealed that the divisions over nationality policy in the borderlands were not straightforward reflections of a split between Russian and local communists. The meeting brought together leading communists of all of the major Soviet nationalities, together with members of the Communist Party of the Soviet Union (CPSU) Central Committee and Politburo. What emerged was that in almost all regions there were clearly identifiable 'National Lefts' and 'National Rights'. The National Lefts were non-Russians who frequently associated with the internationalist Russians in their regions and insisted on a more centralised state. The National Rights covered a broad spectrum from those who agreed with Lenin on the need to display tact in order to win over the non-Russian population to those who were essentially nationalists themselves. The split between these factions was particularly acute and took on an organised form in places of mixed population such as Tashkent, the Tatar republic or Crimea. The representatives of the Party leadership – Stalin, Trotsky and Frunze – tried at this meeting to steer a middle course, but came out against Great Russian chauvinism (i.e., the National Lefts) as posing the greater danger at the time.[14]

MORE DISPUTES

The spectre of Great Russian chauvinism and the need to recruit non-Russian cadres pushed the party leadership to embrace the non-Russian nationalists and to strengthen the institutions of national-territorial autonomy. Eventually they were to design a new form of

[14] B. F. Sultanbekov (ed.), *Tainy nationsal'noi politiki TsK RKP: stenograficheskii otchet sekretnogo IV soveshchaniia TsK RKP, 1923 g.* (Moscow: INSAN, 1992).

Soviet federalism. But this direction was not without its difficulties. The end of the Civil War and introduction of the NEP heralded, it was hoped, a new era of stability and recovery, the cornerstone of which was the worker–peasant alliance. But, just as peasants rebelled in the Russian countryside throughout 1921, so there were constant reminders that not all non-Russians had accepted Soviet power or given up hope of national independence. The Basmachi movement continued to disrupt Central Asia for most of the 1920s, and Makhno's forces remained active in Ukraine until August 1921. Nationalist groupings continued to organise, underground or semi-legally, but mostly under the watchful eyes of the security services, the OGPU.[15] On top of this, the policies that had evolved over the course of the Civil War had not been thought out in advance, and involved new departures in terms of Marxist theory, with all the tensions that involved. In particular, the new policy implied a tolerance of nationalism and co-operation with nationalists who Marxists had previously dismissed as bourgeois in both attitude and background.

Stalin was close to Lenin on the national question, but there were subtle differences that were to evolve into an open dispute between the two.[16] From 1918 Stalin stressed that the nationality policies the

[15] The monthly OGPU reports (*svodki*) prepared for Soviet leaders included separate sections on the activities of nationalists throughout the 1920s. They are published in: G. N. Sevost'yanov (ed.), '*Sovershenno sekretno*': *Lubianka – Stalinu o polozhenii v stranye*, 12 vols. (Moscow: Institut Rossiiskoi istorii RAN, 2001–8).

[16] There is a wide range of views on the differences between Lenin and Stalin on the national question. For an account that ascribes completely opposing policies to them, see Nigel Harris, *National Liberation* (London: Penguin, 1990), 71–72. Richard Pipes, *The Formation of the Soviet Union*, points out some differences but essentially sees Stalin as carrying on Lenin's policy, as does Stephen Blank, *The Sorcerer as Apprentice: Stalin as Commissar of Nationalities, 1917–1924* (Westport, CT: Westview Press, 1994). For more detailed discussion of this question, see Erik van Ree, 'Stalin and the National Question', *Revolutionary Russia* (1994), 7, 2, 214–38, and Moshe Lewin, *Lenin's Last Struggle* (London: Pluto Press, 1975).

Soviet regime was pursuing were a response to the 'backwardness' of non-Russians, with the implication that this was a temporary, developmental stage. All the same, the two shared the vision of territorial self-rule and national development as the best way of incorporating non-Russians into the Soviet project. But Stalin never showed quite the same sensitivity to the non-Russian nationalities as Lenin did. For Stalin, his policies provided practical solutions, whereas Lenin was equally concerned with the way they were received both at home and internationally. As Lenin had explained to Shaumian, it was 'the psychology' that mattered. Stalin also had other concerns. With his military duties coming to an end, in 1920 Stalin turned his attention to running Narkomnats, which he had left in the hands of deputies for much of the Civil War.[17] This was his main political base until he took up the post of general secretary of the CPSU in 1922. Although Narkomnats was less important than the commissariats involved in industry, security and defence, it derived considerable power from the authority it wielded over the autonomous republics and regions of the Russian Soviet Federative Socialist Republic (RSFSR). Its remit was limited to the RSFSR, however, as long as the other Soviet republics remained formally independent. Stalin could not even claim to be the CPSU's leading policy-maker and theoretician on the national question, since this position belonged to Lenin himself. As far as relations with the other Soviet republics went, major decisions were taken by the CPSU Politburo and, while Stalin had considerable input in those decisions, in formal terms his opinion counted for no more than that of any other Politburo member. Bringing the non-Russian republics under his control would have considerably increased his political

---

[17] In spite of the common perception of Stalin as the 'architect' of early Soviet nationality policies, there is little evidence that he took his duties as commissar for nationalities altogether seriously until 1922. See Blank, *Sorcerer as Apprentice*.

status, a matter that was gaining in importance the more Lenin's health declined.[18]

The two clashed over the issue of how the four Soviet entities (the RSFSR, Ukraine, Belorussia and the Transcaucasian Federation comprising Armenia, Azerbaijan and Georgia) should be unified into a single state. Stalin favoured a simple extension of the model of national-territorial autonomy which had already been applied in the RSFSR. So Ukraine, for example, would become an autonomous republic of the RSFSR. Stalin was the head of the commission that was looking into the future structure of the Soviet state in the autumn of 1922, and drew up plans along these lines. He even secured the support of Ukraine and Armenia, and qualified support from Georgia and Azerbaijan, though the Georgian communists felt it was too soon to implement the project. Serious differences emerged on points of detail within the commission, and in late September Lenin acquainted himself with the commission's work. After a meeting with Stalin lasting two hours and forty minutes, Lenin wrote to Lev Kamenev that 'Stalin has already agreed to make one concession – in paragraph one, instead of "adhesion" to the RSFSR, to say "formal union with the RSFSR into a union of Soviet republics of Europe and Asia".'[19] Lenin went on to clarify explicitly that he was now talking about a federation of equals, not a unitary state with subordinate autonomous territories. The difference was not as great as it may seem – under both projects, the republics would enjoy self-rule in areas such as culture and education, and broad rights to vary practices and legislation in areas such as justice and agriculture. But economic policy would be

---

[18] For elaboration of this argument, see Jeremy Smith, 'Stalin as Commissar for Nationalities', in Sarah Davies and James Harris (eds.), *Stalin: A New History* (Cambridge University Press, 2005), 45–62.

[19] Lenin, *Polnoe sobranie*, vol. XLV, 211.

co-ordinated and there would only be one foreign policy. And, of course, the Communist Party would in practice maintain its control everywhere. The immediate difference was mainly one of presentation – were the national republics going to appear to be swallowed up by Russia, or to be entering a union with it as equals? Stalin accepted Lenin's suggestion, but confronted the leader directly over a number of minor points and accused him, in a letter to the Central Committee, of 'national liberalism'.[20]

The disagreements over Stalin's 'autonomisation project' were illustrative of the concern Lenin showed for the international reception of his Party's nationality policy. The compromise arrived at led eventually to the title of 'Union of Soviet Socialist Republics'. But a more serious crisis over nationality policy was just over the horizon. While Stalin was not directly involved in this, it gave Lenin greater reason than ever to fear that mistreatment of national minorities, whether dressed up as internationalism or just Russian arrogance, could seriously undermine his socialist project. The scene of this crisis was the republic of Georgia, which had held out longer than anywhere else against Soviet power and where the continuing appeal of nationalism had led Lenin to call for a policy of 'Special Concessions'. In spite of this warning, over the course of 1921 a series of disputes had arisen between the Communist Party of Georgia, led by Budu Mdivani and Fillip Makharadze, and the Caucasian Bureau of the CPSU (Kavburo) headed by Sergo Ordzhonikidze. Most of these disputes concerned the respective powers of the Soviet Georgian government and the Federal Union of Soviet Socialist Republics of Transcaucasia, which had been formed from Armenia, Azerbaijan and Georgia in March 1922. The Georgian government acted as if Georgia were a completely

[20] RGASPI, f. 5, op. 2, d. 28, ll. 23–4.

separate state, setting up border controls and setting ethnic criteria for citizenship, while the Kavburo sought to bring the security forces (the Cheka), army and economy of Georgia directly under its control.

When it came to the proposal to incorporate Georgia, as part of the Transcaucasian Federation, into the USSR, the Georgian leaders complained vociferously but were dismissed out of hand by Lenin and other leaders. The day after receiving Lenin's telegram rebuffing their protests, 22 October 1922, nine of the eleven members of the Central Committee of the Communist Party of Georgia resigned in protest at the Transcaucasian Committee's (Zakkraikom – the successor to the Kavburo) decision to expel a number of oppositionists from Tbilisi. One of the Georgians who resigned, M. Okudzhava, wrote to Lenin detailing a number of cases of physical and verbal abuse against himself by Ordzhonikidze. This prompted the Central Committee of the Russian Communist Party to send a commission to Tbilisi to investigate, led by the head of the Cheka Felix Dzerzhinsky. Not fully trusting Dzerzhinsky, Lenin himself sent Politburo member Alexei Rykov to Tbilisi soon after. Rykov happened to witness an event which led Lenin to take the affair even more seriously – at a social gathering, Ordzhonikidze struck another Georgian communist, Akakii Kabakhidze.

Dzerzhinsky's commission cleared Ordzhonikidze and the Zakkraikom.[21] But the affair clearly disturbed Lenin, who was on the verge of pursuing it further when ill health struck him down on the night of 15–16 December and brought his active political life to an end. But his concern was sufficient for him to dictate his 'Notes

---

[21] For fuller accounts of the Georgian Affair, see Lewin, *Lenin's Last Struggle*; Jeremy Smith, 'The Georgian Affair of 1922'.

on the Question of Nationalities or "Autonomisation"' on the night of 30–31 December. Together with his famous 'Testament', this was Lenin's last major political intervention. The events in Georgia led Lenin to view his earlier dispute with Stalin in a different light, and to doubt whether Great Russian attitudes might not destroy his plans for a Soviet federation. He called for strict rules on language rights and self-government for the republics, and for exemplary punishment against Ordzhonikidze. In late January, Lenin asked his secretaries to compile a full report on the affair. Lenin was too ill to act on the findings of this report, which sided fully with the Georgian communists, and instead handed it over to Trotsky. In Lenin's absence, Stalin was responsible for seeing through the creation of the USSR. While he was not himself directly implicated in the Georgian Affair, at exactly this time he fell out with Lenin over his handling of Lenin's medical treatment and his rudeness to Lenin's wife Nadezhda Krupskaya, while the political struggle between Stalin and Trotsky was beginning to heat up.

The stage was set for a major confrontation at the Twelfth Congress of the Russian Communist Party, which met in mid April 1923. But Lenin's notes on the national question were over-shadowed by his Testament, in which he criticised all of the Party's leading figures, especially Stalin. Trotsky bowed out of the fight on the nationalities question, and it was left to the Georgians to make their case with half-hearted support from the leader of Soviet Ukraine Khristian Rakovsky, Mirsaid Sultangaliev (days before his arrest), and Nikolai Bukharin. At a separate meeting to the main congress, which included delegates specially invited from the republics and autonomous units, Stalin came under more sustained attack for his theses on the national question. Trotsky again reneged on his instructions from Lenin and refused to enter the fray, but the sustained pressure of the republican delegates, backed up by leading

Bolsheviks such as Mikhail Frunze, led to a number of amendments to Stalin's original theses. These included condemnation of talk about the superiority of Russian culture; a policy of preferential industrial investment in the non-Russian regions; a commitment to allow republican commissariats to operate independently; insistence on the permanence of the national republics; equality of each of the republics in the new federal structures; guarantees on the status of national languages; and the organisation of national military units.[22]

Lenin and Stalin were not so far apart on their conception of the best form for centralising the Soviet republics, and their biggest arguments were over other issues.[23] But the Georgian Affair confirmed what had already become apparent in the autumn of 1922. Stalin and others were, in Lenin's eyes, insufficiently sensitive to the consequences of behaviour which could be pounced on by Great Russian chauvinists who, Lenin argued, still played a major role in the Soviet administration. Such behaviour and attitudes not only threatened to alienate the non-Russians, but would lose the Soviets the respect and inspiration which Lenin saw as essential to his policy of spreading the revolution internationally, with his attention now shifting from Central and Eastern Europe towards the colonial and semi-colonial regions of Asia, Africa and the Middle East. Although Lenin's theses were not published at the time, their contents were sufficiently well known to imbue with confidence and the authority that went along with Lenin's endorsement those delegates who pushed through the amendments to Stalin's theses on the national question. These amendments represented a significant shift away from the largely declaratory tenor of Stalin's proposals,

---

[22] Jeremy Smith, *The Bolsheviks*, 213–28.
[23] Robert Service, *Lenin: A Political Life*, vol III, *The Iron Ring* (Basingstoke: Macmillan, 1995), 268–82.

and endowed the republics and the federation with concrete characteristics.

On the eve of the formation of the USSR, the Russian communists had a policy which made the union neither an administrative convenience nor a federal facade. The republics were to have real powers and rights, and their existence was to embody national development under the guidance of the Communist Party. These decisions determined the course of the national question in the 1920s, and many of them remained relevant through to 1991. The Fourth Conference of the Central Committee with Responsible Party Workers, convened from 9–12 June to discuss the Sultangaliev Affair, was not able to influence the structure of the USSR, but provided another forum at which the National Lefts and Rights could fight out their differences, and both sides could criticise the leadership. Stalin was more in control of proceedings than he had been in April, but his clear statements that Great Russian chauvinism now presented a greater threat than local nationalism showed how far he had needed to amend his own position. Overall, the conference confirmed the language, governance and cadre policies that had been brought into the Party Programme by the Twelfth Congress.

THE FORMATION OF THE USSR

The debates that raged in the Communist Party from the autumn of 1922 to the summer of 1923 arose from the need to formalise relations between the legally independent Soviet republics. The principles of federation which evolved over the second half of 1922 were formally approved through a Treaty of Union between the RSFSR, Ukraine, Belorussia and the Soviet Federation of Transcaucasia. The constitution that was worked out after the

Twelfth Party Congress organised authority according to a three-level schema: those areas which were the preserve of the federal centre in Moscow; those for which each republic had its own responsibility, but where the republican commissariats were subjected to federal commissariats in Moscow; and those where the republics on their own were responsible for policy. In the first category were foreign affairs, defence, foreign trade, communications, and post and telegraphs. Commissariats of finance, food, economy, labour, control and inspection, and state security existed at both the republic and federal levels. Internal affairs, justice, enlightenment, health, social welfare and nationality affairs were left to the commissariats of individual republics.[24] Each republic would govern through its own Supreme Soviet, and the federal government, the Central Executive Committee, was elected by a Congress of Soviets. The CEC was divided into two houses along the lines of bicameral systems in western democracies: the Soviet of the Union (or Federal Soviet), which debated and passed legislation, and an 'Upper House' – the Soviet of Nationalities where each republic was represented according to status rather than size. Each of the union republics and each of the autonomous republics of the RSFSR had five members, while each autonomous region of the RSFSR and each of the five autonomous republics and regions of Transcaucasia had one member.[25] Overall, this gave representatives from the RSFSR three times as many votes as those from the other three republics put together, albeit mostly from non-Russian regions. The Soviet of Nationalities in theory had equal legislative

[24] Ben Fowkes, *The Disintegration of the Soviet Union: A Study in the Rise and Triumph of Nationalism* (Basingstoke: Macmillan, 1997), 44.

[25] Hélène Carrère d'Encausse, *The Great Challenge: Nationalities and the Bolshevik State, 1917–1930* (New York: Holmes and Meier, 1992), 134.

rights to the Soviet of the Union. Under the original constitution, the USSR had four presidents – one from each republic.

With the adoption of this constitution on 31 January 1924, the USSR came into being. Simultaneously, the Communist Party of the Soviet Union was formed. Ukraine, Belorussia, Armenia, Azerbaijan and Georgia each also had its own Communist Party, but there was no separate communist organisation for the RSFSR. The CPSU retained the tradition of democratic centralism, and the nationalities had no especial rights within its overall structures.[26]

Disputes among leading Bolsheviks went back to pre-war times and were part of a lively debate in the Marxist movement across Europe, in which the protagonists were Otto Bauer, Karl Renner, Karl Kautsky and Rosa Luxemburg as well as Lenin and other Bolsheviks. But the Civil War and early years of Soviet power provided these disputes with an especially sharp edge, not only because now there was an opportunity to put policy into practice, but also because Russians and non-Russians alike in the border-lands adopted positions which could be aligned with those of the different leaders, but which were based as much on conflicting national interests and prejudices as on theoretical niceties. National interests in this context included economic and other resource interests, and the outcome of the struggle at the centre was to have profound implications for the distribution of land and political power in the peripheries. On balance, the 'internation-alist' tendency was stronger in the soviets in the non-Russian regions, and the victory of the Leninist line, backed by the

---

[26] For the significance of the absence of a Russian Communist Party, see Geoffrey Hosking, *Rulers and Victims: The Russians in the Soviet Union* (Cambridge, MA: Harvard University Press, 2006).

National Rights, involved a considerable political effort when it came to implementation. Although the policies of nation-building, federalism and *korenizatsiia* which emerged were put in place, they faced enormous opposition and the development of the Soviet nations in the 1920s did not proceed smoothly or without opposition.

CHAPTER FOUR

Nation-building the Soviet way

In creating the USSR and a series of autonomous territories, the Bolsheviks had put territoriality at the heart of their nationality policy. But the course of the debates leading up to this had further implications. As the struggle between 'National Lefts' and 'National Rights' developed in the course of 1922 and 1923, the Rights came out, by and large, on top at the centre and thereby in the peripheries. Delegates returned from the June 1923 special conference to their republics and regions armed with a clear mandate to continue and deepen the process of national consolidation and nation-building. They set about this task with a will, and enlisted national intellectuals and cultural producers in the project. Where they proved insufficiently strong to override the objections of (mostly Russian) local Party members and officials, they were able to call on the centre to support them. While support usually was forthcoming, it was still not always sufficient to overcome opposition. The process of nation-building was, therefore, accompanied by political and, occasionally, violent struggle. Meanwhile, nationalist or religious opponents of Bolshevism continued to try to undermine Soviet rule, occasionally by open rebellion. The policies of *korenizatsiia* and nation-building were therefore being squeezed from two directions, but ultimately prevailed. In a short period of time, by the end of the 1920s people who had not really thought in national terms before the First World War found that they now had a national language, a

73

national culture, national histories and national political structures –
in short, they had become members of a nation.

NATIONAL BORDERS

With the territorial principle at the heart of nationality policy, the
exact location of republican borders became an issue for claims and
counterclaims before and after the USSR was formed. The many
complex border questions in the South Caucasus were mostly
resolved by a Conference on Regulating the Internal Borders of
Transcaucasia, which met in July 1921. But the conference devolved
several of the trickier problems to commissions composed of representatives of all the nationalities living in mixed areas and experts
sent from Moscow. The negotiations of these commissions were
frequently tortuous but generally arrived at detailed agreements
which tried, as far as was practicable, to draw borders between
villages of different nationalities.[1]

In a similar vein, numerous adjustments were made to the
borders of Ukraine and the RSFSR. Belorussia proved a more
difficult case, mainly because of the difficulty of establishing
whether individual villages were Belorussian or Russian, given
the mixed nature of dialects there and overlapping self-identification
by inhabitants. Having lost substantial territory as a result of the
Soviet–Polish war in 1921, Belorussian leaders successfully lobbied
to extend their territory further to the east and south, leading to a
series of enlargements that more than doubled the area and trebled
the population of the republic between 1921 and 1926. These
expansions were achieved against the opposition of Ukrainian and
regional Russian authorities, and often against the wishes of the

---

[1] Jeremy Smith, *The Bolsheviks*, 66–8.

local population who did not consider themselves Belorussian.[2] In the case of Belorussia, the question of the economic viability of the republic was taken into consideration alongside the ethnographic principle.[3]

NAGORNO KARABAKH

Most of the border issues which were a source of conflict between the independent states of the South Caucasus in 1918–1920 were settled in 1921, although this did not bring an end to cross-border raids by peasants and inter-republic disputes – providing one of the reasons for the creation of a Soviet Transcaucasian Federation in 1922. Nagorno Karabakh had been the most difficult question to resolve and, after several changes of mind, a decision was taken by the Caucasian Bureau of the Communist Party on 5 July 1921 to leave Nagorno Karabakh as an autonomous region within the borders of Azerbaijan. It took a further two years for this status to be confirmed; not only were there protests to contend with from the Armenian side, but the authorities in Azerbaijan dragged their feet over forming the autonomous region.[4]

The momentous consequences of this decision were to be fully felt only sixty-five years later, although it was contested for much of the post-war period. At least for the remainder of the 1920s, however, peace returned to the region. Autonomy protected the rights

[2] In some cases parts of the population were considered to be russified Belorussians, who should be made to revert their national status, but the weak level of Belorussian national consciousness played a role. According to an apocryphal story, a delegation of peasants visited Stalin at this time to complain about their enforced belorussification. Without being aware of it, they were speaking in fluent Belorussian.

[3] Francine Hirsch, *Empire of Nations: Ethnographic Knowledge and the Making of the Soviet Union* (Ithaca: Cornell University Press, 2005), 150–5; Jan Zaprudnik, *Belarus: At a Crossroads in History* (Boulder, CO: Westview, 1993), 78.

[4] Imranli, *Sozdanie Armyanskogo gosudarstva*, 168–70.

of Armenians in Nagorno Karabakh so effectively that a number of
Armenian villages in the surrounding area, facing discrimination by
Azerbaijan's authorities, demanded to be included within the auton-
omous region.[5]

THE DELIMITATION OF CENTRAL ASIA

Soviet nation-building faced its greatest challenge in Central Asia.
Local inhabitants before the revolution were more likely to define
themselves by language, region, religion or clan than by ethnicity or
nation. As these categories did not always coincide, individuals
often subscribed to several overlapping identities.[6] While border-
making and the creation of national institutions elsewhere were
largely driven by local nationalities, in Central Asia a huge army of
Soviet ethnographers and civil servants studied the area, supported
by a small number of national intellectuals. Given the ethnic complexity of the region and low levels of national consciousness, this
was to some extent an artificial process. A Kyrgyz Autonomous
Soviet Socialist Republic had already been created in 1920, recon-
stituted as the Kazakh ASSR in 1925, and a Kara-Kyrgyz
Autonomous Region in 1924, renamed the Kyrgyz Autonomous
Region in 1925 and upgraded to a Kyrgyz ASSR in 1926.[7] The
remainder of Central Asia was still known as Soviet Turkestan,

[5] 'Obzor politicheskogo sostoianiia SSSR za sentiabr' 1925 gg., prilozheniia no. 4', in
Sevost'yanor (ed.) '*sovershenno sekretno*', vol. III, part 2, pp. 552–3.
[6] Francine Hirsch, 'Toward an Empire of Nations: Border-Making and the Formation of
Soviet National Identities', *Russian Review*, 59, (April 2000), 214.
[7] The confusing renaming of these regions reflects the difficulties involved in identifying
separate national groups in Central Asia. Before and after the revolution, most of the
native inhabitants of the steppe were known as Kyrgyz, and were divided by ethnologists
into Kazakh-Kyrgyz and Kara-Kyrgyz. It was only with the delimitation that these groups
were given and retained their modern titles of Kazakh and Kyrgyz respectively. From this
point on, I use the modern terminology for the five republics – Kazakhstan, Kyrgyzstan,
Uzbekistan, Turkmenistan and Tajikistan.

taking its name from the former tsarist province, until 1925, when it was divided into the Turkmen and Uzbek Soviet Socialist Republics. The smaller republics of Khorezm and Bukhara, both former separate emirates, were included in this process. Within the borders of the new Uzbekistan, a Tajik ASSR was created, which was upgraded to a separate republic in 1930.

The first tasks were to decide on what national groups should be consolidated in separate republics, and to create standard languages. The most difficult case was Uzbekistan, where dozens of tribes and dialects had no sense of unity beyond Turkism and Islam. Before the revolution, different languages could be found in use at the same time but with different functions – a literary Chagatai or Old Uzbek language, Farsi in administration and Arabic as a popular dialect in many areas. Scholars from Russia collected linguistic data and debated the merits of various candidates for the standardised language, but in the end the decision was political. Against the wishes of most Uzbek intellectuals, the urban dialect most widely employed in Tashkent was selected as the closest one could get to a proletarian language.[8] Turkmen communists who had sided with the Bolsheviks in the Civil War and were joined by a larger number of Turkmen intellectuals were the most enthusiastic supporters of the delimitation. Their aim all along had been to create a Turkmen nation, and now they seized the opportunity to unite the Turkmen population of Turkestan, Bukhara and Khiva in a largely self-sufficient republic where they were not subject to the discrimination they felt Turkmen had suffered at the hands of other political leaders.[9]

[8] Shiriin Akiner, 'Uzbekistan: Republic of Many Tongues', in Michael Kirkwood (ed.), *Language Planning in the Soviet Union* (Basingstoke: Macmillan, 1989), 100–6.
[9] Adrienne Lynn Edgar, *Tribal Nation: The Making of Soviet Turkmenistan* (Princeton University Press, 2006), 53–5.

The delimitation was agreed by a decree of the Central Committee of the CPSU on 25 February 1924. For the remainder of the year, officials of the Turkestan, Khiva and Bukhara communist parties worked out the details under the supervision of the Central Asian Bureau of the CPSU. Inevitably, leaders of the new republics jostled to take territory from each other. Ethnographers adjudicated where there were competing claims, but so complex was the region that some anomalies resulted from the process, in some cases because of distortions created by the influence of local communists, but more often because within one small region distinct village communities existed alongside each other. A further complication was that much of the population, including most Kazakhs, were nomads with no fixed dwelling. Kazakh villages were left in Uzbekistan, Uzbeks found themselves on the Kyrgyz side of the border and so on. During the delimitation process itself, and in the months and years following its official completion in February 1925, the regional authorities and Moscow were inundated with complaints from communities complaining that they had ended up on the wrong side of the new borders. Towns posed a particular problem as, especially in the mixed Fergana valley, their population often differed from the people of the surrounding villages. The Central Asian Bureau, which was the ultimate arbiter over disputed territories, was also sympathetic to the argument that each republic needed a sufficient urban industrial base within its territory in order to develop economically and socially. So the Fergana towns of Jalalabad and Osh went to Kyrgyzstan, while Andijan, Margilan and other towns were in Uzbekistan.[10]

Such complaints involved more than just ethnic pride. Although the Uzbek and other national categories were entirely new to most

---

[10] Hirsch, *Empire of Nations*, 168.

of the citizens who were now labelled with them, those citizens as well as the republic and local authorities were remarkably quick to adopt them and use them to their advantage. In a very short time, members of the titular nationality were receiving preferential treatment in investment, jobs and educational and cultural facilities – so much so that many individuals and villages, especially those who were unclear about their own national status, proclaimed themselves members of the titular nationality even when objective criteria suggested they were not. The converse of this was that non-titulars were subject to negative discrimination, particularly in the provision of schools, literature including newspapers, and community buildings. Thus, Uzbeks in Kyrgyzstan were told 'It is a Kyrgyz state and you are obliged to study Kyrgyz.' Complaints of police harassment, unfair treatment in the courts and being forced to pay higher taxes were also common.[11] Ethnic conflict over resources such as land continued to affect the region in these mixed areas.

Self-interest and local rivalry therefore accelerated the rapid adoption of distinct national identities, and the process was given further impetus by the actions of census-takers in 1926. There were well-documented cases of census-takers, either on their own initiative or under pressure from local authorities, manipulating the answers to the question on nationality to favour their own group. They were often able to do so because the respondents themselves did not know to what nationality they belonged. A more generally significant consequence of the census was that it forced individuals to self-identify according to an official list of nationalities. This affected small tribes in Siberia and elsewhere but was particularly important in Central Asia where the categories also matched up with the recently formed political formations.[12]

[11] Hirsch, 'Toward an Empire', 215–18. [12] Hirsch, *Empire of Nations*, 104, 123–31.

The consolidation of nationhood in Central Asia was further aided by the national cultural policies of the 1920s. For this, the active support of intellectuals and artists who already had a commitment to the national idea was essential, and these were not in altogether short supply. The 'new' nations were not entirely artificial creations, and the Revolution and Civil War had already shown how, in other parts of the Russian Empire, national feeling could spread rapidly from a relatively small base of intellectuals to embrace a much wider population, including peasants. The nationality policies of the Soviet state aided this process in Central Asia by associating territorial administrative structures and a number of material and cultural advantages to nations. The main purpose of the delimitation, then, was to put the population of Central Asia into national categories which could then be used to build socialism at the local level. Communist officials argued with some justification that the process of nation-formation was already underway in Central Asia in any case, and that by accelerating the process they would also hasten the modernisation of the region. Further benefits were that it would remove some of the causes of ethnic conflict (although this was not how it worked out) and that it would help the Soviet cause abroad, especially in nearby countries where Turkmen, Uzbeks and others outside the Soviet Union would appreciate the achievements of their fellow nationals in establishing national territories.[13]

---

[13] Edgar, *Tribal Nation*, 45–7. Until Soviet archives were opened up and revealed the thinking and processes behind the delimitation, a much more common interpretation was that delimitation resulted from a policy of divide-and-rule whereby the potential for Muslim resistance to Soviet rule would be weakened. See, for example, Carrère d'Encausse, *The Great Challenge*, 177–8; other scholars have found support for the 'divide-and-rule' account in their analysis of archival materials: Stephen Sabol, 'The Creation of Soviet Central Asia: The 1924 National Delimitation', *Central Asian Survey*, 14, 2 (1995), 225–41.

AFFIRMATIVE ACTION AND OPPOSITION

The policy of attracting individuals and organisations who were sympathetic to Bolshevik programmes considerably influenced the nationalities experience in the 1920s. The former leading Bundists Moishe Rafes, Alexander Chemeriskii and Ester Frumkina (who had opposed merging with the Bolsheviks) all took leading positions in the Jewish section (Yevsektiia) of the CPSU.[14] They also exercised considerable influence in the People's Commissariat for Nationality Affairs as well as in other commissariats, such as that for enlightenment, where Frumkina headed a section on pre-school education for national minorities. Little significance can be attached to the Jewishness of several leading members of the CPSU, who had long abandoned any roots they may have had in Jewish communities. But by 1922 there were about 20,000 Jewish communists, nearly 5.2% of the total. Almost 3,000 of these were former Bundists while more were attracted to the Bolsheviks from other Jewish organisations, in spite of the fact that before late 1917 Bolshevik penetration of the Jewish population, especially in rural areas, was weak compared to other specifically Jewish parties. In areas where there were Jewish villages and other compact communities Jews made up a significant force in the administration. Thus in 1921 they made up 19.9% of the personnel of the Commissariat of Justice in Ukraine, and were also influential in government in Belorussia and Crimea.[15]

More regularly, however, it was the prevalent nationality in each republic that was encouraged to contribute personnel to the new structures, and the membership of the former socialist parties played a major part in this. In Ukraine, two former Borotbists, Hryhorii

---

[14] Gitelman, *Jewish Nationality*, 513–15. [15] Levin, *The Jews in the Soviet Union*, vol. I, 47.

Hrynko and Oleksander Shumskyi, were elected to the Central Committee of the Ukrainian Communist Party in 1920 as part of the deal that saw the liquidation of the Borotbist party, and were given senior government posts in 1923, with Shumskyi becoming commissar for education. In the same year, with the vigorous encouragement of Moscow, Ukraine embarked on a policy of 'ukrainisation'. This policy effectively abandoned the formal equality of Russian and Ukrainian in the republic and aimed, first, at introducing Ukrainian into all schools, urban as well as rural, and then at making Ukrainian the sole language of government administration, followed by the Communist Party, army and trade unions. The idea was that by spreading the Ukrainian language to the towns and cities, the split between the Russian towns and Ukrainian villages which had characterised the Civil War years would be overcome.[16] Government officials in some departments were given as little as six months to learn the language, while non-Ukrainian speakers could not get access to new state employment at all. The leading Bolshevik Lazar Kaganovich was appointed First Secretary of the Ukrainian Communist Party in March 1923 partly in order to push through the ukrainisation policy. He vigorously pursued the ukrainisation of the Communist Party as well as the state institutions. As well as ensuring that all Party publications and newspapers were in Ukrainian, Kaganovich ordered Party members to study Ukrainian, while all street signs and public notices were to be in Ukrainian. Ukrainians were actively encouraged to join the Communist Party and were given preference in promotion, leading

[16] Terry Martin, *The Affirmative Action Empire: Nations and Nationalism in the Soviet Union, 1923–1939* (Ithaca: Cornell University Press, 2001), 81. Martin's use of the term 'affirmative action' to describe policies of this sort. But the notion had been deployed much earlier by scholars investigating the national republics in the late Soviet period: Ellen Jones and Fred W. Grupp, 'Modernisation and Ethnic Equalisation in the USSR', *Soviet Studies*, 36, 2 (April 1984), 159–60.

to a significant rise in the number of Ukrainian speakers holding senior posts. Eventually, Party and state officials were subject to dismissal if they could not sufficiently master the Ukrainian language. But in spite of a host of legislation and pressure from both Moscow and Kiev, the ukrainisation campaign fell victim to passive resistance, mostly from within the Communist Party of Ukraine. By 1927, 263 government employees had been fired for their failure to master Ukrainian,[17] but this represented only the tip of the iceberg, and the policy of ukrainisation was formally abandoned in 1932.

Affirmative action in Central Asia had another obstacle to surmount before it even encountered such passive resistance. This was the acute shortage of literate, educated members of the local nationality, which made it impossible to fill a majority of administrative positions. In Uzbekistan, a year after delimitation, only 3.8 per cent of Uzbeks were literate in the standardised version of Uzbek that was proposed for the republic.[18] In Turkmenistan, the inability of the republic to find suitably educated candidates to fill the seven places reserved for Turkmen women at the Central Asian Communist University in Tashkent led to the search being broadened to any healthy Turkmen women who would 'liquidate their illiteracy' just before taking up their studies.[19] Even before delimitation, however, considerable success had been achieved in building up a communist party and administrative apparatus that was staffed largely by Muslims. In 1922 half of the members of the Communist Party of Turkestan were Muslims, and by 1924 eight of twenty-one members of its Central Committee were Muslims. At

---

[17] *Ibid.*, 75–98.
[18] Edward A. Allworth, *The Modern Uzbeks: From the Fourteenth Century to the Present* (Stanford: Hoover Institution Press, 1990), 203.
[19] Edgar, *Tribal Nation*, 70.

the more local level, they held a majority of leading posts.[20] In
Central Asia Muslims were still under-represented in overall
Communist Party membership, as may have been expected of
nationalities which were still a minority in the towns. But this was
also true of Georgians in Georgia, where Bolshevism had always
been weak and those who had previously been associated with the
Menshevik regime were excluded from Communist Party membership. Armenians, Russians and Ossetians were much more likely to
join the Communist Party, and in 1927 Georgians made up only
55% of the membership of the Georgian Communist Party,[21] while
constituting 67% of the population. Promotion of the local nationality in the government apparatus extended to the autonomous
republics and regions of the RSFSR, but administration was less
fully nativised than in the union republics. Thus, in Tatarstan, the
proportion of Tatars in the central government bureaucracy grew
from 7.8% in 1921 to 35.4% in 1930[22] – a substantial increase, but
still well short of their composition of 44.9% of the overall population of the autonomous republic. In general, however, affirmative action ensured that the local nationality predominated in the
middle and higher layers of the Party and state apparatus. In 1927,
the representation of local nationalities in the soviet executive
committees of the union republics was at its lowest in
Turkmenistan (68.3%) and at its highest in Armenia (80.5%).[23] By
the end of the decade, in all of the Soviet republics leadership was
firmly in the hands of members of the local nationality.

[20] S. A. Nazarov, *Rukovodstvo TsK RKP partynim stroitel'stvom v Sredney Azii* (Tashkent:
Izdatelstvo Uzbekistan, 1972), 288–9; Carrère d'Encausse, *The Great Challenge*, 143.
[21] Stephen Jones, 'The Establishment of Soviet Power in Transcaucasia: The Case of
Georgia, 1921–1928', *Soviet Studies*, 40, 4 (1988), 625.
[22] Martin, *The Affirmative Action Empire*, 146.
[23] *Natsional'naia politika VKP(b) v tsifrakh* (Moscow: Kommunisticheskaia Akademiia,
1930), 209–12.

RESISTANCE

The single most significant rebellion against Soviet power after 1923 was a revolt in Georgia in August 1924. In spite of the fact that the Mensheviks and other parties had enjoyed considerably more support than the Bolsheviks before they were banned in August 1923, the revolt failed to mobilise a large part of the population or to seriously threaten the Soviets. The rebels were able to gain control of the western region of Guria for a few days, where peasants had a strong tradition of revolt and where the economic crisis continued to hit the rural poor. But the rebels' organisations had been extensively infiltrated by the OGPU, and the hoped-for support from abroad did not materialise. Up to 4,000 rebels were killed or executed, and many more were sent to prison camps afterwards.[24]

More prolonged resistance remained in Central Asia. The Basmachi revolt or *Basmachestvo* had its origins in the Kokand massacre of February 1918, and was not finally extinguished until 1928. Originally organised by survivors of the Kokand government, the *Basmachestvo* took on the character of a broad movement rather than an organised rebellion. Focussed on the Fergana valley, Lokai and Bukhara, the Basmachi were organised in small bands operating independently of each other, based on clan or family loyalties, led by a warlord and carrying out raids targeting Russian property and institutions. Basmachi fighters were mostly not full-time rebels, and reportedly returned to work their fields by day after conducting raids by night. This loose organisation made them hard to defeat as they were able to melt away into the desert or pastureland. On the other hand it also reduced the overall threat they posed. Although the *Basmachestvo* numbered some 18,000 men

[24] Stephen Jones, 'The Establishment of Soviet Power', 632–33.

at its height in 1922, it was unable to mount the sort of co-ordinated
attack that might have posed a serious threat to Soviet power.[25]

The *Basmachestvo* cannot really be characterised as a national
movement: inasmuch as it had any overall appeal this was based on
Islam, but it had no political programme and suffered from the
absence of a clear sense of national identity with its potential to
mobilise.[26] Even the arrival of the Turkish general Enver Pasha,
with his dreams of pan-Turkic unity, to take command of the
movement in 1921 failed to stimulate a clear demand for independence from Russian rule. Enver himself was killed in an engagement
with Red Army cavalry in August 1922. From 1923 a military
campaign by the Red Army commander Mikhail Frunze combined
with the opportunities for Muslims to advance politically and satisfy
many of their grievances under the policies of *korenizatsiia* undermined what was left of the movement. Although armed bands
continued to adopt the Basmachi label for another five years, for
the most part they were little more than bandits in pursuit of plunder
and revenge, and engaged against each other as often as against
Russian settlers or the Soviet authorities.

Ethnic conflict continued to erupt sporadically in Central Asia,
especially Kazakhstan, along with the North Caucasus, throughout
the 1920s. Mostly these episodes were between locals and Russians,
although occasionally non-Russian nationalities engaged in fights
with each other. Disputes over rights to land and water usage were
the most common cause of conflict, followed by border disputes
arising from the delimitation. On occasion, mass brawls, sometimes
fuelled by alcohol, broke out between different ethnic groups at
market places and bazaars, which is where they most frequently

[25] Marie Broxup, 'The Basmachi', *Central Asian Survey*, 2, 1 (1983), 57–82.
[26] Mustafa Chokaev, 'The Basmaji Movement in Turkestan', *Asiatic Review*, 24, 78 (1928),
287–8.

came into contact. In the North Caucasus, cross-border raids by farmers on horseback carrying off livestock and other goods were not unheard of. As nation-building progressed, clearly the property of other nationalities came to be regarded as legitimate targets of such raids.[27]

A practice that invoked particularly hostile reactions and sporadic revolt in Central Asia was the unveiling of women. The symbolic act of emancipating women through unveiling became a key Bolshevik policy; in the absence of any clear class differentiation, women became a 'surrogate proletariat' and the campaign to remove the veil took the place of class struggle as a way of modernising attitudes. In the first place, the unveiling of their own wives and daughters was set as a test of loyalty for Muslim communists, many of whom expressed considerable disquiet out of fear for their own reputations or even violence, or because it went against their own beliefs. Strict disciplinary measures were brought to bear against Party members who failed to unveil their own wives.[28] Where the veil was not such an issue, the Soviets sought to promote the liberation of women through attacking other customs such as the practice of paying bridewealth by the groom's family to the bride's, restricting the economic and personal independence of women.[29] Muslims protested through resolutions, organising public meetings, refusal to obey laws restricting traditional practices, and open revolt. Violent responses often focussed on the women themselves, thousands of whom were beaten, raped

[27] Jeremy Smith, 'Nation Building and National Conflict in the USSR in the 1920s', *Ab Imperio*, no. 3, 2001, 246–60.

[28] Douglas Northrop, 'Languages of Loyalty: Gender, Politics and Party Supervision in Uzbekistan, 1927–1941', *Russian Review*, 59 (April 2000), 179–200.

[29] Adrienne Lynn Edgar, 'Emancipation of the Unveiled: Turkmen Women under Soviet Rule, 1924–1929', *Russian Review*, 62 (January 2003), 138–9.

or even murdered for taking advantage of new emancipatory laws.[30] Refusal to implement laws, or finding creative ways to subvert or circumvent them, meant that such practices continued well into the 1930s in one form or another.[31]

In the campaign to emancipate women in Central Asia, the Communist Party leadership had to resort constantly to sharp disciplinary measures against its own members locally. Having encouraged non-Russian communists to recruit locals to the Communist Party and pursue a nation-building agenda, the Soviets found that the apparatus they were relying on both to take on Russian opposition and to implement its policies in the republics had its own idea of what the national variant of communism should look like. National communism developed its own logic, and while for now the leaders were to back the national communists against their opponents locally, by the end of the 1920s nationalising policies had threatened to take over from the socialist project, leading inexorably to the first of a series of wide-ranging purges which were intended to rein back the national forces which the Bolsheviks themselves had unleashed.

THE SHUMSKYI AFFAIR, 1926–1927

Although Central Asia experienced the most severe difficulties of this sort, it was in Ukraine that things first came to a head. Faced with widespread passive resistance on the part of Russian officials, Kaganovich began to relax the drive towards ukrainisation from 1925 onwards. But this relaxation provoked a corresponding resistance from those Ukrainian communists who had wholeheartedly

---

[30] *Ibid.*, 119.
[31] Douglas Northrop, 'Subaltern Dialogues: Subversion and Resistance in Soviet Uzbek Family Law', *Slavic Review*, 60, 1 (Spring 2001), 123–7.

embraced ukrainisation, prominent among them the former Socialist Revolutionary Borotbists who had come over to the Bolsheviks in the early 1920s. The leading figure in this tendency was Oleksander Shumskyi, who used his position as commissar for education to press for the continued expansion of education in Ukrainian schools and called for further measures to promote Ukrainian in the Party and state apparatus. Shumskyi clashed openly with Kaganovich at a meeting of the Ukrainian Politburo in March 1926, accusing ethnic Russians of dominating Party life and showing condescension and hostility towards Ukrainian communists. Shumskyi appealed directly to Stalin, asking for the replacement of Kaganovich by an ethnic Ukrainian. Kaganovich responded with evidence that Shumskyi was associated with Ukrainian communists who proposed a pro-European orientation for Ukraine. Shumskyi's political past was also used against him in the political struggles that followed. More serious was his close involvement with the Communist Party of Western Ukraine, which had been seeking to spread communism among the Ukrainian population of Poland. This organisation's unequivocal condemnation of the leadership of the Ukrainian Communist Party, and support for Shumskyi, led to the dissolution of its leadership in early 1928. By then, Kaganovich had already succeeded in having Shumskyi removed as commissar for education and sent away from Ukraine to a minor post in Saratov in 1927.

In the course of this affair, Stalin made clear that there were limits to ukrainisation and *korenizatsiia* generally: these policies were aimed at the Soviet apparatus but not at the Russian proletariat, who should also benefit from the policy of free national development.[32] This, at least, was not how the policy had generally been

---

[32] Martin, *The Affirmative Action Empire*, 212–28.

interpreted and implemented by national communists throughout
the Soviet Union. They had taken it as giving a free hand to
promote discriminatory employment and land practices and to
impose the national culture on the whole population of the national
republics. The hostile attitude this provoked among Russians and
other minorities has been well documented. The Shumskyi Affair
indicated that the pressure from these minorities had combined with
growing concern at the increasingly independent line being taken
by national leaders to prompt a change in tack by the Soviet
leadership, one which was to lead to far more severe measures
against national political and cultural elites two years later and
throughout the 1930s.[33]

LANGUAGE AND EDUCATION

At the heart of the nation-building process was language. Linguistic
criteria were the main proxy for national identity used in drawing
up republics' borders, and where uniform spoken or written forms
of the national language were not established, they had to be
created. The Soviets employed ethnographers and linguists who
had held academic and government posts before the Revolution,
and created bodies such as the Commission for the Study of the
Tribal Composition of the Population to examine in depth the
ethnographic composition of the former empire and make recommendations as to what combinations might constitute national
groups, where their borders were to be drawn and what languages
they should speak.[34] For the Bashkirs, Kyrgyz, Karakalpaks,
Kabardins, Balkars, Chechens, Ingush, Circassians, Karachais and
Ossetians, literary traditions were explored in order to find the most

---

[33] *Ibid.*   [34] For an extremely detailed account, see Hirsch, *Empire of Nations*.

suitable forms of written language.[35] Although tsarist-era experts were entrusted with much of the work on language, the most influential figure in the creation and standardisation of local languages was a Marxist, Nikolai Marr, who saw language standardisation for each people as the first step on the road to a hybridisation of languages which would eventually produce the sole common language of the socialist future.[36] Marr also supervised the creation of new alphabets for languages which lacked them, but in the long term he supported the promotion of the Latin alphabet for all languages, rejecting Cyrillic as too closely enmeshed with Russia's capitalist past. Reformist Muslim intellectuals in the nineteenth century had supported transferring from the Arabic to the Latin alphabet, and Azerbaijan's new leaders concurred on the basis that it would differentiate Azerbaijan from Turkey and Iran and strengthen ties with Russia, introducing the Latin alphabet from 1924, a move which the other Turkic republics reluctantly followed from 1928.[37]

Having established standard languages and their written forms, the key was for the population to adopt them, and this was to be achieved through the education system. As soon as the Civil War was over, education became a leading priority for the Soviet regime as a whole. In 1918, responsibility for non-Russian education was transferred from the Commissariat for Nationality Affairs (Narkomnats) to the Commissariat for Enlightenment (Narkompros). This boosted the cause of national education, as Narkompros had far greater resources at its disposal and its leaders were enthusiastic supporters of the principle of native-language

---

[35] Carrère d'Encausse, *The Great Challenge*, 178–80.
[36] Simon Crisp, 'Soviet Language Planning 1917–1953', in Kirkwood (ed.), *Language Planning*, 37.
[37] Altstadt, *The Azerbaijani Turks*, 124; Rorlich, *The Volga Tatars*, 151.

education. Education was an even greater priority for the newly
created Soviet republics in the early 1920s. In 1923, the Georgian
Soviet government spent 48% of its entire budget on the Ministry of
Enlightenment.[38] As a result of tsarist policies, schools in non-
Russian regions were generally even sparser in number than in
the Russian countryside, but over the course of the 1920s the
number of national schools grew at a correspondingly faster rate.
By 1927, the educational authorities could boast that in each of the
union republics more than 90% of school-age children from the
titular nationality were receiving instruction in their own language.
The same did not hold for all of the autonomous republics and the
figure was substantially lower in the autonomous regions (where
bilingual education was the general rule), but 90% or more of
Kazakhs, Kyrgyz, Crimean Tatars, Germans, Tatars and Chuvash
were educated in their mother tongue.[39]

During the course of the transfer of responsibility for national
education from Narkomnats to Narkompros, national communists
expressed some concern that, while Narkompros was committed on
the language of education, its officials were less interested in local
variations in curriculum content. After 1923, however, the republics
did enjoy full authority over their education systems, and the
development of local studies of history is one of the clearest
indications of the way national cultures, even ideologies, were
free to develop for most of the 1920s. In Moscow, the head of the
Institute of Red Professors, Mikhail Pokrovsky, led a school of
historians which condemned the Russian Empire for its colonial
exploitation of the borderlands. This message was taken up with
enthusiasm by non-Russian historians, whose ranks were swelled by

---

[38] Stephen Jones, 'The Establishment of Soviet Power', 627.
[39] Simeon Dimanshtein (ed.), *Natsional'naia politika VKP(b)* (Moscow, 1930), 278–9.

émigré academics and intellectuals who returned to the Soviet
Union in large numbers in the 1920s in order to play their part in
the nation-building project. Most prominent among these was
Mykhailo Hrushevskyi, who as head of the Ukrainian Central
Rada had opposed the October Revolution and declared
Ukraine's independence from Soviet Russia in 1917. As an active
member of the Ukrainian Socialist Revolutionary Party in exile
from 1919, he was critical of the Bolshevik regime, but with many of
his colleagues came to accept that Bolshevism represented the future
of socialism in Ukraine and, with *korenizatsiia* in full swing, returned
to his country in 1924. There he headed the historical/philological
section of the Ukrainian Academy of Sciences and produced his
monumental *History of Ukraine-Rus*, which portrayed the history of
Ukraine in terms of a constant struggle against Russian domina-
tion.[40] While condemning Russian imperialism, the new national
histories were based around the heroic exploits of leaders of resistance against Russian colonialism such as Imam Shamil, as well as
heroes from a more distant past, such as Timur (Tamerlane), who
was claimed by Kazakh historians.

CULTURE

History was not the only area where national culture was transformed in the 1920s. With the standardisation of literary languages
and their spread through the education system, older national
literatures were revived and new ones created throughout the
1920s. National epics were a clear marker of nationhood. Shota
Rustaveli's twelfth-century Georgian epic *The Knight in the Panther*

---

[40] Orest Subtelny, *Ukraine: A History* (University of Toronto Press, 1989), 398–9; Carrère
d'Encausse, *The Great Challenge*, 193.

Skin was revived and translated into many of the languages of the Soviet Union; likewise the huge Kyrgyz *Epic of Manas*, which was adapted to represent Manas himself as a national Kyrgyz, and the Kazakh epic poem *Kyz Zhivbek*.

New forms of poetry, music, literature and painting flourished in all of the republics, taking inspiration from earlier cultural traditions but adapting them to forms that were both more modern and accessible to a wide audience. Music presented an especially challenging area for the development of national culture. The base material for national music was provided by folk melodies, but these were by nature considered 'backwards', and to serve the cultural needs of the new Soviet nations they needed to be transformed into symphonic or operatic forms.[41] In Kazakhstan, ethnographers collected and published a large collection of Kazakh folk songs in the mid 1920s, which formed the basic material with which Kazakh musicians could work. The spirit behind these efforts was summed up by the editor of a Kazakh newspaper in 1923: 'Of course, every people should have its own style, its own general characteristics. This exists in Kazakh music.'[42] In Azerbaijan, before the First World War Uzeyir Hajibeyov had already gained a reputation as a progressive musician, whose operas angered conservative Azerbaijanis. In the 1920s, he was given a number of important positions in the Azerbaijani political and cultural systems. As head of the Baku State Conservatory of Music, Hajibeyov brought in musicians from Russia and elsewhere to teach young Azerbaijani musicians. Flourishing *mugam* opera was attacked by

---

[41] Kiril Tomoff, 'Uzbek Music's Separate Path: Interpreting "Anticosmopolitanism" in Stalinist Central Asia, 1949–1952', *Russian Review*, 63 (April 2004), 218.

[42] Cited in Michael Rouland, 'A Nation on Stage: Music and the 1936 Festival of Kazak Arts', in Neil Edmunds (ed.), *Soviet Music and Society under Lenin and Stalin: The Baton and Sickle* (London: Routledge, 2004), 186–7.

politicians in the late 1920s as 'bourgeois and provincial', but Hajibeyov ensured that a synthesis between traditional and European music flourished, on the one hand introducing choral music which had no place in Azerbaijani tradition, and on the other hand introducing folk instruments into symphonic orchestras.[43] Instruments played an important role in the development of national music. In Soviet Karelia, the kantele was the basis of musical development which incorporated traditional forms of folk song. Songs and kantele music could be performed by non-professional individuals and hence were regarded as both national and proletarian.[44]

All of the new national musical styles were based on traditional music but adapted to modern, European-style forms, a process that Russian composers such as Borodin had already explored in the nineteenth century.[45] In Central Asia, which also suffered from a lack of suitably trained musicians, different nationalities could lay claim to the same musical traditions and the creation of distinct musics for each republic was to some extent mediated by Russian composers. In music, as in other areas of cultural production, innovation came from national artists who supported the broad aims of Bolshevism but the whole process enjoyed the active support and encouragement of central Soviet cultural institutions. Nation-building was, then, a centrally sponsored project but one whose execution rested on the activity of non-Russian intellectuals and political leaders.

---

[43] Matthew O'Brien, 'Uzeyir Hajibeyov and His Role in the Development of Musical Life in Azerbaijan', in Edmunds (ed.), *Soviet Music*, 209–19.

[44] Pekka Suutari, 'Going beyond the Border: National Cultural Policy and the Development of Musical Life in Soviet Karelia, 1920–1940', in Edmunds (ed.), *Soviet Music*, 167–74.

[45] Tomoff, 'Uzbek Music's Separate Path', 217.

The Bolsheviks had more or less stumbled on the policies of *korenizatsiia* during the Civil War and its aftermath. Lenin's policies were taken up with enthusiasm by non-Russian leaders who, at least until 1926, enjoyed the regular support of the Soviet centre. What is even more remarkable is the enthusiasm with which ordinary non-Russians adopted the national message even in those areas where national identity had previously been weak or non-existent. Especially in the towns but even in the villages, people enrolled for adult literacy courses and flocked to concerts, plays and poetry readings. For all that the New Economic Policy did not entirely switch off official rhetoric about the continuing class struggle, politics was increasingly conducted on a national rather than a class basis. In reaction to this, Russians and other minorities vigorously pursued their national claims, which was one of the causes for a dramatic change of direction at the end of the 1920s.

CHAPTER FIVE

Surviving the Stalinist onslaught, 1928–1941

Two decrees of the CPSU Politburo in December 1932 marked a significant shift in the policies of nation-building and *korenizatsiia*. The first concerned the grain collections crisis in Ukraine and the North Caucasus, and blamed the policies of ukrainisation for disguising the activities of 'kulaks, former officers, Petliurites and supporters of the Kuban Rada' to sabotage the collections;

instead of a correct Bolshevik implementation of the nationalities policy, in many Ukrainian regions Ukrainization was carried out mechanically, without considering the specifics of each district, without a careful choice of Bolshevik Ukrainian cadres. This made it easy for bourgeois-nationalist elements, Petliurites and others to create a legal cover for their counter-revolutionary cells and organizations.[1]

A second decree formally brought an end to the policy of ukrainisation. In reality, these decrees, which were issued in the context of agricultural difficulties, reflected a change in direction that had already been evident for four years. By the end of 1932, most of the prominent national communists of the 1920s had been removed and many of them arrested. An assault against the Pokrovsky school of history and national historians was already underway. The implementation of collectivisation had uprooted the cultural basis of peasant life for Russians and non-Russians alike. Kazakh nomads

---

[1] Martin, *The Affirmative Action Empire*, 303.

had suffered especial horrors, and the Ukrainian countryside was about to plunge into the worst famine in its history.

The policies of collectivisation and forced industrialisation in the 1930s transformed forever the social character of the Soviet Union. Russians were caught up in this process as much as non-Russians, but Stalin paid particular attention to the nationalities. The republics were successively purged even before the Great Terror of 1937–1938, and when the Terror did erupt, special categories of victims were assigned according to nationality. From the chaos of the 1930s a new kind of state with a different relationship to society emerged, and the centre–republic relationship was, for the moment, resolved firmly in favour of the centre. The ideological switch to a more Russian-oriented culture weakened but did not eliminate national cultures, while the language policy in education did not change much. Significantly, for both the regime and its population, a new conceptualisation of nationality emerged which portrayed nations as primordial and with fixed, enduring characteristics.

PURGES

Veli Ibragimov had been one of the first prominent Muslims to go over to the Bolsheviks after the Revolution, and was active in organising an underground communist movement in Crimea during the White occupation of Anton Denikin and Pyotr Wrangel. Since 1920, he had been head of the government of the Crimean ASSR. His arrest in January 1928 signalled the beginning of a new direction for the Soviet regime, which had rarely moved against senior officials in the republics since the Civil War. A further 3,500 Crimean Tatars, many of them communists, were arrested and shot, imprisoned or exiled. Ibragimov himself was executed. In the same year, more than 2,000 communists received the death penalty in Tatarstan, and arrests were widespread in Uzbekistan and Kazakhstan.[2]

The numerous Muslim national communists purged in 1928 were suspected of collusion with Mirsaid Sultangaliev, who had already been charged with anti-Soviet activity in 1923 and was now accused of resuming his conspiratorial activities and arrested for a second time in November 1928 at the time of the Tatarstan purge. The Crimean purge coincided with the Shakhty trial of engineers accused of sabotage, which has been widely regarded as marking the beginning of the new turn in Stalin's regime. But unlike in Shakhty, in the republics it was the communists who were under investigation, and it did not take long for this process to spread to non-Muslim nationalities. In the course of 1929, hundreds of Ukrainian academics and intellectuals were arrested on suspicion of belonging to a Union for the Liberation of Ukraine (SVU). Forty-five leading members of this supposed group were put on trial in March 1930 at the Kharkiv Opera House. The public nature of this trial was emphasised by extensive coverage in the Soviet and Ukrainian press. The defendants at the SVU trial came from the Ukrainian Academy of Sciences, the Ukrainian Autocephalous Church, a variety of intellectuals and former members of non-Bolshevik parties. There were no communists among the defendants, but many were among those who had earlier left Soviet Ukraine only to return in order to participate in the national project of the 1920s. Secret police (OGPU) preparations for the trial involved the elaborate concoction of a history of the SVU and, in a foretaste of procedures for Stalin's Great Terror of 1937–1938, the extraction of confessions under torture, which would then be used

---

[2] Ariel Cohen, *Russian Imperialism: Development and Crisis* (Westport, CT: Praeger, 1996), 84; Rorlich, *The Volga Tatars*, 155; Shirin Akiner, *The Formation of Kazakh Identity from Tribe to Nation-State* (London: Royal Institute of International Affairs, 1995), 43.

to implicate others and lead to new arrests. Candidates for the show trial were selected in order to represent a range of professions and tendencies that the trial was designed to denounce.[3] Four of the defendants were sentenced to ten years' imprisonment, with lesser prison sentences or suspended sentences for the remainder. Although many of the defendants were rearrested after a year or later in the 1930s, and died in prison or were shot, these were lenient initial sentences both by later standards and by comparison with the 1928 Muslim communist purges. But the message of the trial was clear: non-Party intellectuals were now universally suspect, and the era of uncontrolled nation-building was at an end.

At the same time as the fabrication of the SVU plot, a thorough investigation of the implementation of nationalities policies throughout the USSR was underway. As a part of this investigation, in the summer of 1929 Volodymyr Zatonskyi sent a detailed report to Stalin and Ordzhonikidze condemning the communist leadership in Belorussia. Most disturbingly for the leaders, he noted that 'I have seen all kinds of things in Ukraine, but the degree of animosity towards Moscow that oozes out at every gathering of writers or academics here [in Belorussia] is greater by several degrees than the most frenzied nationalism of the Petliura movement in 1918. A large number of Communists are caught up in this chauvinist intoxication.'[4] Zatonskyi's primary targets were intellectuals of backgrounds similar to those being rounded up in Ukraine, but he also charged the communist leadership in the republic with supporting and encouraging their activities. He accused communists of being swept up in the wave of cultural nationalism that now characterised the republic, including communists who were not ethnic Belorussians. Between late 1929 and September 1930, dozens of

---

[3] Martin, *The Affirmative Action Empire*, 250–4.   [4] *Ibid.*, 262.

members of the Belorussian Academy of Sciences were arrested, along with Belorussian communists, among them the commissar of agriculture, Dmitri Prioshchepov, the commissar of education, Anton Balitskii, and the former head of the government press department, Alexander Adamovich. A Union for the Liberation of Belorussia (SVB), similar to the SVU, was invented, centred on the Belorussian Academy of Science. In all, 108 supposed members were arrested, most of whom were sentenced to exile in Siberia and the Far East.

There were a number of developments in 1928 that may have influenced these attacks on republican political and intellectual elites. A rupture with Britain had caused rumours of impending war to sweep across the Soviet Union, and the leadership was increasingly nervous about the international situation. Poland was looking more and more threatening under the leadership of Jozef Pilsudski, and both the SVU and the SVB were charged with preparing to organise a rising behind Soviet lines in the event of a war with Poland. This charge was clearly a fabrication, but international tensions may well have focussed the regime's attention on the extent to which national development was getting out of hand and threatening to take whole areas of the borderlands away from Moscow's control. The year 1928 was also the beginning of the first of the five-year plans in industry, while a looming crisis in agriculture, which was eventually to pave the way to collectivisation, was another reason for re-establishing central authority. The Belorussian and Ukrainian trials were launched soon after Stalin's political defeat of Bukharin, which cemented Stalin's power at the centre. Trotsky together with his leading supporters, who had the sympathy of a number of national communists, had already been expelled from the CPSU at the end of 1927. This was the beginning of the 'cultural revolution' of 1928–1932 which was to transform the

Soviet economy and society at all levels. Among the beneficiaries of the new turn were upwardly mobile and ideologically motivated young workers, mostly Russian. This group overlapped with those Russian workers in the republics who had been complaining vociferously about the discriminatory policies that held them back there. These developments need to be considered alongside Zatonskyi's comments about the degree to which nationalism was dictating events in the republics, although this was hardly news. The national agenda had been dominating politics in the Soviet republics for years, but in Stalin's new world it was class struggle, a forward surge in the economy and a militant commitment to 'progress' that came to dominate.

In any case, the days of the national communists were numbered. In Azerbaijan a campaign against former Musavatists and 'national deviation' was in full swing by 1930.[5] The leadership of the Transcaucasian Party organisations was reorganised twice in the course of six months from the end of 1929 to mid 1930, and again in 1931.[6] Further 'conspiracies' were uncovered in Belorussia and Ukraine between 1931 and 1933. Another purge in Ukraine in 1933 cast the old Bolshevik Mykola Skrypnyk as the lead national deviationist. Skrypnyk shot himself on 7 July 1933. Almost all of the surviving former Borotbists were purged.[7] Shumskyi was arrested in the same year and sentenced to ten years' hard labour. Purges took place in Uzbekistan, Kyrgyzstan, Turkmenistan and Tajikistan, where 66 per cent of Communist Party members were expelled in 1934.[8] Almost all of the national communists of the 1920s had been purged by 1933. Edward Gylling, the Finnish communist

---

[5] Altstadt, *The Azerbaijani Turks*, 132–41.
[6] Suny, *Making of the Georgian Nation*, 245, 249–50, 255.
[7] Martin, *The Affirmative Action Empire*, 345–9.
[8] Nahaylo and Swoboda, *Soviet Disunion*, 72–3.

leader of Soviet Karelia, survived in his position until 1935. The popular leader of Abkhazia, Nestor Lakoba, died in suspicious circumstances in 1936. The Communist Party organisations in all of the republics were purged from top to bottom at one time or another, and often more than once, between 1928 and 1936, before the leaders who had replaced the national communists were themselves swept up in Stalin's Great Terror.

COLLECTIVISATION

The collectivisation of agriculture was introduced in the republics at the same time as Russia, from 1928 onwards. Used to a significant degree of self-rule, however, many leaderships, such as those of Georgia, argued that their conditions differed from those in Russia and that collectivisation should be introduced in different ways. Any sign of holding back the pace of agricultural transformation was condemned by Moscow, particularly after the acceleration of collectivisation in the course of 1930. Many of the early national purges were connected directly to the reluctance of leaders to implement collectivisation fully. They were correct, up to a point, in insisting that collective farming was wholly inappropriate for certain forms of agriculture, and was, for many peoples, even more unsuitable than in Russia, with its traditions of the peasant commune (*mir*). Collectivisation extended to all forms of food production, including fishing and reindeer herding – the traditional occupations of many small peoples in the Far North.[9] But such arguments carried no weight in the heady atmosphere of 1930–1932, and collectivisation was imposed regardless.

[9] Andrei Golovnev and Gail Osherenko, *Siberian Survival: The Nenets and Their Story* (Ithaca: Cornell University Press, 1999).

Collectivisation and the cultural revolution were accompanied by a renewed onslaught on religious organisations. This time, unlike during the Civil War and early 1920s, it was not just the Russian Orthodox Church that was a target. The anti-religion decrees of 1929 affected mosques and synagogues as much as churches. Kiev, with its large Jewish population, was left for a time without a single synagogue. The number of mosques in the Soviet Union fell from more than 26,000 in 1921 to just over 1,000 by the start of the Great Patriotic War in 1941. In Central Asia and other Muslim regions the war against the kulak became entwined with the war against the mullah.

As a consequence, opposition to collectivisation was more widespread and more serious in many non-Russian regions than elsewhere. Flight, across a border or into mountains or forests, was the most common form of passive resistance. Destruction of livestock, a severe problem across the Soviet Union, was particularly common among people who raised animals for a living. Occasionally, popular opposition could delay or prevent the full implementation of collectivisation. In Abkhazia peasant protests prevailed on Abkhaz leader Nestor Lakoba to impose a more moderate form of collectivisation, with no dekulakisation and with horses allowed to remain private property.[10] But resistance to collectivisation took an armed form in the North Caucasus, especially in the Chechen and Ingush republics, where local officials were murdered and remote villages held out against collectivisation throughout the 1930s.

---

[10] Timothy Blauvelt, 'Abkhazia: Patronage and Power in the Stalin Era', *Nationalities Papers*, 35, 2 (2007), 212.

SEDENTARISATION

The effects of collectivisation were especially harsh in Kazakhstan because of a combination of the nomadic way of life and local political conditions. In the late 1920s, 77 per cent of Kazakhs were classified as nomadic or semi-nomadic. Although Kazakh nomads were herdsmen dealing in livestock, they traded with settled Russian peasants, and grain provided their staple diet. Most Kazakh nomads were extremely poor and, in spite of efforts to educate children in the context of a nomadic way of life, largely illiterate. A campaign against rich owners of livestock in 1927–1928, which also aimed at breaking the traditional hierarchical clan structures, was abused by local officials who also imposed heavy taxes on already hard-pressed herdsmen. As they sold horses and other livestock in an effort to meet these obligations, prices for animals plummeted, sending the herdsmen into even greater poverty. Thousands of Kazakhs fled across the border into China.

So the Kazakh countryside was already in crisis before the campaign against nomadism began. Collectivisation of European settlers was already in progress, and grain requisitions from them were further affecting the living standards of Kazakhs by December 1929, when the Central Committee of the Kazakh section of the CPSU decreed the sedentarisation of all nomads – forcing them to settle and adapt to new methods of agriculture in collective farms. The decision was based on a political decision as much as on the needs of collectivisation. It was presented as a positive move that would benefit the Kazakhs by resolving their dependence on European grain producers as well as reducing ethnic tensions. As construction projects stuttered and herdsmen resisted the sedentarisation decree, little progress was made in 1930, while about 51,000 families of 'dekulakised' peasants from Russia began to arrive in

Kazakhstan after being exiled from Russia, bringing additional pressures on scarce food supplies.

What sealed the fate of the Kazakh herdsmen was a series of decisions in early 1932 to socialise livestock farming. About a quarter of the population – 1.5 million people – were forced into huge collective farms together with their animals. These farms were built on land unsuitable for rearing livestock, and large numbers died from hunger and disease. Farmers slaughtered their herds in protest at their sedentarisation, while all the time animals were taken to towns in Russia in fulfilment of the requirements of the first five-year plan. Between the first half of 1929 and 1934, the number of animals in Kazakhstan fell from 4,133,100 to 431,727 – a drop of almost 90 per cent. The disappearance of the livestock herds and growing pressure on grain supplies led to a horrific famine in Kazakhstan that lasted from 1931 to 1933. In all, between 1929 and 1934 the population of Kazakhstan fell from 6.5 million to 5 million through a combination of famine, flight across the border and migration to towns in Russia.[11]

Sedentarisation and collectivisation in Kazakhstan resulted not only in massive loss of life, but also destroyed a centuries-old way of life and the culture that was associated with it. While the famine appears to have been the result of incompetence and ill-thought-out implementation of drastic policies, the decision to sedentarise and the callousness of implementation underlined the new priorities of the regime. Not only did the economy come first, but also national development was no longer to be organic and was taken out of the hands of national communists.

[11] Niccolò Planciola, 'Famine in the Steppe: The Collectivization of Agriculture and the Kazak Herdsmen, 1928–1934', *Cahiers du Monde russe*, 45, 1–2 (2004), 168.

THE UKRAINIAN FAMINE

Difficulties in counting the numbers of Kazakh herdsmen and of evaluating the impact of flight and migration in 1931–1933 have made an accurate rendering of the exact impact of the famine there on the population problematic. In the case of the Ukrainian famine, the question of the numbers of victims and the reason for so many deaths has become a matter of intense academic debate which has had political ramifications. In post-Soviet Ukraine the *Holodomor* (the Ukrainian word for 'death by hunger') has regularly been portrayed as a deliberate attempt by Stalin to commit genocide against the Ukrainian people. The famine was a forbidden topic in the Soviet Union until the late 1980s, so it was the work of western historians that came under scrutiny. For Ukrainian nationalists anxious to promote a narrative of national suffering, those who downplayed the numbers of dead or seemed to excuse Stalin's role in the crisis were guilty of pandering to Stalinism, while ever greater estimates of the death rate were seized on as proof of their position.

The reputation of journalists who disputed the existence of the famine at the time has also become embroiled in this argument. In March 1933 Welsh journalist Gareth Jones reported on the famine for the *Manchester Guardian*. His reports were denounced as fabrications by American journalist Walter Duranty, who in turn was attacked by Jones' *Guardian* colleague Malcolm Muggeridge. In the early 2000s, Ukrainian émigrés organised a vociferous campaign, ultimately without success, to revoke the Pulitzer Prize awarded to Duranty for another piece he had published in 1932, although the campaign did bring to public attention the inaccuracy of Duranty's reporting on the famine. The Ukrainian government was not involved in this campaign but in later years, especially after the Orange Revolution of 2004, the government of the former Soviet state became more involved in the issue of the *Holodomor*. Given the politicised nature of this question and the role it came to play in later post-Soviet nation-building, as well as the difficulty of reaching a balanced conclusion about the causes of the famine in the face of such conflicting scholarship, in a departure from the practice elsewhere in this book this section will include an account of the development of opposing historiographical approaches.

There is no disagreement among western scholars about the fact that a terrible famine occurred, with its main impact in Ukraine, in 1932–1933. What is disputed are (1) the number of dead; (2) the extent to which the famine affected urban and non-Ukrainian areas as well as the Ukrainian countryside; and (3) whether the famine was deliberately engineered by Stalin or the consequence of a poor harvest caused by unfavourable climatic conditions and worsened by the impact of collectivisation. The famine was first discussed at an academic conference in Quebec in 1983, which rejected the notion that the famine was genocidal.[12] The first full-length western study was Robert Conquest's *Harvest of Sorrow*. Using demographic data, Conquest suggested at a conservative estimate that there were, in total, at least 13.5 million deaths as the result of the collectivisation and the 1932–1933 famine, although in a later edition of the book he raised this figure to 14.5 million deaths. Of these, he attributes about 6 million to the famine – 5 million in Ukraine and 1 million in the North Caucasus.[13] A further million, he estimated, died in the separate Kazakh famine. In a 1984 article, James E. Mace put the figures higher, at 7.5 million Ukrainians.[14] Both the figures

[12] Yaroslav Bilinsky, 'Was the Ukrainian Famine of 1932–1933 Genocide?', *Journal of Genocide Research*, 1, 2 (1999), 147.

[13] Robert Conquest, *The Harvest of Sorrow: Soviet Collectivization and the Terror-Famine* (Edmonton: University of Alberta Press, 1986).

[14] James E. Mace, 'Famine and Nationalism in Soviet Ukraine', *Problems of Communism*, 33, 3 (1984), 37–50.

and, especially, the presumption that the famine was deliberate were challenged in 1991 by the economic historian Mark Tauger. From a reading of extensive data, Tauger argued that the harvest in 1932 was much lower than official figures suggested – so low that famine was unavoidable.[15] In a subsequent exchange of letters between Conquest and Tauger, the battle-lines were drawn. In addition to disagreements over figures, questions were raised about the reliability of Soviet émigré accounts, reports that border guards prevented Ukrainians leaving or food being brought in, and the availability of food reserves which the regime might have used to relieve the famine.[16]

In 1999 Yaroslav Bilinsky drew more explicit attention to another part of the argument, that Stalin himself 'was known as a Ukrainophobe'.[17] But most of the subsequent debate focussed on numbers of victims and the availability of grain. In 1995 the results of detailed archival work were published by Robert Davies, Mark Tauger and Stephen Wheatcroft, which showed that in 1932 the Politburo became increasingly alarmed about the amount of grain available for distribution in the USSR as a whole, and that grain stocks were running much lower than usual. They conclude that while the relatively small reserves could have been used to save millions of peasant lives, Stalin and the Politburo would also have feared that emptying the grain reserves could have led to famine in the cities and the army.[18]

In a subsequent book, Davies and Wheatcroft argued that the famine was the long-term product of Stalin's industrialisation

---

[15] Mark B. Tauger, 'The 1932 Harvest and the Famine of 1933', *Slavic Review*, 50, 1 (1991), 70–89.
[16] 'Letters', *Slavic Review*, 51, 1 (1992), 192–4, and 53, 1 (1994), 318–20.
[17] Bilinsky, 'Was the Ukrainian Famine', 153.
[18] R. W. Davies, M. B. Tauger and S. G. Wheatcroft, 'Stalin, Grain Stocks and the Famine of 1932–1933', *Slavic Review*, 54, 3 (1995), 642–57.

policies and mistaken assessments of agriculture, which combined with a poor harvest to create the conditions for famine. While arguing that more could have been done to alleviate the famine, they point to small amounts of extra grain being provided to Ukraine and the North Caucasus in 1933 in response to the crisis.[19] Wheatcroft later argued that the true figure for famine deaths in Ukraine was closer to 3.5 million.

Several other scholars have taken part in this debate, with a wide array of opinions and interpretations being expressed in the absence of any consensus over the basic facts. Some of the largest estimates of victims can be dismissed as exaggerations, and it seems that somewhere between 3.5 million and 7 million Ukrainian peasants died in the famine. It also seems likely that the regime might have done more to alleviate the famine, but that some degree of famine was in any case likely in 1932–1933 and that, belatedly, small efforts were made to relieve its worst effects. This does not answer the question of whether there was a deliberate effort to break the Ukrainian peasantry through allowing them to bear the brunt of the famine. Bilinsky's evidence for Stalin's Ukrainophobia is unconvincing, and what has influenced historians more are assessments of Stalin's mass deportations of smaller nationalities from the North Caucasus and Crimea in 1944. Leaving aside for now whether the deportations amounted to attempted genocide, Chapter 7 shows that the personal prejudices of Stalin and Beria probably played at least some role in the deportations. So might not Stalin have held a similar grudge against Ukraine?

---

[19] R. W. Davies and Stephen Wheatcroft, *The Years of Hunger: Soviet Agriculture, 1931–1933* (Basingstoke: Palgrave, 2004). For a summary of their arguments, see R. W. Davies and Stephen G. Wheatcroft, 'Stalin and the Soviet Famine of 1932–1933: A Reply to Ellman', *Europe-Asia Studies*, 58, 4 (2006), 625–33.

On the other hand, Stalin's attitude to ukrainisation for most of the 1920s would not support this, but by the end of the decade he had turned viciously on Ukrainian cultural and political leaders. The Ukrainian famine, like the Kazakh famine, was an enormous tragedy that left a huge scar on certain nationalities in particular. If nothing else, the circumstances in which they had been allowed to develop show how far priorities had shifted since the highpoint of nation-building in the 1920s.

INDUSTRY

The first two five-year plans (1928–1937) had two immediate impacts on the Soviet republics. The first was a massive level of investment in industry, and the second was the creation or reinforcement of regional economic specialisation. The most important secondary effects were demographic, both in terms of overall ethnic balance and a shift in population from the countryside to the towns. Ukraine received 20 per cent of all investment under the first five-year plan. Of 1,500 new industrial plants, 400 were located there, including the mass Dnieper hydroelectric dam project, begun in 1932. Another 1,000 plants were constructed in Ukraine under the second plan, and 600 under the short-lived third.[20] Investment was allocated to Ukraine and Russia at proportionally much higher rates than elsewhere, but in parts of the Soviet Union purely rural societies developed industry in a very short time.

In Ukraine, investment focussed on the production of raw materials, especially coal, while most manufacturing remained in Russia. Hence the Ukrainian industrial economy was, from the start, entirely interconnected with that of Russia and other republics. Azerbaijan's position as the major producer of oil for the Soviet

[20] Subtelny, *Ukraine*, 405–6.

Union was confirmed, but new fields were opened in the Russian North and East partly in order to restrict dependency on Azerbaijan for fuel. Central Asia became another specialised producer of raw materials, in this case cotton, and again was drawn into a relationship of economic interdependence with Russia, where most textiles factories were located. Eventually more than 90 per cent of cotton production in Uzbekistan was sent to other republics. By the same token, the transformation of land from grain and livestock production to industrial cotton production made Uzbekistan entirely dependent on other republics for food supplies.[21]

Whether this kind of industrial specialisation amounted to a colonial policy is a moot point.[22] Certainly the concentration of raw material production in the peripheries, and of final manufacturers in Russia, meant that more skilled labour, and hence a more educated workforce, was concentrated in Russia. Many enterprise managers in the republics were sent from Russia, but in the absence of full research, anecdotal evidence of this practice is not sufficient to conclude it was a general rule. Conversely, Russia became dependent on the peripheries for its own prosperity, at least until the vast resources of Siberia were opened up and exploited. The location of raw materials thousands of miles away from where they could be processed was one of many irrational features of the plans, one which upset the fulfilment of planned production in spite of heavy investment in transport at the same time. At the very least, we can say that no effort was made to promote self-sufficient industrial complexes in the republics, and it seems likely that the promotion of mutual interdependence was deliberate.

The demographic impact of industrialisation on the ethnic composition of republics varied. In four of the five Central Asian

---

[21] Neil J. Melvin, *Uzbekistan: Transition to Authoritarianism on the Silk Road* (Amsterdam: OPA, 2000), 22.

[22] For this interpretation, see Subtelny, *Ukraine*, 407.

Table 5.1 *Ethnic and urban change in the republics under the impact of industrialisation, 1926–1939*

Republic	Percentage of Russians in population		Percentage of entire population urbanised	
	1926	1939	1926	1939
USSR Total	47.0	52.4	18	32
RSFSR	77.8	83.4	18	33
Ukraine	8.6	10.4	19	34
Belorussia	4.9	4.3	17	21
Georgia	3.6	8.7	22	30
Armenia	2.3	4.0	19	29
Azerbaijan	9.6	16.5	28	36
Kazakhstan	21.2	40.3	9	28
Uzbekistan	5.2	11.5	22	23
Turkmenistan	7.4	18.6	14	33
Kyrgyzstan	11.6	20.8	12	19
Tajikistan	0.6	9.1	10	17

Source: Robert J. Kaiser, *The Geography of Nationalism in Russia and the USSR* (Princeton University Press, 1994), 118, 122.

republics, the Russian share of the population roughly doubled as skilled workers and administrators were sent to the region, reaching as high as 40.3% in Kazakhstan. In Tajikistan the Russian presence had been negligible, but rose from 0.6% to 9.1% of the total population between 1926 and 1939. Numbers doubled in Armenia and Georgia, but from a fairly small base, and in Azerbaijan the proportion of Russians rose from 9.6% to 16.5%. Elsewhere, in Ukraine the change was small and in Belorussia the proportion of Russians actually fell. The highest influx of Russians appears to have taken place in the North Caucasus.[23] Apart from Ukraine, Kazakhstan and Turkmenistan, the growth of the urban population

[23] Robert J. Kaiser, *The Geography of Nationalism in Russia and the USSR* (Princeton University Press, 1994), 119.

was slower than the average for the USSR, and these were the three republics that had seen the largest depopulation of the countryside as a result of sedentarisation and famine. Already in the 1930s and through to the 1950s, however, most titular nationalities increased, and in some cases quite dramatically, their share in the urban population. So a number of things were happening. Russians were arriving in most of the republics in large numbers, to build factories and housing and to work and live in them. But there was also a more dramatic move from the surrounding countryside to the towns which was greatly increasing the numbers of non-Russian industrial workers. At the same time, and especially during and after the Second World War, non-Russian minorities were increasingly persuaded or forced to move to their 'own' republics. Thus in Georgia, both Georgians and Russians increased their share of the urban population between 1926 and 1959, mostly at the expense of Armenians and other minorities, who left Georgia altogether. It is hard to discern any grand design at work here in the 1930s – managed population movement was more a feature of the post-war years. But the character of towns was changed, in terms of size, industrial base and ethnic balance, and the overall effect was, in the long run, to transform the national question in the USSR from a peasant question to an urban one.

HISTORY

The attacks on national historians, many of who were caught up in the early purges, led for a while to a hiatus in official portrayals of national history. In the course of the 1930s a new, state-sponsored historiography emerged, which erased or condemned non-Russian historical heroes while restoring the reputation of Russian ones – Peter the Great, Alexander Nevskii and so on. The non-Russian peripheries were now portrayed as having benefitted from Russian imperial rule, which began the process of raising them up from a backward, undeveloped condition, a process which was now completed by Stalin's revolution. Russian history and Russian culture were now at the heart of Soviet ideology, and the non-national 'Soviet man' that official rhetoric was beginning to embrace was to be centred on Russian culture.

This process started not so much from a consideration of nationality factors, but from a perception that the emphasis in education on social sciences in the 1920s had affected what little history was being taught, and that textbooks which served up generalisations about class struggle and social development contained little that would be understood or remembered by school pupils. As the rhetoric of class struggle died down and the international situation became more tense, history was restored to the core of attempts to rally the population of the Soviet Union around a unifying message. Patriotism, dismissed in the 1920s as a bourgeois device to mislead workers, was made acceptable by Stalin in a speech in 1931. While acknowledging Marx and Engels' famous phrase from the Communist Manifesto that 'the workers have no fatherland', Stalin argued that 'now, since we've overthrown capitalism and power belongs to the working class, we have a fatherland and will defend its independence'. This line of argument was taken up by propagandists in subsequent years, and informed the Commissariat of Education's new history curriculum, issued in 1933. Politburo member Andrei Bubnov was tasked with discussing details and planning publications with historians and others, but it was Stalin who settled how the issue of nationality would be handled. According to a participant at a joint meeting of the Politburo with historians in March 1934, after rubbishing existing Soviet history textbooks, Stalin called for new textbooks 'on antiquity, the middle ages, modern times, the history of the USSR, and the history of the colonised and enslaved peoples'. Bubnov suggested 'perhaps not [the history of] the USSR, but the history of the peoples of Russia?' To this, Stalin responded 'no, the history of the USSR ... the Russian people in the past gathered the other peoples together and have begun that sort of gathering again now'.[24]

This line of thought coloured the doctrine of the 'Friendship of Peoples' which emerged in 1935. While the doctrine acknowledged the multi-national character of the USSR, in statement after statement the 'leading role' of the ethnic Russian people was emphasised. Russian thinkers, writers, inventors, generals and politicians were extolled for their contribution to world culture and history. Battles from wars against foreign powers from the eighteenth and nineteenth centuries and earlier came to occupy a place parallel to the victories of the Civil War.

Where did these explicit references to the superiority of the Russian people leave the non-Russian nationalities in history and culture? With specific reference to the incorporation of non-Russians into the tsar's empire, the leading ideologist of the Communist Party, Andrei Zhdanov, himself proposed a 'lesser-evil' argument, that peoples such as Ukrainians and Georgians were better off under Russian rule than under Polish or Turkish rule. But historians of the USSR found it more practical to leave out the non-Russians altogether. A. V. Shestakov's 1937 *Short Course on the History of the USSR* is a case in point, paying no separate attention to non-Russians.[25]

[24] David Brandenberger, *National Bolshevism: Stalinist Mass Culture and the Formation of Modern Russian National Identity, 1931–1956* (Cambridge, MA: Harvard University Press, 2002), 34, 47.
[25] *Ibid.*, 43–56.

Another move cemented the superiority of Russian culture – a decree of 13 March 1938 making the study of Russian compulsory in all schools. This did not amount to a russification of the school system, since it only required the study of Russian as a second language for non-Russians, and in actual fact only confirmed what was standard practice already. The number of schools with non-Russian languages as the language of instruction was maintained and even expanded.[26] But symbolically this legislation was significant, as it put into law for the first time a hierarchical relationship between the languages of the Soviet Union.

PRIMORDIALISM

In the course of the 1930s, the flourishing national cultures of the 1920s were brought more closely within the orbit of all-USSR cultural institutions, whose currency was Socialist Realism. While this did not mean an end to national culture, it did alter its character away from the experimental and innovative forms of the 1920s, as was the case for Russian culture. But there was a further shift in the direction national culture was pushed. Traditional national costumes were the subject of museum exhibitions, and national musicians were invited to perform and take part in competitions in Moscow, where the cultural diversity of the Soviet Union provided a constant source of entertainment for Party leaders, educated society and workers. In a closely controlled process, national culture became rooted in an eternal past, with little or no modern dynamic.

---

[26] Peter A. Blitstein, 'Nation-Building or Russification? Obligatory Russian Instruction in the Soviet Non-Russian School, 1938–1953', in Ronald Grigor Suny and Terry Martin (eds.), *A State of Nations: Empire and Nation-Making in the Age of Lenin and Stalin* (Oxford University Press, 2001), 253.

What underpinned this celebration of 'national kitsch' was a new conception of nationality that departed sharply from standard Marxist models. Instead of nations being seen as relatively modern constructs, they were viewed as eternal and unchanging, with specific characteristics marking out different nations. Research institutes engaged in the study of ethnography and ancient history proliferated and flourished, reinforcing the notion that modern nations in the USSR had ancient roots. In the process, the number of recognised nationalities was drastically cut, and a great deal of this scientific work was devoted to consolidating nationalities into larger groups.[27] While the number of official nationalities was still greater than the number of national territories in the USSR's federal structure, the two began to converge. One implication of this, and a major reason for the shift, was that it consolidated the Russian character of the RSFSR. But a further impact was that it portrayed the other nationalities, especially those rooted in consolidated territories, as timeless and therefore, by implication, incapable of full assimilation. A more sophisticated view of nationality was pioneered by writers such as Lev Gumilev, and was closely associated to the broader ideas of Eurasianism. Not only was Eurasia distinctive as a region, but the different nationalities living on its territories were also adapted genetically to the geographical and climatic conditions.[28]

To some extent the shift to a primordial understanding of nationality was a logical outcome of broader ideological changes in the 1930s. Collectivisation and the elimination of the kulak had brought to an end the period of class struggle in Russian history. Citizens were no longer defined by class since all were proletarians,

[27] Hirsch, *Empire of Nations*, 204–27.
[28] Mark Bassin, 'Nurture *Is* Nature: Lev Gumilev and the Ecology of Ethnicity', *Slavic Review*, 68, 4 (2009), 872–97.

and nationality replaced class. Nationality was inscribed in passports, in census questionnaires, in biographies and on all official forms. The turn to primordialism was also assisted by the promotion in the 1920s of pre-revolutionary Russian ethnographers and other academics who already shared this worldview and who, with the national intelligentsias swept aside, now found an open field for their ideas. Primordialism was, then, a natural outgrowth of earlier policies combined with the new ideological turn of the 1930s. There is no evidence that it was premeditated, but it was to have important consequences both in the late 1930s and in the Brezhnev era.[29]

TERROR

The story of Stalin's Great Terror in the Soviet republics is a dreadful and repetitive one. To tell it in full would amount, as it did for Russians, to tales of knocks on the door in the night, disappearance, torture and confessions, along with the endless list of names of those caught up in the purge. Explaining the inexplicable has, in this case, taxed historians for decades, and no consensus has emerged on the reasons for the Terror.[30] Suffice it to say that, with the exceptions of only Azerbaijan and Georgia, in 1937–1938 every single leader of every republic, autonomous republic and autonomous region was purged. In most cases, two or more successive first secretaries fell victim to the purges. The same was true of many Russian regions, but the Terror seems to have fallen especially severely on the republican elites, and came on top of the successive purges that had been rolled out since 1928.

[29] Martin, *The Affirmative Action Empire*, 442–51.
[30] For a range of opinions, see J. Arch Getty and Roberta T. Manning (eds.), *Stalinist Terror: New Perspectives* (Cambridge University Press, 1993). Extensive archival work on the Terror since then has done little to clarify the reasons behind it.

The Terror also affected the new propaganda of Soviet patriotism, as one after another the useable heroes of the recent past were arrested or their memories discredited. Textbooks and popular works on contemporary history posed particular problems, and numerous new works had to be withdrawn from circulation and discarded or rewritten. Works celebrating the building of socialism in the national republics were as badly hit as any. The pictorial volume *Uzbekistan at Ten Years*, which first appeared in Russian in 1934, had to be considerably revised for publication in Uzbek the following year after the fall of Abel Enukidze. Also removed from the later third edition were purge victims F. Khodzhaev, A. Ikramov, A. A. Tsekher, D. Abikova, A. Babaev and T. Khodzhaev.[31] The effects of the purges were to strengthen the standing of more remote heroes, from medieval and tsarist times, as opposed to the heroes of the revolution.

There was another, specifically national, dimension to Stalin's Terror. A Politburo decree of January 1938 extended an 'operation for the destruction of espionage and sabotage contingents made up of Poles, Latvians, Germans, Estonians, Finns, Greeks, Iranians, Kharbintsy, Chinese and Romanians, both foreign subjects and Soviet citizens'. This was just one of a series of decrees demanding 'national operations' against members of diaspora nationalities within the Soviet Union. The national operations against these minorities account for a very high proportion of the overall victims of the Terror: in two years from 1936 to 1938, more than 1.5 million members of these categories were arrested, and they accounted for 247,157 executions during the Terror – 36 per cent of the total.[32] Considering that these were, numerically, rather minor nationalities

---

[31] Brandenberger, *National Bolshevism*, 38–9.
[32] Martin, *The Affirmative Action Empire*, 335–8.

in Soviet terms, these figures are extraordinary. Two factors in particular combined to explain the national operations: the first was the fear of impending war, with which the Terror was intimately connected, and the possibility that the Soviet Union might find itself undermined by internal enemies once the fighting started. This converged with the predominance by then of a primordial view of nationality, which suggested that national traits were stronger than citizenship ties, indicating by a cruel logic that co-nationals of potential enemy states were themselves enemies. This logic of primordialism was to lie behind another of Stalin's greatest crimes, the national deportations of the Second World War.

Over the course of nine years, Stalin had abandoned many of the policies of the 1920s, had overturned the basis of peasant national culture, had overseen successive changes of leadership in the republics and had rewritten Russian history and put the Russians at the heart of the Soviet project. And yet the federal structure of the USSR remained in place, national languages continued to dominate in non-Russian regions and national cultures were the object of affectionate study and public presentation. Cities across the Soviet Union were in upheaval and were swelled by Russians and non-Russians alike, and increased education and literacy made the changing urban landscape the centre of national life. However circumscribed that life was, and however cowed the population and especially its intellectual and political elites were by the Terror, most non-Russians continued to see themselves in national terms, and indeed were encouraged to do so by the passport regime introduced in 1932. National identity survived, and was to be given a new lease of life in the course of the Second World War; it emerged changed but intact after the leader's death.

CHAPTER SIX

The Great Patriotic War and after

The Soviet Union's eventual victory in the Great Patriotic War of 1941–1945 came at the expense of suffering and loss of life on an unimaginable scale. Compared to combined US and British losses of well under a million people overall, the Soviet Union lost, according to latest estimates, between 25 and 30 million lives, the majority of those civilian. While no breakdown of casualties by nationality exists, Russians made up the bulk of the Red Army and no doubt figured heavily among the military losses. For non-Russians, nevertheless, a number of aspects of the wartime experience suggest that in many cases national suffering was higher than for the Russians. This was most obviously the case for those peoples – Germans, Tatars from Crimea, Balkars, Chechens, Cherkess, Ingush, Kalmyks, and Karachais from the North Caucasus, and Meskhetians from the South Caucasus – who suffered wholesale deportations from their territories and relocation in special settlements, as will be discussed in Chapter 7. The first front of the Great Patriotic War was in Belorussia and Ukraine, whose population suffered not only the ravages of invasion but a ruthless occupation. Although some German leaders advocated turning the Belorussians and Ukrainians against the Russians, the pull of Nazi racial ideology proved too strong, and all Slavs were treated as *Untermenschen*. Further to the north, the Estonians, Latvians and Lithuanians were subjected to occupation first by the Soviets in 1939–1941, next by the

Nazis and then again by a vengeful Soviet Union. And in all of the occupied territories, the Jewish population was wiped out under the Final Solution, which the Nazis arrived at six months after the invasion of the USSR, and which may have been implemented first in Lithuania.[1]

Even for the nationalities far away from the front line, the adoption or, rather, readoption of symbols and practices previously associated with the Russian Empire, including recognition of the spiritual role of the Russian Orthodox Church, was a further development of the turn towards Russia of the 1930s which was finally summed up in Stalin's famous end-of-war toast to 'above all, the Russian people'. After the war's end, those Soviet Jews who had survived the Holocaust were subjected to a new round of Soviet persecution, while the ascendancy of Russian culture also seemed connected to a new round of purges in the republics towards the end of the 1940s. But the war also transformed the atmosphere for those non-Russians who were not directly persecuted by either the Nazis or Stalin. The war effort required the mobilisation of the entire population of the USSR, and local versions of the wartime reorientation of ideology raised non-Russian historical figures to heroic status. The role of non-Russians in the defence of the Soviet Union was specifically celebrated. In the occupied territories, communist partisans and less organised forms of local resistance added to the pantheon of national myths and heroes, although these had to be counterbalanced against acts of collaboration. Some national partisans fought against both Nazis and Soviets. In general, defeat of the Nazis led to immense suffering but also gave rise to a renewal of hope and expectation among most of the Soviet population.

---

[1] Dina Porat, 'The Holocaust in Lithuania: Some Unique Aspects', in David Cesarani (ed.), *The Final Solution: Origins and Implementation* (London: Routledge, 2002), 159.

In spite of the russocentric nature of much of the official victory rhetoric, the other nationalities, some of whom had reformed their national military units towards the end of the war, felt a justified pride in their role in the defeat of fascism. Any notion that a national revival might follow was resisted by the centre, which also had to contend with the incorporation of the newly acquired Polish territories and the three Baltic states. As long as Stalin was alive, the hope of renewal came up against a stagnant and conservative ideology. But at the grass-roots level, national feeling was resurgent.

INVASION

Hitler launched Operation Barbarossa on 22 June 1941 along a broad front. The main initial thrust saw the whole of Belorussia, Lithuania and Latvia occupied within a matter of weeks. The drive of the Wehrmacht through Belorussia on the road to Moscow brought it to Smolensk, the first major city on Russian territory, which fell on 16 July. Despite the loss of two mechanised corps and almost 200,000 troops, the Soviets put up sufficient resistance to slow the advance and thwart an attempted encirclement, allowing more than 100,000 Red Army troops to escape and defend the road to Moscow. This failure led Hitler to abandon his direct drive to Moscow and to focus on weakening the Soviet Union economically. This meant advancing on the industrial centre of Leningrad in the north and on Ukraine to the south, which was an important economic region itself as well as lying on the path to the oilfields of the Caucasus. The Southwestern Front was commanded by the hero of the Russian Civil War, Semyon Budyonny, and the future Soviet leader Nikita Khrushchev was the army's political commissar in Kiev. They were fortunate to escape with their lives, unlike the front commander Mikhail Kirponos, who perished trying to escape the encirclement which trapped almost half a million Red Army troops – probably the largest encirclement in history up to that point.

It had taken barely three months for the Wehrmacht to complete the occupation of the western and Baltic republics of the Soviet Union. By 13 October, it was within 90 miles of Moscow, but from that point on the German advance began to fade. From 5 December 1941 the Germans were in retreat from Moscow. The decisive turn in the war did not take place until the end of the Battle of Stalingrad in February 1943, while the siege of Leningrad, begun about the same time as the encirclement of Kiev, lasted into 1944. Thus, while the bloodiest, most prolonged engagements of the eastern front were focussed on the Russian cities of Leningrad and Stalingrad, non-Russian regions – specifically Ukraine, Belorussia, the three Baltic republics and parts of the North Caucasus – bore the brunt of the German occupation. This tested the nationality policies of both the Soviets and Nazi Germany, since the problem of supplying the frontline troops and maintaining communications to Berlin were heavily affected by the attitude of the local population.

It was also in these occupied territories that most of the partisan units operated, and while some of these were Red partisans, loyal to and sponsored by Stalin's regime, in other units nationalism was the driving motive and hence loyalty was ambivalent, and many partisans continued to oppose the Soviets after the Germans were driven out. As the Red Army recaptured territory, further military engagements were fought, including the second battle of Kiev from October to December 1943. The 'liberated' territory included all of the lands that had been sovietised in 1939–1941, but even within the former borders of the USSR direct collaboration with the Nazis and indirect complicity in the Holocaust emphasised the anti-Soviet potential of nationalism. That nationalism did not make more headway in response to freedom from Soviet rule had much to do with the policies of the occupiers.

OCCUPATION AND RESISTANCE

Hitler's policies towards the Soviet Union were driven by the overwhelming belief in the evils of Bolshevism, the perception that the Russian Revolution and subsequent regime were inspired by Jews, and the Nazi conviction that Russians were an inferior race. Nazi ideology, never crystal clear at the best of times, was especially confused over the Slavs – were Ukrainians, Belorussians and other Slavs essentially equivalent to the Russians? How far were non-communist Slavs to be differentiated from members of the Communist Party? And if communism was led by Jews, was there some longer-term hope for Slavs under a different leadership? Ultimately the racism of the Nazis led to all Slavs being treated with contempt, and opportunities for the occupiers to exploit national differences in the western region were squandered. This contrasted with the approach in the occupied regions of the North Caucasus, where collaboration and the deployment of local administrative structures was far more widespread.

Racial ideology was not the only source of confusion for the occupiers, who also had strong economic incentives for conquering the USSR. In the long term, according to Hitler's view, space was needed to provide farming land for the Aryan population. In the short term, the Soviet Union could provide resources that were essential to the war effort – food and fuel. The Nazis were divided internally over the treatment of the occupied populations, and even clearer splits were evident between the more ideologically motivated SS and the German army, which was concerned more with order and with control of material resources. Occupation policy and behaviour had important consequences not only for the German war effort, but also for the national development of parts of the population. On the one hand, Ukrainians and Belorussians were driven to embrace the popular myths associated with the eventual victory in the Great Patriotic War, although for some the war provided an opportunity for a national resurgence. On the other hand, smaller peoples, especially in the North Caucasus, had a taste of some of the freedoms which they had not enjoyed since the 1920s.

For Hitler himself, there was nothing really to distinguish economic from racial principles: 'Our guiding principle must be that these people have but one justification for existence – to be of use to us economically.'[2] 'These people' here refers to the Slavs as a whole, whose lack of any human rights was confirmed by the ideology of the *Untermensch*. While the German forces were initially welcomed in many Ukrainian villages as liberators from communism and collectivised agriculture, any illusions were soon abandoned. Communists were rounded up and shot, food and goods were requisitioned without compensation, and fit men were taken as slave labour back to the Reich.

The perception of a reign of Nazi terror throughout the occupied countryside may be misleading, however. Although the Germans granted neither the self-rule nor the return to private agriculture that nationalists and many ordinary peasants hoped for, the practical tasks of administering such a large territory meant that strict control was enforced mostly in the cities and along the main communication routes to the front line. In many rural areas, the Germans were hardly seen at all, and local government and even law enforcement

[2] Quoted in Alexander Dallin, *German Rule in Russia 1941–1945: A Study of Occupation Policies*, 2nd edn (Boulder, CO: Westview Press, 1981), 45.

rested in the hands of willing collaborators. Of these there were many – former kulaks, priests, intellectuals and others who had a sufficient grudge against the Soviet regime. But in some cases, lack of alternatives and the need for some continuity led to even low-level Communist Party officials being spared and retaining some administrative functions.[3]

Although the use of willing locals in occupied Belorussia and Ukraine was born out of necessity, by contrast, rule through locals was official policy in non-Slav areas. Although the occupation of the North Caucasus was relatively brief (1942–1943) and the Germans never succeeded in the key war aim of advancing into the South Caucasus and capturing the oilfields of Baku, they succeeded in putting local administrative structures in place that were informed by an altogether different way of thinking than was the case in the West. In the North Caucasus, the Karachais were governed by a Karachai National Committee under the leadership of a local peasant, and similar forms of local government were set up for the Kabardins and Balkars. Mosques were reopened and Muslims were allowed to perform rituals, celebrate religious holidays and engage in other practices that had effectively been banned since the early 1930s. Consequently the welcome granted to the invading forces in many villages did not fade over time as it did in Ukraine.

One reason for the different experience of occupation was that in the North Caucasus, which remained an active field of military operations for most of the time it was occupied, administration stayed in the hands of the army, which was less trapped by ideological considerations. Hitler had no plans to colonise this region with Aryans. The practical advantages of securing peacefully the

---

[3] Alexander Hill, *The War behind the Eastern Front: The Soviet Partisan Movement in North-West Russia 1941–1944* (London: Routledge, 2005), 47–51.

supply lines for the German advance towards Baku also provided powerful arguments for a lighter touch. But there was also a strong ideological component to local policies. The peoples of the Caucasus were subjected to racial stereotypes no less than others, but in this region they were mostly positive: Georgians were 'freedom-loving, brave and proud', Armenians 'industrious, enterprising and peaceful' and all of the peoples of the region had a 'highly developed sense of honour, pride and sensitivity'. Moreover, they had a greater history of resistance to both tsarist and Soviet rule than could be seen practically anywhere else, a fact which counted for a lot in German eyes.[4]

Although abuses still happened, German commanders tried to encourage an accommodating attitude to the population of the North Caucasus. In an order issued at the start of the offensive in the North Caucasus, Field Marshal Wilhelm von List gave these instructions to his troops:

(1) The population of the Caucasus should be treated as friendly nations, except when they show themselves to be anti-German.

(2) The aspirations of the Mountaineers to do away with the collective system [of farming] should not be hindered in any way.

(3) The reopening of houses of worship of all confessions and the cultivation of religious customs and traditions [are] to be allowed.

(4) Property is to be respected and requisitioned goods should be paid for.

---

[4] Alexander R. Alexiev, 'Soviet Nationalities in German Wartime Strategy, 1941–1945', in Alexander R. Alexiev and S. Enders Wimbush (eds.), *Ethnic Minorities in the Red Army: Asset or Liability?* (Boulder, CO: Westview, 1988), 97.

(5) The trust of the population is to be won by exemplary conduct. Its collaboration is of great importance in the mountainous area which is difficult to control militarily, and can also
considerably facilitate the further advance of the German
troops.

(6) All necessary war measures causing hardship to the population
should be explained and justified.

(7) The honour of the Caucasus women should be especially
respected.[5]

In spite of this attitude and the institution of limited organs of self-
government in the North Caucasus, the non-Russians who lived
there were not sufficiently trusted to be granted independence even
on a puppet-regime basis, as had been the case in several occupied
countries of Eastern Europe. Only the ethnic Germans, a number of
whom lived in industrial areas of Ukraine, were regarded as fully
reliable, but most of these had already been deported by the Soviets
before the German armies arrived, and those who remained were
few in number and had no significant experience. Several did
collaborate, but with little impact, and fled with the German forces
at the end of the war.[6]

Granting a certain amount of self-rule to the peoples of the
Caucasus, and instructing occupying troops in how to show respect
to them was, above all, in line with a policy whose aim was to ensure
that Russian dominion could never be re-established over the area
of the former empire once the Soviet government was overthrown.
According to the Nazis, the peoples of the Caucasus, who had
already proved resistant to Russian and Soviet rule, needed little

[5] *Ibid.*, 98.
[6] Hiroaki Kuromiya, *Freedom and Terror in the Donbas: A Ukrainian–Russian Borderland, 1870s–1990s* (Cambridge University Press, 1998), 282–3.

encouragement to break off former ties and pursue a separate course. The possibility of a resurgent Russian state at some point in the future would have been even more remote if the other Slavs – primarily the Ukrainians and Belorussians – could be split off from the Russians. But on this point the Nazis were divided. Shortly after the 1941 invasion, Alfred Rosenberg was appointed head of the ministry responsible for administering the occupied regions in the East – the Reichsministerium für die besetzten Ostgebiete. Although he shared the racialist theories that were fundamental to Nazism, Rosenberg saw a distinction between Russians and other Slavs and recognised the potential to divide them politically:

The aim of our policy, to me, therefore, appears to lie in this direction: to resume, in an intelligent manner and sure of our aim, the aspirations to liberation of all these peoples and to give them shape in certain forms of states, i.e. to cut state formations out of the giant territory of the Soviet Union and to build them up against Moscow, so as to free the German Reich of the Eastern nightmare for centuries to come.[7]

Up to a point, this strategy informed the administrative division of the occupied territories, which were to be split into four Reichkommissariats: Reichkommissariat Ostland (comprising the Baltic region and Belorussia), Reichkommissariat Ukraine, Reichkommissariat Moscow and Reichkommissariat Caucasus. The Ukrainian and Caucasus Reichkommissariats in particular were designed to play on national feeling and encouraging separatism. While the success of the policy in the Caucasus was limited by the brevity of the occupation and the failure to advance beyond the Caucasus mountains, in Ukraine it was thwarted by the nature of the occupation. Although Rosenberg's policy implied a certain tolerance towards Ukrainians and their national aspirations, the

---

[7] Rosenberg's address to his staff on 20 June 1941, in Dallin, *German Rule*, 54.

appointment of the more fanatical Eric Koch as Reich commissar for Ukraine ensured that Ukrainians would be treated every bit as badly as Russians. Koch's attitude was summed up in a statement to a conference in Rovno in August 1942:

The attitude of the Germans in [Ukraine] must be governed by the fact that we deal with a people which is inferior in every respect. Contact with the Ukrainians is therefore out of the question. Social contact is not permitted; sexual intercourse will be severely punished ... There must be no acts of sentimentality. This people must be governed by us by iron force, so as to help us to win the war now. We have not liberated it to bring blessings on Ukraine but to secure for Germany the necessary living space and a source of food.[8]

Koch expressed his personal feelings even more forcefully on another occasion: 'If I find a Ukrainian who is worthy of sitting at the same table as me, I must have him shot.'[9] Although Rosenberg was formally Koch's superior, the latter's personal connections to Martin Bormann and Hermann Göring gave him considerable influence in the leadership of the Nazi Party and his ideas, in any case, were close to those of Hitler. For Koch, all Slavs were subhuman, the Ukrainian intelligentsia had to be eliminated altogether, and any idea of compromise with the Ukrainian population was dismissed. Under his influence, Rosenberg's administrative scheme was abandoned and Ukrainian territory was dismembered. Through executions and harsh treatment, about 1.3 million Soviet prisoners of war died on Ukrainian territory. From early 1942, Koch sent his police to round up young Ukrainians for slave labour back in Germany, numbering some 2.3 million by the end of the war. Ukrainian cities were left without food, and thousands fled the cities for the countryside.[10]

[8] *Ibid.*, 143.   [9] Subtelny, *Ukraine*, 467.   [10] *Ibid.*

To some extent, Belorussians were not treated as brutally as the Ukrainians. Nazi ideologists held that the Belorussians had a different racial lineage from the Russians and Ukrainians, while their historical development also differed fundamentally as they had escaped Mongol rule and benefitted from subjection to the Polish–Lithuanian Commonwealth in the sixteenth and seventeenth centuries. The commissar for Belorussia, Wilhelm Kube, was, up to his assassination in September 1943, less extreme than Koch, maintaining that Belorussians could be saved from the influence of Bolshevism and act as a buffer between Russia and Europe. Belorussia was not granted self-rule and Kube intended that national development would be allowed 'only to the extent that they shall be capable of forming a wall against Muscovy and the Eastern Steppe'.[11] Belorussia lacked any local fascist movement, but that part of the population that had lived on the territory annexed by the Soviet Union in 1939 provided a body of willing collaborators who were employed more extensively in the administration than was common elsewhere in the occupied territories. In the course of 1942, almost 300,000 men were recruited to a local police force, the Schutzmannschaft, in Belorussia, Ukraine and the Baltic states.[12] A number of these units, especially in Latvia, went on to play a major role in executing the Holocaust against the Jews.[13]

The destruction of Soviet Jewry began immediately after the German invasion. Four groups of special forces – the Einsatzgruppen – consisting of up to 1,000 specially prepared Germans and backed up by Ukrainians, Belorussians, Estonians, Latvians and Lithuanians followed in the wake of the Wehrmacht.

[11] Kube's speech of 7 July 1942, in Dallin, *German Rule*, 204.
[12] Martin Dean, *Collaboration in the Holocaust: Crimes of the Local Police in Belorussia and Ukraine, 1941–1944* (New York: St Martin's Press, 2000), 60.
[13] *Ibid.*, 62–3.

In the first months of the war, they targeted Jewish communities, rounding up and exterminating Jews. On 29–30 September 1941, more than 33,000 Jews were killed at the infamous Babi Yar ravine in Ukraine near Kiev. Many of the Jews who escaped the initial onslaught were later trapped in Crimea, where they had fled, and which was cleared entirely of Jews by April 1942. These were just the most prominent of a series of atrocities. The few Jewish ghettos that were set up in cities such as Minsk were eventually destroyed and their populations killed by mid 1943. In all, close to 2 million Jews were murdered in the Soviet Union, and the long-established Jewish communities of Ukraine, Belorussia and Lithuania were eliminated.[14]

NATIONAL PARTISANS

The Nazis' distrust of Ukrainians and Belorussians prevented them taking this collaboration any further. In western Ukraine the Organisation of Ukrainian Nationalists (OUN), founded in 1929, embraced a Ukrainian nationalism that was characterised by extreme anti-Semitism and an antagonism towards Russia which the Soviet occupation of 1939 only reinforced. The OUN hoped for the support of Nazi Germany, and immediately after Operation Barbarossa was launched its leaders raced to Lviv and declared an independent 'revived Ukrainian state [which] will co-operate closely with National-Socialist Great Germany . . . the Ukrainian National Revolutionary Army, to be formed on Ukrainian soil, will henceforth fight along with the Allied German Army against

[14] Levin, *The Jews in the Soviet Union*, vol. I, 398–419; Yitzhak Arad, *The Holocaust in the Soviet Union* (Lincoln: University of Nebraska Press, 2009).

Muscovite occupation for a Sovereign United Ukrainian State and a new order in the whole world'.[15]

This open avowal of fascist aims and the common antipathy towards Jews and Russians were not enough to win the OUN German support. The political and military leader of its more radical wing, Stepan Bandera, together with other OUN leaders, was arrested by the Germans in 1941. The military wing of the OUN, which attracted substantial popular support, found itself fighting at various times against both the Germans and the Soviets. In 1943 they were regularised as the Ukrainian Insurgent Army, or UPA. Out of desperation, in 1944 the Germans released Bandera and other nationalist leaders and formed a Ukrainian National Committee, one of whose tasks was to establish a liaison with the UPA partisans, who now numbered as many as 90,000 men. The committee failed to establish control over the UPA, however, and it continued to operate independently against first the Germans and then the Soviets, continuing to hold out in the forests of western Ukraine until the mid 1950s.

The UPA and other nationalist partisan groups fought either alongside or in rivalry with Soviet-backed partisans. As the Germans advanced on Stalingrad in September 1942, Stalin approved an order 'On the Tasks of the Partisan Movement', which explicitly broadened the partisan movement to include, among other elements, ethnic units. As the war progressed, partisan units tended to be dominated by the nationality of the area in which they were operating, reflecting a somewhat ambiguous position. On the one hand, partisan units were organised, led and supplied with munitions by a Soviet Central Staff. On the other hand they relied on the local population for shelter and food. The national names

[15] Wilson, *The Ukrainians*, 132.

given to many partisan units, combined with the heroic myths that grew up around them, could act as a source of national pride as much as showing the solidarity of the Soviet peoples in the struggle against fascism. In Ukraine, rivalry between nationalist and Soviet partisans was at its most intense. Although for the most part individuals joined whichever group offered the best chance of putting up a fight in their locality rather than choosing between the two, the Soviets made every effort to promote theirs as the true Ukrainian partisans. Partisan groups active on Ukrainian territory were named as Ukrainian units (such as Sidor Kovpak's 1st Ukrainian Division), but consisted of only a minority of ethnic Ukrainians. All the same, they were portrayed as the heirs to the Ukrainian Cossack tradition and were given a separate Ukrainian staff in recognition of their special national role.[16]

The partisan movement itself contributed to a spiralling circle of violence in the occupation. As well as brutal reprisals against the civilian population in direct response to partisan activities, the Nazis used the threat of partisans to build on the anti-Semitic and anti-Slav feelings of German soldiers to further brutalise them and induce complete disregard for the lives and welfare of Jews and Slavs.[17]

Divisions between official, Soviet-backed partisans and more independent nationalist units were even more evident in the Baltic region. Towards the end of the war, hopes and rumours of an Anglo-American intervention against the Soviets once victory against Hitler had been achieved played a large part in encouraging

---

[16] Kenneth Slepyan, 'The People's Avengers: The Partisan Movement', in David R. Stone (ed.), *The Soviet Union at War, 1941–1945* (Barnsley: Pen and Sword, 2010), 172.

[17] Truman Anderson, 'Incident at Baranivka: German Reprisals and the Soviet Partisan Movement in Ukraine, October–December 1941', *Journal of Modern History*, 71, 3 (September 1999), 591.

Estonians, Latvians and Lithuanians to join the national partisan groups. As the Germans were driven out, these were active in attacking Soviet institutions and disrupting the renewed sovietisation drive. In Latvia the Latvian National Partisan Union (LNPA) and the Latvian Fatherland Guards Union (LTSpA) prevented local soviets from meeting, carried out numerous acts of sabotage and in some regions instituted their own document checks. Ideological divisions abounded within and between these groups – some of which owed their allegiance to the Latvian Central Council, which was backed by the western Allies, while others had previously collaborated with the Nazis. While attitudes to fascism may have been at the core of disagreements, at the tactical level the national partisans were divided over whether to escalate the armed struggle or to adopt a more passive policy that relied on pressure applied to the Soviet regime by the United Nations. The more militant LNPA succeeded in disrupting Soviet elections in February 1946 in districts where it was strong, but the divisions between the partisans meant this was not repeated across the country. Although the partisan movement continued to hold out against Soviet power until the late 1940s, the popular movement of the summer of 1945 had, a year later, dwindled to a few bands of diehard nationalists who, once the prospect of Allied intervention had disappeared, had no chance of restoring independence.[18]

The experience of Nazi occupation had a number of consequences. The brutal policies of the occupation ensured that most of the population turned away from nationalism and further embraced Soviet power. This was particularly significant in Ukraine, where it denied any possibility of the nationalist movement based in

---

[18] Geoffrey Swain, 'Divided We Fall: Division within the National Partisans of Vidzeme and Latgale, Fall 1945', *Journal of Baltic Studies*, 38, 2 (June 2007), 195–214.

recently sovietised western Ukraine spreading its appeal to the east. Hence, the UPA remained isolated and largely confined to the west, while the pro-fascist OUN sought too late to moderate its policies and broaden its appeal. In the Baltic republics, the Germans were rather more successful in exploiting ethnic and ideological divisions, involving nationalist organisations and individuals in the Holocaust and playing on anti-Soviet feelings. Whether this actually increased levels of nationalism and had any impact on the character of the Soviet reoccupation is open to question since, as we shall see in Chapter 8, hostility to Soviet rule hardly needed any encouragement. The partisan movement throughout the occupied territories furnished both the Soviet regime and the nationalist movements with a set of myths that underpinned existing divisions. For the most part, however, the national partisans, while displaying extraordinary courage and resourcefulness in holding out for years after the end of the war, dwindled in size and popular appeal from mid 1945 as the Soviets re-established control with an iron grip, capitalised on the bad feeling left by the Nazi occupation, and supplemented the legitimacy conferred on Stalin's regime by the defeat of Hitler with a series of messages aimed at the Soviet population as a whole as well as at individual nationalities.

PATRIOTISM AND PROPAGANDA

Two weeks after the defeat of Hitler, Stalin famously raised a toast at a reception for Red Army commanders to 'the Soviet people and, above all, to the Russian people, the most outstanding of all the nations that make up the Soviet Union ... the directing force among all the peoples of our country'.[19] The Russian people, once

[19] J. V. Stalin, *Works*, 18 vols. (London: Red Star Press, 1986), vol. XVI, 54.

Ukraine and Belorussia were occupied, made up the overwhelming majority of the population on which the war effort relied, and had seen a number of concessions to national symbolism and feeling during the course of the war, and especially around the time of the battle of Stalingrad in 1942–1943. These included the restoration of some prestige and authority for the Russian Orthodox Church (in return for the patriarch's support for the war) and the use of epaulettes for officers and other symbols of the old tsarist Russian regime. In one of the most important speeches of the war, on the 1941 anniversary of the Russian Revolution, Stalin had appealed to the achievements of exclusively Russian military heroes.[20]

In spite of this singling out of the Russian people for especial praise, non-Russians were also able to taste a revival in national culture and prestige. Stalin's early war speeches also emphasised the Soviet friendship of peoples, and the multi-ethnic harmony of Soviet society was contrasted to Hitler's racialist state.[21] Renewed praise was also heaped on non-Russian historical figures, especially those with a military pedigree. In support of the parallels drawn between the Ukrainian partisans and the Cossacks, in October 1943 a medal was struck in honour of the Cossack leader who had led Ukraine into the Russian Empire in the seventeenth century, Hetman Bohdan Khmelnytski. Imam Shamil, the leader of the resistance to Russian rule in the North Caucasus in the nineteenth century, was restored to favour. Even before the official rehabilitation of Shamil, the former Civil War hero and now commander of the Southern Front Marshal Budyonny, used the example of Shamil to inspire a division of Russian troops: 'Look at these

[20] Simon, *Nationalism*, 181.
[21] David Brandenberger, '"It Is Imperative to Advance Russian Nationonalism as the First Priority": Debates within the Stalinist Ideological Establishment, 1941–1945', in Suny and Martin (eds.), *A State of Nations*, 277.

mountaineers. Their fathers and grandfathers, under the leadership of the great Shamil, fought bravely for twenty-five years to defend their independence against tsarist Russia. Let that be an example to you and show you how one fights for the Fatherland.'[22] The Tatar khan Edighe, who had sacked Moscow in the Middle Ages, was likewise lauded as a national hero,[23] and the reputation of Timur was revived in Central Asia.[24] The non-Russians also experienced something of a national cultural revival during the war years, with many works that had been repressed in the 1930s now returning to favour. In Central Asia, poets were allowed to celebrate their national historic achievements and to laud their national homelands as well as praising Stalin and the Soviet Union.

NATIONAL MILITARY UNITS

The armed forces remained a melting pot where the fraternal ties of all of the peoples of the Soviet Union were reinforced and shown off before the world. The message of the brotherhood of nations was reinforced by a staged photo opportunity at the end of the war, when the Red Flag was raised above the Reichstag in Berlin by two ordinary soldiers – a Russian, M. A. Yegorov, and a Georgian, M. V. Kantaria. But the inconsistencies of Soviet nationality policy were once again underlined by the reintroduction of national units in the Red Army, which had been abolished only in 1938. The first national units arose in the Baltic republics and were based on the old national armies that had existed under independence. But a decree of November 1941 formalised and extended the policy on creating

---

[22] Abdurahman Avtorkhanov, 'The Chechens and Ingush during the Soviet Period and Its Antecedents', in Marie Broxup (ed.), *The North Caucasus Barrier: The Russian Advance towards the Muslim World* (London: Hurst & Co., 1992), 180.
[23] Harris, *National Liberation*, 138–9.   [24] Allworth, *The Modern Uzbeks*, 242.

national military units, and between sixty-two and eighty national divisions or brigades were created during the course of the war. Some 700,000 men took part in these brigades which, when combined with the Ukrainian and Belorussian partisan units, meant that all of the major (i.e. those which had their own union republics) nationalities were represented by organised military formations, as well as some smaller ones such as the Bashkirs and Kalmyks. Even the Chechens and Ingush had their own national unit until their mass deportations.[25] National military units figured prominently in Soviet propaganda surrounding key battles such as Moscow, Stalingrad and Kursk. For example, the Kazakh Division's role in the defence of Moscow attracted particular attention.[26]

The portrayal of national heroes and celebration of the feats of non-Russian military units did not go unopposed and took place amid a certain ideological confusion that resulted from the wartime effort to mobilise the population by any means. While Russian patriotic values were being celebrated by Stalin and others, in the republics propagandists and writers took it as read that they now had a freer hand in celebrating national themes, but this did not always go unopposed. The most serious dispute concerned a new *History of the Kazakh SSR from the Earliest Times to Our Days*, which was published in 1943. The book celebrated the rebellion of Sultan Kenesary Kasymov against Russian rule in the 1830s and 1840s, as well as other instances of revolt. The clear contradiction between this history and a similar history of the Bashkirs, on the one hand, and the official glorification of the Russian past, on the other, did not go unnoticed in the highest circles. After they were condemned

[25] Susan L. Curran and Dmitry Ponomareff, 'Managing the Ethnic Factor in the Russian and Soviet Armed Forces: An Historical Overview', in Alexiev and Wimbush (eds.), *Ethnic Minorities*, 51–61.
[26] Akiner, *The Formation of Kazakh Identity*, 49.

by Russian historians and officials in the propaganda department of the CPSU, the leading communists Alexander Shcherbakov, Georgi Malenkov, Andrei Zhdanov and even Stalin became involved in the argument between two schools of history. For most of the war, however, the dispute remained unresolved, and contradictory versions of history were in circulation, both types serving the purpose of appealing to the national pride of different parts of the population.[27] But as the Soviet victory in the war began to look inevitable, in August 1944 a decree of the Central Committee of the CPSU condemned the celebration of Khan Edighe and signalled an end to this phase of the flourishing of national history.[28]

AFTER THE WAR

At the war's end, the Soviet population believed that the victory over Hitler, achieved at enormous loss of life and great personal endeavour by practically every family in the USSR, would lead to a new era in which the needs of consumers would receive more attention, and where personal rights would be respected in place of the arbitrariness of the 1930s and the individual sacrifice of the war years. For the nationalities, the revival of national myths and heroes and the achievements of partisan or regular national military units added a national element to this sense of expectation. Between 1946 and 1950 Stalin oversaw the establishment of a new world order, and arrests, deportations and collectivisation created massive upheavals in the new Soviet territories of Estonia, Latvia, Lithuania, western Ukraine and Moldova (see Chapter 8), while

---

[27] Brandenberger, 'Debates', 279–81.

[28] Victor A. Shnirelman, *Who Gets the Past? Competition for Ancestors among Non-Russian Intellectuals in Russia* (Baltimore: Johns Hopkins University Press, 1996), 7.

the struggle against national partisan units continued mostly in the same areas. But for the most part the non-Russian republics enjoyed a period of stability in which there were very few changes in leadership, and national languages and cultures were able to consolidate.

As long as Stalin was alive, however, nationality policy was subject to arbitrary swings. The most disturbing feature of this period was the growth of official anti-Semitism. Even at the height of the war and with the Jewish Anti-Fascist Committee in full swing, the number of Jews in leading positions in central cultural institutions was being reduced as a matter of policy, while a senior member of the State Cinema Committee complained about the prominent 'Semitic features' of the actress Faina Ranevskaya when she was given a leading role in Sergei Eisenstein's film, *Ivan the Terrible*.[29] While it seems paradoxical that senior officials should have adopted such anti-Semitic positions just at the time when the Soviet Union was presenting itself as the defender of Jewry against Hitler, the open embrace of Russian nationalism at the centre may have emboldened certain individuals. As yet, however, there was nothing to suggest that the demotion of Jews had official sanction from the top. Once the war was over, however, a number of Jews were removed from the press agency Sovinformburo. In January 1948, the head of the Jewish Anti-Fascist Committee, Solomon Mikhoels, died in mysterious circumstances. The creation of the state of Israel in 1948, with its clear pro-American orientation at a time when the Cold War was heating up, gave further impetus to a more determined policy against the remaining Soviet Jews and the prominence they had achieved through wartime activity. The

[29] Hosking, *Rulers and Victims*, 263.

Jewish Anti-Fascist Committee was closed down in November 1948 and many of its leading members arrested.

This marked the beginning of a campaign against 'cosmopolitanism' that saw not only the arrest of prominent Soviet Jews, but also the closure of theatres and other cultural institutions.[30] Speeches and newspaper articles raised the spectre of an international Jewish conspiracy to overthrow Soviet power. In early 1953 a number of senior Kremlin doctors, all with Jewish names, were arrested and accused of having caused the deaths of former Politburo members Zhdanov and Shcherbakov and of plotting to kill Stalin and other leaders. There is some suggestion that Stalin was preparing to deport all of the Soviet Union's Jews to Siberia, and that this plan as well as the persecution of the Kremlin doctors was prevented only by his death on 5 March 1953.[31]

While Jews were singled out for this kind of treatment, between 1950 and 1953 the overall relative stability that had marked the immediate post-war years in the Soviet republics began to unravel. In Georgia in 1951–1952 thousands of officials were purged and many arrested, including a large number of leaders of the Georgian Communist Party who came from the Mingrelian region, which was also the home base of Lavrenti Beria. Beria was then head of the security police of the USSR, but as the former boss of the Party organisations in the South Caucasus he had appointed many of the officials in Georgia and had shown a marked preference for fellow Mingrelians. The Mingrelian Affair, launched on Stalin's own initiative, therefore seriously undermined Beria's basis of support in Georgia at a time when Stalin was becoming suspicious of his

---

[30] Levin, *The Jews in the Soviet Union*, vol. I, 488–525; vol. II, 527–50.

[31] Iakov Etinger, 'The Doctors' Plot: Stalin's Solution to the Jewish Question', in Yaacov Ro'i (ed.), *Jews and Jewish Life in Russia and the Soviet Union* (Ilford: Frank Cass, 1995), 103–26.

growing power in Moscow.[32] But there were also signs that Stalin was growing wary of the power bases being built up by leaders in the republics generally, and that the more tolerant attitude to nationalism that had arisen during the war was encouraging a new generation of young people to display nationalist tendencies, while leaders were accused of failing to take sufficient care to integrate them into a Soviet way of thinking. This was particularly the case in Georgia,[33] but in the last years of his life Stalin also instigated major purges in Estonia, Karelia, Kyrgyzstan, Moldova and Uzbekistan.

Viewed from the republics, in many ways late Stalinism was the opposite to the high Stalinism of the 1930s. Stalin's regime had overturned social and cultural relations in the 1930s, and the nationalities were powerless to resist. They were bombarded with mobilising messages to which they had little option but to acquiesce. The war transformed this relationship. The nationalities, like the Russians, emerged with a new sense of pride – much of it pride for the Soviet Union, but also national pride. The relaxation of ideological and cultural controls together with the sense that the sacrifice involved in victory over Hitler would lead to better times ahead fired a mood of expectation that the regime could only disappoint. Suspicion was no less a hallmark of Stalin's last years than it was of his earlier ones, but now it was expressed in a conservative opposition to radical change and an obsession with administrative solutions to perceived dangers. As in the 1930s, nationalism was viewed as one of those dangers, and now it was the Jews, who had undergone a political revival in their wartime activities, who

[32] J. Ducoli, 'The Georgian Purges 1951–1953', *Caucasian Review*, 6 (1958), 54–61; Amy Knight, *Beria: Stalin's First Lieutenant* (Princeton University Press, 1993), 159–64; Yoram Gorlizki and Oleg Khlevniuk, *Cold Peace: Stalin and the Soviet Ruling Circle, 1945–1953* (Oxford University Press, 2005), 109–13.

[33] Politburo proceedings of 29 October 1951, RGASPI, f. 17, op. 3, d. 1091.

bore the brunt of Stalin's suspicions. For the other nationalities, the confused ideological messages of this era contrasted with the simplicity of the single wartime imperative, in which everything was subordinate to the cause of victory. The result was a frustration and resentment that lay behind an upsurge of national feeling that followed Stalin's death.

CHAPTER SEVEN

Deportations

The previous chapter sketched some of the broad experiences of the non-Russian nationalities during and after the Second World War. There was considerable variation across the Soviet Union, with the western and North Caucasus nationalities who suffered German occupation experiencing the war differently from other national-ities, while the Jews faced persecution of different sorts by the Nazis during the war and by the Soviets after it. But two further groups of nationalities deserve especial attention. In this chapter, the fate of the relatively small nationalities from the Caucasus and Crimea who were deported *en masse* from their home republics or regions in 1944 is examined, while the next chapter looks at the nationalities who were incorporated into the Soviet Union, first under the terms of the Molotov–Ribbentrop pact in 1939–1940, and again at the end of the war as the Red Army drove out the occupying Germans – Estonians, Latvians, Lithuanians, the Ukrainians and Belorussians whose territory was annexed from Poland, and the Moldovans of Romania. Both sets of nationalities are important not just to com-plete the picture of the nationalities experience in the 1940s, but also because of their lasting impact and eventual contribution to the break-up of the USSR. The population of the Baltic republics played a direct role in the demise of the Soviet Union, but the deported peoples also presented a constant reminder of the mass scale of repression under Stalin and affected late Soviet politics in several ways. How to manage them was one of the first questions to be addressed by Nikita Khrushchev under destalinisation, but those who were still denied the right to return to their homelands pressed their demands by letter, petition and demonstration right through to the 1980s, while those who did return contributed to some of the ethnic conflicts that marked the final years of Soviet rule. Not least, the Chechens, hardened by their experience of exile, ensured that the relatively peaceful break-up of the Soviet Union would eventually sink the new Russian Federation into internal and bloody warfare.

THE OPERATIONS

Seven-year-old Ayshe Seytmuratova was woken by her mother on the night of 17/18 May 1944 and taken from her home:

They packed us barefoot and cold, dressed only in pyjamas, into railcars and sent us off to Central Asia, along with the entire Crimean Tatar people. We Crimean Tatars call these Soviet railcars 'crematoria on wheels' . . . so we were transported for weeks without proper food or medical attention. There was not even any fresh air, for the doors and windows were bolted shut. For days on end corpses lay alongside the living . . . And only in the sands of Kazakhstan did the transport guards open the doors, so as to toss out the corpses alongside the railway. They did not give us time to bury our dead. Many people went insane . . . We, the Crimean Tatar children of the 1940s, grew up under the conditions of cruel state-sponsored terror on reservations – that has naturally left a deep imprint on our hearts.[1]

Many such testimonies survive, and the experience was repeated for almost a million people from the North Caucasus and Crimea over the coming year. The process started in a way which, if not actually

[1] Ayshe Seytmuratova, 'The Elders of the New National Movement: Recollections', in Edward A. Allworth (ed.), *The Tatars of Crimea: Return to the Homeland*, 2nd edn (Durham, NC: Duke University Press, 1998), 155.

justifiable, was at least understandable and has often been compared with the USA's incarcerations of ethnic Japanese in the course of the Second World War. On 26 August 1941, two months after the German invasion of the USSR, the Soviet government ordered the resettlement of 500,000 Germans inhabiting the Autonomous Republic of the Volga Germans 'without exception, both townsmen and the rural population'. The deportation was carried out within a matter of days.[2] These Soviet citizens were mostly descendants of settlers who had been brought to the Volga region by Russian empress Catherine the Great in the second half of the eighteenth century. As guests of the empress, they were given special linguistic, cultural and religious rights which (apart from religion) were maintained under Soviet rule. Recognised as a distinct nationality inhabiting a compact area (as opposed to more recent German immigrants who were scattered around the Soviet Union), they were granted an autonomous republic in 1924. As such, they had no ties with Germany itself, but they spoke German and were no doubt aware of their ethnic ties, and this made them sufficiently suspect in Stalin's eyes to warrant their wholesale removal to a supervised special regime.

The arrest and removal of ethnic Germans had begun during Stalin's Great Terror in 1937 when, with the prospect of a European war looming, the arrest of all Germans working in the military, chemicals, electricity and construction sectors was ordered. Further categories of Germans were added, and by the end of 1939 some 70,000 ethnic Germans had been arrested. Many of these were Soviet citizens, but this was a more targeted campaign, mostly against more recent arrivals in the USSR, and starting with those in sensitive

---

[2] Irina Mukhina, 'Germans of the Soviet Union: Ethnic Identity, Tragic Reality' (unpublished Ph.D thesis, Boston College, 2005), 65–73.

Table 7.1 *Peoples deported from their home republics in 1943–1944*

Nationality	Population in republic/region (1939 census)	Date of deportation
Karachais	73,000	2 November 1943
Kalmyks	131,000	27 December 1943
Chechens	408,000	23 February 1944
Ingush	92,000	February 1944
Balkars	43,000	8 March 1944
Crimean Tatars	202,000	18 May 1944
Meskhetian Turks	200,000	15 November 1944

Source: Isabelle Kreindler, 'The Soviet Deported Nationalities: A Summary and an Update', *Soviet Studies*, 38, 3 (1986), 387.

industries.[3] It is a clear indictment of the scale and horror of the later deportations that this exercise of Terror against 70,000 Germans appears relatively insignificant and even semi-rational.

The remainder of the wartime deportations occurred in 1943–1944 as the Red Army recaptured territory from the Germans and were followed by the NKVD forces that carried out the operations. Thus, these deportations were in essence a settling of scores rather than a pre-emptive move against possible traitors. The bare facts of the later deportations are summarised in Table 7.1. The Karachais, Kalmyks, Chechens, Ingush and Balkars each comprised the main national group in one of the autonomous regions or republics in the North Caucasus, although two of them shared the name and population of their republic with a second nationality – the Karachais with the Cherkess, and the Balkars with the Kabardins. The Tatars made up some 25 per cent of the population of the Crimean peninsula, which at that time was part of the RSFSR. The

---

[3] *Ibid.*, 63–6.

Meskhetian Turks were inhabitants of Georgia, Muslims descended from Turks but also from the local Meskhet population.

BASIS OF DEPORTATIONS

All of these peoples were Muslim by religion, but what they had in common more significantly was that all had lived under German occupation and had been granted a role in administering the occupied regions. Karachais, Kabardins and Balkars had taken part in local government and had wasted no time in ridding themselves of collective agriculture. In all cases, however, larger numbers had served in the Red Army than had worked willingly for the Germans.

But there were more scores to settle than just acts of collaboration with the Germans. The peoples of the Caucasus mountains had held out more determinedly than anybody else against Russian rule in the nineteenth century, and in the twentieth the Chechens and Ingush in particular had been troublesome for the Soviets, rebelling regularly throughout the 1930s, particularly in response to the collectivisation of 1929, which disrupted traditional structures. As recently as 1940, even before the German invasion, the popular Chechen writer Hassan Israilov led a rebellion which gained control of most of the mountains and spread in 1942 as the Soviets withdrew troops to fight against Hitler's forces. Israilov's clear aim was to liberate the Chechens and other peoples of the North Caucasus from Soviet rule. Although Israilov made some common cause with the Germans – in committing acts of sabotage in the oilfields of Chechnya, for example – differing aims and ideologies made close collaboration difficult. The rising was put down by the Soviets through aerial bombing raids in 1942.[4]

---

[4] Amjad Jaimoukha, *The Chechens: A Handbook* (London and New York: RoutledgeCurzon, 2005), 55–6.

If the history of resistance combined with reprisals for Israilov's revolt were sufficient cause to solve the problems posed by the Chechens and Ingush once and for all by wholesale deportation, then reprisals for perceived collaboration with the Germans on its own appears to have motivated the removal of the Tatars from Crimea. The order of 11 May 1944 stipulated that

Crimean Tatars betrayed the Homeland, deserted units of the Red Army defending Crimea, and went over to the side of the enemy. They joined volunteer Tatar military units, formed by the Germans, battling against the Red Army; in the period of the occupation in Crimea, taking part in German punitive detachments with German fascist troops, Crimean Tatars were especially distinguished by their beastly reprisals in regard to Soviet partisans and also aided the German occupiers in organizing the business of forcibly driving Soviet citizens into German slavery and that of the mass execution of Soviet individuals.[5]

Up to 20,000 Tatars had joined the Wehrmacht as volunteers and others served in the local police force, denouncing partisans and communists and taking part in some atrocities. But these numbers were a small part of the overall population that eventually faced deportation, and were outweighed by those who served loyally in the Red Army. Tatars were also active in the partisan movement under the occupation.[6] Moreover, just ten days before this order was issued, Beria had reported to Stalin about the activities of German-sponsored fascist Russian and Ukrainian organisations in Crimea.[7] While members of these groups were arrested, ethnic Russians and Ukrainians as a whole faced no recriminations for

---

[5] 'Postanovlenie GKO no. 5859', State Defence Committee, Moscow, 11 May 1944, in Allworth (ed.), *Tatars of Crimea*, 154.

[6] Brian Glyn Williams, 'Hidden Ethnocide in the Soviet Muslim Borderlands: The Ethnic Cleansing of the Crimean Tatars', *Journal of Genocide Research*, 4, 3 (2002), 358–9.

[7] A. N. Yakovlev (ed.), *Lubianka. Stalin i NKVD-NKGB-GUKR 'Smersh'. 1939–mart 1946* (Moscow: Materik, 2006), 423–5.

collaboration. The Karachais were likewise charged with collaboration with the Germans, but were also being held to account for supporting the White General Denikin during the Russian Civil War as well as for rebellious activities in the 1930s.[8]

While collaboration with the Germans and acts of rebellion against Soviet power appear to have been the main motivation for the deportations, punishment was neither proportional nor consistent. At least some Kabardins had collaborated with the Germans, and yet not only did they escape national punishment, they actually benefitted from the opportunity to acquire land and property as well as political influence following the expulsion of the Balkars. While it is impossible to fully rule out hidden agendas behind actions which seem to make little sense against a background of a war for survival with Germany, we should not be too surprised to find irrational or disproportionate behaviour on the part of Stalin's regime in this kind of situation. Beginning with the drafting of ambitious five-year plans and the campaign to collectivise agriculture at the end of the 1920s, the Soviet Union had preferred to do things on a grand scale. This was generally true of a number of areas of Soviet policy, but two considerations in particular point to propensities which may help understand the deportations. First, the security of the Soviet state in what was perceived as an encirclement by hostile capitalist powers was a question of survival, and any possibility that internal forces might provide succour to external enemies provoked a harsh response. After all, one of Stalin's closest associates Vyacheslav Molotov affirmed to the end of his days that the Great Terror of 1936–1938 was a justified response to the presence of traitors constituting a 'fifth column' in the Soviet rear at a time of impending

---

[8] Walter Comins-Richmond, 'The Deportation of the Karachays', *Journal of Genocide Research*, 4, 3 (2002), 432.

war. The presence in the rear of a significant number of people who had already collaborated with the enemy was going to provoke an equally disproportionate response. Secondly, as discussed in Chapter 5, the Soviets had by now moved towards a far more rigid, primordial view of nationality than Lenin had held. It was a short step to associate particular nations with specific character traits. If the political or intellectual elites of a nationality had been prepared to betray the motherland and work for Hitler's Nazis, how could the rest of that nation be trusted?

A further factor that helps in understanding the deportations is that such extreme measures were hardly unknown in Russian history. In 1864, after finally subjugating the North Caucasus, Tsar Alexander II's government had deported large numbers of Cherkess, Chechens, Ossetians, Abkhaz and others to Turkey.[9] The Circassians or Adyghes were expelled in their entirety from the empire. About two-thirds of the Tatar population of Crimea had already been forced into emigration under the Russian Empire. These measures had been intended to clear space for Russian settlers who would provide a loyal population, at the same time as breaking up nationalities whose hostility to Russian imperial rule posed, in the minds of the empire's rulers, a threat to its stability. Smaller-scale resettlements in order to improve the territorial compactness of nationalities had accompanied some of the early Soviet demarcations of national territories. As well as ethnic Germans, in the years leading up to the war ethnic Chinese and Koreans had been moved away from the border regions as a pre-emptive measure. And there were aspects of the Great Terror which took a national character, with operations aiming at rounding up specified numbers of various nationalities (see Chapter 5).

---

[9] Avtorkhanov, 'The Chechens and Ingush', 150.

While tsarist and Soviet precedents together with consideration of Soviet attitudes to nationality help to understand the deportations, they fail to fully make sense of operations which occupied some 120,000 NKVD agents and 180 railway trains at a time when the war with Hitler was still to be conclusively won. While deportation fell short of Hitler's final solution for the Jews, the aim seems to have been to destroy these selected nationalities as nations by denying them a common territory and removing them altogether from the basis of their national cultures. These momentous decisions appear to have been taken with remarkable casualness – the decision to deport the Balkars seems to have been an afterthought to the deportation of the Chechens and Ingush, with Beria advising Stalin that such an operation could be carried out conveniently as sufficient NKVD operatives were still in the area.[10]

JOURNEY TO EXILE

As noted, about 120,000 NKVD agents were involved in the Chechen and Ingush operations,[11] and it seems that it was much the same forces that were involved in each of the others. Chechens faced a nineteen-day journey in crowded wagons to their place of exile. Typhus was rampant, and many died on the way. At the infrequent stops on the journey, the wagon occupants would crowd around the doors to get a rare gasp of air while Soviet soldiers dragged out the bodies of the dead and left them by the side of the tracks. There was little food and water and no hygiene, and for Chechen women the shame of relieving themselves through a hole

---

[10] *Tak eto bylo: natsional'nye repressii v SSSR 1919–1952 gody* (Moscow: INSAN, 1993), 265.

[11] Birgit Bauer, 'Chechens and the Survival of Their Cultural Identity in Exile', *Journal of Genocide Research*, 4, 3 (2002), 389.

in the floor in front of men was too great to contemplate.[12]
Karachais were held for three days before being loaded on to trains,
ninety to a wagon.[13] These horrific tales of the journey away from
their homelands are repeated for all of the deported nationalities.
Thousands died, although earlier reports of up to half of the
population perishing on the journey appear to have been
exaggerations.

Most of the deportees were sent to Kazakhstan, with large
numbers also going to Siberia. The local NKVD were given
responsibility for the new arrivals, but were given less than a
month's notice. Chaos accompanied their arrival at their final
destination. As one Kazakh guard recalled the arrival of
Chechens, 'There was great noise, screams. People didn't recognise
each other and got lost, family members had been sent in a different
car. They looked terrible, like prisoners. They had nothing with
them, except their clothes.' Next they were divided into groups of
twenty or thirty and sent to different locations.[14] While some of
these smaller groups ended up in the same settlements, or at least
areas close to each other, in general they were widely dispersed.
The 68,938 deported Karachais were split between 550 different
settlements. Half of these were children and most of the adults were
women, reflecting both the local demographic and the particular
wartime situation. As soldiers of the deported nationalities were
removed from the Red Army and sent into exile, the male population grew over the coming year. Deportees often found there was

[12] *Ibid.*, p. 388. Later accounts by Chechen victims of the deportations frequently claimed
that women died of ruptured bladders rather than relieve themselves, but it seems this
would be medically impossible.
[13] Comins-Richmond, 'The Deportation', 433.
[14] Michaela Pohl, '"It Cannot Be that Our Graves Will Be Here": The Survival of Chechen
and Ingush Deportees in Kazakhstan, 1944–1957', *Journal of Genocide Research*, 4, 3
(2002), 404.

no accommodation waiting for them, and if they were lucky they were housed in barracks and later built their own dugouts and mud huts. Shortages of water and the presence of malaria (which the deportees were unaccustomed to dealing with) spread disease among an already weak and ill population.[15]

EXILE

Famine and disease hit all the deportees, and probably accounted for more deaths than the journey itself. Not only were local officials unprepared, but the new arrivals were often treated with hostility by the local population. Crimean Tatars, most of whom were resettled in Uzbekistan, seem to have encountered a particularly adverse reception.[16] In Kazakhstan, where memories of their own treatment by Stalin in the early 1930s were still strong among the locals and where ties of religion counted for much, deportees sometimes received more favourable treatment:

The local people, especially those of Kazakh nationality, people of the Muslim faith, shared each piece of bread with us, although, it's true, they were extremely poor themselves. I will never forget the Ismuldinovs . . . In 1946 and 1947 I herded horses on the outlying pastures, and lived in their family. The mother, Nazam, always put a larger piece of bread in front of me than in front of her own sons.[17]

But Chechens and Ingush also had difficulty in gaining acceptance, not least because of the negative stereotypes attached to those nationalities, which were further stoked by rumours spread by the NKVD in advance of their arrival. Until 1956, the new settlers lived

[15] Comins-Richmond, 'The Deportation', 433–4.
[16] Ann Sheehy and Bohdan Nahaylo, *The Crimean Tatars, Volga Germans and Meskhetians: Soviet Treatment of Some National Minorities* (London: Minority Rights Group, 1960), 8.
[17] Pohl, '"It Cannot Be"', 405.

in Special Settlements. They were forbidden to depart more than three kilometres from their villages, and were policed by a special section of the NKVD rather than being restricted by walls and fences. For many of those who had been deported, who were used to working in mountain pastures, adapting to settled agriculture or factory work proved too difficult. Those who failed to adapt to a full-time job were the lowest priority when it came to the distribution of food, adding to the existing problems of malnutrition and disease. Under these conditions, between their arrival in 1944 and 1949, 23.2% of the Chechens, Ingush, Balkars and Karachais, 20.7% of the Kalmyks, 10.1% of Crimean Tatars and 8.9% of Germans died according to NKVD reports,[18] although some estimates are much higher.[19]

Deportees were treated with contempt and disdain by many local officials, but the NKVD sections that were mostly responsible for their fate generally sought to find ways to improve the situation. Gradually, the new communities settled into a regular way of life. Permanent buildings and farms were constructed, and health care improved. Some deportees were even active in the Communist Party, but for the most part the exile groups, neglected by authority after the war, built their own communities and remained largely estranged from the world around them. Inefficient registration procedures made it possible for the exiles to keep their children out of the official education system. Children were brought up within their own settlements, and the traditions and customs of their people were carefully nurtured.

The most remarkable and unexpected feature of the exile was the way in which the deported people not only survived, but flourished culturally. The closed nature of the regimes under which they were

[18] *Ibid.*, 404–7.   [19] Sheehy and Nahaylo, *The Crimean Tatars*, 8–9.

held contributed to this, but the shared experience of tragedy and suffering also bound the exile communities together. Even before restrictions on movement were relaxed after Stalin's death, separated communities found ways to communicate with each other and to share survival strategies. To a strong sense of national solidarity cemented by shared trauma was added intense hatred of the Soviet regime which had caused this calamity, a hatred that was to persist after the enforced exile was brought to an end.

RETURN

Khrushchev's Secret Speech of February 1956 included a denunciation of Stalin and Beria's wartime deportations. A December 1956 resolution of the Central Committee (CC) of the CPSU provided for the orderly and gradual repatriation of the Caucasian peoples. In January 1957 the Kalmyk ASSR was restored along with the Chechen–Ingush ASSR, although this was reduced in size with some of its territory remaining in the North Ossetian ASSR. Although the authorities anticipated an orderly return, they were powerless to resist the spontaneous movement of a majority of the deportees, who clogged up railway stations for months in an effort to return and reclaim their ancestral homes. Since many of these had been taken over by Russians and other North Caucasian people, clashes erupted on the return of the exiles, but for the most part the recent immigrants moved out and the returnees were able to resume their pre-war life.

The spontaneous rapid return of exiles created confusion in the North Caucasus, and official prohibitions on the place of resettlement proved unenforceable. As a consequence, thousands of Ingush returned to their former homes in the Prigorodnyi region and the city of Prigorodnyi itself, which was now the capital of North

Ossetia. Restrictions on residence permits were introduced by the Soviet government in March 1982 in an effort to ease the over-crowding of the region, but many Ingush simply failed to register themselves. Conflicts over land and housing burst out sporadically throughout the late Soviet period, and erupted into full-scale ethnic conflict in 1992.[20]

While the Kalmyks, Chechens, Ingush, Karachais and Balkars had their territories restored by the decrees of 1956 and were able to return over the following years, the same pardon was not extended to the Crimean Tatars, Germans and Meskhetians. The Germans were not even mentioned in the Secret Speech, and had to wait until 1964 for their political rehabilitation. The cause of the Germans – who were deported earlier and more dispersed than the other deported nationalities – never achieved wide recognition, and the main strategy adopted by many of them was to take advantage of German citizenship laws and, especially after the unification of Germany in 1990, emigration provided the easiest way out. The Meskhetians were freed of the Special Settler restrictions by a separate decree of 1956, but were denied the right to return to their homeland until 1968. Even then, while a decree of April 1968 recognised this right on paper, no practical arrangements were made for their return and the Georgian authorities refused to accept them. Some families did manage to return to Georgia, but not to the districts they had originally inhabited. A movement to emigrate to Turkey was thwarted, and most Meskhetians and their descendants have remained in Uzbekistan and Kazakhstan.[21]

The fate of the Crimean Tatars received most publicity in the late Soviet period. They, too, were freed from the Special Settler regime

---

[20] Valery Tishkov, *Ethnicity, Nationalism and Conflict in and after the Soviet Union: The Mind Aflame* (London: Sage, 1997), 168–9.

[21] Sheehy and Nahaylo, *The Crimean Tatars*, 24–7.

in 1956 but were refused the right to return to Crimea. Tatar land had been rapidly resettled by Russians and Ukrainians, and the integration of the peninsula into Ukraine had already caused strains with the Russian population. In addition, Crimea was the site of the main Soviet naval bases for the Black Sea and was key for security purposes. Following the logic of the same prejudices that had underlain the original deportations, the Soviet leadership were unwilling to allow the return of a people whose loyalty might be suspect. In any case, their numbers were much greater than those of other deported peoples. Those who did return illegally were often met by violence and intimidation from the recently arrived Slavic population. Of all the deported peoples, the campaign of the Crimean Tatars was the most persistent and most publicised throughout the Brezhnev and Gorbachev eras. The Tatar community in Uzbekistan was well organised and led, and its demands were not always opposed by the Uzbek leadership, which would have been happy to see the Tatars leave. Between 1962 and 1965, the primary tactic was to send delegations to Moscow in the hope of prevailing with a logical argument that the Crimean Tatars were in an analogous situation to the other deported peoples and should enjoy the right to return. Continuously rebuffed in these reproaches, the leaders of the Crimean Tatars resorted to a more open and mass campaign. In December 1973 a letter signed by 7,000 people was delivered to the Politburo demanding restitution for Stalin's injustice. Subsequent petitions and letter-writing campaigns, and occasional demonstrations in Uzbekistan and Moscow, brought the plight of the Tatars to the attention of the United Nations and the international community, as well as the Soviet dissident movement whose leading figure, Andrei Sakharov, took up the Tatar cause in 1979. The Tatars were faced with harassment and official violence, and their leaders were arrested and sent to prison camps. The Tatar movement tried to take advantage of the more open policies of *perestroika*, but a July 1987 demonstration in Moscow was broken up by charging riot police. Shortly after this incident Gorbachev did, finally, relent and grant the Crimean Tatars the right to return. Up to a quarter of a million eventually did so, creating population and property pressures on the peninsula which are still not fully resolved.

Stalin's wartime national deportations were motivated by a combination of fear, prejudice and opportunism. While the population of the targeted nationalities was massively depleted by the deportations and first years of exile, if the intention was to destroy them physically or culturally then in this aim they failed. Most of the surviving deported peoples returned to their original homelands with a stronger sense of national solidarity than they had had when they left, sustained by a narrative of national trauma for peoples who had already proved their cohesion and resilience. The persecution of these peoples has never been forgotten, and with the break-up of the USSR this experience provided one of the motivations for separatism in the North Caucasus. The first president of post-Soviet Chechnya, Djokhar Dudaev, was deported as a small baby, and his successors Zelimkhan Yandarbiev and Aslan Maskhadov were both born in Kazakhstan. The deportations were seen in Chechnya as one part of a consistent '300-year war' against the Chechen people.[22] Stalin's greatest crimes against nationalities took the longest to forget. While the remainder of the Soviet nationalities were able to revive rapidly after Stalin's death, for the deported nations the sores of the deportations continued to fester up to the end of the USSR and beyond.

[22] Vicken Cheterian, *War and Peace in the Caucasus: Ethnic Conflict and the New Geopolitics* (New York: Columbia University Press, 2008), 225.

CHAPTER EIGHT

Territorial expansion and the Baltic exception

The aftermath of the Great Patriotic War was a period of rebuilding, but did not bring an end to the suffering of the Soviet peoples, many of whom faced renewed persecution at the hands of Stalin's regime. A further consequence of the defeat of Hitler was the emergence of the Soviet Union as one of the world's great powers. While it did not take long for the newly formed friendship between the USSR, Great Britain and the USA to deteriorate into Cold War, the Allied victory allowed a breathing space in which Stalin could redraw the borders of Eastern Europe and impose favourable communist regimes in territories liberated from the Germans, without any opposition from the other great powers. This included the incorporation of Estonia, Latvia and Lithuania into the USSR, where they were ultimately to present a formidable challenge to the integrity of the Soviet Union. This chapter describes this process and some of its consequences but, before doing so, it is necessary to go back to the end of the Russian Civil War and examine developments in the Baltic states which gained their independence from Russian rule at that time.

INDEPENDENT ESTONIA, LATVIA AND LITHUANIA

Soviet recognition of the three independent Baltic states in 1920 resulted from the particular circumstances of the Russian Civil War

163

at the time, as described in Chapter 2. Support for the Bolsheviks remained strong, especially in the cities, and for the time being the possibility of further revolution remained a hope for Soviet Russia, and a fear for the new governments of Estonia, Latvia and Lithuania, as well as for the major international powers. Applications by all three countries to join the League of Nations in 1920 were rejected largely as a result of the anticipation that the League might become embroiled in military confrontation with Soviet Russia if it accepted the vulnerable states as members, at a time when the Entente powers were winding up their intervention in the Russian Civil War. Although the Allied Supreme Command formally recognised Estonia and Latvia in January 1921, senior diplomats, in spite of their own sympathies, privately admitted that some sort of incorporation of the three states into Russia at some point in the future was almost inevitable.[1] But the Bolsheviks' military losses against Poland and the confirmation of the existing order in northeastern Europe in the Treaty of Riga, signed between Soviet Russia, Soviet Ukraine and Poland in March 1921, persuaded the Russian communists to limit their intervention to support for the local communist parties until 1939. Estonia, Latvia and Lithuania joined the new countries that had emerged in Eastern Europe from the rubble of the Austro-Hungarian Empire, in building new states with a strong national element to them.

As in Eastern Europe, this process was not without difficulties. None of the three was ethnically homogeneous, there was little tradition of democratic participation or structures to draw on, and all were riven by the class divisions that had been accentuated in the course of the Russian Revolution. Economic life was severely disrupted by the loss of Russian markets and by the redistribution

[1] Kirby, *The Baltic World*, 286.

of land which was necessary both to assure the support of poor peasants and to replace the dominance of the barons who had been swept aside in 1917.[2] In these difficult circumstances, the Baltic states were tasked with creating a political system from scratch; with promoting a sense of national identity and unity from a small intellectual base and in the face of a large rural and radicalised urban population; with building up a national economy; and with managing international relations from a position of weakness and encirclement not just by Soviet Russia, but also by an aggressive Poland. None of these tasks could be accomplished in isolation from the others – social peace depended crucially on economic policies, while nation-building had to be achieved without antagonising potentially hostile neighbours. Politically, the experience of democracy was limited and all three countries ended up under semi-dictatorial regimes. But social, educational and economic achievements were substantial.

Economic reform was accomplished by formalising the seizures of land that had accompanied the Russian Revolution. The mostly German landowners were given little in the way of compensation, and the distribution of land in all three states, especially in Estonia and Latvia, was, by comparison with other contemporary European countries and even later communist systems, remarkably egalitarian.[3] The region's industry, which had grown massively during the last decades of tsarist rule, collapsed under the impact of war and revolution, and when it did recover, it did so in a different direction from before. The Baltic region had not only prospered through access to Russian markets before the war, but had also played a key

[2] Romuald J. Misiunas and Rein Taagepera, *The Baltic States: Years of Dependence, 1940–1980* (Berkeley: University of California Press, 1983), 10.

[3] Rein Taagepera, 'Inequality Indices for Baltic Farm Size Distribution, 1929–1940', *Journal of Baltic Studies*, 3, 1 (Spring 1972), 26–34.

role in the Russian Empire's external trading, much of which was directed through Riga. The new states turned to developing production primarily for the domestic market, although exports remained important. Most efforts were aimed at building up small-scale industry related to agricultural·production, but state-led investment in mineral extraction and associated industries such as chemicals also led to healthy economic growth. The economy of Lithuania, for example, grew by an average of 5 per cent per year in the inter-war period.[4] Much of this growth was catch-up, however. The early land reforms had more impact than later industrialisation in their effect on the social composition of the three countries, all of which remained predominantly rural up to 1939 and beyond. The westward orientation of exports also made the economies vulnerable to the impact of the great depression of the 1930s, giving further impetus to the growth of authoritarianism in all three countries.

Perversely, the constitutional orders adopted in the early 1920s were aimed at preventing such authoritarianism. Following the French model, constitutions were framed in order to ensure that a strong, single-chamber parliament was the dominant force in politics while the executive remained weak. In Lithuania, it was another aspect of French constitutionalism that undermined parliamentary rule – the separation of church and state. In May 1926 a minority government of socialists and populists led by Mykolas Sleževičius began to implement socialist secular policies which were unpopular with much of the Lithuanian population. The government depended on the support of ethnic minorities, and measures which benefitted the Polish minority together with anti-religious policies fomented popular discontent. The final straw was an attempt to

---

[4] Thomas Lane, *Lithuania: Stepping Westward* (London: Routledge, 2001), 29.

reorganise the army and its officer corps, prompting senior military figures to launch a coup on 17 December 1926. Army officers overthrew Sleževičius and President Kazys Grinius, replacing them with Augustinas Voldemaras and Antanas Smetona respectively. Voldemaras and Smetona were the two leading figures in an organisation called Iron Wolf (Geležinis Vilkas), a paramilitary organisation with parallels to Hitler's later Nazi Party, although its anti-German creed prevented any co-operation. This duumvirate did not last long, however, and Smetona rapidly gained the upper hand, dismissing parliament in 1927, promulgating a new, presidential constitution in May 1928, and finally dismissing Voldemaras in 1929. Smetona banned political organisations including the Iron Wolf, although it remained active as an underground movement.[5]

The new constitutional models enjoyed more success in Estonia and Latvia. But political inexperience combined with social fragmentation in the early years led to a profusion of political parties and consequently an unstable legislature. In Estonia, fourteen parties were represented in the hundred-seat 1923 parliament, the largest of which – the Farmers' Union – held only twenty-three seats. The complexity of coalition politics ensured that, between 1919 and 1933, the government changed every eight months on average. Weak central authority encouraged radical groups to seek power by a variety of constitutional and extra-constitutional means. An attempted communist takeover in Tallinn in December 1924 was defeated by force and followed by brutal repressions. The economic downturn of the early 1930s resulted in a surge in popular support for the rightwing League of Veterans of the War of Freedom (Vabs or Vaps). With the support of popular pressure, Vabs succeeded, at

[5] Nicholas Hope, 'Interwar Statehood: Symbol and Reality', in Graham Smith (ed.), *The Baltic States: The National Self-Determination of Estonia, Latvia and Lithuania* (London: Macmillan, 1996), 61–2.

the third attempt, in getting parliamentary approval for a new constitution which granted extraordinary powers to an elected president.

As preparations for the elections were underway, it became clear that a Vabs candidate was likely to win, which would have left the country in the hands of a radical populist movement. Under the terms of the new constitution, Prime Minister Konstantin Päts became acting president until the elections were held and, in a surprise move, assumed that the new constitutional provisions regarding the presidency applied to him in his temporary capacity. In March 1934 he declared martial law, arrested 400 leading members of Vabs, and postponed all elections indefinitely. With the passive support of all the moderate political parties, who feared Vabs above all, Päts ruled by decree until 1938. Under a new constitution introduced in 1936, there was a return to some form of electoral democracy, but only Päts' Popular Front for Implementation of the Constitution was allowed to field candidates as a party, ensuring that Päts himself would remain president under the indirect electoral procedure.[6]

Like Estonia, Latvia's constitution makers created a single-chamber hundred-seat parliament (Saeima), this time with an indirectly elected president. Lists of candidates rather than formal political parties formed the basis of electoral competition, leading to an even greater fragmentation – in the four elections held between 1922 and 1934, between 88 and 141 lists were submitted, but only between 46 and 93 of these won representation. Fractions formed in the parliament based on these lists, but none ever achieved a majority. The strong socialist tradition in Latvia ensured

---

[6] Rein Taagepera, *Estonia: Return to Independence* (Boulder, CO: Westview Press, 1993), 53–8.

that the Social Democrats remained the largest party ahead of the Agrarian Union, but they usually stayed out of government as they eschewed entering coalitions. Consequently, the less-well-supported Agrarian Union became the dominant force in politics, providing three of four inter-war presidents and entering eleven of thirteen coalition cabinets, in ten of which the prime minister was from the Union. As the economy took a downturn and the international situation appeared more threatening in the early 1930s, calls for a stronger presidency grew in frequency, as they had in Estonia. But unlike in Estonia, constitutional efforts led by the Agrarian Union to create a strong presidency failed in the face of opposition from most other parties. What followed was an outright military coup, backed by the army and the National Guard, on 15 May 1934. The coup was led by the Agrarian Union's Kārlis Ulmanis, who disbanded parliament, banned political parties including his own, and appointed a cabinet under his leadership. Two years later, he further assumed the presidency on the expiry of the term of office of the incumbent, Alberts Kviesis.[7]

Estonia and Latvia had, before succumbing to authoritarianism, enjoyed some experience of democracy, and at least in Estonia elections and other signs of democracy were returning to public life on the eve of the Soviet takeover. Authoritarianism resulted from sharp political cleavages and the failure of the experiment in ultra-democracy to achieve stable government. By contrast, Lithuania did not have long to develop democratic traditions.

While all three of the Baltic countries came under authoritarian rule between the wars, they were not subject to any of the Terror and extremes of repression that characterised Hitler's and Stalin's

---

[7] Andrejs Plakans, *The Latvians: A Short History* (Stanford: Hoover Institution Press, 1995), 126–33.

regimes. Radical parties – notably the communists – faced persecution throughout, and at periods all party activities were banned. But compared with some of their contemporaries in Central and Eastern Europe, and other parts of the world, the regimes of Päts, Ulmanis and Smetona were relatively mild, avoiding extremes of nationalism, militarism and personality cults. Ethnic minorities were not persecuted, though in some cases they did see their economic and political influence gradually curtailed. Free primary school education was introduced in all three states in the early 1920s, and social welfare provision expanded to a level which was not far off that of the Scandinavian countries.[8]

INTERNATIONAL DEVELOPMENTS AND THE MOLOTOV–RIBBENTROP PACT

Estonia, Latvia and Lithuania, flanked by the two pariah powers of inter-war Europe, Germany in one direction and the Soviet Union in the other, followed an international policy of studied neutrality. The three did conclude a Baltic Entente with each other in 1934, but this was the only significant sign of regional co-operation and fell well short of a military alliance. Although common interests were manifest, the priority was not to do anything that might provoke the larger neighbours, and different fears predominated: a resurgent and aggressive Germany appeared the greater threat to Lithuania and Latvia, while further to the east Estonians were more wary of the Soviets. External economic activity was oriented around the Baltic Sea and, among the major powers, Great Britain was seen as the most important supporter of the Baltic states, because of its naval presence in the region but also because of trade links and its attitude

---

[8] Hope, 'Interwar Statehood', 50–9.

towards independence at the end of the First World War. Britain was lukewarm in making commitments towards these three small countries, however, and as a matter of survival all three sought to appease both Germany and the Soviet Union. Non-aggression treaties were concluded with the USSR by Lithuania in 1926 and by Estonia and Latvia in 1932. Belatedly, all three signed similar agreements with Germany in the first half of 1939.[9]

The precariousness of the position of the three countries was underlined by a threat from a smaller neighbour. In March 1938, Eastern Europe came close to its own, local war, over an incident on the Polish–Lithuanian border. Poland and Lithuania had been at odds over the status of Vilnius since it had been occupied by Polish troops in 1920, and had no diplomatic relations as a result. Days after Hitler's *Anschluss* achieved the incorporation of Austria into Germany, the Polish media whipped up a frenzy over the fatal shooting of a border guard, Stanislaw Serafin, by Lithuanian troops. This led eventually to a Polish ultimatum to the Lithuanian government in Kaunas to establish formal diplomatic ties or face military action. Lithuania's rapid acceptance of the Polish terms avoided a further deterioration in the crisis.[10]

But as the great powers headed inexorably towards war following Hitler's rise to power and the rearming of Germany, the Baltic states faced far greater threats than Poland. There was little alternative to a policy of appeasement, which led Lithuania to cede the region of Klaipéda to Germany on Hitler's insistence in March 1939. But Stalin's Soviet Union, with an eye on greater access to and security in the Baltic Sea, was more interested in the Baltic region than was Nazi Germany. Although the Soviet patriotism of the 1930s was

[9] Misiunas and Taagepera, *The Baltic States*, 13–14.
[10] Alfred Erich Senn, 'The Polish Ultimatum to Lithuania, March 1938', *Journal of Baltic Studies*, 13, 2 (Summer 1982), 144–56.

derived in part from the doctrine of 'socialism in one country' and contained no explicitly annexationist messages, the fact that parts of the Russian Empire had escaped Soviet control was not lost on the regime's policy makers, providing a further, ideological, rationale for taking over the region as well as for attacking Finland. Strategically, reincorporating the Baltic region, including at least the eastern part of Finland, made sense as such a move would restore the more easily defended borders that had been achieved by Peter the Great and would move Leningrad further from the front line in any future war with the West.[11] Stalin may also have had a personal motive for restoring the western borders of the former Russian Empire, especially territories in western Poland: Stalin himself had played a part (and been blamed by Lenin) for the disaster of the 1920–1921 Soviet–Polish War, which had resulted in the loss of territory with largely Ukrainian and Belorussian rural populations. In 1925 Stalin had personally sequestered parts of the archives related to these events, and during the negotiations with Germany the German foreign minister, Joachim von Ribbentrop, alluded several times to the Soviet losses, suggesting that this was, indeed, a point that still rankled with the general secretary of the CPSU.[12]

Awareness of the Soviet threat lay behind the agreements between Estonia, Latvia and Lithuania on the one hand and Germany on the other in early 1939, and the sympathy of Britain and France towards the Baltic states was one of the factors that held up a tripartite agreement between the two western countries and the Soviet Union. Hitler had no such qualms, and the fact that, as Stalin

[11] Robert Edwards, *White Death: Russia's War on Finland 1939–1940* (London: Phoenix, 2007), 28–9.
[12] Dmitri Volkogonov, *Stalin: Triumph and Tragedy* (Rocklin, CA: Prima Publishing, 1996), 361.

reported to his Politburo on 19 August, 'Germany is giving us complete freedom of action in the Baltic states and does not object to the return of Bessarabia to the USSR'[13] was a key reason for the signing of the pact agreed between the respective German and Soviet foreign ministers, von Ribbentrop and Vyacheslav Molotov, four days later.

The 'Treaty of Non-Aggression between Germany and the Soviet Union', signed late at night on 23 August 1939, was ostensibly a ten-year promise on the part of both sides not to engage in military action against each other, individually or in alliance with other powers. A separate agreement also covered trade. But in a secret protocol that was not made public at the time, and which the Soviets admitted to only late in the 1980s, Nazi Germany and the Communist USSR also agreed on a division of Eastern Europe into spheres of interest:

In the event of a territorial and political transformation in the territories belonging to the Baltic states (Finland, Estonia, Latvia, Lithuania) the northern frontier of Lithuania shall represent the frontier of the spheres of interest both of Germany and the USSR ... In the event of a territorial and political transformation of the territories belonging to the Polish state, the spheres of interest of both Germany and the USSR shall be bounded approximately by the line of the rivers Narev, Vistula and San ... With regard to South-Eastern Europe, the Soviet side emphasizes its interest in Bessarabia. The German side declares complete political disinterest in these territories.[14]

It was clearly understood that either side was free to bring about such a 'territorial and political transformation' within their sphere and, just as Hitler was able to launch his invasion of western Poland in the knowledge that this would trigger war with France and Great

---

[13] 'Stalin Provokes the War' (Stalin's speech to the Politburo of 19 August 1939), in Richard Sakwa (ed.), *The Rise and Fall of the Soviet Union, 1917–1991* (London: Routledge, 1999), 226.

[14] 'The Nazi–Soviet Pact,' in Sakwa (ed.), *Rise and Fall*, 119.

Britain while the USSR stood aside, Stalin also knew he had a free hand to expand Soviet territory.

THE FIRST ANNEXATIONS

On 17 September 1939 Soviet forces entered Poland from the east, capturing Vilnius two days later. Hitler had launched his invasion from the West eighteen days earlier, and the already depleted Polish army offered little resistance to the Red Army. Polish resistance ended on 6 October, and by November the Soviet Union was able to declare that the population of the entire eastern part of Poland assigned to it by agreement with the Germans were now Soviet citizens. A majority of these new citizens were not ethnic Poles – about two-thirds were a mix of Ukrainians, Belorussians and Jews. The Soviet attack was presented to the public and to the invading forces as a war to liberate oppressed Ukrainians and Belorussians. In order to reinforce this message, Ukrainian Red Army units were prominent in the attack, and they were commanded by the ethnic Ukrainian Semyon Timoshenko. This was no more than a facade, but all the same many peasants, who had felt the oppression of Polish landlords, welcomed the invading troops. They were organised into peasant militias and workers' guards, revolutionary councils were formed and rigged elections were held for soviets. On the basis of these, the People's Assembly of Western Ukraine asked, on 24 October, to be incorporated into the USSR as part of the Ukrainian Republic. Industry was taken over by the Soviet state and a start was made on the collectivisation of land, although only 13 per cent of the land had been collectivised by the time of the German invasion of 1941.[15]

---

[15] Ronald Grigor Suny, *The Soviet Experiment: Russia, the USSR, and the Successor States* (Oxford University Press, 1998), 303.

Even before the invasion of Poland was complete, the Soviets began to put pressure on the Estonian government. On 24 September, Estonian foreign minister Kaarel Selter was summoned by Molotov and asked to agree a military pact and mutual assistance agreement which would allow for the stationing of Soviet troops in Estonia. After two days of hasty negotiations, the Estonian government agreed to the demands. A pact was signed on 28 September, with Stalin assuring the Estonians that he would respect their sovereignty. At exactly the same time, Molotov was renegotiating the pact with Germany so as to bring Lithuania into the Soviet sphere as well. Lithuania was granted the city of Vilnius, to which it had aspired since 1921, in return for a mutual assistance pact. Latvia signed a pact similar to the Estonian one, having been more or less overtly threatened with invasion should they refuse.

Although the Soviet invasion of Finland in November 1939, in the face of Finnish refusal to agree similar terms, soon became bogged down, the smaller Baltic states were in no position to offer similar resistance, and their western allies were now mired in a war with Germany. A faint hope that the Soviets would stick to the terms of the pacts and leave national governments intact while conducting military operations from their bases may also have contributed to acceptance of the Soviet terms, but in general politicians in Estonia, Latvia and Lithuania were pessimistic about the outlook for the future. In the early months there were several violations of the agreements from the Soviet side, and hostility towards Soviet troops went undisguised. But, formally, relations remained correct. In May 1940, however, the Soviet government began to interfere in the composition of the government of Lithuania and the Soviet press launched a campaign accusing the Baltic states of harbouring sympathies for the Allies. Smetona argued for Lithuania to resist renewed political pressure but, unable to gain the support of other members of the government, he resigned his office of president and went abroad, ending up in the USA, where he died in 1944. Red Army troops began to occupy strategic positions in Lithuania on 15 June, and ultimatums demanding the creation of new governments were delivered to Estonia and Latvia the next day. With no ready alternatives available, all three governments soon capitulated. New governments were formed from lists approved by Moscow, and in mid July elections were held under the control of communists. In spite of the small size of the communist parties, manipulation and falsification ensured victory for them and their docile sympathisers in all three countries.[16] The newly elected assemblies duly voted to apply for admission to the USSR on 21–22 July, a request that was formally agreed to by the USSR Supreme Soviet in early August 1940. Nationalisation of industry, the expropriation of large bank accounts and the confiscation of large estates soon followed.

Although the initial Soviet incorporation of the Baltic states followed, on the surface, more or less legal and constitutional lines rather than resulting from outright invasion, as had happened to Poland, it was clear to the entire population that change had been forced on them by an outside power which would have used military force had acquiescence not been forthcoming. While some of the population, notably the urban and rural poor, communists and left-wing Jews, looked forward to some improvements under Soviet rule, they were soon disabused as Moscow dictated policy and personnel.[17] For most Estonians, Latvians and Lithuanians, the initial sovietisation brought to an end a period of independence which, for all its failings in terms of political

---

[16] David Kirby, 'Incorporation: The Molotov–Ribbentrop Pact', in Smith (ed.), *The Baltic States*, 73–9.
[17] Kirby, *The Baltic World*, 357.

developments, had allowed national cultures to flourish and had resulted in considerable advances in the economic and social spheres.

SOVIETISATION OF THE BALTIC REPUBLICS

The first period of Soviet rule over the Baltic republics lasted less than a year. Lithuania and Latvia were among the first regions to fall to the Wehrmacht following the German invasion of the Soviet Union on 22 June 1941. Before the German army could arrive, popular risings drove the Red Army out of Lithuania altogether, took control of Riga for a day and caused substantial casualties in Estonia. Although some of the population extended a warm welcome to the Nazis, and many people with far-right sympathies actively collaborated throughout the German occupation, Nazi plans to germanise the Baltic region and its subjection to a single Reichskommissariat which also included Belorussia soon dispelled any illusions that Nazi occupation would bring any benefits compared to Soviet rule. While Estonians, Latvians and Lithuanians were not treated as badly as Slavs were elsewhere in the Soviet Union, they were not much better off and could take little comfort from this relative advantage.[18] Meanwhile, for the Jews of the region there was no escape, and some of the worst excesses of the Holocaust were witnessed here. But while the brutality of the Nazi occupation drove many to embrace communism, substantial numbers joined partisan groups which were opposed to both the Nazis and the Soviets, resisting sovietisation long after the Germans had left the scene.

[18] Dallinn, *German Rule*, 182–98.

After the Red Army returned in 1944–1945, the sovietisation policies of 1940–1941 were renewed, but with some differences and at a slow pace. The cautious rate of change can be attributed in part to the disruptive activities of the Forest Brotherhoods (as the anti-Soviet partisan groups were known after the Second World War), but also to a reluctance to engage immediately in a frontal attack on a hostile local population at a time when the security services were exhausted by war and the regime had other priorities. Mistrust of people who had lived under independent states and then under Nazi occupation, even those who avowed their support for communism, meant that Moscow was reluctant to rely on local cadres to implement policies, preferring instead to bring in outsiders both to the administration and to the security organs. Inasmuch as local cadres were developed, there was a marked preference for Russians, even though they were a minority of the population in the Baltic republics, even more so after the transfer of the largely Russian eastern districts of Estonia to the RSFSR, which for a while left Estonia with a 93 per cent ethnic Estonian population.[19]

Legitimisation of the regime through the standard process of single-candidate elections took some time to organise. Supreme Soviets in each republic were elected in February 1947, and local soviet elections almost a year later. In Latvia and Lithuania the First Secretaries of the communist parties from 1940 – Jānis Kalnbērzins and Antanas Sniečkus – were restored, while in Estonia the disgraced Karl Säre was replaced by Nikolai Karotamm. In each case, an ethnic Russian Second Secretary was appointed and enjoyed considerable authority and the ear of Moscow. The work of these leaders was supervised by special bureaus for Estonia, Latvia and Lithuania,

---

[19] David J. Smith, *Estonia: Independence and European Integration* (London: Routledge, 2001), 37–8.

which were established by the Politburo of the CPSU in November or December 1944. These consisted of Moscow-based officials who received copies of all reports seen by senior members of the republics' communist parties as well as secret police reports. They carried out regular inspections of the work of ministries, drew up their own recommendations for local reorganisation and monitored all senior appointments. They also played a large role in major programmes such as land redistribution and the fight against partisans. The detailed activities of these bureaus meant that, in the first years of Soviet power, the republican leaders enjoyed considerably less independent authority than was the case elsewhere.[20] At lower levels of the Communist Party and administration, distrust of locals competed with the need to recruit officials with knowledge of the local language. In Latvia and Estonia, this dilemma could be partly solved by dispatching tens of thousands of ethnic Latvians and Estonians whose ancestors had migrated to Russia during or before the First World War. There was no similar pool of Lithuanians, so a large number of Russians held important ministerial and lower posts, and a smaller but nonetheless significant Russian presence was felt in the ranks of officials in the other republics. Communist Party membership overall remained relatively low and disproportionately made up of members of national minorities. By 1949 only about one-third of the members of the communist parties in all three republics were from the local nationality: 0.3% of Lithuanians and 0.7% of Estonians and Latvians had joined by then, well below the Soviet average of over 3%.[21]

The confiscation of land above a 30-hectare norm per farm (in some cases 20 hectares) was carried out in a short time, but its

[20] Geoffrey Swain, '"Cleaning up Soviet Latvia": The Bureau for Latvia (Latburo), 1944–1947', in Olaf Mertelsmann (ed.), *The Sovietization of the Baltic States, 1940–1956* (Tartu: Kleio, 2003), 67–74.

[21] Misiunas and Taagepera, *The Baltic States*, 74–78.

redistribution and the creation of collective and state farms took rather longer. Landless and poor farmers were able to apply for new land allocations, but seem to have been reluctant to do so, in part out of fear of retribution – immediately from guerrillas, or in the future should Soviet power fail and the former landowners be restored. So small were most land allotments that they remained practically unviable. Meanwhile taxation on larger landholdings (classified as belonging to kulaks) was progressively increased, in some cases up to 75 per cent of official earnings, and in practice even higher. Lists of kulaks were drawn up for tax purposes, which would later be used for their deportation.[22] Thus, both poor and better-off farmers were provided with incentives to join collective farms, and early in 1949 the rate of collectivisation began to accelerate rapidly.[23] But in March 1949 membership of collective farms remained below 10 per cent in each republic, and the regime decided to embark on a more radical programme of collectivisation.

MASS DEPORTATIONS

The principal method used to accelerate collectivisation in the Baltic republics was the mass deportation of those identified as kulaks. In some ways, this was one in a series of waves of deportations that began in 1940 and continued after the second Soviet occupation in 1944, although the 1949 deportations were on a much larger scale. While the methods of deportation were similar to those that had been applied to smaller peoples in the course of the Second World War, they differed in character from those covered in Chapter 7. The aim was not to remove entire ethnic groups but was targeted

[22] Anu-Mai Köll, 'Tender Wolves: Identification and Persecution of Kulaks in Viljandimaa 1940–1949', in Mertelsmann (ed.), *Sovietization of the Baltic States*, 132–3.
[23] Misiunas and Taagepera, *The Baltic States*, 91–6.

against specific categories – initially political figures from the pre-war order, members of the upper classes and nationalist intellec-tuals; then individuals and their families who had been associated with the Nazi occupying forces; and finally wealthy farmers. The earlier deportations had more in common with the various anti-clerical, anti-bourgeois and anti-elite campaigns of the 1920s, while the 1949 deportations resembled more the anti-kulak persecutions that accompanied collectivisation in the 1930s. The security forces had refined their methods during the wartime deportations, and so the Baltic deportations were achieved more quickly and effectively than earlier campaigns.

The first large-scale arrests and deportations were carried out in connection with the elections of July 1940. By agreement with Hitler, 16,000 ethnic Germans who had remained in the Baltic republics were removed to German territory in January 1941. In May of that year, Beria drew up a plan 'On measures for purging the Lithuanian SSR of anti-Soviet, criminal and socially dangerous elements', which was soon extended to cover Estonia and Latvia. Under these orders, political activists, members of the nobility, industrialists, officers of the former tsarist or later national armies, clergymen, police officers, those with foreign ties, and leading civil servants were arrested, sentenced to between five and eight years in prison camps and a further twenty years of exile from their home republics – some 10,000 Estonians, 17,000 Latvians and 18,000 Lithuanians in all. In 1944–1945 the focus was on deporting anyone associated with nationalist partisan move-ments in Ukraine, Belorussia, Estonia, Latvia and Lithuania together with members of their families. In all, 260,000 people were deported from these regions at that time, most of them from western Ukraine.[24]

---

[24] Pavel Polyan, *Ne po svoei vole . . . Istoriya i geografiya prinuditel'nykh migratsii v SSSR* (Moscow: OGI-Memorial, 2001), 99–100, 130–1.

In January 1949 the Soviet Council of Ministers sanctioned the renewed deportation of more than 94,000 'bourgeois nationalists' and their families from the Baltic republics. In practice, the operations included some intellectuals but were focussed on the lists of kulaks which had been drawn up in preceding years. The deportations were carried out between 18 and 28 March, and a majority of the deportees sent to the Omsk, Amur, Krasnoyarsk and Irkutsk regions in Siberia were women and children.[25]

In all, 203,590 individuals were deported from the three Baltic republics in 1940–1953.[26] This was a substantial proportion of the overall population in 1950 of 5,611,000 (1,097,000 for Estonia, 1,944,000 for Latvia, 2,570,000 for Lithuania). Most of these were better-off farmers, but the pre-war intellectual, political, military and economic elites were also included in their entirety, along with key public figures such as clergymen and civil servants. The removal of these individuals contributed to economic difficulties in both town and country, as did resistance to collectivisation which, as in Russia in the 1930s, included the widespread slaughter of livestock. Farming suffered as a result. Soviet statistics show a massive leap forward in industrial and overall economic development in the post-war years, with annual double-digit industrial

[25] *Ibid.*, 139.

[26] *Ibid.*, p. 140. These figures are based on relatively recent investigation of archival documents in Moscow, and have been supported by a number of studies by Estonian, Latvian and Lithuanian historians, with the governments of the post-Soviet Baltic states actively promoting accurate research into these questions (see e.g. Andres Kasekamp, 'Book Review: David J. Smith, *Estonia: Independence and European Integration*, and Walter C. Clemens Jr, *The Baltic Transformed: Complexity Theory and European Security*', Välisministeerium (Estonian Ministry of Foreign Affairs) 2001, www.vm.ee/ ?q=en/node/4046). These figures are considerably lower than earlier estimates, such as those of 61,000 Estonians, 35,000 Latvians and 39,000 Lithuanians in 1940; in 1945–1949, a further 320,000 Lithuanians, 60,000 Estonians and 110,000 Latvians, or a total of 625,000. See Aleksandras Shtroma, 'The Baltic States as Soviet Republics: Tensions and Contradictions', in Smith (ed.), *The Baltic States*, 87; Misiunas and Taagepera, *The Baltic States*, 70, 96.

growth recorded in successive years from 1946 to 1955. These figures were clearly distorted, however, and in the minds of most Estonians, Latvians and Lithuanians, living standards were worse in the post-war years than before the war.[27] Educational provision and social services were also high before the war, meaning that there was little to be gained from the implementation of Soviet policies in these areas. The fact that so few individuals were ready to seize the opportunities provided by Communist Party membership is just one indication of how resented Soviet power was, lacking as it did any tangible benefits for the population of the Baltic republics.

POST-WAR ANNEXATION OF THE UKRAINIAN AND BELORUSSIAN LANDS OF POLAND

The lands seized from Poland in 1939 and squeezed out of Romania in 1940 came up for discussion at the Yalta conference between Stalin, Franklin D. Roosevelt and Winston Churchill in February 1945, and again at the Potsdam conference of July–August. With the other Allies either disinterested or unable to do anything, approval was forthcoming for Stalin's plan to redraw the borders of Poland, adding land to the west at the expense of Germany, and expanding the Ukrainian and Belorussian SSRs westward at the expense of Poland up to the so-called Curzon Line. In fact, in 1919–1920 the British politician Lord Curzon had drawn up two versions of this line, which proposed the demarcation of territory between Poland and either Russia or an independent Galician state in the context of the Paris Peace Conference, but which had been made redundant by the Polish–Soviet war and the 1921 Treaty of Riga. It

---

[27] Olaf Mertelsmann, 'Was There a Stalinist Industrialization in the Baltic Republics? Estonia – an Example', in Mertelsmann (ed.), *Sovietization of the Baltic States*, 151–70.

was the more western of these two lines that was agreed on at Yalta and Potsdam. This included the important city of Lviv, which had never been part of the Russian Empire, in the Ukrainian SSR. The Bukovyna region of Czechoslovakia was also now included in Ukraine. Thus the Soviet Union expanded to include some lands which had never experienced Russian, let alone Soviet, rule, and a population which, while ethnically mostly Ukrainian and Belorussian, were culturally far apart from their ethnic brethren to the east. Weakening Poland fitted Stalin's agenda at a time when its future was unclear, while the inclusion of important industrial centres in newly acquired territory was in line with earlier Soviet demarcation policies.

While there were strategic and historical reasons for the new border, the move also needs to be understood in the context of the Soviet leadership's preference for containing the USSR's non-Russians in more or less ethnically homogeneous republics (with the exception of the large Russian populations in most of them), as discussed in Chapters 5 and 7. This preference was underlined by a massive, compulsory, exchange of populations conducted on an ethnic basis. Between 1944 and 1946 about a million Poles moved out of the newly annexed territories into Poland, while over half a million Ukrainians moved in the opposite direction. Overall, Ukraine had gained about 110,000 square kilometres of territory and 7,000,000 inhabitants. Most of these were ethnic Ukrainians, but in order to ensure some sort of reliable political presence in western Ukraine, a huge influx of ethnic Russians to the region was organised in the post-war years, reaching some 330,000 by 1959.[28]

A specific problem confronted by the new authorities in western Ukraine was that most of the population adhered to the Greek

---

[28] Subtelny, *Ukraine*, 483–4.

Catholic Church, which continued to maintain ties to Rome. A campaign against the church began as early as November 1944, and in March 1946 a Soviet-engineered synod revoked all ties with Rome and 'reunited' the Greek Catholic Church in Ukraine with the Russian Orthodox Church. Thousands of priests were suppressed, but this was just the tip of the iceberg. The new Soviet authorities were faced with an intelligentsia that had been the focus of Ukrainian national identity before and after the Russian Revolution, and a culture that was in many ways more alien than those that had developed in the Baltic states over twenty years of independence, while the resistance of the OUN partisans continued to harry the regimes on both sides of the border. Stalin turned to his usual strategy of mass repression, and hundreds of thousands of western Ukrainians were killed or deported in the post-war years.[29]

CREATION OF THE REPUBLIC OF MOLDOVA

The Moldovan Autonomous Soviet Socialist Republic was created in the west of Soviet Ukraine on 12 October 1924. The ethnic Moldovans were closely related to Romanians across the border, speaking much the same language. Although Moldovans made up less than a third of the population of the ASSR (Ukrainians were almost 50 per cent), the republic served a useful propaganda role in appealing to the poor peasants of Romania or, more specifically, of Bessarabia.[30] A distinct Moldovan culture was nursed by the Soviet regime in the 1920s and early 1930s, and the adoption of the Cyrillic alphabet further emphasised distinctions between Romanian and Moldovan. But in 1932 the alphabet reverted to a Latin script,

[29] Wilson, *The Ukrainians*, 149.　　[30] Martin, *The Affirmative Action Empire*, 274–75.

signalling a renewed effort to appeal to the oppressed population of Romania.

Much of Bessarabia was annexed by the Soviets in 1940 (in line with the Molotov–Ribbentrop Pact), only to be overrun by Romanian troops in 1941, who then proceeded to cross the boundary of the Dniester river to reunite Bessarabia under Romanian rule. With the return of the Red Army in 1945, however, Moldova was expanded to include former Romanian territory, with the Soviet–Romanian border established along the Prut river by a treaty of 1947. At the same time Moldova lost some of its former territory to Ukraine, those regions that were inhabited mostly by Ukrainians, and a strip of territory to the east of the Dniester was added to it. Moldova had already been upgraded to the status of a full union republic on 2 August 1940, and now it embraced part of the former Moldovan ASSR, part of former Romania and part of former Ukraine. The new borders no longer allowed any direct access to either the Danube or the Black Sea, which were now in the hands of the more reliable Ukrainian SSR. More significantly, the new republic was more ethnically homogeneous than its autonomous predecessor, with 68.8 per cent of its population Moldovan. But this population remained politically and culturally divided, and does to this day, between heirs of Ottoman and Romanian rule on the one hand, and of imperial Russian and Soviet rule on the other.[31]

THE REPUBLIC OF TUVA

A less recognisable expansion of territory occurred in 1944 on the southern Siberian border with Mongolia. Although effectively existing

---

[31] Charles King, *The Moldovans: Romania, Russia, and the Politics of Culture* (Stanford: Hoover Institution Press, 1999), 91–5.

as a protectorate of both the Russian Empire and the Soviet Union, Tuva had been formally independent between 1921 and 1944. It was then quietly taken over by the Soviets, who transformed it within years. Previously, 85 per cent of the population had been nomadic cattle, horse, sheep and reindeer herders. But a brutal collectivisation of agriculture was completed by 1955, and in the meantime thousands of Russians and Ukrainians settled there and built the city of Kyzyl.[32]

In all of these cases sovietisation was accompanied by repression on a massive scale, and in most of them it was conducted against populations who had already suffered at the hands of Hitler and the Gestapo. There were few if any tangible material gains as a result of sovietisation, while the cultural and political impact deeply affected well-established nations. The Estonians, Latvians, Lithuanians and western Ukrainians had developed national identities before the First World War which were relatively strong for the region. The period of independence that followed for the three Baltic states further cemented that identity, which was also nailed on to institutional forms, albeit politically authoritarian ones. For the western Ukrainians, it may not have been immediately clear that Soviet rule would be any worse than Polish rule, but intense persecution, an influx of Russians and treatment as junior partners to the eastern Ukrainians to whom the westerners had always felt culturally superior were to provide lasting sources of tension. Similar considerations apply to the Moldovans, while Tuvans may not have had a strong sense of national identity, but were wedded to a traditional lifestyle which was destroyed by sovietisation. But it was the newly formed Soviet republics of Estonia, Latvia and Lithuania that proved most exceptional and most troublesome for the Kremlin

[32] Victor L. Mote, *Siberia: Worlds Apart* (Boulder, CO: Westview Press, 1998), 123–4.

for the remainder of the Soviet period, with only Georgia rivalling them, and hence this chapter has paid added attention to their pre-Soviet experience. For the Baltic population, experience of democracy was limited, but at least basic rights had been observed. The economic impact of sovietisation may be ambiguous, but what was clear above all was that the Estonians, Latvians and Lithuanians had lost something which they had fought for and clung on to, their independence. Discourses and slogans about Soviet occupation and the desire for independence were to dominate protest in these three republics from the time of destalinisation in the 1950s right through to the collapse of the USSR, in which they played no small part.

CHAPTER NINE

Destalinisation and the revival
of the republics

Stalin's death on 5 March 1953 meant far more than just a change of face at the top of the Soviet system. The frustrated hopes that had arisen after victory over fascism in the Great Patriotic War now came to the fore again. The political uncertainty that followed the unprecedented death of a Soviet tyrant encouraged different interests in Soviet society to trade support for individual leaders and the institutions they headed in return for policies that favoured their interests. As politics consolidated around the CPSU its leader, Nikita Khrushchev, pursued a utopian programme of reforms which aimed at improving the life circumstances of Soviet citizens, not only in a material sense but also in terms of rights, political participation and justice. Participation was to be on terms dictated by the centre, and fell well short of genuine democracy, and Khrushchev encountered many unintended consequences of his policies, particularly after the relative openness signalled by his Secret Speech of February 1956. Throughout his tenure of the post of First Secretary of the CPSU, Khrushchev played a risky game of alternating between favouring, reining in and putting down various interests, a tactic which ultimately left him with no support when a concerted effort to remove him from office was made in 1964. Thus the nationalities experience of the mid to late 1950s and the early 1960s consisted of a series of episodes of mobilisation (either spontaneous or state-led), and inconsistent policies from the centre which at times increased, and at times diminished, the ability of the Soviet republics to deal with their own affairs. Faced with this inconsistency and the unpredictability of national responses, efforts to promote an ideology of the 'merger of nations' failed to have any real impact or to inspire new attitudes.

The 1950s was also the decade in which the USSR became an urban society – more Soviet citizens lived in towns and cities than in the countryside for the first time. While most of the non-Russian republics remained rural to a greater or lesser degree, it was increasingly the cities that were determining national character. The cities tended more and more to become national melting pots, and no longer represented bastions of Russian or russified people and culture in a sea of non-Russian countryside as they had at the time of the Russian Revolution. Under the Virgin Lands campaign the earlier population tendency was actually reversed, with Russian and Ukrainian settlers taking over the countryside surrounding largely Kazakh towns. Intellectuals and artists born and educated under Soviet rule were able to embrace a national message, whether they kept that message within the confines of Soviet ideological correctness or took it beyond those limits and contributed an important element to the early Soviet dissident movement. Economic and social reform also entailed large-scale migration within the USSR, from country to town but also between republics. Some of this migration was a spontaneous consequence of the spread of employment opportunities, but some of it resulted from deliberate policy. Either way, the consequence was a change in the national composition of several of the union republics, and especially the autonomous republics and regions. These issues will be discussed in more depth in Chapter 10, but it must be noted that they had their origins in the Khrushchev period.

CONTENDING FOR POWER AFTER STALIN'S DEATH

Among the interests for whose support the contenders for power now competed, the national republics were among the most important. Stalin had frequently and ruthlessly intervened in the composition of the political and intellectual leadership in the republics in the last three years of his life precisely because they were sufficiently removed from the day-to-day control of the centre that powerful groupings were beginning to consolidate there. Recognising this, Soviet leaders saw the republics as an important base of support. In constitutional terms, the non-Russians also contributed a large proportion of votes to the Supreme Soviet of the USSR and the Central Committee of the CPSU. Finally, a number of the leading political figures in Moscow had their political backgrounds in one or more of the republics and still enjoyed strong links there. Foremost among these were Lavrenti Beria, who had headed the Communist Party organisations in Georgia and then the whole South Caucasus before moving to Moscow and taking over the key security institution, the NKVD, and Nikita Khrushchev, who had twice served as party leader in Ukraine and combined his network of protégés and supporters there with the network he had built up as head of the Moscow city communist organisations to create a basis of support that was unrivalled by any other leader.[1]

Within days of Stalin's death, the release of the Jewish doctors accused in the Doctors' Plot signalled an end to both the arbitrariness and the overt anti-Semitism of Stalin's regime. It seems likely that a consensus was easily reached among all the surviving leaders on this point, but Beria quickly emerged as the driving force in a

[1] Nikolai Mitrokhin, 'The Rise of Political Clans in the Era of Nikita Khrushchev: The First Phase, 1953–1959', in Jeremy Smith and Melanie Ilic (eds.), *Khrushchev in the Kremlin: Policy and Government in the Soviet Union, 1953–1964* (London: Routledge, 2011), 26–40.

number of policy areas, among them nationality policy. Although a notorious monster and sadist when it came to his personal life and police duties Beria was, in communist terms, a relative economic liberal and in some political areas, especially where he saw personal advantage, he was open to approaches that were radically different from Stalin's. Beginning with western Ukraine, where half a million people had been persecuted by the state in the newly occupied region between 1944 and 1952, Beria instigated a wholesale reorganisation of the Communist Party which spread as far as the leadership of the whole of the Ukrainian republic. The Russian Leonid Mel'nikov was replaced by the Ukrainian Alexei Kirichenko as First Secretary of the Ukrainian Communist Party on the same day that the Politburo introduced measures to increase the proportion of ethnic Ukrainians in local organisations in western Ukraine. Similar measures were introduced in Lithuania in May 1953. Here a thinking similar to that behind *korenizatsiia* in the 1920s was apparent: if the local soviet and Communist Party apparatus were given a national character, bourgeois nationalism – signs of which were increasing – would be undermined. A month later, similar measures were proposed for Belorussia, but the replacement there of the Russian First Secretary by a Belorussian was never enacted, suggesting there was already opposition to such a policy among the leadership.[2] Beria also succeeded in strengthening both his own position and the representation of the South Caucasus at the highest level by having the First Secretary of the Communist Party of Azerbaijan, Mir Jafar Bagirov, promoted to the Presidium of the Central Committee (as the Politburo was known from 1952 to 1966).[3] Beria, anxious to improve relations with the capitalist

[2] Rudol'f Pikhoya, *Moskva. Kreml'. Vlast': Sorok let posle voyny 1945–1985* (Moscow: Rus'-Olimp, Astrel'AST, 2007), 241–6.
[3] E. Ismailov, *Azerbaidzhan: 1953–1956: pervye gody 'ottepeli'* (Baku: Adil'ogly, 2006), 19.

world, also floated the idea of ceding some of the territory seized from Eastern Europe, Finland and Japan.

Although Beria's colleagues never really abandoned these mild, pro-nationality cadre policies, they did figure among the charges levelled against him following his arrest on 26 June 1953. He was accused, among other things, of inspiring nationalism in the republics. Many of Beria's associates in Georgia, including those who had previously been caught up in the Mingrelian Affair but who Beria had had time to restore to favour, were persecuted anew. Khrushchev himself took a direct interest in the affairs of the South Caucasus, instituting a review of education of Abkhaz children, which had remained georgianised since Beria's time as leader in Georgia. Beria himself was shot secretly in December. Bagirov, who had taken over the post of First Secretary in Azerbaijan in 1933 and was thus the only holder of such a post from any republic not only to survive, but also to play a large part in implementing, Stalin's Terror, was arrested not long after Beria and eventually shot in 1956. Nevertheless, the principle introduced by Beria that the First Secretary in each republic should be a member of the titular nationality, while not always observed,[4] was sufficiently general that its violation by Mikhail Gorbachev in 1986 provoked one of the first crises of his rule.

TRANSFER OF CRIMEA AND NATIONAL ANNIVERSARIES

Not long after Beria's execution, an important territorial change affected the Ukrainian SSR. Early in 1954, the Councils of Ministers of both the RSFSR and Ukraine came to an agreement over the transfer of the territory of Crimea from the RSFSR to Ukraine. This

---

[4] For example, the Russian Leonid Brezhnev became First Secretary in Kazakhstan in 1955.

move was ratified by the Supreme Soviets of both republics and, eventually, by the Supreme Soviet of the USSR on 26 April. The move was ostensibly carried out to celebrate the friendship of the Ukrainian and Russian peoples on the 300th anniversary of the Treaty of Pereyaslav (under which Ukrainian territory first came under the dominion of the Russian tsar). It is frequently referred to as Khrushchev's 'gift' to Ukraine, but there is no direct evidence to link Khrushchev (who did not attend any of the key meetings) to this decision. The political complexities of the period allow for plenty of speculation as to the real motives behind the change: Khrushchev was, by then, in control of the main bodies of the CPSU and owed a lot to the support of his previous co-workers in Ukraine, but the initiative for the move appears to have come from the RSFSR Council of Ministers, over which he had little influence. The chairman of the Supreme Soviet of the USSR, Klim Voroshilov, summed up the reasoning behind the transfer: 'Considering the commonality of the economies, the territorial proximity and the close economic and cultural ties between the Crimean province and the Ukrainian SSR'. The measure was carried out in accordance with the constitutions of the two republics and the USSR.[5] While it may have served to increase the loyalty of the population of Ukraine to the USSR, it was also a neat solution to the status of a territory rich in economic potential but which had seen its population reduced to a little over 200,000 by the wartime deportation of the Tatar population. The economic and infrastructural benefits of linking the peninsula to Ukraine, with which it had its only land connection, were obvious, and Crimea held a special place in Ukrainian national history given its emphasis on its

---

[5] Volodymyr G. Butkevych, 'Who Has A Right to Crimea', 1992, www.infoukes.com/ history/crimea/page-12.html.

Cossack heritage. But the switch had a perverse effect of introducing into Ukraine a territory which was predominantly Russian in ethnic and linguistic terms and where Ukrainian cultural institutions and traditions were non-existent.[6]

Several factors were at work behind the decision to transfer Crimea to Ukraine, but this also marked the beginning of a period when national anniversaries were being taken seriously as symbols of the status and significance of the union republics. In 1967, the city of Yerevan enjoyed its 2,750th anniversary, while in 1969 celebrations marked the 2,500th anniversary of the Uzbek city of Samarkand and so on.

THE VIRGIN LANDS CAMPAIGN

One of the earlier reforms personally associated with Khrushchev had a profound impact on the demography and agriculture of Kazakhstan. Following the sedentarisation campaign of the 1930s, much of the land that had previously been used by nomads was no longer in agricultural use. This large area of unfarmed steppe, together with neighbouring regions of Siberia, became the target for the Virgin Lands campaign – an effort to get unused land under cultivation by bringing in thousands of settlers, mostly from Russia and Ukraine. From 1954, 42 million hectares of previously uncultivated land, most of it in northern Kazakhstan, was ploughed and sown. The initial economic benefits and later slump in agricultural output from the Virgin Lands were major factors in the fortunes of Khrushchev's leadership, but they also had a drastic impact on nationality relations.

[6] Wilson, *The Ukrainians*, 150–1.

Between 1 and 2 million settlers arrived in waves in the Virgin Lands in the 1950s, building settlements that were modern and European by the standards of Kazakhstan. Settlers had been told that they were travelling to entirely unpopulated land, and were shocked to discover that members of the 'traitor nationalities' deported by Stalin in 1940–1944 were already there. Mass fights and riots were typical of the early months of settlement, often exacerbated by alcohol and by settlers finding a shortage of work and consequent competition for employment. Kazakhs as well as resettled Chechens, Ingush, Poles and others were involved in this violence. By 1956, when the first successful harvest was brought in by the Virgin Landers, these conflicts had died down. With a shortage of cultural facilities, Slavs, Kazakhs and deported peoples put on their own shows and dances, and frequently attended each others'. Mixed marriages became fairly common. The lifting of the Special Settlement regime in 1956 and the subsequent return of many deportees to the Caucasus further eased ethnic relations. The Virgin Lands campaign brought with it significant (if at first inadequate) infrastructural investment, and even when harvests began to decline in the 1960s the economic benefits remained tangible. Education levels improved and a lively culture, drawing on different traditions, flourished. Europeans were at the forefront in this, however, and not only did the Kazakh share of the population decline in the Virgin Lands regions, but many of their schools were closed and replaced by Russian ones. The legacy for Kazakhstan was, therefore, a mixed one.[7]

---

[7] Michaela Pohl, 'The "Planet of One Hundred Languages": Ethnic Relations and Soviet Identity in the Virgin Lands', in Breyfogle *et al.* (eds.), *Peopling the Russian Periphery*, 238–61.

SOVIET KARELIA

One republic that underwent a drastic change in status in the 1950s was Soviet Karelia. The status of Karelia had always been intimately connected to relations with neighbouring Finland. The Karelian language is closely related to Finnish, to the extent that many Finnish nationalists considered it merely a dialect of Finnish. With the influx of Finnish refugees, including many communists, to Russian Karelia following the White victory in Finland's Civil War in 1918, a Karelian Labourers' Commune was established under the leadership of the Finnish communist Edward Gylling. The Finnish nationalist message was reinterpreted in Marxist terms – Finnish culture and language were more advanced than Karelian, which was a peasant language with no written literary tradition. A campaign of Finnicisation of schools, culture and administration followed so that, by 1932, 99.6 per cent of Finnish children were studying in Finnish schools. In this period Soviet policy in Karelia was aimed mostly at providing a staging post and pole of attraction for any revolutionary crisis which might develop in Finland. But with the worsening international situation of the late 1930s Soviet policy shifted to preparations for war, and on 1 January 1938 Finnish as a language disappeared from the republic to be replaced by a newly standardised Karelian language written in the Cyrillic alphabet. Following the acquisition of parts of Finnish Karelia in the Winter War of 1939–1940, Finnish was again adopted as an official language. More significantly, the Commune was upgraded to a Karelo-Finnish Soviet Socialist Republic – the same status as the other union republics. Renewed war with Finland led to a Finnish occupation of most of Karelia from 1941 to 1944, during which wholesale Finnicisation was reintroduced. After Soviet control was restored in 1944, Finnish continued to be an official language alongside Karelian, and the clear aim of the Karelo-Finnish republic was to form the basis for the future incorporation of Finland. In January 1956, however, Khrushchev reached a further accommodation with the Finns and withdrew Soviet forces from their base at Porkkala, near Helsinki, which had been established on Finnish territory as part of the 1944 peace settlement. With the USSR now entering a period of co-operative and friendly relations, the status of the Karelo-Finnish republic was suddenly downgraded to that of a Karelian Autonomous Republic on 16 July 1956. Foreign policy had already ceased to play much of a role in Soviet nationality policy with the incorporation by Stalin of the Ukrainian and Belorussian parts of Poland, and the Moldovan parts of Romania in 1945. Karelia's status was always a subject of foreign policy, and its downgrading in 1956 had important consequences for future language development and assimilation.[8]

KHRUSHCHEV'S SECRET SPEECH AND GEORGIA

The most immediate policy impact on nationalities of the denunciation of Stalin in Khrushchev's Secret Speech of February 1956 was a review of the fate of the deported nationalities, as discussed in Chapter 7. But the Secret Speech had unintended consequences as well, including a resurgence of nationalism, which gathered momentum in the wake of the crushing of the Hungarian rising later in the year. The Secret Speech and subsequent letter had an immediate impact in Georgia, where Stalin had been born and served his early career as a Bolshevik. In 1954 and 1955, the anniversaries of Stalin's death had been marked by officially backed

---

[8] Paul M. Austin, 'Soviet Karelian: The Language That Failed', *Slavic Review*, 51, 1 (1992), 16–35.

parades and poetry readings in honour of the dead leader. In March 1956, however, these ceremonies were officially banned and further insult was added by rumours that Khrushchev had directly vilified not just the memory of Stalin but the Georgian nation as a whole. The unofficial demonstrations that began on 2 March may have had tacit support from the Georgian Communist Party leadership,[9] but the demonstrations were made up mostly of students motivated by a mixture of national pride, dislike of Khrushchev and regard for the memory of Stalin.[10]

Between 2 and 11 March thousands of young Georgians (and at least some members of other nationalities) took to the streets of Tbilisi, Gori, Batumi, Sukhumi, Kutaisi and other towns in Georgia. For day after day, they gathered at monuments to Stalin and delivered poems and speeches, sang songs and chanted anti-Khrushchev slogans. Tensions were at their highest in Tbilisi, where crowds converged on the Communist Party headquarters and also demanded to meet with a visiting leader of the Chinese Communist Party. Eventually, on the morning of 11 March, Red Army soldiers opened fire on demonstrators in Tbilisi, killing twenty.[11] The shootings left a deep scar on a whole generation of Georgians, and resulted in an immediate increase in ethnic tensions between ethnic Georgians and Russians throughout the republic as well as a mistrust which lasted into the post-Soviet period.

[9] Timothy Blauvelt, 'Status Shift and Ethnic Mobilisation in the March 1956 Events in Georgia', *Europe-Asia Studies*, 61, 4 (June 2009), 651–68.

[10] Some eyewitness testimonies are collected in Lev Lur'e and Irina Malyarova (eds.), *1956 god: seredina veka* (St Petersburg: Neva, 2007), pp. 140–68.

[11] The number of victims is hotly disputed, but the lower figure appears to be confirmed by archival sources. For detailed accounts of these events, see I. Statnikov, *Istochnik* no. 6, 1995; Viktor Kozlov, *Mass Uprisings in the USSR: Protest and Rebellion in the Post-Stalin Years* (New York and London: M. E. Sharpe, 2002), 112–35.

GROWING NATIONAL UNREST

The events in Georgia in March 1956 were a foretaste of the more widespread and threatening mobilisations that were unleashed by the Secret Speech in the satellite communist states of Poland and Hungary later in the year. The bloody suppression of the Hungarian rising in November 1956 underlined the dangers to the Soviet regime of nationalism, and its ability to combine with anti-Soviet feeling and lead to popular mobilisation. In this regard Georgia was exceptional, since the Georgian republic had been under Soviet rule since 1921, although arguably it had never been fully integrated into Soviet culture and ideology. More generally, grass-roots unrest was more likely to emerge among nationalities that had had communist rule imposed on them in recent times, such as the satellite states and, inside the USSR, western Ukraine, Moldova and the three Baltic republics. Although in Moldova reactions to destalinisation did not differ much from the pattern in the rest of the Soviet Union,[12] in the Baltic republics the Secret Speech was like a match to a fuse, and the Hungarian events further aroused the indignation and defiance of opponents of Soviet rule. The strongest reactions came in Lithuania, although here opposition was more covert than in Georgia. Nationalist graffiti became commonplace at Vilnius University and across the republic: 'Long live the revolution in Hungary, let's follow their example!'; 'Lithuanians! Lithuania is for Lithuanians, Russians are occupiers, throw them out!'; 'Give freedom to Lithuania'; 'Let's follow Hungary's example'; 'Down with communists'; 'Russians, get out of Lithuania'. In Estonia similar sentiments were seen daubed on

---

[12] Mark Sandle and Igor Casu, 'Rumours and Uncertainty in the Borderlands: Soviet Moldavia and the Secret Speech, 1956–1957', *Europe-Asia Studies*, 65 (2013).

walls: 'Death to the occupiers'; 'Down with the Russian governors. Death to Russian occupiers. Throw the Russians out of Estonia'. Demonstrating that it had not entirely abandoned the administrative tendencies of the Stalin era, the solutions proposed by the Khrushchev leadership rested mostly on training cadres and ensuring a more proportional ethnic balance in local Communist Party and soviet organisations.[13]

Unrest in Georgia and the Baltic republics occurred at a time when the leadership had most to fear from events in Poland and Hungary, when the ideological confusion caused by Khrushchev's Secret Speech was leading to minor disturbances throughout the USSR (although they never reached the scale of the later rising against Soviet authority in Novocherkassk). That national feeling meant potential trouble in these republics was known to the leadership from the late Stalin years, when it had prompted purges in Estonia and Georgia. It was no surprise that the thaw should lead to occasional manifestations of this sort, and for the time being it was left to the republics to deal with them. Very few reprisals were conducted in Georgia, and the Georgian Communist Party got no more than a slap on the wrist and was empowered to deploy a mixture of concessions and surveillance to keep the situation from recurring.

But already documents of a less expected and in ways more disturbing nature were reaching the Kremlin. These concerned the actions of leading figures in the communist parties of individual republics. Some reports dealt with the failure to implement changes in cadre policies which had already been demanded by Beria in 1953. But others indicated that republican leaders themselves were caught

[13] Jeremy Smith, 'Leadership and Nationalism in the Soviet Republics, 1951–1959', in Smith and Ilic (eds.), *Khrushchev in the Kremlin*, 83–4.

up in the national mood and were implementing national policies that not only supported the local national cause, but were clearly directed against Russians and other local minorities. The most significant cases were in Latvia and Azerbaijan. Late in 1956, reports reached Moscow of the growing displays of nationalism by the Second Secretary of the Communist Party of Latvia, Eduard Berklāvs, the chair of the Latvian Supreme Soviet, Karlis Ozoliņš, and the deputy chair of Latvia's Council of Ministers, Vilis Krūmiņš. They had joined together in condemning the influx of Russians into the capital city Riga, so that 'Riga was becoming a Russian city and losing its national character.' In response, the Latvian leaders were discussing proposals to ensure that Russians who did not learn Latvian within two years would lose their right to stay in the republic.[14]

On 21 August 1956 the Supreme Soviet of Azerbaijan passed a law making Azerbaijani the sole official language of the republic. This brought it into line with the constitutional provisions already in place in the neighbouring republics of Georgia and Armenia. But the change was introduced in Azerbaijan without any consultation with the central authorities and in a way which clearly upset minorities living within the republic. Russians and Armenians, who formed a large part of the population in Nagorno Karabakh and cities such as Baku, Kirovabad, Sumgait and Mingechaur, had grown accustomed to using their own language in the public sphere and now found themselves effectively excluded from political decision-making and unable to fulfil bureaucratic and other func-tions which were henceforth conducted solely in Azerbaijani. The new law was used as a basis for arguments similar to those deployed in Latvia, that Armenians and Russians should be thrown out of

[14] RGANI, f. 5, op. 31, d. 59, ll. 58–9.

senior positions in politics and industry if they could not show a
command of the republic's language. Mirza Ibragimov, chair of the
Supreme Soviet of Azerbaijan, was held primarily responsible for
the passage of the language law, but the recently appointed First
Secretary of the Communist Party of Azerbaijan, Imam Mustafaev,
shared political responsibility.[15]

Some of the general reasons why republican leaders should have
shown such signs of pandering to nationalism are discussed in
Chapter 10, as the phenomenon became more widespread, though
it was more subtly expressed, in the Brezhnev years. There were
particular reasons why this tendency may have been stronger
already in Latvia, where discontent with the Soviet occupation
still rumbled on and where the leadership, which had come to office
immediately after sovietisation and many of whose members had
worked underground as communists in independent Latvia, or as
partisans during the Great Patriotic War, were closely attuned to
the mood of the population. Azerbaijan, as the first Soviet republic
with a Muslim majority, had occupied a special position since
Lenin's time, when it was run by Azerbaijani communists who
were barely integrated into the Bolshevik movement and had
been allowed more freedom to manoeuvre than was the case in
other republics. Long-standing territorial and national rivalry with
neighbouring Armenia, which was soon to become the sole focus of
Azerbaijan's academic output, heightened the popularity of such
nationalist and anti-minority measures.

Although these tendencies became apparent in 1956, not only
were the leadership preoccupied elsewhere, but Khrushchev's own
position was not entirely secure, and he was aware that he might
need to draw on the support of senior figures from the republics at

[15] RGANI, f. 5, op. 31, d. 60, ll. 10–12.

some point in the future. He did not have long to wait for this point to arrive. When the 'anti-Party group' led by Molotov, Malenkov, Kaganovich and others tried to remove Khrushchev at a meeting of the Politburo in May 1957, in a manner similar to that which had brought down Beria, Khrushchev managed to outmanoeuvre them and insist on the matter going to the full Central Committee of the CPSU. He was also able to ensure that Central Committee members from the Russian regions and the Soviet republics were flown in to this hastily convened meeting. Khrushchev's championing of the role of the Party against government institutions in previous years was probably the main factor in ensuring his victory in front of the Central Committee, but he could also count on the support of most of the republican delegates. None of the conspirators had significant experience or contacts in the republics, unlike Khrushchev and Anastas Mikoyan, who remained loyal. The non-interference of earlier years in republican affairs paid off as these delegates rose to support the First Secretary and condemn his opponents.

THE *SOVNARKHOZ* REFORM

With his own position at home stronger than it had ever been and relations with both the western powers and Eastern Europe stabilising, Khrushchev was able to turn his attention and that of the CPSU towards his own agenda. It was after the defeat of the anti-Party group that Khrushchev launched many of his reforms, including instituting a massive housing programme and agricultural reforms, stepping up the space programme, and other initiatives. He also turned his attention to ideology, which was to culminate in the creation of a new Party programme for the CPSU in 1961. Much of Khrushchev's project at this stage was utopian, aimed at improving the living standards of Soviet citizens and closing the developmental, technological and military gap with the USA. But he also sought ways to improve the administration of the Soviet Union. A year later, this was to lead him to tackle head-on the most troublesome of the Soviet republics but, in the immediate afterglow of his defeat of the anti-Party group in 1957, Khrushchev introduced an ambitious economic reform which was to strengthen the powers of the union republics.

This was the *sovnarkhoz* (economic council) reform, which decentralised a large part of economic decision-making and supervision to regional councils. There was a political motive for this, as it involved the abolition or decimation of a number of central Moscow ministries, thus weakening the governmental structure that had acted as a rival to his own base, the CPSU, between 1953 and 1957. But there were also sound economic reasons for the reform. The centrally planned economy had ultimately proved effective at building up the Soviet Union's industrial base in the 1930s and rebuilding it after the war, but did so at the cost of enormous waste and hardship. The costs and limitations of central planning were becoming more and more apparent as the possibilities of mobilising extra manpower and material began to diminish. The *sovnarkhoz* reform, by allowing more local decision-making and a degree of autonomy to factory directors, was supposed to overcome narrow departmentalism in the Moscow ministries, eliminating supply bottlenecks and rigid targets.[16]

Most of the regional economic councils were based in Russia, but each of the republics received its own council and was able to exercise control over most of its enterprises, provided that they each met production and delivery plans which were still laid out centrally

---

[16] Philip Hanson, *The Rise and Fall of the Soviet Economy: An Economic History of the USSR from 1945* (London: Longman, 2003), 58–60.

by the State Planning Commission (Gosplan). Ukraine gained most economic autarchy from this system, as it had several *sovnarkhozy* but also a republic-wide co-ordinating body, Ukrsovnarkhoz, and the regional councils were subject to the control of the republic's own Council of Ministers and Gosplan.

The *sovnarkhoz* system was plagued by inherent problems from the beginning, however. Partly by design, there were few areas of production where the Soviet economy could operate on a fully regional basis. Processing and production plants were typically far away from the site of raw materials, with final assembly plants often somewhere else. Coal from Ukraine and cotton from Central Asia were needed by industry across the Soviet Union. For this reason Gosplan had retained its planning role and mandated individual *sovnarkhozy* to deliver materials and goods to other *sovnarkhozy* according to a fixed schedule. Local planners were supposed not to obtain materials from sources other than those laid down by Gosplan. Hence the problem of supply bottlenecks was not overcome, and in fact a new element was introduced that hampered the flow of supplies. This was termed in Russian *mestnichestvo* – localism – and was particularly associated with the Soviet republics. Given more economic authority locally, republican authorities consistently prioritised the needs of their own republics over scheduled deliveries to other republics. Goods and materials were diverted away from their planned destination even when there should not have been demand locally. Clashes soon developed between the USSR Gosplan and the Ukrainian *sovnarkhozy* and republic Gosplan, which were charged – inevitably, and with some justification – with nationalism.

A valid distinction can be drawn between localism and nationalism. The former might be pursued on a non-national basis and, even where production was organised on the basis of a national republic, the pursuit of local interests might be considered the natural tendency of a bureaucracy anywhere. Nationalism involves something more, an ideological element and a suggestion that members of a particular national group are more deserving than others – either in general or, as in this case, deserving of the fruits of the efforts of co-nationals. In the context of the Soviet republics, some of the rhetoric of republican authorities lent justification to the charge that they were acting out of national interest. The accusation of *mestnichestvo* became more or less synonymous with the accusation of nationalism.

Frustrated by the failure of the *sovnarkhoz* reform to improve economic performance, Khrushchev soon turned his attention elsewhere, in particular to increasing Party supervision of the economy through the division of the Communist Party into agricultural and industrial branches – a move that was eventually to lead to his downfall. Some of the central ministries abolished in 1957 were quickly resurrected, and the *sovnarkhoz* reform was abandoned altogether shortly after Khrushchev's removal from office. But to some extent the damage was already done and was lasting. In Ukraine, which had always been an economic powerhouse of the Soviet Union, the authorities had got used to the idea of exercising a certain degree of control over their own economies, and were never to abandon this power.[17] In the Baltic republics, whose economies were more developed than those of the rest of the Soviet Union in the first place, the taste of autarchy strengthened the tendency to insist on the republics reaping the benefits of their own economic production. A probably unintended consequence of the *sovnarkhoz* reform was that Soviet republics began to develop their own

[17] Nataliya Kibita, 'Moscow–Kiev Relations and the *Sovnarkhoz* Reform', in Smith and Ilic (eds.), *Khrushchev in the Kremlin*, 94–111.

international relations in the economic sphere. Estonia began limited trading and opened up tourism with Finland, and the first ferry route between Tallinn and Helsinki was opened in July 1965. Georgia developed independent contacts with France in wine-making and with India in the tea industry, providing the pretext for a series of previously impossible trips abroad for officials and industry experts. These contacts faded, however, as restrictions on foreign travel were again tightened under Brezhnev.

THE EDUCATION REFORM OF 1958–1959

It may well have been the early manifestations of *mestnichestvo* that persuaded Khrushchev to take on the growing nationalism that was already evident in the republics in 1956. Although his roots were in Ukraine, Khrushchev was from a generation of communists who on the one hand were internationalist, but on the other hand attached particular characteristics to different nationalities and took it for granted that Russian culture was inherently superior to that of other Soviet nationalities. The significance of his frequent references to the 'merger of nations' should not be exaggerated: Khrushchev did not expect national differences to disappear in the near future, but he did regard the development of nationalist tendencies among both citizens and leaders as a step backwards. Although he presented many of his policies as a 'return to Lenin', he could at least feel justified in arguing that, while local nationalism was an inevitable feature of the 1920s, it had no place in a society that was well set on the path to socialism. The turn towards official promotion of Great Russian culture and values under Stalin was a further factor giving him the confidence to take on one of the sacred cows of Leninist nationality policy – the principle that each child should be educated at school in his or her mother tongue.

The Theses on Education published under Khrushchev's name on 14 November 1958 were mostly concerned with updating old-fashioned teaching techniques, bringing more modern and technical subjects into the classroom, and improving the preparedness of pupils for future work by including experience of farm or factory labour as part of the educational curriculum. The reform also standardised education across the USSR, removing the differences that existed, in particular between Soviet republics. During a wide-ranging discussion that preceded publication of the theses, the question of education in schools for non-Russians received some attention. The main problem that was identified was that, whereas Russian children in the RSFSR were required to study one foreign language, Russian pupils in other republics had to learn a foreign language plus the language of the republic they lived in, whereas nationals living in their own republics had to study Russian as well as another language. This meant that most pupils in the non-Russian republics were studying one more subject than Russian pupils in Russia, at the expense of hours devoted to other subjects. In addition, the question was now raised of teaching national history as well as Russian history. The solution most commonly proposed from the republics, and which was already in force in Estonia, Latvia and elsewhere, was to require pupils to stay on at school for an additional year if they studied in the national schools.

The solution of this problem proposed by Khrushchev was quite different, as laid down in Article 19 of the Theses:

The question ought to be considered of giving parents the right to send their children to a school where the language of their choice is used. If a child attends a school where instruction is conducted in the language of one of the Union or autonomous republics, he may, if he wishes, take up the Russian language. And vice versa, if a child attends a Russian school, he may, if he so desires, study the language of one of the Union or autonomous republics.[18]

This article appears to have come as a bolt from the blue. Such an approach had not figured in any of the correspondence with the republics before the theses were published, and there is no record of it having been discussed at the Presidium. There were hints that the regime was interested in promoting a single *lingua franca* for the Soviet Union, and such a development was endorsed by a resolution of the USSR Academy of Sciences in June 1958.[19] But at no point did this enter broader official discourse. As late as September a report signed by two senior education officials, the minister of education for the RSFSR and the president of the Academy of Pedagogical Science, discussed the possibility of extending the period of education in non-Russian schools but did not consider other options. Given the moves to strengthen the role of the national language in Azerbaijan and Latvia in 1956, Khrushchev must have known that this proposal would provoke a furore from the republics. The democratic pretensions of Article 19 must be treated with heavy cynicism in the Soviet context, and to most outsiders the implication of the article was that non-Russian children would take up a Russian-language education in large numbers, with the encouragement of parents anxious for the later career advancement of their offspring. Although technically Article 19 allowed non-Russian children in national schools to drop the study of Russian as a second language, it was clearly recognised that this was wholly impractical and undesirable for children with any ambition whatsoever, and it was strongly suspected that the real

[18] English translation of the full theses in George S. Counts, *Khrushchev and the Central Committee Speak on Education* (University of Pittsburgh Press, 1959), 45–6.
[19] Isabelle Kreindler, 'Soviet Language Planning since 1953', in Kirkwood (ed.), *Language Planning*, 48.

intention was that an expanding network of Russian-language schools would drop the teaching of the main language of the republic.

This interpretation seems to have been shared by republic leaders, for whom the national school was one clear area of republican authority and something which ensured the survival of the nation linguistically. While Lenin had never been entirely consistent in his attitude to the Russian and non-Russian languages, a preference for education in the mother tongue had long been accepted as a fixed aspect of Lenin's nationality policy. When the proposal came up for discussion at a session of the USSR Supreme Soviet in December 1958, it was openly opposed by the senior representatives from Estonia, Latvia, Lithuania, Armenia and Georgia. Delegates from Belorussia and Ukraine also raised objections. Nevertheless, the measure was carried at the Supreme Soviet and, in line with usual practice at the time, individual republics were left to draw up and pass their own laws. The Law on Education passed at the Supreme Soviet of Latvia on 17 March 1959 deferred the decision on the overall length of school study to a later date, while not making any mention of Khrushchev's principle of parental choice in the language of study. The law passed in Azerbaijan also failed to clearly articulate this principle. While in Azerbaijan this amounted to brazen defiance, in Latvia a breakdown in communication appears to have contributed to their dissent, as efforts to contact the CC CPSU secretariat for clarification in the days leading up to the enactment of the legislation failed.[20]

---

[20] Jeremy Smith, 'Republican Authority and Khrushchev's Education Reform in Latvia and Estonia, 1958–1959', in Mertelsmann (ed.), *Sovietization of the Baltic States*, 249.

PURGES IN LATVIA AND AZERBAIJAN

Although both Latvia and Azerbaijan were constitutionally entitled to decide on their own education law and, as in other republics, could claim overwhelming public support for their versions, Khrushchev had invested too much in his plans for education to tolerate such defiance. It is quite possible that the Kremlin leaders had made up their minds already to sort out the Communist Party leadership in Latvia and Azerbaijan, whose increasingly nationalistic stance had been brought to their notice at least as early as 1956. A CC CPSU commission was sent to Riga on 21 June. As well as addressing the school reform, the numerous deviations of Berklāvs and others over the course of the decade were brought up again. In addition to the pressures brought to bear on Russian officials to learn Latvian, a list of charges was brought up which included the reduction of Russian-speaking places at universities, attempts to block doctors trained in Latvia from working in other republics, a discriminatory passport regime in Riga and failure to highlight the 'friendship of peoples' or pay sufficient attention to the contribution of Russians to the victory over Hitler in official propaganda.[21]

Berklāvs was dismissed immediately and cast into the political wilderness, eventually to return as a democratic member of parliament under *perestroika* and in post-Soviet Latvia. By the end of the year, Latvian First Secretary Jānis Kalnbērziņš, chair of the Latvian Council of Trade Unions Indriks Pinksis, and chair of the Latvian Council of Ministers since 1940 Vilis Lācis had all been dismissed.[22]

---

[21] Archive of the Communist Party of Latvia, f. 101, op. 22, d. 48a, ll. 20–27, 50.

[22] An alternative interpretation, drawing heavily on the memoirs and later interviews of Berklāvs and others, sees the Latvian purge as engineered by Red Army officers and conservatives in the CPSU Politburo against Khrushchev's wishes: William Prigge, 'The Latvian Purges of 1959: A Revision Study', *Journal of Baltic Studies*, 35, 3 (2004), 211–30.

On 1 July, on the same day that the Riga commission reported its findings, the question of the leadership of Azerbaijan was brought up at a Presidium meeting in Moscow, which was also attended by First Secretary of the Communist Party of Azerbaijan, Imam Mustafaev. Charges of economic mismanagement, nationalism (refusal to meet oil deliveries to other republics) and use of nationalist propaganda (which exaggerated the historic role of Azerbaijanis while neglecting that of Armenians and Russians) were added to those relating to language and discrimination on the basis of nationality. Sadykh Ragimov and Mirza Ibragimov were identified as the main culprits, but by the end of the year Mustafaev had joined them and a long list of senior officials in losing their positions.[23]

Khrushchev's determination to seize control of events in the republics was underlined by a series of other purges. S. Babaev had been removed as First Secretary in Turkmenistan in December 1958, followed by Uzbek First Secretary S. Kamalov in March 1959. In April–May 1961 First Secretaries were replaced in Moldova, Kyrgyzstan and Tajikistan, where other officials were also purged. Promoting officials on the basis of nationality, which had been established as normal practice in the 1920s and reconfirmed in the early post-Stalin years, was now seen as an offence, and corruption also played a part at a time when the regime was especially sensitive to the possible abuses afforded by the *sovnarkhoz* reform and which had embarrassed the leadership in the infamous Ryazan Affair, in which production and live stock figures were fabricated to an extreme degree. The promotion of non-Russians in the central leadership also slowed down markedly after the dismissal in May

[23] *Arkhivy Kremlya: Prezidium TsK KPSS 1954–1964*, vol. I, *Chernovye protokol'nye zapisi zasedanii Stenogrammy* (Moscow: Rosspen, 2003) 357–87.

1960 of the Ukrainian Alexei Kirichenko from his positions in the Presidium and the CC Secretariat, after he was identified with a policy of ukrainising the Communist Party in the Ukrainian SSR.

In the last years of his hold on power, Khrushchev took encouragement from his defeat of the Azerbaijani and Latvian leaders, and the acquiescence of the others, to raise the tempo of rhetoric about the 'merger of nations', which was enshrined in the new Communist Party Programme of 1961.[24] But in reality this was a pyrrhic victory. With Khrushchev's attention turned elsewhere, republican leaders continued to build their national bases as they had done before 1958. Even the education reform had little impact in the republics. In Estonia the leadership, which had reluctantly deferred to central insistence in passing its education law, took steps to ensure that Estonian children continued to attend Estonian schools. The Central Committee received dozens of complaints from Ukraine about the non-availability of Russian-language schools and other violations of the new policy, but the Ukrainian leaders excused each of these complaints, and the central authorities did nothing to pursue them. By 1964, the production of non-Russian school textbooks had actually increased across all the republics, and there was even an increase in the number of Russian children studying at national schools.[25]

Khrushchev's education reform, the several republican purges and a renewed rhetorical emphasis on the 'merger of nations' may appear on the surface to amount to a policy of russification. Several of Khrushchev's Presidium colleagues were clearly inclined to

[24] Alexander Titov, 'The 1961 Party Programme and the Fate of Khrushchev's Reforms', in Melanie Ilic and Jeremy Smith (eds.), *Soviet State and Society under Nikita Khrushchev* (London: Routledge, 2009), 14–15.

[25] Harry Lipset, 'The Status of National Minority Languages in Soviet Education', *Soviet Studies*, 19, 2 (1967), 183–4, 188.

promote the Russian language and culture, as discussed in Chapter 10, and some of Khrushchev's moves may have been designed as a sop to them. There is little to suggest, however, that Khrushchev himself was particularly interested in a russfication programme as such. What concerned him above all was the need to close the gap between the Soviet Union and the advanced western countries, and he was convinced of his own ability to achieve this. His moves against the national republics in the later part of his rule can be placed alongside successive efforts to reform the party and state apparatuses to bring them more firmly under his control as instruments of reform. Destalinisation had unleashed several forces in the communist bloc which threatened to diminish his control and, after the Hungarian revolt had been suppressed and the conservative old guard in the CPSU leadership defeated, the republics remained as the most likely source of obstruction to his schemes.

Stability and national development: the Brezhnev years, 1964–1982

The Brezhnev era (1964–1982) has been characterised as one of stagnation, and with some obvious justification: during the eighteen years when Leonid Brezhnev was general secretary of the CPSU, only sixteen new appointments were made to full membership of the highest decision-making body, the Politburo of the Central Committee of the CPSU. This does not, however, do justice to the many changes that were going on below the level of the top leadership, where society was developing in ways which eventually outstripped the comfortable complacency of the ageing leadership. This was also an active time in Soviet foreign policy, with the Cold War reaching new heights but also going through periods of calm, and the leadership often preoccupied with events in Eastern Europe, culminating in the Prague Spring of 1968. But the regime generally eschewed major policy upheavals. Many of Khrushchev's innovations reached fulfilment in the years after his ouster, while others were quickly dropped. In the latter category, and of particular concern for the non-Russian nationalities, were the *sovnarkhoz* reform of 1957, abandoned in 1965, and the education reform of 1958–1959, which was quietly allowed to recede into irrelevance. Instances of large-scale unrest were rare, with the economy maintaining (by global standards) reasonable but not spectacular growth rates until the late 1980s. Although economic growth eventually lagged behind that of the major western economies and the

limitations of the planned economy were already apparent, technological improvements and rising oil prices allowed for a greater
emphasis on consumer goods, with many families now able to own
refrigerators and televisions for the first time. Improved consumption levels (though low by western standards) did much to account
for the stability of the time. Social stability was also underlined by
the urbanisation of most of the country and universally high levels
of education.

Non-Russian citizens of the Soviet Union shared in this stability, but the politics of stagnation had contradictory effects on the
nationalities. As slow as turnover was among the leadership in
Moscow, at the top levels it became increasingly russified.
Although a number of non-Russians were promoted to the
Politburo in the first six years of Brezhnev's leadership, of the
eight new full members appointed between 1971 and Brezhnev's
death in 1982, all were Slavs, seven Russians and only one
Ukrainian. But Brezhnev's regime followed more closely the
principle that the First Secretary of the Communist Party in
each republic should be a national of that republic, and longevity
in office for members of the Politburo was matched if not sur-
passed for the leaders of the union republics: Heidar Aliev led
Azerbaijan from 1969 to 1982, Petr Masherov headed the
Communist Party of Belorussia from 1965 to 1980, Vasili
Mzhavanadze and Eduard Shevardnadze occupied the top post in
Georgia between them from 1953 to 1985, Dinmukhamed Kunaev
held the Kazakh post with a brief interruption from 1960 to 1986,
Turdakun Usubaliev in Kyrgyzstan from 1961 to 1985, Avgust
Voss in Latvia from 1966 to 1984, Ivan Bodyul in Moldova from
1961 to 1980, Jabar Rasulov in Tajikistan from 1961 to 1982,
Mukhamednazar Gapurov in Turkmenistan from 1969 to 1985,
Sharaf Rashidov in Uzbekistan from 1959 to 1983, Peter Shelest

followed by Vladimir Shcherbitsky in Ukraine from 1963 to 1989.
Ivan Käbin held his post in Estonia from 1950 to 1978 and, longest
of all, Antanas Sniečkus was appointed First Secretary in
Lithuania by Stalin upon sovietisation in 1940 and remained in
that post until 1974.[1] A confused or, rather, indifferent nationality
policy at the top allowed these leaders considerable leeway with
the affairs of their own republics and, boosted by the confidence
that stability of tenure engendered, they showed a marked tendency to build up their own power bases and underpin them by
developing the national character of their republics.

This tendency was reinforced by pressures from below.
Relaxation of controls on the production of culture encouraged
the development of national art, music, literature and cinema,
around which a national intelligentsia consolidated. Complaints
over perceived national inequalities, interference from the centre,
and inconsistencies over, in particular, language status elicited a
vociferous response from these national intelligentsias, who also
began to compete with each other over historical and territorial
claims. Nationalists became an important part of the growing dissident movement, and added national rights to the demand for
human rights. Demands for independence became more common
and were sometimes expressed in underground political or even
terrorist movements. On occasion, as in Georgia in 1978, interference from the centre was met by mass mobilisation on the streets.
Demographic change also had a profound and inconsistent effect on
the republics, with migration in and out of Russia providing opportunities but also discord.

---

[1] For useful lists of First Secretaries in each of the Soviet republics, see Yu. V. Goryachev,
  *Tsentral'nyi komitet KPSS, VKP(b), RKP(b), RSDRP(b): istoriko-biograficheskiy spra-
  vochnik* (Moscow: Parad, 2005), 442–7.

BREZHNEV'S NATIONALITY POLICY AND THE
SOVIET PEOPLE

Leonid Brezhnev was born and educated in Ukraine, where he remained for the earlier part of his political career, and he also did stints as party leader in Moldova and Kazakhstan in 1950–1952 and 1954–1956 respectively. In spite of this, his writings display little interest in the national question. When he and his colleagues removed Khrushchev from power in 1964, no mention of the national question was made in the long list of accusations against the First Secretary. National leaders had failed to come to Khrushchev's defence in 1964 as they had done in 1957 and, anxious not to antagonise the republics, the new leaders dropped the rhetoric of the merger of nations. Within a year of removing Khrushchev, the new leadership restored the practice of publishing Supreme Soviet laws in the languages of all the republics, which had been abandoned in 1960, and granted chairmen of the republics' Supreme Soviets, Councils of Ministers, Supreme Courts and planning committees automatic membership of the corresponding USSR organs.[2] In one of his first major speeches as party leader, at the XXIII Congress of the CPSU in March 1966, Brezhnev emphasised that 'the Party will continue to show solicitude for the interests and the national characteristics of each people' but otherwise avoided the question.[3]

The impression that the Brezhnev period (or, more accurately, the period beginning in the late Khrushchev years) was one of russification and the acceleration of the disappearance of national differences rests largely on rhetoric, which became more and more pervasive, about 'the Soviet People – the New Historical

---

[2] Suny, *Making of the Georgian Nation*, 294.
[3] Nahaylo and Swoboda, *Soviet Disunion*, 153.

Community of Peoples'. How this worked out in practical terms as far as language and culture are concerned is discussed later in this chapter. Here it is worth pointing out that Brezhnev's policy was not at all clear on what this meant. He himself claimed that Soviet culture was 'a culture socialist in content, in its main direction of development, *multifaceted in its national forms*, and international in its spirit and character'.[4] In other words, reflecting Stalin's slogan of 'national in form, socialist in content', Brezhnev repudiated the notion that the Soviet people would form a single nationality sharing a single language. At most, they would share a common culture expressed in different forms and different languages.

For the most part, Brezhnev maintained a tactful neutrality on the national question. But around him a fierce and ultimately unresolved debate raged about the future of nationality and, in particular, of the role of the Russian language. Echoing some of the choruses of the late Stalin years, journals and newspapers extolled the greatness and cultural superiority of the Russian language, and argued its indispensability as the common language of communication in the Soviet Union: 'Because of its richness and diversity, Russian is quite an extraordinary treasure chest of the accomplishments of civilization', wrote V. Kuznetsov in the newspaper of the Communist Party of Ukraine in 1972.[5] But these opinions did not go unopposed. In 1966 the Georgian F. Eligulashvili noted sarcastically that 'knowing Russian could of course be useful . . . neither would it do any harm to know English, French, German'.[6] The official Party line was to steer a delicate

---

[4] Isabelle Kreindler, 'The Changing Status of Russian in the Soviet Union', *International Journal of the Sociology of Language*, 33 (1982), 17. The italics are mine.

[5] Cited in Fowkes, *The Disintegration of the Soviet Union*, 96.

[6] Cited in Kreindler, 'Changing Status', 16.

course between calls for a greater drawing together (*sblizheniye*) of the Soviet peoples while avoiding accusations of pursuing assimilation. An editorial in the principal theoretical journal *Kommunist* cautioned in September 1969 that 'the drawing together of Soviet nations and their internationalist unity should not be regarded as fusion. The removal of all national differences is a long process, which cannot be achieved except after the complete victory of communism in the world and its consolidation' and went on to warn that 'indifference and nihilism as regards national problems cannot be tolerated'.[7]

Overall, however, the tone of ideological discussions came increasingly to favour the further promotion of the Russian language. More than just a useful *lingua franca*, Russian was held to be the language which best conveyed the messages of communism as originally formulated, and hence was to be more widely used in education. Its use was linked to the greatness of Russian culture and so, according to a perverse logic, greater mastery of Russian would enhance the national development of the non-Russians. Finally, Russian would help promote the unity and collective strength of the peoples of the multi-national Soviet state.[8] This was reflected in policies aimed at further promoting the teaching of Russian and exerting more central control over the school system in the republics. Although the CPSU leadership rarely went on record to promote russifying measures, it is well known that, from the Khrushchev period onwards, a number of key figures in the Politburo and Central Committee were clearly inclined towards Russian nationalism, and with their encouragement Russian

[7] Cited in Nahaylo and Swoboda, *Soviet Disunion*, 168.
[8] Kreindler, 'Changing Status', 18–20.

nationalist movements grew and were able to spread their ideas through journals such as *Molodaia gvardiia* and *Nash sovremennik.*[9]

NATIONAL CULTURE FLOURISHES

The rather uncertain messages coming from the top, combined with the assurance of stability, encouraged the further production of national culture which had already been launched during the Khrushchev thaw. Throughout the Khrushchev and Brezhnev periods the journal *Druzhba narodov* published translations of poetry from all the non-Russian republics, as well as from abroad, into Russian. This official effort to place national cultures within the context of mutual appreciation and the Brotherhood of Nations could not contain the more determinedly nationally oriented culture which was produced either under the auspices of or in defiance of the republican communist authorities. Leading the way in Ukraine was the young poet Vasyl Simonenko, who died age 29 in 1963. He challenged the notion of cultural ties of Ukraine and Russia with the line 'Let America and Russia be silent when I talk to you [Ukraine].'[10] Simonenko and other poets, writers, and artists of the 'sixties generation' operated semi-legally, meeting in each other's apartments and at the Club of Creative Youth in Kiev, and contributed to *samizdat* publications. *Samizdat* that went beyond the purely cultural, like Ivan Dziuba's *Internationalism or Russification?* and the journal *Ukrainian Herald*, edited by Vyacheslav Chornovil and then Stepan Khmara, faced official

[9] Nikolai Mitrokhin, *Russkaya partiya: dvizhenie russkikh natsionalistov v SSSR 1953–1985 gody* (Moscow: Novoe Literaturnoe Obozrenie, 2003); Simon Cosgrove, *Russian Nationalism and the Politics of Soviet Literature: The Case of* Nash Sovremmenik, *1981–1991* (Basingstoke: Palgrave, 2004).

[10] Ludmilla Alexeyeva, *Soviet Dissent: Contemporary Movements for National, Religious, and Human Rights* (Middletown, CI: Wesleyan University Press, 1985), 31–2.

persecution (Chornovil was arrested in 1972).[11] But public poetry readings, concerts of Ukrainian music and exhibitions of folk and modern art were tolerated. At times open support for Ukrainian national culture, and a preference for Ukrainian over Russian in written works, was expressed by the republic's leaders including First Secretary Peter Shelest, who declared his admiration for the Ukrainian Cossacks and defended Ukrainian national writers.[12] In Uzbekistan official support for a new generation of national poets extended to a special effort to promote female poets.[13]

The most popular cultural medium of the time was cinema, and in Georgia and Kyrgyzstan national cinema flourished. The Gruzia film studio was one of the most productive in the USSR, and in the 1960s and 1970s up to sixty Georgian films were being produced each year. They included the works of Sergei Paradjanov, who celebrated not just Georgian but other Caucasian values and histories, and Tengiz Abuladze, whose celebrated film *Repentance* was a thinly disguised condemnation of Lavrenti Beria. Abuladze profited from the protection of Georgia's First Secretary Eduard Shevardnadze but Paradjanov, like many of the Ukrainian cultural figures, faced periodic persecution throughout the 1970s and 1980s.[14] While Georgia had a long tradition of film-making predating the Russian Revolution, in Kyrgyzstan the first film studio was opened only in 1942. In the 'Golden Age' of Kyrgyz cinema in the 1960s, directors such as Melis Ubukeev, Tolomush Okeev, Bolot Shamshiev and Gannadi Bazarov focussed on historical themes which emphasised the Kyrgyz attachment to their native land and

---

[11] Andrew Wilson, *Ukrainian Nationalism in the 1990s: A Minority Faith* (Cambridge University Press, 1997), 54–5.
[12] Nahaylo and Swoboda, *Soviet Disunion*, 168–9.
[13] Allworth, *The Modern Uzbeks*, 316–19.
[14] Charles King, *The Ghost of Freedom: A History of the Caucasus* (Oxford University Press, 2008), 207–11.

the affinity of the Kyrgyz nation to nature. While their films do not shy away from the conflict between tradition and modernity and the challenges of building socialism, through tales of personal trauma, bravery and eventual triumph against the odds they clearly celebrate and commemorate the Kyrgyz nation.[15]

In Azerbaijan under Heidar Aliev, the Azerbaijan Writers' Union sponsored an official version of culture and history through the pages of its monthly journal *A*z*erbaijan*. Earlier on, this had consisted of accounts of progressive historical and literary figures with the emphasis on Russian influence over Azerbaijani culture, but from about 1979 onwards a different tone was clearly apparent. A discussion of Azerbaijani Turkish literature 'from Nizami to Saib Tabrizi' established a strong local culture predating the Russian presence. Poems celebrated the Homeland, with an emphasis on the local landscape and nature, as well as the importance of the Azerbaijani language, as in Sabir Rustemkhanli's poem 'Thank You, My Mother Tongue':

> Thank you, my mother tongue,
> You never left me helpless or alone . . .

This particular poem stresses the precedence of language as a national unifier prior to the advent of Islam, and also makes reference to Karabakh as an inseparable part of Azerbaijan, in line with the new turn in historic competition discussed below. The Republic of Azerbaijan provides an intriguing example of a leader, Heidar Aliev, who personally took care to show his support for the official Moscow line while, at the same time, promoting the separate Azerbaijani identity through cultural production.[16] I return to this theme later in the chapter.

[15] Sally N. Cummings, 'Soviet Rule, Nation and Film: The Kyrgyz "Wonder" Years', *Nations and Nationalism*, 15, 4 (October 2009), 636–57.
[16] Altstadt, *The A*z*erbaijani Turks*, 188–91.

Smaller nationalities also enjoyed something of a cultural revival. In the most populous and powerful autonomous republic, the Tatar ASSR, cultural revival was based on the richness of the Tatar language, the Islamic cultural heritage and the distant history of Kazan. Novels and poems of the 1960s and 1970s, such as G. Bashir's novel *My Home Is a Green Cradle*, celebrated the endurance of Tatar national traditions and folk culture. This cultural upsurge took place in official channels, with *samizdat* unheard of before 1977, when the Tatar national movement began to take on a more political and dissident form.[17] Karelian national culture focussed on traditional costumes, dance and handicrafts.[18] In Siberia the Buryats revived festivals of art and literature and also pursued cultural contacts with Mongolia, in spite of official disapproval of the link. In Yakutia, a Canadian writer visiting in the 1960s noted that Yakut writers were 'not anti-Russian' but 'unabashedly pro-Yakut'.[19] Occasionally, official backing for national culture extended to the smallest nationalities. On the island of Sakhalin, at a time when the tiny Nivkh and Orok communities were experiencing rapid decline, a publishing house was established which 'issued popular local histories for national consumption'.[20]

NATIONAL HISTORIES IN COMPETITION

The encouragement given to intellectuals to pursue national agendas in the republics took a peculiar twist among academics,

[17] Rorlich, *The Volga Tatars*, 161–75.

[18] Tuulikki Kurki, 'The Modern Soviet Man Looks Back: Images and Narratives of Soviet Karelia', in Pekka Suutari and Yury Shikalov (eds.), *Karelia Written and Sung: Representations of Locality in Soviet and Russian Contexts* (Helsinki: Kikimora Publications, 2010), 100.

[19] James Forsyth, *A History of the Peoples of Siberia: Russia's North Asian Colony 1581–1990* (Cambridge University Press, 1992), 377–80.

[20] Bruce Grant, *In the Soviet House of Culture: A Century of Perestroikas* (Princeton University Press, 1995), 117.

especially in the Caucasus, which had serious consequences for the break-up of the USSR and developments since.

Armenian and Azerbaijani historians debated the ancient settlement of the region of Karabakh and its upper reaches, Nagorno (Mountainous) Karabakh. Much of the debate raged over the nature and legacy of the 'Caucasian Albanians'. Little is known about this long-disappeared people, who once inhabited the eastern parts of the South Caucasus. From 1960 onwards Azerbaijani historians, led by Igrar Aliev and Ziya Buniatov, argued that the descendants of the Caucasian Albanians had been subjected to Turkic influences before the seventh century AD. The Armenians who had inhabited Karabakh for a long time were, they claimed, armenianised Albanians who were thus truly ethnic Azerbaijanis. Although Karabakh was littered with Christian buildings and monuments, pursuing this logic Buniatov claimed that really they were part of Azerbaijani culture. Most Armenian inhabitants of Soviet Karabakh were, according to Azerbaijani intellectuals, relative newcomers whose ancestors had been settled there by imperial Russia after 1825, consequent to the Treaty of Turkmanchai that marked the end of the Russo-Persian War in 1828. Armenian historians and ethnographers riposted that most of the new Armenian settlers went elsewhere in the Russian Empire, and claimed that Armenian settlement of Karabakh preceded the advent of the Caucasian Albanians and that the region remained culturally continuous since the fifth century AD, and sought to find roots to the ancient Armenian kingdom stretching back as far as the Nairi civilization in the thirteenth century BC. While some support for both sets of arguments could be adduced from sketchy evidence, neither side showed much regard for historical accuracy.

As early as the 1930s, when Abkhazia was becoming more fully integrated into Georgia, Georgian historians began to describe the medieval Abkhaz Kingdom as ethnically Georgian and as a west Georgian state. Others argued that the Abkhaz had migrated from the North Caucasus as late as the seventeenth century, and so were relative newcomers to the region. In the late Stalin period, when Georgia was still involved in a policy of georgianisation in Abkhazia, the message from politicians to academics was unmistakeable. In 1951 M. K. Delba, chair of the Council of Ministers of Abkhazia, condemned the earlier Soviet linguist Nikolai Marr for treating the Abkhaz as a separate people and insisted that 'Abkhazians as a Georgian tribe [had been] an integral part of the Georgian people throughout all their history.'[21] Pavle Ingorovqa, who had been a major influence in the discussions of Abkhazia in the 1930s, published a new book in 1954 which went even further in seeking to demonstrate that Abkhaz were only a Georgian tribe. This sparked off a new round of debate between Abkhaz and Georgian scholars. In 1964 a book that sought to show how much the Abkhaz language had been influenced by Georgia highlighted the overlaps between academia and politics: the author, director of the Abkhaz Research Institute Kh. S. Bgazhba, was the brother of the First Secretary of the Abkhaz regional branch of the Communist Party of Georgia.

As the ethnic Abkhaz gained more control over institutions in Abkhazia, these views were formally condemned in Tbilisi, Moscow and Sukhumi, but continued to influence Georgian writers, who carried on arguing that Abkhazia had been an integral part of the Kingdom of Georgia.[22] In the years leading up to Georgian independence and, afterwards, war with Abkhazia and South Ossetia, these messages became ever more stridently pronounced. Abkhaz

---

[21] Victor A. Shnirelman, *The Value of the Past: Myths, Identity and Politics in Transcaucasia* (Osaka: National Museum of Ethnology, 2001), Senri Ethnological Studies no. 57, 240–1.
[22] *Ibid.*, 208–10, 242–58.

historians claimed that the ancestors of the Abkhaz had been present in their territory since the first few centuries AD, and saw proof of separate Abkhaz statehood in the separate Russian annexations of Georgia and Abkhazia in 1801 and 1810 respectively.[23] Territorial claims based on thinly supported or spurious historical assertions were evident on a smaller scale in the North Caucasus, where Ingush described the village of Angusht as the 'grandfatherland of the Ingush', while Ossetian archaeologists claimed descent from the Alans who, it was advanced, had occupied the whole North Caucasus.[24]

In Soviet Moldova, the crucial arguments of linguists and historians were directed not against another Soviet republic, but against another socialist state – Romania. The key task of academics was to prove the separateness of the Moldovan language and national identity from that of Romania, and they pitted themselves not just against Romanian and émigré scholars, but also against western studies.[25] The efforts of academics did not, in this case, contribute to national tensions directly as they did in the Caucasus. But they were partially successful in establishing an atmosphere of opposition to unification with Romania when the opportunity might have arisen in the 1990s, while on the other hand the idea of the common cultural and linguistic heritage did remain sufficiently alive to play a role in the conflict between the left- and right-bank populations after independence.

For the entire Soviet period, academics – like artists – were unable to disentangle themselves from politics. But whereas under Stalin they had served the dictates of the ruler's idiosyncratic cultural and political tastes, in the Brezhnev era they increasingly

---

[23] For discussion of these historical disputes, see Cheterian, *War and Peace*, 49–70.
[24] Tishkov, *Ethnicity, Nationalism and Conflict*, 15.   [25] King, *The Moldovans*, 112–14.

served the national cause. To some extent, this was even true of the RSFSR, where a considerable proportion of linguists devoted themselves to extolling the virtues of the Russian language. But it was more the case in the non-Russian republics, where both academics and cultural producers revived the national past and glorified the national present. This contributed to the further consolidation of a sense of nationhood which the federal structure of the USSR had already institutionalised. It was not unimportant in the growth and popularity of secession movements in the 1980s, although where the national cultural and historical turn threatened to undermine the notion of the friendship of peoples – specifically the friendship of Russian with non-Russian peoples – as happened in Ukraine under Shelest, the centre was more likely to intervene. In some areas, most notably the Caucasus, what fuelled national pride elsewhere fuelled national rivalry and even hatred. Exactly why and under whose prompting academics should have taken such a direction remains unresearched. Territorial competition was not new, and it may simply be that academics were seeking to advance their careers by capitalising on disputes which had not been resolved in the 1920s. In any case, the more strident and dishonest efforts to rewrite history were the most extreme manifestation of a direction which historians were pursuing elsewhere in the USSR.

NATIONAL DISSIDENTS

On 5 December 1965, a demonstration took place on Pushkin Square in Moscow under the slogan 'Respect the Soviet Constitution!' This event is regarded as the birth of the Soviet human rights movement. Three and a half years later the Initiative Group to Defend Human Rights in the USSR was formed in Moscow, giving the movement organisational form. The group's first document mentioned the persecution of participants in the national movements in Ukraine and the Baltic republics, and among the Crimean Tatars, who were still in exile. The Moscow Human Rights Committee, formed in 1970, also took up these questions. The Moscow Helsinki Watch Group was formed in 1976, basing its message around the Soviet Union's failure to observe the terms of the Helsinki Final Act, signed by the USSR and thirty-four other states in 1975, and which included agreements on the observance of human rights. The Moscow Helsinki Group was shortly copied by activists in Ukraine, Lithuania, Georgia and Armenia.

The Moscow Helsinki Group maintained links with the groups in the republics, and announced and publicised the activities and persecution of the other organisations. But this was a rare case of co-ordination among the dissidents of the Soviet Union, and was limited in its scope. Direct links between the various national movements were unheard of, and this lack of contact was only partially overcome during Gorbachev's *glasnost'*.[26] Human rights were the only area on which a number of the many dissident organisations could find common cause. The nationalities question, in particular, remained divisive among dissidents. While prominent Russian dissidents such as the physicist Andrei Sakharov did refer to the problems accruing from the implementation of Soviet nationality policies, most Russian dissidents ignored the question or, in the case of Russian nationalist groups, vigorously opposed demands for secession.[27]

The national dissident movements predated the emergence of the Russian human rights movement and, while they borrowed the language of rights, for most nationalists human rights were

[26] Alexeyeva, *Soviet Dissent*, 16–18.   [27] Nahaylo and Swoboda, *Soviet Disunion*, 161–5.

equivalent to national rights over language or secession. This differing conception of rights and the hostile attitude of some Russian activists would have presented difficulties for the USSR-wide co-ordination of the dissident movement, but the activities of the KGB and other security organs in any case made such co-ordination next to impossible. Hence, the dissident movement developed separately in each republic, and was at its strongest in Ukraine, Armenia, Georgia, Estonia, Latvia and Lithuania.

Members of the 'sixties generation' in Ukraine had to contend both with an ambivalent official attitude towards themselves and with the legacy of wartime nationalist development. While some of the wartime leaders of the Ukrainian national movement had been tainted by collaboration with the hated Nazis, members of the OUN-UPA waged their struggle both against the German occupiers and the Soviet 'liberators', and enjoyed considerable popular support, especially in western Ukraine. Underground groups continued to operate in the west after the defeat of the OUN, but the futility of underground struggle combined with the possibilities that appeared to be opened up by Khrushchev's thaw to convince many nationalists that peaceful dissent was the way forward. The Ukrainian Workers' and Peasants' Union, formed in western Ukraine in 1958, persisted in a radical demand for independence, but based its call for secession on the legal possibilities offered by the official Soviet constitution.

Mobilising around demands based on Soviet legality was to become a consistent feature of the later main Soviet dissident movement. The sixties generation followed this tradition and was of an altogether different character from the OUN-UPA. It was led by intellectuals who had grown up under Soviet rule, who engaged in cultural activity as much as in political dissent. A wave of arrests among these intellectuals shortly after Khrushchev's downfall forced the movement into more direct political opposition, culminating in the arrest of the young journalist Vyacheslav Chornovil in August 1966. Chornovil had compiled a dossier of violations of official legality in Ukraine and published them as the first Ukrainian *samizdat*. Underground publications flourished in the following years and were supplemented by works written by prisoners in the Gulag camps. Chornovil and Dziuba were the leading lights of the dissident movement until 1972 when, following Chornovil's second arrest, Stepan Khmara emerged as the leader of a more radical movement which was ready to go beyond the bounds of socialist legality. This new radical wing of Ukrainian nationalism claimed the mantle of the OUN-UPA, but had little success in establishing organised underground activity. Individual acts of protest were more dramatic: on 5 December 1968 Vasyl Makukh burned himself to death in the centre of Kiev, shouting out 'Long live free Ukraine!', while Mykola Breslavs'kyi's similar attempt at self-immolation the following February was unsuccessful.[28]

The dissident movement in the three Baltic republics was able to feed off popular discontent which, as discussed in Chapter 9, was still abundant in the 1950s. But attempts to create underground nationalist cells were generally short-lived and ineffective, and an organised dissident movement did not really emerge until the 1970s. In Lithuania, a dissident movement of 'folklorists' focussed on cultural and historical themes, but was repressed in 1974.[29] A more lasting dissident movement crystallised around the Catholic Church, which had been virtually destroyed by Stalin following the occupation of Lithuania, but which was allowed to revive somewhat under Khrushchev. Under Brezhnev, demands for the observance

[28] Wilson, *Ukrainian Nationalism*, 52–6; Nahaylo and Swoboda, 156–8, 163.
[29] Alexeyeva, *Soviet Dissent*, 66.

of the constitutional rights of believers were accompanied by the organisation of secret religious services and the emergence of *samizdat* publications such as the *Chronicle of the Catholic Church in Lithuania*, which was started in 1972 and was regularly quoted on Vatican Radio. This and other religious publications, such as *God and the Homeland* and *The Way of Truth*, existed alongside secular *samizdat* publications such as *The Champion* and *The Bell*. What stands out about Lithuania is that the appeal of Catholicism brought the Catholic movement closer to the broader population and served as a common point across a wide range of divergent views, including those professed by purely secular dissidents.[30]

In Armenia, the dissident movement focussed initially on maintaining and reviving Armenian historical and cultural traditions. The popular resonance of these issues was illustrated by a mass demonstration marking the fiftieth anniversary of the genocide of Turkish Armenians, organised in Yerevan on 24 April 1965. Unlike other dissident movements, however, the Armenians did not confine themselves to appeals for national rights. The movement was divided on the whole issue of national independence, with the historic dependence on Russia in face of the threat from Turkey still holding sway over many nationalists. Secondly, as well as memorialising the genocide, a key aim of the national movement was the unification of historic Armenian territories. At the 1965 demonstration, the demand for the reunification of Turkish territories was raised, but increasingly dissidents turned their attention to the Soviet territories belonging to the Azerbaijan Republic – Nagorno Karabakh and Nakhichevan. The National Unity Party

---

[30] Mark Nash, 'The "Exceptional" Church: Religious Freedom and the Catholic Church in Russia' (unpublished Ph.D dissertation, University of Birmingham, 2007), 124–6; Michael Bourdeaux, *Land of Crosses* (Chulmleigh: Augustine Publishing Co., 1979); Alexeyeva, *Soviet Dissent*, 66–7.

(NUP), organised in 1967, raised this as their core demand, and in June 1965 thirteen prominent Armenian intellectuals petitioned Moscow for the transfer of Karabakh to Armenia. Further petitions and *samizdat* publications on the topic appeared, and in 1968 the first violent clashes since sovietisation took place in the Karabakh town of Stepanakert.

The Armenian movement was also distinguished by the alleged or actual resort to terrorist activities. In January 1974, an NUP member, Razmik Zohrapyan, burned Lenin's portrait in the centre of Yerevan. More seriously, three years later the NUP was accused of masterminding the bombing of the Moscow Pervomaiskaya metro station, which left seven dead and thirty-seven wounded, and of planning a similar attack at the Kursk station in October. Three Armenians were executed for these bombings.[31] A series of explosions also occurred in Georgia in the mid 1970s. Although most of these appear to have been connected to criminal gangs or a response to Shevardnadze's anti-corruption drive, at least one bomber, Vladimir Zhvania, seems to have been politically motivated. He was executed in January 1977.

Such acts were exceptional, however, and for the most part national dissidents followed their Russian counterparts in issuing demands and organising petitions calling for the observance of Soviet and international law in recognising national and human rights. The Helsinki Final Act gave a further legal impetus to this approach, and the Helsinki Groups in different republics became, after 1976, the major focus for information and activity at home and abroad. *Samizdat* publication was the main activity of dissidents in both Russia and the republics, and it served a dual purpose. On the

---

[31] Simon Payaslian, *The History of Armenia* (Basingstoke and New York: Palgrave Macmillan, 2007), 185–6.

one hand these works served as a source of information for domestic activists and the population at large, but they were also frequently smuggled out of the country as a way of informing the international community about the true situation in the USSR. For the nationalities, this function was particularly important, as they could appeal to large and often well-funded and influential émigré communities in Europe and North America. The Jewish émigré community was the most powerful and unique in having a state, Israel, outside the USSR to which it could appeal directly. But the Armenian and other communities also had electoral muscle and personal influence, while the Lithuanian dissident movement was able to gain the attention of the Vatican. While the general public in the West remained largely ignorant of Soviet nationality affairs until the explosion of unrest in the late 1980s, and the national question played an insignificant role in the Cold War, diaspora groups remained acutely aware of the situation in their homelands and on occasion were able to gain the attention of major western powers.

OPEN PROTEST

Samizdat publication and distribution, letters of protest and petitions were the regular activities of national dissidents, but public group protests were not unknown. One American scholar was able to analyse 321 open national protests between 1965 and 1978, getting most of his information from *samizdat* publications. Over three-quarters of these were by Jews (54.2%) and Crimean Tatars (22.4%) demanding the right to live in Israel and Crimea respectively, and 41.7% of the protests analysed took place inside the RSFSR.[32]

---

[32] David Kowalewski, 'National Rights Protest in the Brezhnev Era: Some Determinants of Success', *Ethnic and Racial Studies*, 4, 2 (April 1981), 175–88.

Elsewhere, protests of note broke out in the Prigorodnyi district of North Ossetia in 1973, around the demand for the region to be returned to the Chechen–Ingush Autonomous Republic. In Lithuania, the self-immolation of an 18-year-old schoolboy, Romas Kalanta, triggered two days of demonstrations in the city of Kaunas in May 1972. A few days later, in a more passive display of solidarity, spectators refused to stand for the Soviet anthem at a volleyball match in Vilnius. Sports events became a regular focus for political demonstrations in Lithuania, with one numbering up to 15,000 participants in 1977.

In Georgia, protests by students, especially in Tbilisi, became a regular occurrence from the mid 1960s.[33] Perhaps the best known, and certainly most successful, public protest took place in Georgia in 1978. A draft constitution of the Georgian SSR, prepared in conjunction with the discussions for a new constitution of the USSR, included Russian and other languages in addition to Georgian as the official languages of the republic. In response, following a petition campaign up to 5,000 people, mostly students, took to the streets in Tbilisi until First Secretary Shevardnadze announced that the proposal had been dropped. This apparent protest against a russifying move was in fact double-edged: the change would have strengthened the linguistic position of Georgia's minorities – Abkhaz, Ossetians, Armenians and so on – who made up about a third of the population and did not speak Georgian as a first language. A series of demonstrations in Abkhazia in the same year, in part motivated by the victory of the Tbilisi demonstrators, won some concessions, but these fell short of the demand for separation from Georgia or equal status for the Abkhaz language.[34]

---

[33] Alexeyeva, *Soviet Dissent*, 68–9, 108–9.
[34] Cheterian, *War and Peace*, 160–1; Suny, *Making of the Georgian Nation*, 309.

In the absence of a free press and opinion surveys, it is always difficult to judge the extent of particular attitudes and beliefs among the population of the Soviet Union. Assessments of national assertiveness in the USSR necessarily focus on the activities of small numbers of people and are based on anecdotal evidence or that presented by *samizdat* publications which, given the agendas of their authors, must be handled with some care. On occasion, the numbers involved in petitions or open protest were impressive by Soviet standards, but still involved a small minority of the total population. Activists generally represent the views of a far greater number under any political system, and it can be argued that this is even more true under a system where the risks of openly expressing opposition views were so great. But all the same it is difficult to extrapolate how widely shared were the views of dissidents and protestors.

Care should also be taken when reading back from the national movements of the late 1980s to arrive at the conclusion that national discontent was bubbling away throughout the Soviet period. At least it cannot be denied that among the two nationalities of the Soviet Union that were most active on a regular basis – Jews and Crimean Tatars – the demand for national rights was widespread. With some confidence, we can say that in the three Baltic republics the perception of sovietisation as a form of occupation continued to hold sway among most of the national populations. In Georgia, students formed the core of a national movement which was given expression by intellectuals. Elsewhere, national movements were largely confined to intellectuals. For broader assessments of the direction national identity in the republics was going, we need to look at the more tangential evidence of language retention and other data. Before doing so, however, the crucial role of the official leaderships and the national infrastructures they built in the republics need to be examined.

NATIONAL REPUBLICAN LEADERSHIP AND NATIONAL INFRASTRUCTURES

The republican Communist Party First Secretaries listed in the introduction to this chapter owed their longevity in office to a combination of factors: the stance of non-interference adopted by the Brezhnev leadership and its general policy of 'stability of cadres' allowed leaders to remain in post as long as their health allowed and they did not rock the boat too much. But it was equally important that these leaders were able to build a solid base for their own power in the republic. This meant, first, pursuing policies that appealed to a substantial portion of the population, including its political and intellectual elites. Since the titular nationality constituted a clear majority of the population in each of the union republics, it was generally to the majority nationality that the leaders appealed. Secondly, it meant appointing to key positions a group of supporters whose loyalty could be counted on, and it helped if these supporters could identify with the leader. Being of the same nationality was an important starting point, but closer affiliations were often sought. Family members, personal acquaintances of long standing, common members of ethnic subgroups and in Central Asia members of the leader's clan were generally preferred in important appointments. This approach gave rise to a series of 'national mafias'[35] running each republic, each of whose members would in turn lean on their own networks. Among other advantages, this allowed republican leaders to argue for their own indispensability in holding these governing networks together and to discourage other contenders from bidding for their positions.

---

[35] Suny, *Revenge of the Past*. The following discussion owes much to the inspiration of Suny's book.

As well as the republican First Secretaries, other senior posts came to be dominated by members of the titular nationality who generally enjoyed longevity in office. In Ukraine, 88% of Politburo members were ethnic Ukrainians in 1979, while the proportion of ethnic Ukrainian provincial party secretaries in the republic rose from 84% in 1966 to 96% in 1980, against an ethnic Ukrainian share in the overall population of only 74% in the middle of this period. Only in Belorussia and Moldova were the dominant ethnic group under-represented in proportion to their share of the population.[36]

Pure self-interest is not necessarily the only, or the best, explanation of the policy choices made by republican leaders. Personal biographies are important given the extensive powers each had. Unlike the previous generation of leaders, all of those appointed First Secretary after 1953 were born shortly before or in the decade after the 1917 Revolution. They had no memory of the revolution or the utopian days of the 1920s, but they were also too young to be at all politically active during the excesses of Stalin's Terror (which, if anything, created the space for their subsequent rise through the ranks). As for the slightly younger generation of Mikhail Gorbachev, the Great Patriotic War was a key formative influence, and they were approaching their political peak amid the atmosphere of hope, renewal and growing nationalism that accompanied Khrushchev's thaw. Feelings of both Soviet and national patriotism were, most likely, not alien to any of them. And once such leaders had come into office in the republics, isolated events such as the March 1956 demonstrations in Georgia or the broader phenomenon of national dissidence could not help leaving their mark. If the dissident movement was, indeed, a symptom of broader national

---

[36] Ben Fowkes, 'The National Question in the Soviet Union under Leonid Brezhnev: Policy and Response', in Edwin Bacon and Mark Sandle (eds.), *Brezhnev Reconsidered* (Basingstoke: Palgrave Macmillan, 2002), 69.

aspirations, then this pressure was sure to be felt at a time when the emphasis was on stability and gradual development towards communism.

In at least one case, pressures of the local environment appear to have counted more than personal biography. Ivan Käbin was born in Estonia in 1905 but was brought up in Russia and served his political career in Moscow and the St Petersburg region until 1944. Although an ethnic Estonian, he hardly spoke any Estonian and his appointment as First Secretary of the Communist Party of Estonia in 1950 was viewed as a move to strengthen Moscow's control over the republic. After appearing to cave in over the language provisions of Khrushchev's education reform in 1959, however, he tactfully saw to it that Estonian remained the main language of instruction for Estonian children, ensuring after Khrushchev was removed from office that Estonia retained the eleven-year school system. He himself made great efforts to learn Estonian and to speak it in public, and was generally regarded as a skilful defender of Estonian national cultural and language interests at a time when Estonia was facing dilution of the national population by the mass settlement of Russians in the republic.[37]

Another leader who can be considered to have acted in response to environmental pressures was Eduard Shevardnadze. As head of the Georgian Komsomol in Kutaisi in 1956, he was intensely aware of the potential for mobilisation among Georgian youth, but also impressed Moscow with his handling of the March events. He was appointed to replace Mzhavanadze as First Secretary of the Georgian Communist Party in September 1972, with the solid

---

[37] Toivo U. Raun, *Estonia and the Estonians* (Stanford: Hoover Institution Press, 1987), 192, 212; Jaan Pennar, 'Soviet Nationality Policy and the Estonian Communist Elite', in Tonu Parming and Elmar Jarveson (eds.), *A Case Study of a Soviet Republic: The Estonian SSR* (Boulder, CO: Westview Press, 1978), 123.

backing of Moscow and a clear brief to tackle the corruption and nepotism that had become endemic in Georgian politics. He set about this task with enthusiasm, conducting wide-scale purges in the political and academic systems, while at the same time condemning 'national narrow-mindedness and isolation' and tackling head-on the perceived nationalism in culture, history writing and language policy. But so ingrained was corruption that Shevardnadze eventually appears to have accepted its permanent role, and his capitulation to demonstrators over the status of the Georgian language in 1978 was followed by another concession to students demonstrating over the sacking of a popular professor in March 1981. Under his leadership, Georgia went as far as conducting public opinion polls and basing policy decisions on their outcome. Shevardnadze did not always give in to nationalist pressures, however, resisting protests against the stipulation that all doctoral dissertations must be submitted in Russian in 1975. Like Käbin, his success lay in promoting a national agenda in the republic while simultaneously satisfying his overlords in Moscow.[38]

Heidar Aliev in Azerbaijan followed a career trajectory similar to Shevardnadze's. He was more active behind the scenes than Shevardnadze in promoting national culture, but was equally successful in sending the right messages to Moscow, ensuring his hold on the republic by both placating the CPSU leadership and promoting an elaborate network of loyal followers in the administrative, cultural and academic institutions of the republic. He had more in common, however, with the leaders of Central Asian republics in carefully nurturing a personality cult which was to stand him in good stead on his return to power following independence.

---

[38] Suny, *Making of the Georgian Nation*, 306–10.

What these two – Aliev and Shevardnadze – shared was the rare distinction of being non-Slavs who achieved promotion to the CPSU Politburo in the years between Khrushchev and Gorbachev. For most republican leaders, it appeared that during the Brezhnev years there was a glass ceiling which, while allowing them to rule with relatively little interference over their own republics, meant they were always subject to the whims of the Kremlin and could never achieve higher office. The feeling of subordinate status was reinforced by the offhand treatment of even the highest officials from the republics on their visits to Moscow, and the fact that they still needed permission from a special department of the CPSU Central Committee to take trips abroad.[39] These facts encouraged leaders to make the most of their leadership positions locally.

Whatever the reasons behind it, the systems that developed around these leaders generally involved two tendencies: one was corruption, a phenomenon that was common enough in Brezhnev's USSR but which reached outlandish proportions in Georgia under Mzhavanadze and in Central Asia. The other was the pursuit of a national agenda. This was displayed in a number of ways. Tacit or open support for academics, writers and artists to pursue national themes has already been discussed. Another area was in language policy, whether it be defending the official status of the national language, as Shevardnadze did only under pressure but leaders in the Baltic republics, Armenia and Azerbaijan did of their own volition, or quietly ensuring that education was implemented in a way which favoured the national language. But perhaps the clearest indication of an official national agenda was the way that architecture, city planning, and other elements of urban and national

[39] Tishkov, *Ethnicity, Nationalism and Conflict*, 44–5.

infrastructure reflected a national character. The small town of Yerevan was reconstructed as a republic capital in the 1920s according to a city plan and including new architectural styles that were declared the national Armenian style, as developed by the architect Alexander Tamanian. This process was taken further in the 1960s with the construction of further buildings and the inauguration of a monument commemorating the genocide in 1967, which was also the year in which the 2,750th anniversary of the city was celebrated. By the 1970s Yerevan resembled a national capital, with all the attendant infrastructure, and a distinctive national architectural style.[40]

While the transformation of Yerevan was the most dramatic, the process was repeated elsewhere, with distinctive and grand buildings springing up in all the republic capitals or, as was the case in Baku, older buildings dating from the oil boom years of the late nineteenth and early twentieth centuries being assigned to the use of Soviet political and cultural institutions. A glance at the Academy of Sciences buildings in each republic, many of which were built in the 1950s and 1960s, gives a clear indication of the differing national architectural styles which flourished in the centres of capital cities at a time when much of Soviet architecture was uniform and uninspiring. By the end of the Brezhnev era, each capital was home to at least one of each of the buildings typical of European capital cities – an opera house, a state theatre, national museum and so on, as well as Supreme Soviet and other government buildings. By 1984, while Russia boasted only two metro systems (Moscow and St Petersburg), metros had been opened in Kiev, Tbilisi, Kharkiv, Baku, Tashkent, Yerevan and Minsk – in that order, which also

[40] Taline Ter Minassian, *Erevan, la construction d'une capitale à l'époque soviétique* (Presses Universitaires de Rennes, 2007).

gives an indication of the relative importance of each republic in official eyes. As well as the physical infrastructure, each republic enjoyed a full set of its own artistic and academic institutions – an Academy of Sciences, a Union of Writers, a Union of Artists and so on. With the partial exception of Ukraine, where separate regional centres can be identified, these national infrastructural and institutional developments were concentrated in the capital cities, which also became the focus for road, rail and air communications.

In short, by the 1980s each republic was led by a national ruling elite, had a distinctive and flourishing national intelligentsia, both official and dissident, was teaching national history in schools (after 1960) and was centred on a capital city that held most of the characteristics and infrastructure of the capital of an independent European country. The extent to which this held true varied considerably between republics – Minsk, for example, was an increasingly russified city, while national development perhaps went furthest in the three South Caucasian republics. But, by the time of Gorbachev's *glasnost'*, in many respects the republics resembled modern nation-states.

THE PERSISTENCE OF NATIONAL LANGUAGE

For all that the leaderships in the republics adopted and promoted many of the attributes of nationhood, two pressures in particular worked on the populations of the republics so as to weaken their national identity. The first was demographic change. Rural inhabitants continued to move into cities which, in many areas away from the capitals, had a long-established Russian character. At the same time, Russians and other Slavs arrived in the non-Russian republics in several waves of state-sponsored migration, as they had in the 1930s, and transformed even rural areas into Russian-dominated

Table 10.1 *Proportion of titular nationality as percentage of total population of each republic, 1939–1989*

Republic	1939	1959	1989
RSFSR	83.4	83.3	81.5
Ukraine	73.5	76.8	72.7
Belorussia	82.9	81.1	77.9
Estonia	–	74.6	61.5
Latvia	–	62.0	52.0
Lithuania	–	79.3	79.6
Moldova	–	65.4	64.5
Georgia	61.4	64.3	70.1
Azerbaijan	58.4	67.5	82.7
Armenia	82.8	88.0	93.3
Kazakhstan	38.2	30.0	39.7
Uzbekistan	64.4	62.1	71.4
Kyrgyzstan	51.7	40.5	52.4
Tajikistan	59.6	53.1	62.3
Turkmenistan	59.2	60.9	72.0

Source: Robert J. Kaiser, *The Geography of Nationalism in Russia and the USSR* (Princeton University Press, 1994), 116, 174.

ones. This was especially the case in Kazakhstan, Estonia and Latvia, and less so in Georgia, Azerbaijan and Armenia, where there was actually an outmigration of ethnic Russians in the 1960s–1980s (see Table 10.1). The second pressure came from opportunities for social and geographical mobility, which rested on a command of Russian. The predominance of Russian in higher education in most republics (Azerbaijan was a notable exception) and the availability of senior party posts as well as technical and managerial roles only to Russian speakers provided a strong incentive for parents to send their children to Russian-language schools. It was this pressure that Khrushchev had hoped to capitalise on with his 1958 school reform. A further factor that might have been expected to encourage the disappearance of national languages, had Marxist theory on the question proved correct, was that by the late Soviet period social and economic differentiation, or variations in levels of development, between nationalities had all but disappeared.[41] These pressures probably played a bigger role in promoting russification than all of the official propaganda about the Soviet people and the hand-wringing in Moscow academic circles about the need to improve levels of command of the Russian language. If there was an official policy of russification, it was applied mostly in Ukraine and Belorussia, and even then only sporadically and inconsistently – the language used in advertisements on the Kiev metro changed four times in the 1970s and 1980s.[42]

With these pressures pitched against the natural desire to retain the mother tongue and the prevailing national atmosphere in the republics, there was no inevitability about linguistic russification. As already noted, the 1958 reform appears to have made little difference to the number of pupils receiving Russian-language instruction outside the RSFSR, and under the impact of nationalising policies an increasing number of Russians were actually attending local-language schools.[43] By the late Soviet period, city dwellers in Ukraine were much more likely to be studying at Russian-language schools than was the case in the countryside.[44] Although the teaching of Russian as a second language had been long-established in practice (and by law since 1938) the level to which it was actually

[41] Tishkov, *Ethnicity, Nationalism and Conflict*, 39.
[42] V. Alpatov, *150 iazykov i politika 1917–1997* (Moscow: Institut Vostokovedeniia RAN, 1997), 111.
[43] Harry Lipset, 'The Status of National Minority Languages in Soviet Education', *Soviet Studies*, 19, 2, 1967, 183–4, 188.
[44] Nigel Grant, 'Linguistic and Ethnic Minorities in the USSR: Educational Policies and Developments', in J. J. Tomiak (ed.), *Soviet Education in the 1980s* (London: Croom Helm, 1983), 28.

taught varied enormously. In many rural areas, recruitment of teachers qualified to teach Russian proved difficult. Anecdotal evidence suggests that particular problems persisted in teaching Russian in Central Asia – teachers of Russian sent to pedagogical institutes in Moscow and St Petersburg for training reportedly had a very poor command of the Russian language themselves. Hardly surprising, then, that school children in the Central Asian republics were leaving school with barely any working knowledge of Russian. The problems of teaching and learning Russian in non-Russian schools were admitted in a further school reform in 1984, but this was never fully implemented and had little impact.[45]

The evidence for native-language retention comes mostly from comparison of successive Soviet censuses. These censuses, which relied on responses given by Soviet citizens and, to some extent, the interpretation and recording of the census-takers, need to be treated with some caution. But, if anything, they might be expected to exaggerate knowledge of Russian. The censuses do indicate that, between 1959 and 1989, the number of respondents claiming fluency in the language indicated by their official nationality did in fact fall in all republics except Armenia and Azerbaijan. But in most cases this fall was by less than 1 percentage point. The exceptions were among Belorussians, where native language use fell by 13.3 percentage points over the thirty-year period, followed by Ukrainians (6.6 percentage points) and Moldovans (3.6 percentage points). Among all the major nationalities apart from Belorussians and Ukrainians, native-language retention ran at well over 90% in 1989 (see Table 10.2).

---

[45] Michael Kirkwood, '*Glasnost*', "the National Question" and Soviet Language Policy', *Soviet Studies* (1991), 43, 1, 67.

Table 10.2 *Language retention and russification of major Soviet nationalities in own republic, 1959–1989, percentage of titular nationality*

Republic	Republic language as first language		Russian as first language	
	1959	1989	1959	1989
RSFSR	99.8	99.8	99.8	99.8
Estonia	95.2	95.5	4.7	4.4
Latvia	95.1	94.8	4.6	5.0
Lithuania	97.8	97.7	1.2	1.8
Ukraine	87.7	81.1	12.2	18.8
Belorussia	84.2	70.9	15.3	28.5
Moldavia	95.2	91.6	3.6	7.4
Georgia	98.6	98.2	1.3	1.7
Azerbaijan	97.6	97.7	1.2	1.7
Armenia	89.9	91.7	8.3	7.6
Kazakhstan	98.4	97.0	1.2	2.2
Kyrgyzstan	98.7	97.8	0.3	0.6
Uzbekistan	98.4	98.3	0.5	0.7
Tajikistan	98.1	97.7	0.5	0.8
Turkmenistan	98.9	98.5	0.6	1.0
Bashkiria	61.9	72.3	2.6	11.2
Tatar	92.1	83.6	7.0	15.6
Buryatia	94.9	86.3	5.1	13.6
Kabardin	97.9	97.2	1.9	2.6
Balkaria	97.0	93.6	2.2	5.4
Karelia	71.3	47.8	28.5	51.8
Komi	89.3	70.4	10.5	29.5
Mari	95.1	80.8	4.6	18.8
Udmurtia	89.1	69.6	10.7	30.0
Chechenia	98.8	98.1	1.0	1.7
Ingushetia	97.9	96.9	1.9	2.8
Yakutia	97.5	93.8	2.4	6.1
Abkhazia	95.0	93.5	3.1	4.9

Source: Robert J. Kaiser, *The Geography of Nationalism in Russia and the USSR* (Princeton University Press, 1994), 266–8.

Table 10.3 *Knowledge of Russian and republic national language by republic, 1989*

Republic	Nationality	% in population of republic	% with knowledge of languages Russian	Republic main language
Armenia	Armenian	93	45	–
	Azerbaijani	3	19	7
	Kurd	2	7	75
	Russian	2	–	33
Azerbaijan	Azerbaijani	83	32	–
	Russian	6	–	15
	Armenian	6	69	7
	Lezgin	2	29	54
	Avar	1	9	70
Belorussia	Belorussian	78	80	–
	Russian	13	–	27
	Poles	4	82	67
Estonia	Estonian	62	35	–
	Russian	30	–	15
	Ukrainian	3	94	8
Georgia	Georgian	70	32	–
	Armenian	8	52	26
	Russian	6	–	24
	Azerbaijani	6	35	10
	Ossetian	3	39	54
	Greek	2	80	20
	Abkhaz	2	82	3
Kazakhstan	Kazakh	40	64	–
	Russian	38	–	9
	German	6	96	7
	Ukrainian	5	96	6
	Uzbek	2	55	10
	Tatar	2	92	7
Kyrgyzstan	Kyrgyz	52	37	–
	Russian	22	–	12
	Uzbek	13	39	4
	Ukrainian	3	94	2
	German	2	95	0.3
Latvia	Latvian	52	68	–
	Russian	34	–	22
	Belorussian	5	86	18

Table 10.3 (*cont.*)

Republic	Nationality	% in population of republic	% with knowledge of languages Russian	Republic main language
Lithuania	Lithuanian	80	38	–
	Russian	9	–	38
	Polish	7	67	21
	Belorussian	2	89	21
Moldavia	Moldavian	65	58	–
	Ukrainian	14	80	14
	Russian	13	–	12
	Gagauz	4	80	6
Tajikistan	Tajik	62	31	–
	Uzbek	24	22	17
	Russian	8	–	4
	Tatar	1	88	3
	Kyrgyz	1	19	13
Turkmenistan	Turkmen	72	28	–
	Russian	10	–	2
	Uzbek	9	29	16
	Kazakh	3	41	18
	Tatar	1	87	8
	Ukrainian	1	92	2
Ukraine	Ukrainian	73	72	–
	Russian	22	–	34
	Jewish	1	98	49
Uzbekistan	Uzbek	71	27	–
	Russian	8	–	5
	Tajik	5	18	42
	Kazakh	4	31	15
	Tatar	2	81	12
	Karakalpak	2	20	6

Source: Data from the 1989 Soviet census summarised in Valery Tishkov, *Ethnicity, Nationalism and Conflict in and after the Soviet Union: The Mind Aflame* (London: Sage, 1997), 90–1.
[*Note:* Tishkov argues that knowledge of Russian was most likely somewhat under-reported in all republics except those of Central Asia, where it was over-reported in the census, while mutual understanding among Turkic peoples of Central Asia was likely to have been under-reported].

Even successive Soviet efforts to improve the knowledge of Russian as a second language had failed. In 1989, only 32% of Georgians living in Georgia claimed knowledge of Russian, 31% of Tajiks in Tajikistan, 28% of Turkmen in Turkmenistan and 27% of Uzbeks in Uzbekistan. At the other end of the scale, 64% of Kazakhs in Kazakhstan, 72% of Ukrainians in Ukraine and 80% of Belorussians in Belorussia claimed at least some knowledge of Russian (see Table 10.3).

In most cases knowledge of Russian as a second language had advanced considerably over the previous thirty years, but comparison of the census data of 1970, 1979 and 1989 suggests that the process was slowing down by the 1980s.[46] Linguistic and cultural russification was considerably higher among non-Russians living outside their home republics, although even then Uzbeks and Kazakhs living outside their republics (most of them in other Central Asian republics, but including many living in Russia) showed low levels of command of Russian. Only in Ukraine and Belorussia was Russian making significant inroads in the late Soviet period. Overall, if there was a conflict between a russifying programme sponsored by the Soviet centre and a nationalising programme sponsored by the republics, it was clearly the republics that were winning out.

ECONOMIC AND DEMOGRAPHIC DEVELOPMENT

In 1921, Leon Trotsky proclaimed that the Soviets would pursue a regional investment policy which favoured the less-developed, and especially the underdeveloped non-Russian, regions of the USSR. This policy of evening out differences was enshrined in the 1961

[46] Kaiser, *Geography of Nationalism*, 289.

CPSU Party Programme, and in 1972, at the time of the fiftieth anniversary of the creation of the USSR, Brezhnev claimed that the aim of equalisation across the Soviet Union had already been achieved. But the evidence appeared to go against this: although the non-Russian republics benefitted from rapid economic growth throughout the post-war period, far from catching up with the RSFSR in developmental terms, they were seeing the gap grow on most indicators. Between 1959 and 1967, most state capital investment was concentrated in the Northwest of the USSR, Siberia and the Far East. Only the Baltic republics, Ukraine and Kazakhstan enjoyed more than the USSR average rate of investment. In other words, economic investment was focussed primarily on those areas where industry was already most developed, or on special priority areas like Siberia.[47] Nothing was being done to overcome the legacy of the 1930s when many non-Russian areas, notably Central Asia, were devoted to the production of raw materials. The continuous focus on defence needs was one reason for concentrating industry in central areas, but the republics had not helped their cause with their response when they had been granted more economic responsibility under the *sovnarkhoz* reform. For all the power and influence republic leaders were able to wield locally, this is one illustration of their powerlessness when it came to lobbying the central authorities. Some republics, notably Georgia, had standards of living and income higher than these official figures suggest largely because of unrecorded black market activity. But the failure to attract investment from the official planning system was a serious setback for all of these economies.

[47] Robert A. Lewis, Richard H. Rowland and Ralph S. Clem, *Nationality and Population Change in Russia and the USSR: An Evaluation of Census Data, 1897–1970* (New York: Praeger Publishers, 1976), 116–22.

The rapid growth of Central Asia's population caused panic among certain ethnologists who looked ahead with trepidation to the day when the Muslim population would outnumber the Slavic population of the USSR. Russian nationalists and some political leaders also took note of these trends and urged serious policy initiatives to stem them. Western observers predicted massive out-migration from Central Asia to European Russia, leading to 'ethnic mixing and [its] attendant problems',[48] while the first predictions of the demise of the USSR were based on this population pressure.[49] As it turned out, ethnic conflict and a break-up of the federal structure did ensue, but for altogether different reasons.

AUTONOMOUS REPUBLICS AND REGIONS

The autonomous republics were the scenes of the worst ethnic tensions, especially in the North Caucasus, but also in Yakutia, where an influx of Russians made abuse and brawling an everyday occurrence, and where troops had to be called in on one occasion in 1979 to quell ethnic rioting.[50] The autonomous republics and regions of the RSFSR were unable to pursue the same nationalising policies as the union republics for a number of reasons. First, there was an entirely different demographic structure. By 1959, the titular nationality was already a minority or only a bare majority in almost all autonomous units of the RSFSR (the exceptions were Chuvashia, Tuvinia and multi-ethnic Dagestan), and this did not change much over the next twenty years.[51] Second, while there were

---

[48] *Ibid.*, 381.
[49] Hélène Carrère d'Encausse, *L'empire éclaté* (Paris: Flammarion, 1978).
[50] Forsyth, *A History of the Peoples of Siberia*, 381.
[51] Kaiser, *Geography of Nationalism*, 174–5. The exception was the Chechen–Ingush republic, where the chechen and Ingush share of the population rose in this period from 41.1% to 64.6% as a result of the return of deportees.

cases of longevity in office to rival those of the union republics (Timbora Mal'bakhov held the post of First Secretary in the Kabardino-Balkar regional committee of the CPSU from 1957 to 1985), as a rule turnover was much more frequent.[52] In any case, these were leaders of regional branches of the CPSU and did not have their own separate Party organisations beneath them, and were subject to far closer supervision from the centre. Although separate national cultures did flourish within the RSFSR, the autonomous republics and regions did not have the cultural or economic tools, needed for nation-building, which were available in the larger republics.

Language development took an altogether different direction in the RSFSR. Apart from in the Tatar and Bashkir republics, Russian was the language of instruction after the first couple of grades. While most non-Russians still claimed their national language as their first language, in many cases the numbers dropped considerably over the Brezhnev period, while the numbers claiming Russian as a first language rose correspondingly. By 1979, in contrast to the union republics, the vast majority of nationals in the RSFSR claimed either Russian as a first language or fluency in Russian as a second language.[53]

The contrast between the headway made by linguistic russification in the RSFSR contrasted starkly with the lack of progress in the union republics. The Brezhnev leadership's unwillingness to engage in struggle with the peripheries at a time when stability was the main keyword was one reason for the steady growth of national cultures and institutions. The attitude of the republican leaders, the free hand they were given and the length of time they were afforded to

---

[52] Goryachev, *Tsentral'nyi Komitet KPSS*, 472–8.
[53] Grant, 'Linguistic and Ethnic Minorities in the USSR Developments', 44; Kaiser, *Geography of Nationalism*, 266–7, 290–2.

pursue national projects were more important. In spite of the restrictive nature of the Brezhnev regime and the ever-growing intrusiveness of the KGB, the population was very aware of developments in Eastern Europe, in the developing world (where nationalist forces were celebrated in official propaganda and received material support) and in Europe. The activities of dissidents and the growing incursion of a discourse of rights encouraged the national populations to absorb the national messages of leaders and cultural producers, and to exert pressure on them to go further in that direction. Nations singularly failed to wither away or merge, and the idea of a universal *Homo sovieticus* was a stillborn one. In the Brezhnev years, the national republics developed sufficient national characteristics both to make them a focus of turmoil in the Gorbachev years and to allow them to emerge from the rubble of the USSR as ready-made nation-states.

CHAPTER ELEVEN

From reform to dissolution, 1982–1991

Speaking on the sixtieth anniversary of the creation of the USSR in 1982, Yuri Andropov affirmed the Soviet state's commitment to the economic and social equalisation of the different nationalities of the USSR. He had nothing to say about any putative 'drawing together' or 'merger' of nations. Effectively, he was confirming in rhetoric the situation that already existed in practice, and committed the regime to completing the process of equalisation through quota systems in higher education and other forms of affirmative action.[1] Such policies were typical of Andropov's cautious approach to reform, a need for which he clearly recognised, but nationality relations were not at the top of his agenda. His successor as general secretary, Konstantin Chernenko, was an avowed supporter of the increasing use of the Russian language in national schools, but his efforts to make changes in this direction met with the same fate as those of his predecessors.[2] Little affected the nationalities experience, then, during the short reigns of these two heirs of Brezhnev. But the situation was to develop in an entirely new direction not long after Chernenko's death, and the appointment as general secretary of the CC of the CPSU of a young leader who, until recently, had been working in the Russian provinces.

---

[1] Jones and Grupp, 'Modernisation and Ethnic Equalisation in the USSR', 159–60.
[2] Nahaylo and Swoboda, *Soviet Disunion*, 221–30.

MIKHAIL GORBACHEV

Assessments of the Soviet Union's seventh and final leader Mikhail Gorbachev have yet to move towards any consensus, not least because he recorded what most commentators regarded as his greatest achievement – the end of state communism in Europe – as a result of a series of misjudgements and errors. More specifically, it is still not entirely clear whether or not he came to the Kremlin as general secretary with a clear agenda for far-reaching reform, or if this is a path he took in response to particular circumstances and on an *ad hoc* basis. On 10 March 1985, the day before his appointment as general secretary of the CPSU, he reportedly told his wife Raisa that 'life demands action, and has done so for a long time'.[3] On the other hand, early attempts at change were mostly tentative and rested on the administrative methods that were typical of Soviet leaders. On the national question Gorbachev appeared, in retrospect, hopelessly utopian: the national question was, in his opinion, solved in the USSR and the nations of the Soviet Union constituted 'a single family – the Soviet people'. At the time, however, such an assessment may not have been as naïve as it now seems. Most of the Soviet republics had been led by the same man for some years, and these leaders, as described in Chapter 10, had created a stable cultural base for the republics. Ethnic tensions were mostly limited to rivalry at sporting events, taunts and sometimes brawls erupting at mixed schools, in bars or just in queues.[4]

There are signs that Gorbachev not only failed to understand the nature and potential for nationalism, but he also seriously misjudged the mood and position of the people who had most influence

[3] Dmitri Volkogonov, *The Rise and Fall of the Soviet Empire: Political Leaders from Lenin to Gorbachev* (London: HarperCollins, 1999), 445.
[4] Rasma Karklins, *Ethnic Relations in the USSR* (London: HarperCollins, 1986), 68–71.

in the implementation of nationality policy – the leaders of the Soviet republics. On a trip to Ukraine shortly after becoming general secretary, Gorbachev criticised the performance of key Ukrainian industries and agriculture in front of the republic's leaders. In his memoirs, Gorbachev refers to the 'detailed but tedious accounts ... "from the provinces"' delivered by Kunaev and Shcherbitsky at the XXVII Congress of the CPSU in February 1986. At the same Congress, he openly put down Eduard Shevardnadze, already a Politburo member, for his fawning attitude.[5] Reflecting later on the problems in Ukraine, Gorbachev came to the conclusion that he was then 'under the illusion that we could successfully solve new problems and produce radical reforms while keeping the same leaders', and realised too late that this generation had 'exhausted their potential'.[6] Gorbachev's continuing belief that the obstructiveness of individual leaders in the republics was what thwarted his programmes there was typical of a Soviet bureaucrat. Though not without some truth, this analysis failed to take account of the dynamic between leaders and citizens that had established nationalism as a deep-rooted factor in the republics. Clumsily displaying his own contempt for these leaders offended not just them personally, but also the nations they represented.

In fact, in terms of age that generation of republican leaders was only slightly older than Gorbachev's own (Shevardnadze was the youngest, and only four years older than Gorbachev). But that small age difference had given them a greater taste of politics in the late Stalin years and, more significantly, the experience in the republics was very different from that of Moscow-based or Russian regional party officials. Gorbachev's generation of bureaucrats and politicians had been affected by both the Great Patriotic

[5] Mikhail Gorbachev, *Memoirs* (London: Doubleday, 1995), 176, 187.   [6] *Ibid.*, 177.

War in their childhood and by Khrushchev's thaw in their early political career. For these reasons it was more reform-oriented than the Brezhnev generation.[7] But the republic leaders had reached the pinnacle in their republics at an early age, and had built up around them elaborate networks, cultural systems and infrastructures that were less familiar in central Russia. In Gorbachev's world, the Communist Party was divided between reformers and conservatives, and he failed to account for the ability of republican leaders to act as national leaders. The apparent calm in the USSR when it came to the national question was the product of a system that rested on national structures, not because the national question had become obsolete.

RIOTS IN YAKUTIA AND ALMATY

What Gorbachev did recognise was that corruption was, if anything, worse in the national republics than at the centre, and it was in tackling this issue that he first became aware of the potential for national mobilisation. In May 1986, fighting broke out between Sakha (Yakut) students and local Russians in Yakutsk, the capital of the Autonomous Republic of Yakutia. Police intervention appeared to favour the Russians, and led to serious injuries to several Sakha young women. Three days of demonstrations followed, which began to raise national issues alongside demands to tackle corruption and other reform agendas that the Sakha demonstrators

---

[7] While most earlier accounts portrayed lower-level and regional party bureaucrats as conservative opponents of Gorbachev's reforms, Jerry Hough's more detailed study highlights the reformist inclinations of Gorbachev's contemporaries, including leading regional figures: Jerry F. Hough, *Democratization and Revolution in the USSR, 1985–1991* (Washington, DC: Brookings Institution Press, 1997), 55–60. The question of whether attitudes to reform in the *perestroika* period were more likely to be influenced by personal biography or by position within the system has yet to be properly investigated.

believed Gorbachev had promised but failed to deliver in their republic. The response of local authorities was to punish demonstrators and increase the number of Slavic students at the university, while failing to take any measures against the Russian perpetrators of the original violence.[8] In December of the same year, after coming under attack from his own colleagues in the Central Committee of the Communist Party of Kazakhstan, Dinmukhamed Kunaev was removed as First Secretary, bringing to an end twenty-six years of his political dominance in Kazakhstan. There is no reason to suppose that Gorbachev was using Kazakhstan as a testing ground for taking on entrenched national interests in the republics – his aim was to tackle corruption and, to some extent, Brezhnevite inertia, and he was egged on by rival political factions in Kazakhstan. But the removal of Kunaev – exacerbated by replacing him with a Russian from outside the republic, Gennadi Kolbin – unleashed both the rival, clan-based factions and popular national feeling in Kazakhstan. Personal supporters of Kunaev may have been responsible for organising the days of rioting in Almaty that followed, but there is no doubt that interference in a republic which had grown accustomed to going its own way, and imposing an outsider as leader, struck against the national basis on which the Soviet republics were by then constructed.[9] Possibly hundreds of rioters were killed in Almaty, and the experience there and in Yakutsk led Gorbachev to take greater care with his cadres policies after that. He continued, however, to

---

[8] Marjorie Mandelstam Balzer and Uliana Alekseevna Vinokurova, 'Nationalism, Interethnic Relations and Federalism: The Case of the Sakha Republic (Yakutia)', *Europe-Asia Studies*, 48 (1996), 108.

[9] Martha Brill Olcott, 'Kazakhstan: Pushing for Eurasia', in Ian Bremmer and Ray Taras (eds.), *New States, New Politics: Building the Post-Soviet Nations* (Cambridge University Press, 1997), 552.

view the difficulties in the national republics as stemming princi-
pally from corruption and entrenched interests.

ENVIRONMENTAL MOVEMENTS IN THE REPUBLICS

The Communist Party leaders in the republics had, in effect, put
themselves at the head of the nation long before Gorbachev came to
power. As Gorbachev loosened controls on the expression of oppo-
sitional ideas, initially it was difficult to oppose national interests to
Soviet power since the two were so closely intertwined in the Soviet
system. Opponents of communism could not instinctively turn
towards nationalism, since within the framework of the federal
union republics the national agenda was already taken in hand by
the local leaderships and cultural institutions. Instead, and perhaps
surprisingly, it was around environmental concerns that opposition
groups first crystallised. In the Baltic states, long-standing environmental grievances – construction of a new hydroelectric dam and
pollution from a phosphates plant – attracted protest. Pollution in
Lake Sevan in Armenia and the gradual disappearance of the Aral
Sea in Central Asia also served as focal points for local activists.
There are a number of reasons why the environment may have
attracted particular attention on the peripheries of the Soviet Union.
By deliberate design, much of the more polluting industry, and
some of the grander projects such as the diversion of Central Asia's
rivers, had been located in the republics and away from central
Russia. Nature and landscape featured heavily in the national
cultures of a number of republics which flourished from the 1950s
onwards, in part because the physical landscape was a politically
safer repository for national affection than were national heroes.
The fact that these were local issues, which may have affected large
areas of particular republics but did not cross republic borders, was

another reason that they attracted nationalists rather than environmentalists or, rather, there was little distinction between the two.

Protest over the environment was in part inspired by the rise of the environmental movement in the West, and its initiators were genuinely concerned by the damage that Soviet policies had caused to the natural environment and that directly impacted on local conditions of life. But there was an added attraction in that such movements as a form of protest both avoided the ideological quagmire left by the Soviet regime's appropriation of the language of class struggle,[10] and allowed for protest against local leaders who might clamp down harder on expressions of nationalism that were not sanctioned by themselves. In any case, environmental groups, often having their origins in single-issue campaigns, quickly became a focus for broader protests that gradually acquired a national form.[11] The role of the republics' communist leaders in these early movements can be seen, in retrospect, to have been indicative of the dynamic that the national movement was to assume under *glasnost'*. In some cases, spontaneous and somewhat subversive grass-roots movements were adopted by republican leaders in order to exert pressure on the Moscow authorities. This official support, which may have been intended as a short-term tactic in which the movements were used as pawns in a broader political game, provided the encouragement which allowed the movements to flourish and to adopt broader and increasingly radical demands. This in turn forced leaders to choose between turning against a wave which they had

[10] Suny, *Revenge of the Past*, 125–6.
[11] Geoffrey Hosking, 'The Beginnings of Independent Political Activity', in Geoffrey Hosking, Jonathan Aves and Peter Duncan (eds.), *The Road to Post-Communism: Independent Political Movements in the Soviet Union 1985–1991* (London: Pinter, 1992), 1–28.

initially endorsed but which had gotten out of hand, or of riding along atop that wave. More often than not, they chose the latter.

A prime example of the way an environmental movement developed into a national one, and how republican authorities reacted, is found in Lithuania. From the late 1970s, Lithuanian scientists unobtrusively opposed plans to build the Soviet Union's largest nuclear power station at Ignalina. They achieved some success in having the plans for the size of the plant scaled down. In 1985 the Soviet government revealed plans to drill for oil off the Baltic coast, which would have damaged the popular resort near Neda. At this stage, the same scientists joined forces with cultural figures in opposition to both projects on environmental grounds. As Lithuania was slow to respond to the policy of *glasnost'*, no public appeal was made until 1988, but in late 1987 an independent environmental association, the Žemyna Club, was formed, and obtained recognition from two key official organisations, the Lithuanian Komsomol and the Lithuanian Academy of Sciences. At the club's founding congress in February 1988, discussion moved from environmental issues to complaints about the Soviet centre's colonial treatment of Lithuania.

The Lithuanian Communist Party initially sought to stifle the organisation, but was weakened in its opposition by the alternative stance taken by two of its supposedly subordinate bodies, the Komsomol and the Academy of Sciences. When the Communist Party tried to defuse the situation by holding open meetings and seeking to portray itself as a supporter of efforts to minimise the environmental impact of Ignalina, they only managed to spur on the increasingly nationalistic tone of the open forums organised by the Žemyna Club. Responding to this popular side, the Lithuanian Communist Party threw itself fully behind the environmentalists in May 1988. The Žemyna Club escalated attempts to clearly link the

environmental and national causes, referring to the threat of genocide and assaults on Lithuanian national identity. In June, the
Lithuanian Movement for Perestroika was founded on the initiative
of the head of the Žemyna Club, Zigmas Vaišvila. It soon became
known as Sajudis, and was the Lithuanian version of the popular
fronts that were springing up elsewhere. Sajudis took over the
Ignalina issue as one of its key campaigns, and some of the largest
nationalist demonstrations it organised in 1988 focussed specifically
on environmental issues.[12]

Environmental issues were also used by the Soviet leadership to
undermine the position of local leaders. This was the case in
Armenia when an article attacking the Armenian leadership over
its handling of pollutants from chemical plants in Yerevan appeared
in the Soviet journal *Literaturnaya gazeta* in July 1987. The article
appeared to have been centrally sanctioned, and went beyond the
immediate environmental issues to a broad attack on corruption in
the Armenian Communist Party.[13] This encouraged large-scale
demonstrations over the issue, as well as over the pollution of
Lake Sevan, in September and October. In this case, too, the
movement developed its own momentum and adopted an increasingly patriotic tone, raising demands over national rights.[14]

While these movements arose around long-standing but relatively little-known issues (apart from the drying up of the Aral Sea,
which was so dramatic that it was evident from satellite pictures),
two major catastrophes had substantial impacts on the Soviet Union
and internationally, and also on national consciousness in the

---

[12] Jane I. Dawson, *Eco-Nationalism: Anti-Nuclear Activism and National Identity in Russia, Lithuania, and Ukraine* (Durham, NC: Duke University Press, 1996), 34–61.

[13] Pierre Verluise, *Armenia in Crisis: The 1988 Earthquake* (Detroit: Wayne State University Press, 1995), 84–5.

[14] Suny, *Looking toward Ararat*, 196.

regions they affected. The explosion of a reactor core at the Chernobyl nuclear power plant in Ukraine on 26 April 1986 was one of the major factors that prompted Gorbachev to turn his policy of *glasnost'* (or openness) from rhetoric into words, so obvious was it that the culture of secrecy had made the impact of the disaster worse than it needed to be. It also had a devastating impact not just in Ukraine, where the accident took place, but across a wide area affected by radioactive fall-out which travelled as far north as Scandinavia. The fact that only the westernmost parts of the RSFSR were affected was an accident of geography and meteorology. While the Baltic republics and Ukraine were affected, the worst of the impact was felt in Belorussia, where the scars can be felt to this day. All the indicators are that, as at the time of the revolution and in the 1920s, Belorussia displayed the least developed sense of national identity of any of the Soviet republics in the 1980s.[15] The Chernobyl disaster dramatically increased levels of nationalist activism in the republic, however.

Protest movements spawned by Chernobyl were further boosted in the summer of 1988 by the discovery of mass graves of victims of Stalin's Terror in Kuropaty Woods near Minsk. In spite of its weak precedents, the Belorussian national movement was able to organise before those of the Baltic republics. The first informal groups arose in the spring of 1987, and by the end of the year thirty such groups came together to form a consolidated national movement. By the time of the Belorussian election campaign of February 1990, nationalists were able to mobilise demonstrations of more than 100,000 people. In the case of Belorussia, the republican authorities did show signs of capitulating to some of the national demands, for example

---

[15] As indicated, for example, by relatively lower rates of language retention and higher rates of intermarriage; see Chapter 10.

by taking measures to restore the declining fortunes of the Belorussian language, but for the most part they pursued a policy of repression against the national movement rather than giving it encouragement as happened elsewhere. This appears to account for the relative weakness of the Belorussian national movement in 1991 and the continuing opposition of the republic's leaders to the break-up of the Soviet Union until after the failed August 1991 coup.[16]

The other major catastrophe was the Armenian earthquake of December 1988. Coming at the height of nationalist protest across the Soviet Union, in the short term its impact was to reduce levels of mass nationalist activity, not only in Armenia but also across the USSR as protestors observed a period of respect for Armenia's dead. It had two longer-term impacts, however. First, it internationalised the Armenian national movement as relief efforts drew heavily on the support offered by the Armenia diaspora in Europe, North America and elsewhere, which also gave the diaspora the opportunity to become involved in the politics of the national movement. Secondly, although the earthquake itself could not be blamed on the Soviet authorities in the way the Chernobyl disaster could, the weakness of buildings and other structures exposed by the earthquake and contributing to the death toll were partly due to features of the Soviet planning system, and the response from the Soviet Union was slow and weak, as it had been after Chernobyl. This increased the resolve of many Armenians that they could manage their own affairs better if separated from the USSR, a lesson which was also taken on board by other republics.[17]

[16] Mark R. Beissinger, *Nationalist Mobilization and the Collapse of the Soviet State* (Cambridge University Press, 2002), 252–7.
[17] Suny, *Looking toward Ararat*, 210–17.

TERRITORIAL DISPUTES

In the Baltic republics, the environmental movement developed into a full-scale independence movement, but before then in Armenia the national movement took a different direction. The question of the status of Nagorno Karabakh had reappeared in Armenia in the Brezhnev years, becoming the central question raised by Armenian intellectuals and at the core of disputes between Armenian and Azerbaijani historians and archaeologists (see Chapter 10). The demand for the transfer of the territory to the Armenian republic became the key question for the burgeoning national movement in the second half of 1987, and appeared to have the backing of powerful figures including Anastas Mikoyan's son Sergei, and Gorbachev's chief economic adviser Abel Aganbegyan. A demonstration in the Karabakh village of Chardakhly was attacked towards the end of the year, which gave further fuel to the unification movement. In the strongest display of nationalism yet, up to a quarter of a million people demonstrated in Yerevan in February 1988, while the Karabakh regional soviet adopted a resolution and obtained 80,000 signatures on a petition demanding unification with Armenia. This was an autonomous political movement that succeeded in uniting Armenians in Karabakh, Armenia and Russia, and which was able to make use of official Soviet structures for the first time without authorisation from above.[18]

Two days after the Karabakh Soviet resolution, the backlash began in the towns of Hadrut and Askeran, where Azerbaijanis from nearby Aghdam arrived to 'restore order'. Two of the Azerbaijanis were killed by police tasked with dealing with the disorder. Six days later, on 28 February 1988, violence broke out in Sumgait, near

---

[18] Cheterian, *War and Peace*, 94.

Baku – a city built in the 1940s and with a mixed Azerbaijani and Armenian population which was already suffering from the economic crisis that was beginning to develop in the Soviet Union, leading to high unemployment and a shortage of housing. It is unclear whether the slaughter of Armenians was carried out by locals or recent Azerbaijani refugees from Armenia, and whether or not these events had the backing of the Soviet KGB or army.[19] In any event, over the course of three days, gangs of Azerbaijanis broke into Armenian apartments, hauled Armenians off buses and out of public places, systematically raped and killed them and set fire to property. Officially, there were thirty-two victims of the massacre – twenty-six Armenian and six Azerbaijani – but unofficial Armenian estimates range as high as 450.[20]

The Sumgait massacre raised the heat in both Armenia and Azerbaijan, where the question of Karabakh's status became the main issue for the national movement. In Azerbaijan, in spite of the academic disputes of the 1960s and 1970s, this was a new development, as most of the public attention had been focussed by nationalists on the Azerbaijani population across the border in Iran. The Sumgait events shocked most Azerbaijanis, but by November 1988 anti-Armenian feeling had risen sufficiently to fuel mass demonstrations in the capital Baku and elsewhere. In March 1989 the Azerbaijani Popular Front was formed and concerned itself mostly with protests over Karabakh, organizing blockades of goods and fuel between the two republics. In November 1989 more attacks on Armenians took place in Kirovabad, another industrial city in Azerbaijan. By that time, Armenians were fleeing from Azerbaijan

---

[19] For a discussion of conflicting accounts of the Sumgait massacre, see Cheterian, *War and Peace*, 101–9.

[20] Thomas de Waal, *Black Garden: Armenia and Azerbaijan through Peace and War* (New York University Press, 2004), 32–41.

and Azerbaijanis were moving in the other direction. Although most of the Armenian population of Baku had left, after a series of demonstrations there on 14 January 1990 a radical group moved to the Armenian quarter and carried out a massacre among those that were left. Those that survived were airlifted out shortly after.

In connection with these events, there had been a complete breakdown of law and order in Baku, which was virtually controlled by the Popular Front. In response, a Red Army force of around 26,000 troops entered the city on the night of 19–20 January, destroying barricades and clashing with Azerbaijanis, more than 120 of whom were killed.[21] 'Black Sunday', as it became known in Azerbaijan, was by far the most large-scale Soviet operation in response to ethnic conflict, and it was followed by Karabakh itself being put under virtual occupation.

In Georgia's autonomous territories of Abkhazia and South Ossetia, separatism developed more slowly and with less violence. Fifty-eight leading members of the Abkhaz Communist Party signed a letter demanding secession from Georgia in June 1988, and the following March the first mass meetings took place to support this demand. As in Azerbaijan, it was the reaction of the Georgian national movement that led to an escalation in the situation. Demonstrations opposing the Abkhaz demands were held in Tbilisi, peaking at 100,000 people on 8 April 1989. The demonstrations were not sanctioned by the Georgian Communist Party, and the next day its leader Jumbar Patiashvili called in the Red Army, which attacked the demonstrations, leaving nineteen dead. In this case it was the intervention of Soviet armed forces against peaceful demonstrators, rather than inter-ethnic clashes, that

---

[21] According to the independent commission 'Shield': Altstadt, *The Azerbaijani Turks*, 213–16.

escalated the violence. The immediate effect was not so much to inflame Georgian–Abkhaz hostilities as to cement the determination of the Georgian national movement to secure independence, an aspiration that now had overwhelming support in the republic.

Different factors were at work when conflict between Uzbeks and Kyrgyz broke out in the summer of 1990 in the Osh region of Kyrgyzstan. Although the request for regional autonomy or even a redrawing of the border between Kyrgyzstan and Uzbekistan was raised by the regional Uzbek movement Adalat, formed in 1990, the violence had more to do with purely local factors.[22] Osh was a highly industrialised region and had been badly hit by the economic crisis affecting the Soviet Union. High unemployment and lack of available housing space are classic ingredients of conflict in ethnically mixed areas. Outside the towns, rivalry over land, then in short supply, fuelled competition between ethnic groups. In the region as a whole, Kyrgyz comprised 60% of the population, Uzbeks 26%, and Russians 6% of the population. But more Uzbeks lived in the cities, and they heavily outnumbered Kyrgyz in Osh city by 46% to 24%, with Russians making up a further 20%, while Uzbeks were in a majority in a number of other towns. Corruption and administrative incompetence also contributed to tensions, and the situation across the republic was exacerbated by the growing nationalist tendency of its Kyrgyz leaders, who upset a delicate balance in the allocation of senior jobs between members of the three ethnic groups which had been in place for decades. Ethnic violence erupted in Osh city on 4 June 1990 and spread to other cities and villages the following day. By 10 June at least 120 Uzbeks, 50 Kyrgyz and 1 Russian had died in the clashes.[23]

---

[22] Glenn E. Curtis, 'Kyrgyzstan: A Country Study', in Lydia M. Buyers (ed.), *Central Asia in Focus: Political and Economic Issues* (Hauppauge, NY: Nova Science Publishers, 2003), 120.

[23] Tishkov, *Ethnicity, Nationalism and Conflict*, 136–7.

In the Osh conflict, Uzbeks conducted most of the violence in the towns but Kyrgyz retaliated in force in the surrounding countryside as news spread. While republican leaders were not involved in the direct sense that they were in Armenia, Azerbaijan or Georgia, the growing assertiveness of the Kyrgyz leadership had contributed to the developing crisis. The sudden eruption of violence here, in the absence of long-standing territorial or political disputes, can be attributed to rapid economic decline. What all of the ethnic conflicts of the late 1980s and early 1990s had in common was the manipulation of the national situation by local and republican elites, which probably was not intended to lead to the sort of violence that emerged in Sumgait, Baku and Osh, but resulted from the national movement developing its own momentum. In all cases the situation was fuelled by growing economic decline leading to greater competition for jobs, housing, land and other resources, exacerbated by an influx of refugees in the case of Azerbaijan. The dynamic of nationalist development – involving elite manipulation, economic decline, indifference or incompetence in the response of the authorities, and a weakening of central power leading to a growing feeling that difficulties needed to be dealt with locally – was not so very different from that of the other republics, but in these cases it took a confrontational, violent course. A crucial difference that should also be recognised is that in each of these cases the competing ethnic groups did not include Russians, as was the case in the Baltic republics and other places where the national movements took on a more peaceful character.

POPULAR FRONTS

Gorbachev's policy of *glasnost'* took a leap forward in the summer of 1988 when he announced that some of the members of a new

Congress of People's Deputies were to be elected in open, compet-
itive elections. The message was unmistakeable and was seized on
by activists as a signal that they could organise with impunity. The
movements that had been developing around environmental issues
in Estonia, Latvia and Lithuania now led to the creation of national
parties or coalitions. The Estonian Popular Front and the Latvian
Popular Front were created not long after Sajudis in Lithuania.
These organizations grew rapidly, membership was open to all, and
many communists joined their ranks. Demonstrations thousands
strong became commonplace in all of the major cities of the Baltic
republics. The focus of many continued to be on the environment,
but protests against communist rule and against individual leaders
were common. As the economy declined, further protests erupted,
but strikes over wages and other conditions were more widespread
than actions over other issues. Although strikes in support of
political demands became frequent, generally a separation was
drawn between economic grievances and national ones. At demonstrations, nationalist demands did not generally accompany economic ones, although those voicing ethno-national desires
frequently also called for liberal reforms.[24] Following the Baltic
example, popular fronts formed in all of the union republics and
several autonomous republics in the second half of 1988. In August
representatives from all over the Soviet Union met in Yalta and
Leningrad to co-ordinate the work of popular fronts.[25]

[24] Beissinger, *Nationalist Mobilization*, 76–9. Beissinger reaches this conclusion by quantify-
ing demonstrations raising ethno-nationalist, liberalising and economic demands, and
combinations of two of these three. While some queries can be made regarding the
distinction, the conclusion is clear enough. Beissinger does point out that in Belorussia,
northern Kazakhstan, eastern Ukraine and western Siberia, economic protest was more
frequent than ethno-nationalist protest, in contrast to the remaining non-Russian regions
of the USSR.

[25] *Ibid.*, pp. 83–5.

There were more demonstrations in 1988 than in any other year, but the highpoint of this participatory movement came in August 1989, on the occasion of the fiftieth anniversary of the Molotov–Ribbentrop Pact which had sealed the future of the three Baltic states as part of the Soviet Union. Activists had spent most of the preceding month mobilising people for the event. On the day of the anniversary, more than a million people linked hands, forming a human chain from the eastern border of Estonia, crossing Estonia, Latvia and Lithuania and ending up at the western border of Lithuania.

The August 1989 demonstration came on the back of a euphoric triumph in the elections to the Congress of People's Deputies, which were held in March. In Latvia and Lithuania the heads of government were among the long lists of senior people within the existing regime in each republic who were heavily defeated at the polls. The mayor of Kiev also lost in his constituency, but the elections were still quite closely controlled in the South Caucasus and Central Asia and, away from the Russian cities of Moscow and Leningrad, it was in the Baltic republics that the most spectacular results occurred.

The elections did have the effect of taking the steam out of popular demonstrations. Aside from the August demonstration, levels of participation and numbers of demonstrations dropped. The popular fronts stepped down from their focus on street demonstrations as the new conditions meant that they could now take their opposition into the legal channels of elections and participation in legislative bodies. The electoral process itself led to a greater level of organisation among nationalists, and successes emboldened the popular fronts. From the time of the March 1989 elections, demands for secession spread from a vocal but small minority to large sections of non-Russians, notably in the Baltic republics, but to some extent in every one of the union republics. In Estonia, 'Citizens' Committees' began to register the names of citizens of independent Estonia between the wars and their descendants, laying the basis for citizenship claims of a future independent state.[26] This was one manifestation of how powerful the discourse of occupation was for the Baltic republics, moving their populations towards the demand for outright independence more quickly than elsewhere. The Estonian, Latvian and Lithuanian popular fronts were all calling openly for secession by August 1989. By the end of the year, all three Supreme Soviets had declared the secret protocols of the 1939 Molotov–Ribbentrop Pact illegal, laying the legal basis for independence.

In all three republics steps were also taken in the course of 1989 to introduce economic changes locally which went beyond Gorbachev's official programme. To some extent these local reforms appealed to nationalists by harking back to pre-war economic structures, but they also built on the real advantages the Baltic economies had over the Soviet average. The economic advantages of secession also had some appeal to the substantial ethnic Russian populations of the Baltic republics. Russian-dominated counter-movements to the popular fronts, the *Interdvizhenii*, were formed in late 1988, but had limited success in mobilising against secession, while there was even active support for independence among a significant number of ethnic Russians.[27]

In the Baltic republics, then, with Georgia not far behind, the mood for independence was growing. But given the limited military resources at their disposal and the unwillingness of the international community to commit itself in what was still an internal affair, it

[26] David J. Smith, *Estonia*, p. 48.
[27] Graham Smith, 'The Resurgence of Nationalism', in Smith (ed.), *The Baltic States*, 129–36.

took a further breakdown of authority at the centre for the aims of the popular fronts to be realised.

THE ROLE OF RUSSIA

It seems perverse to conclude that the republic that perhaps had most to do with the break-up of the USSR was the one that stood at its centre – the RSFSR or, as it now became known, the Russian Federation. Some Russian nationalists, among them Alexander Solzhenitsyn, did conclude that Russian interests were best served by separating Russian territory from the other republics. But for most Russians, the Soviet Union was a source of pride: it was the size of Russian territory and population that gave the Soviet Union its great power status. Even the loss of direct influence over the East European communist states in 1989 was seen by Russians as a betrayal and humiliation.[28]

But it was at the level of institutions, not popular sentiment, that Russia withdrew its support for Gorbachev's continuing efforts to hold the union together. The key here was the contest between Gorbachev and Boris Yeltsin. Yeltsin had been promoted to candidate membership of the Politburo by Gorbachev in 1985, at the same time as he took over the important role of leading the Communist Party organisation for Moscow city. But in 1987 Yeltsin grew frustrated with the pace of reform and, in October, directly criticised the conservative senior Politburo member Yegor Ligachev. At the end of the year and the beginning of 1988 he lost all of his Party positions and appeared to be cast into the political wilderness. But he began a spectacular comeback in the March 1989 elections,

---

[28] Wisła Suraska, *How the Soviet Union Disappeared: An Essay on the Causes of Dissolution* (Durham, NC: Duke University Press, 1999).

starting with a popular campaign to secure nomination and culminating in receiving the support of 89% of voters in Moscow. Although he was leader of a fairly small faction in the USSR Congress, a year later he was elected chairman of a separate RSFSR Congress of People's Deputies. After another year, on 13 June 1991, Yeltsin won 60% of the vote across Russia for a new post of president of Russia. His popularity and legitimacy clearly outstripped Gorbachev's, but in political terms his institutional base was in Russia. It was with the Russian Congress and later presidency that Yeltsin was able to take on Gorbachev and his all-Soviet institutions. In the process, he advanced himself as the spokesman for those republican governments which were beginning to move towards separation. In his efforts to undermine the power of the centre, he even called on the autonomous republics and regions of the RSFSR to 'gobble up as much autonomy as you can'.

Yeltsin was a committed reformer and was willing to work alongside Gorbachev so long as the latter was moving in the right direction. But the language of Russian nationalism which he adopted in 1989–1991 is one of the key reasons for suspecting him of opportunism. Yeltsin had shown little interest in such matters in the past, and his actions in the last year or two of Soviet power seem mainly to have been aimed at securing his own authority against Gorbachev's. In doing so he greatly weakened the centre and encouraged the republics to push their own causes ever harder.

THE 'WAR OF LAWS'

During the course of 1989–1990 popular fronts scored a series of successes in elections at local and republic level. Scores of communists, including senior ones, now threw in their lot with the nationalists. For some this may have been purely a case of seeing which way the wind was blowing, but already for some time the Communist Party organisations in the republics had adopted national stances and this move to the popular fronts was not so unnatural. In the Baltic republics, the more radical nationalists objected to working with communists or even ex-communists, but on the whole a moderate line of co-operation prevailed. Popular fronts were able to exercise so much influence in Estonia, Latvia and Lithuania that the governments of these three republics declared sovereignty in the USSR by the summer of 1989, and by 1990 the Supreme Soviets in all three republics were controlled by the popular fronts. Sovereignty meant that laws passed in the republics took precedence over the laws of the Soviet Union. These proclamations of sovereignty were not recognised by Gorbachev, and indeed were against the Soviet constitution. But as the Baltic republics, joined by Russia and the others, continued to issue their own laws and implement separate programmes, the authority of the centre weakened progressively. Of particular significance was the fact that the Baltic republics were already introducing elements of market reform into the economy, and in October 1990 the Russian parliament adopted a radical '500 days' programme of transformation to a market economy. With each republic pursuing a different economic reform programme in a country as economically integrated as the USSR, economic collapse accelerated exponentially. This added a new edge to protests and strengthened the determination of the popular front leaders to pursue independence.

Declarations of sovereignty were not confined to the union republics of the USSR. *Glasnost'* reawakened concern among peoples of many of the autonomous republics and regions over their demographic and language situations, which had deteriorated during the late Soviet years. For these autonomous units, concern was not so much over the power of the Soviet centre as over the union republics that stood above them in the federal structure – indeed Moscow was increasingly seen as the protector of the status of the smaller titular nationalities. Outside Russia, fears about the new order contributed to the outbreak of violence – in Abkhazia, Nagorno Karabakh and South Ossetia. But some of the republics and regions of the RSFSR, those that were resource-rich or more powerful by virtue of their size or historic identities – Bashkiria, Checheno-Ingushetia, Tatarstan and Sakha – used the political turmoil to advance their own agendas. Gorbachev strengthened their hand with a law of 26 April 1990 which effectively gave autonomous republics a say in running the Soviet federation that was equal to that of the union republics. They were also invited to participate in the drafting of a new Union Treaty on an equal basis.[29]

THE END OF THE SOVIET UNION

Any possibility that the three Baltic republics might be persuaded to stay within the orbit of the USSR was ended by the events of early 1991. The separatist direction of all three was a growing cause of concern for Gorbachev, who in the last months of 1990 promoted a number of conservative figures in the government and Politburo who were determined to keep the Soviet Union together at all costs. Towards the end of the year official denunciations of Lithuania were ratcheted up, fuelled by reports that Lithuanian nationalists had drawn up lists of communists to be executed and had plans to annex territory from other countries.[30] Finally, on 7 January 1991, Soviet paratroopers entered all three republics. At the same time,

---

[29] Hough, *Democratization and Revolution*, 246–8, 381–5.
[30] Martin McCauley, *Gorbachev (Profiles in Power)* (London: Longman, 1998), 198.

demonstrations of ethnic Russians protesting against the secessionist tendencies of the government began to converge on the Supreme
Council building in Vilnius. Called out by the leaders of Sajudis,
thousands of Lithuanians rushed to defend the Supreme Council
and the television station. It was here that, on 12 January, troops
opened fire and killed thirteen Lithuanian demonstrators.

The Red Army had already resorted to lethal force in Tbilisi and
Baku, but it did so in Vilnius at a time when the nationalist movement
was already well organised, and it appeared, in effect, as an attack by
the Soviet government on the government of one of its own republics. The governments of Estonia, Latvia and Lithuania had no
hesitation in declaring their independence, and the international
coverage given to the Vilnius events was one of the reasons that
foreign governments began to give serious consideration to recognising independent statehood should any of the republics break free.
Georgia was not far behind in pressing its claims for independence,
but it still seemed perfectly possible that the remainder of the union
could be saved. As he worked on a new Union Treaty, which would
have given more power to the republics but kept some central control
in place, in March 1991 Gorbachev organised a referendum which
asked voters directly whether they were in favour of keeping together
the USSR. In all of the republics where the referendum was conducted (it was boycotted in Estonia, Latvia, Lithuania, Georgia and
Moldova) the result was a resounding yes.

For conservative forces, it was Gorbachev's willingness to concede too much power to the republics and the threat that some might
secede anyway that proved the final straw. The prospect of a new
Union Treaty being signed on 20 August was what prompted a
group of Politburo and military figures to stage a coup against
Gorbachev while he was away in Crimea. The coup was, unsurprisingly, condemned by the breakaway republics, while only the

Central Asian leaders hesitated and waited to see which way the wind was blowing. As it turned out, the coup was a spectacular failure. Yeltsin further increased his prestige and authority by leading the resistance to the coup, and when Gorbachev did return to Moscow, he faced humiliation at Yeltsin's hands. Crucially, the failed coup seems to have decided the leaders of a number of republics that their own interests and those of their nations were best served separate from the Soviet state with its unpredictable leadership. Gorbachev's last throw of the dice was to offer Yeltsin the presidency of the USSR in return for his commitment to keeping it together, but when Ukrainian leader Leonid Kravchuk told Yeltsin that he no longer supported the unity of the Soviet Union, Yeltsin refused. A new referendum in Ukraine on 1 December this time voted firmly in favour of independence. A meeting between the leaders of Russia, Ukraine and Belarus on 8 December sealed the fate of the USSR. After these three republics agreed to go their separate ways, the remaining republics which had not already declared independence soon followed suit. Finally accepting this, Gorbachev resigned as president of the Soviet Union on 25 December, and on the night of 31 December 1991 the USSR ceased to exist, and its place was taken by fifteen separate states.

Several factors combined to bring about the collapse of communism and the dissolution of the USSR. The national factor was among the more important. In the view of at least some economists, the economic collapse which brought disillusion to numerous Soviet citizens and elites only really took hold quite late in Gorbachev's reign, and was in large part prompted by the divergent economic programmes of the Soviet republics.[31] But it was mostly a

---

[31] Hanson, *Rise and Fall*, 227–36.

combination of two factors that ensured the eruption of the national question in the last years of Soviet rule. First, national feeling that had been running high for some time, especially in the Baltic republics, had been kept in check by a combination of repression, the nationalising policies of republican leaders and a stance of non-interference by the centre. This balance was upset not only by the opening up of a space for free expression, which first took effect in the republics through environmental movements, but also by a renewed interest on the part of the centre in the republics. This was directed initially at corruption, but came to embrace other reform areas being pushed forward by a Soviet leadership that had little understanding of the national question. Secondly, republican elites, after a period of hesitation, generally threw themselves behind the national movements that were developing from below. In some cases the old elites simply put themselves at the head of the movement; in others old elites were pushed aside and replaced by new figures who enjoyed the confidence of nationalists. The attitude of Yeltsin and Russia gave further encouragement to national movements and republic leaders, who were finally pushed over the line by the August 1991 coup if they had not already taken steps towards independence.

CHAPTER TWELVE

Nation-making in the post-Soviet states

By at least early December 1991, it was clear that the days of the Soviet Union were numbered. Under a series of agreements in December the fifteen new states agreed to mutually recognise each other, and the international community was not far behind in accepting their legitimacy and establishing diplomatic ties. Some delays were caused by outstanding territorial claims between the new states, while a number of international organisations and governments hesitated as a result of the experience in the former Yugoslav states, where the readiness of Western governments to welcome the new formations without qualification may have contributed to ethnic violence.[1] International recognition also opened the door to aid and advice: the two were frequently linked as governments sought to reproduce the economic transition from communism that had already taken place in Eastern Europe. While many of the new governments were eager to attract international support, more important were the internal dynamics of political development which varied substantially from country to country. Popular fronts had been at the forefront of the movements for independence, but the distinction between their members and communists was often blurred. Thus the extent to which the new

---

[1] Carl Cavanagh Hodge, 'Botching the Balkans: Germany's Recognition of Slovenia and Croatia', *Ethics and International Affairs*, 12 (1998), 1–18.

leaderships represented a break with the past varied enormously. Each of the post-Soviet states inherited key elements of a national infrastructure from the Soviet period, but what could be built on top of this infrastructure in terms of a new, independent state-based national identity was up for grabs. Early political contests, which in some cases turned violent, were therefore key in determining future developments.

Given the huge variety of experience in the first twenty years of post-Soviet independence, it is not possible here to provide a comprehensive account of the progress of each of the new states. The emphasis in this chapter is on early political and national developments and a selection of key later events that reflect the impact of the Soviet nationalities experience on the post-Soviet independent states.

CIVIL WARS

Violence that erupted in Azerbaijan and Georgia before and after the collapse of the USSR was mostly centred on the separatist conflicts involving Nagorno Karabakh, Abkhazia and South Ossetia, which are dealt with in Chapter 13. But both countries also experienced brief internal civil wars in which the ruling government was overthrown by rival forces from the same ethnic-majority background. Azerbaijan's first democratic election since 1920, held on 7 June 1992, brought to power the leader of the Popular Front, Abulfaz Elchibey. Under his leadership, and with the assistance of Russian forces left behind in the region, Azerbaijan came close in the autumn of 1992 to overwhelming Nagorno Karabakh and defeating the Armenian separatists there. But by the end of the year, Armenian forces were beginning to win back territory, and as a result support for Elchibey declined rapidly. Elchibey already faced opposition from senior members of his government. Heidar Aliev, the former leader of the Communist Party of Azerbaijan, was then in charge of the enclave of Nakhichevan, on the far (south-western) side of Armenia. Aliev refrained from opening a second front with Armenia, a move which would have put a severe strain on Armenia's support for the Karabakh forces, and was steadily building up his own diplomatic relations with Turkey, Russia and even Armenia.

Meanwhile in the capital, Elchibey was faced with treachery on the part of his defence minister, Rahim Gaziev. Gaziev appeared to be conspiring with the army commander Suret Husseinov to engineer military defeats in order to pave the way for the over-throw of the elected president. When the conspiracy was unmasked, on 4 June 1993, Husseinov took the 709th Brigade he commanded to its base in Ganja and refused to follow orders. In Ganja he was able to take control of military equipment and munitions left behind after the withdrawal of the Soviet Fourth Army. When government troops were sent to Ganja to take control of this military hardware, they came into open conflict with Husseinov's forces, leaving around seventy dead. The rebels seized Ganja and then began to march on Baku. With his popular-ity plummeting, nobody was willing to stand up for Elchibey and, rather than plunge the country into a prolonged civil war while the Karabakh conflict still raged, he fled to Nakhichevan on 18 June. Meanwhile, Aliev had already arrived in Baku and engineered his own election as the speaker of the Azerbaijani parliament, a post which entitled him to take over the presidency on Elchibey's departure. On 24 June the parliament appointed Aliev president and Husseinov prime minister. In an orchestrated election, Aliev was confirmed as president with 98.8 per cent of the vote in an election on 3 October.

Azerbaijan continued to suffer military reverses in Karabakh, and Aliev faced a number of challenges to his rule. Another rebellion broke out in the southwest of the country in August 1992, backed again by Gaziev, but was soon defeated. In October 1995, Husseinov organised a coup against Aliev that failed. Husseinov fled to Moscow but was later extradited back to Azerbaijan and imprisoned. In March 1995 Rovshan Javadov, leader of the para-military OPON forces, attempted a military coup but was killed in the subsequent fighting along with dozens of soldiers.[2] From then on, Aliev's control remained unchallenged until his death. It was the Popular Front that had overthrown communism and brought its own candidate, Elchibey, to power in Azerbaijan's first presidential election. But with the chaos caused by the Karabakh conflict and in the face of the threat to order posed by undisciplined military leaders, the same Popular Front assisted Aliev back into power, at Elchibey's expense. Heidar Aliev brought with him many of the personnel of the old Soviet apparatus and established a personal dynasty for the country.

Political conflict in Georgia in the late Soviet and early post-Soviet years was also heavily affected by relations with minority regions, but from the beginning the anti-communist movement was fiercely divided. The former dissident Zviad Gamsakhurdia came to power in elections held in October 1990, which were boycotted by other opposition parties and which followed a violent election campaign during which the offices of two parties were attacked and set on fire. One leading rival politician, Giorgi Chanturia, was fired upon and wounded two days before the elections. After his victory, Gamsakhurdia appointed his own regional prefects to run minority areas, and resorted to force against minorities and against

[2] De Waal, *Black Garden*, 210–15, 251.

Georgian political opponents alike. In May 1991, Gamsakhurdia used his control over the media and the government administration to ensure his election as president of Georgia with 87 per cent of the vote. His popular appeal rested as much on his extreme nationalist messages as on his manipulation of state forces and the media. Competing irregular armed formations had already been created before Gamsakhurdia's election, and when the rebellion of South Ossetia in response to Gamsakhurdia's abolition of autonomous status broke out in early 1991 the stage was set for civil war. Gamsakhurdia's ambivalent position towards the failed August 1991 coup attempt in Moscow prompted the resignation of a number of government ministers and the defection of key supporters, including the leaders of both official and unofficial military formations. The Georgian capital Tbilisi descended into chaos as demonstrations and counter-demonstrations led to violent clashes. In December 1991 an opposition Military Council occupied central Tbilisi and shelled the parliament building where Gamsakhurdia and his supporters were located. An appeal to Soviet forces to defend the president failed to elicit any response, unsurprisingly given his antagonistic attitude to Russia. On 6 January 1992 Gamsakhurdia was forced to flee the country just days after its independence was accepted by Moscow, and he ended up in the Chechen capital Grozny as a guest of Dzhokar Dudaev.

Gamsakhurdia's flight did not bring an immediate end to civil strife in Georgia. The country was in a political and economic mess and the opposition was so divided that it had little recourse but to invite the former communist leader of the republic, and more recently Gorbachev's foreign minister, Eduard Shevardnadze, to reassume the reins of control in Georgia. Shevardnadze's position was weak, however, and depended on the goodwill of competing warlords, while Gamsakhurdia's popularity in the country remained high. The armed forces were in disarray and unreliable, and the government had little control over the country outside Tbilisi, which was itself rife with crime and violent confrontations between rival gangs. Large parts of western Georgia remained under the control of 'Zviadists' loyal to Gamsakhurdia, and the situation became worse following the ill-advised military operation against Abkhazia in August 1992. Abkhaz successes against the Georgian army were achieved with the aid of Zviadists, who were encouraged to seek to restore Gamsakhurdia to power by force. In October 1993 Zviadists overran Poti on the Black Sea coast where they seized a large arms cache and then turned east towards the capital. With Russia now supporting Shevardnadze's army, however, the Zviadist forces were defeated by the end of 1993 and the dead body of Gamsakhurdia himself was found near his stronghold of Zugdidi on 31 December. Corruption, crime and weak government remained as the legacy of this civil war for Georgia, until Shevardnadze was himself overthrown by a peaceful revolution in 2003.[3]

Whereas the civil wars in Azerbaijan and Georgia took place against the background of attempts by minority regions to break away and involved small elite groups competing for power, in Tajikistan the civil war engulfed the whole country and had a greater international aspect, involving direct or indirect participation of military forces and equipment from Russia, Afghanistan and Uzbekistan. Tajikistan had been among the quietest of the Soviet republics during the mass protest phase of *perestroika*, but intense economic deprivation, rabid corruption and regional rivalries laid the basis for violence, which first erupted in February 1990 on the streets of the capital Dushanbe. Triggered by rumours that Armenian refugees were to be settled in already scarce housing in

[3] Cheterian, *War and Peace*, 167–204.

the city, and fuelled by competing political and criminal factions, the riots that lasted for eight days left a couple of dozen dead and hundreds injured.[4]

But this was a small prelude to what was to come. The main phase of the civil war lasted only from May 1992 until early in 1993, but it left up to fifty thousand dead, hundreds of thousands of refugees and a country in ruins. In common with the conflicts elsewhere, the fighting was initiated by a competition for power between the old Soviet elites and competing opposition forces, but it took on a much broader regional dimension, with much of the fighting concentrated in the south of the country. Rakhman Nabiev, from the northern Leninabad province, had served as First Party Secretary of the Soviet republic of Tajikistan from 1982 to 1985 and returned to power in presidential elections in December 1991. He brought with him many of the established Soviet *nomenklatura* as well as allies from his home region, and set about persecuting opposition leaders, including the mayor of Dushanbe, Maksud Ikramov. On 5 May 1992, supporters of Ikramov clashed on the streets of Dushanbe with armed government supporters, leaving some sixty people dead. Ostensibly, the opposition forces were based on an alliance of democrats and Islamists who were opposing the old communist forces. Their strongholds were in the eastern Gorno Badakhshan region and the southern Qurghonteppe (or Kurgan-Tiube in its Russian form) region. As the conflict developed into a regional one, it became easy to dismiss any ideological dimension.[5] The fact that in Soviet times political power was primarily based on leaders from

---

[4] Aziz Niyazi, 'Tajikistan', in Mohiaddin Mesbahi (ed.), *Central Asia and the Caucasus after the Soviet Union* (Gainesville: University Press of Florida, 1994), 173–5.

[5] See, for example, United States Institute of Peace, 'Special Report: The War in Tajikistan Three Years On' (Washington, DC: United States Institute of Peace, November 1995).

Leninabad and Kuliab in the south meant that the regional division reflected earlier access to power and resources, presenting a more complex picture of the alignment of forces. Although it would equally be an oversimplification to portray the conflict as one between the old communist and the new opposition forces, it was both a regional and a political one.

Most of the fighting was concentrated in the South, especially the Kurgan-Tiube region, fuelled by the transportation of arms and militiamen from neighbouring Afghanistan. Faced with the threat of military intervention from Russia and neighbouring Central Asian countries, Nabiev stood down on 7 September 1992. He was briefly succeeded as leader by Akbarsho Iskandarov, but as fighting continued around Dushanbe as well as in the south it was the relatively obscure Kuliabi, Emomali Rakhmonov, who had risen from a regional rural post in the 1980s to become a member of the Supreme Soviet in 1990 and its speaker by the end of 1992, who emerged as the leading figure in the country. Although fighting continued sporadically up until 1997, the death of Nabiev in May 1993 marked an end to the main political struggle, and by November 1994 it was possible to hold elections, in which Rakhmonov was chosen as president.[6]

In Azerbaijan, Georgia and Tajikistan, regional and ethnic factors, the involvement of Russian troops acting outside the orbit of the central army command, and Abkhaz, Armenian and Uzbek military interventions all served to sharpen conflict. But the intensity of military competition arose from what was at stake for the competing forces: the chance to lead a new country in which

---

[6] Gregory Gleason, *The Central Asian States: Discovering Independence* (Boulder, CO: Westview, 1997), 103–10.

the formerly stabilising central authority of the Soviet Union had collapsed.

The civil wars in Azerbaijan, Georgia and Tajikistan were the most extreme manifestations of political struggle that ensued from the collapse of the Soviet Union. But elsewhere similar types of conflict took place in more peaceful forms. Broadly speaking, the new regimes could be divided between those based on old communist elites and those formed from opposition forces. In the Baltic republics of Estonia, Latvia and Lithuania, the popular front movements had been at their strongest and, in spite of efforts by the communist leaderships to fall behind the national movements, new leaders emerged from the opposition to the highest positions of power. Strongly parliamentary constitutions were adopted and elected assemblies were dominated by anti-communist parties. The presidents of all three states were chosen by parliament and had largely symbolic roles, but the choices of the first post-independence presidents are indicative of how far these countries had broken with their political pasts – in Estonia, the writer and film-maker Lennart Meri held the post from 1992 to 2001, while in Lithuania the musician Vytautas Landsbergis, who only entered politics as one of the founders of Sajudis, held the position from the time of Sajudis' victory in 1990 until 1992, when he was temporarily replaced by Algirdas Brazauskas, who then won a popular election in February 1993. Brazauskas had headed the Lithuanian Communist Party, but had been quick to break it away from the CPSU. The first post-independence president of Latvia, Guntis Ulmanis (great-nephew of the pre-war president Kārlis Ulmanis) had also been a member of the Communist Party until 1989, but had served as a lowly economist. In Moldova, the Popular Front swept aside the Communist Party in elections to the Congress of People's Deputies in 1989 and the Supreme Soviet in 1990. The first post-Soviet elections held in February 1994 were a victory for the Agrarian Democratic Party, which included former communists among its leaders and was for a strongly independent Moldova, a message that helped it defeat the pro-Romanian Popular Front. Two years later, the incumbent president Mircea Snegur was defeated by the more pro-Russian Petru Lucinschi. The significance of the 1994 elections in Moldova was that they were the first time anywhere in the post-Soviet states that a sitting parliamentary majority was defeated by purely democratic means. Ukraine was ahead of Moldova in presidential elections, when in the summer of 1994 the nationalist Leonid Kravchuk was defeated by the Russian-speaking Leonid Kuchma in presidential elections.

Elsewhere, the transfer to democracy and a political break with the past were less clear cut. In Armenia, Levon Ter-Petrossian, the leader of the Armenian National Movement, became head of the Supreme Council of Armenia following elections in the summer of 1990, and went on to win presidential elections in 1991 and 1996. With the Karabakh issue dominating Armenian politics, however, he was forced to resign in 1998 after taking a compromising position in negotiations with Azerbaijan, and was replaced by the Karabakh leader Robert Kocharian following elections which were of dubious quality. On 27 October 1999 a group of gunmen stormed into the parliamentary chamber in Yerevan, shooting dead the prime minister, the speaker and six other members of parliament. This incident further heightened the already tense political atmosphere and led to further restrictions on democratic activity, ensuring Kocharian's re-election in 2003 and the election of his chosen successor Serzh Sargsyan in 2008.

Of the Central Asian states, Kyrgyzstan has consistently been viewed as the one most likely to pursue a liberal democratic path, and has equally consistently disappointed. Like many of the political leaders to emerge from the chaotic years of *perestroika*, Askar Akaev was an academic. He joined the Communist Party only in 1981 and was elevated to the post of president of the Kyrgyz Academy of Sciences in 1989. Just a year later, in October 1990, the still relatively unknown Akaev was chosen as president of the Kyrgyz Soviet Socialist Republic as a compromise candidate, after the three leading candidates were all disqualified under the electoral rules then in force, none of them being able to obtain an outright majority in the first two rounds of voting. Akaev's popularity rose rapidly, not least when he resisted pressure from the Communist Party in resolutely opposing the failed Soviet coup in August 1991, and his position was confirmed in a popular vote, where he was unopposed, in October 1991. Even before the end of the Soviet Union, he pursued a vigorous programme of market-oriented economic reform, which had the immediate advantage of attracting high levels of western aid to the poor republic, while maintaining good relations with Russia. With the economy deteriorating and political opponents growing in confidence by the middle of the 1990s, however, Akaev turned to increasingly authoritarian methods to ensure his political survival, disbanding parliament in 1994 and holding presidential elections a year early in December 1995. Akaev won this election with 70 per cent of the vote, but its fairness was seriously questioned. In 1998 Akaev manipulated a decision of the Constitutional Court to allow him to stand for election a third time in 2000, which he duly won, having succeeded in disqualifying his main rivals from running; the election itself was full of irregularities and was deemed unfair by international observers. As his third term in office neared its end, Akaev appeared to be preparing either for another constitutional change to allow him to run again, or to be grooming one of his children to succeed him. Kyrgyzstan seemed to be going the way of other authoritarian regimes in Central Asia before Akaev's overthrow in the Tulip Revolution of 2005.[7]

Other post-Soviet leaders were more successful than Akaev in establishing effectively unchallenged rule and, in one case to date, a dynasty of sorts. In some ways the leaders of Azerbaijan, Belarus (as the former Soviet republic of Belorussia became officially known after independence), Kazakhstan, Turkmenistan and Uzbekistan continued the traditions of the long-serving republican First Secretaries of the Brezhnev era. But now these leaders were officially heads of state and were no longer subject to limitations imposed by Moscow. The personality cults that arose were consequently more extreme than anything that had existed since Stalin's day, and the leaders were not shy of amassing huge personal fortunes and distributing wealth and patronage to relatives, fellow clan members and supporters. In all of these cases, while the formalities of democracy were respectfully observed, true democracy existed only for a fleeting moment if at all. The cult of the leader was also intimately tied in to the nation-building project: while there was an obvious self-interest on the part of these presidents in promoting themselves as the figurehead of the nation, the various cults also proved a rallying point for severely fractured nations and lent a peculiar character to the nature of post-Soviet nationhood in the remaining six states.

In Belarus, Alexander Lukashenko was a former Red Army officer who was elected to parliament in 1990, where he was the

[7] Regine A. Spector, 'The Transformation of Askar Akaev, President of Kyrgyzstan', Berkeley Program in Soviet and Post-Soviet Studies Working Paper Series (Berkeley: University of California, 2004), 3–22.

only deputy to vote against the dissolution of the Soviet Union in December 1991. He rose to further prominence as the chair of the anti-corruption committee of the parliament, from where he succeeded in indicting seventy senior officials, including the speaker of the parliament Stanislav Shushkevich, in 1993. In the first Belarusan presidential elections held in July 1994, Lukashenko stood on a populist platform and won 80.1 per cent of the vote in the second round. He went on to win further elections in 2001, 2006 and 2010, having obtained a change to the constitution abolishing term limits in 2004. The levels of electoral manipulation, intimidation and fraud appeared to increase with each election, and opposition in the form of protests was always met with severe repression. But Lukashenko also managed to retain a high level of popularity through his first three terms in office by adopting a populist stance based on promises of raising living standards, something he was able to achieve as Belarus experienced relative economic growth based in large part on the active support of Russia. Lukashenko also proved adept at dividing potential opponents and keeping political and economic elites dependent on him, while alternating between repression and relaxation in his pursuit of popularity. By 2010, however, Russia's leaders had run out of patience with the increasingly eccentric autocrat and withdrew economic as well as political support. The economy started to deteriorate rapidly as a result, and Lukashenko's popularity suffered at the same time, his approval rating dropping from 53% in December 2010 to 20.5% in September 2011.[8] By the end of 2011 Lukashenko's position looked far less secure than at any time since 1994, and any plans he may have had

---

[8] Inna Bukshtynovich, 'BISS Polling Memo: Belarusians Are in between – But No One Is There to Represent Them', *Belarus Headlines*, issue IV, October 2011, 8.

to ensure his son Viktor would succeed him as president must have
been in doubt.

Where Akaev and, most likely, Lukashenko failed in establishing
a personal dynasty, at least one post-Soviet president succeeded.
When Azerbaijan's President Heidar Aliev began to suffer serious
ill health in 1999, he took steps to ensure a smooth political
succession. While being treated for the second time at the
Cleveland Clinic in the United States at the beginning of October
2003, Aliev resigned the presidency and nominated his son, Ilham,
as the candidate of the ruling Yeni Azerbaijan party for the new
presidential elections already scheduled for 15 October. Ilham duly
won with 76.84 per cent of the vote, and the death of Heidar was
announced as having occurred on 12 December 2003.[9] Heidar Aliev
had risen to power in 1993 out of the chaos of Azerbaijan's civil war,
but unlike many other post-Soviet leaders who reached the highest
positions at a time of crisis, he was no compromise candidate. As
First Secretary of the Communist Party of Azerbaijan from 1969 to
1982, he had built up a strong patron–client network both in Baku
and in his native Nakhichevan, and he returned to Baku as an
experienced, well-supported and powerful leader. Heidar Aliev's
task of consolidating his power was considerably eased by the
discovery in the 1980s of vast reserves of untapped oil around
Baku and in the Caspian Sea. The 'contract of the century' signed
in 1994 between Aliev and a consortium of international oil com-
panies brought in an initial US $18 billion, which represents only a
fraction of the overall foreign investment. This was further boosted
by the discovery of gas reserves at the end of the 1990s, which
provide a continuous large source of revenue for the government in

---

[9] There has been speculation that Heidar actually died much earlier, but that his death was
covered up in order to ensure the election of Ilmar.

the form of taxes and permit fees. Resource wealth has allowed both Alievs to enrich themselves, their family and supporters, as well as to rebuild large parts of the capital city Baku and construct lavish national monuments. While relatively little of this wealth trickled down to the general population, the energy industry at least provided a regular source of employment and living standards were relatively high in terms of the post-Soviet countries. Heidar Aliev's emergence as leader of post-Soviet Azerbaijan from the chaos of civil war and the continuing conflict with Armenia over Nagorno Karabakh allowed him to present himself as the father of a new nation, who even posthumously continued to be officially referred to as the 'nationwide leader'.

National identity in post-Soviet Azerbaijan rests in large part, then, on the cult of the Alievs, alongside a sense of embattlement and victimisation and a virulent hatred of Armenia and Armenians as long as a fifth of the territory of Azerbaijan is occupied by Armenian forces. The cult of Heidar Aliev, begun before his death, was broadened and deepened by Ilham, who renamed the main airport of Baku after Heidar in 2004 and ensured the construction of extravagant statues of his father not only across Azerbaijan but abroad as well. Members of the Aliev family circle and a broader network based on the Alievs' home region of Nakhichevan held privileged positions not just in the political system but in major areas of the economy such as tourism and construction. The Alievs have backed up their personal cults with an authoritarian approach to ruling the country. Although opposition groups remained lively in Azerbaijan, they stayed weak and divided, with no strong alternative leader emerging, and were subjected to regular police harassment and the banning or violent dispersal of political demonstrations. Elections have been held regularly but have always been criticised by international observers both for unfairness in the registration of candidates and campaigning, and for irregularities on election days themselves. Hopes that Ilmar Aliev and his wife Mehriban might liberalise politics have proved mostly unfounded. Although oil and gas revenues were set to decline as the twenty-first century progressed, there has been little sign of Ilmar Aliev's authority being challenged, and the removal of constitutional limits on the number of terms an individual might serve as president suggests that he anticipates ruling for a long time to come.[10]

Personality cults and authoritarian rule became characteristic of all of the energy-rich countries of the former Soviet south. Nursultan Nazarbayev became First Secretary of the Communist Party of Kazakhstan in 1989, having played a part in the removal of Dinmukhamed Kunaev from that position in 1986. In April 1990 he was chosen as president by the Supreme Soviet of the republic, and was confirmed in his post by 91.5 per cent of the popular vote when he stood unopposed in December 1991. After winning more popular votes (again unopposed) in 1995, 1999 and 2005, in 2007 Nazarbayev secured a constitutional change allowing him to serve an indefinite number of terms as president (while the two-term limit still applied to everyone else). Revenues from oil and gas have helped sustain Nazarbayev in power, and while his commitment to democratisation and the fight against corruption remained dubious, Kazakhstan kept up an open dialogue with the European Union and other international bodies over its human rights record and received the prestigious accolade of holding the chairmanship of the Organization for Security and Co-operation in Europe in 2010.

[10] International Crisis Group, 'Azerbaijan: Vulnerable Stability', International Crisis Group Europe Report no. 207, 3 September 2010.

Elections remained tightly managed, however, and Nazarbayev ensured that the country stayed firmly under the control of himself and his inner circle. His grip on the country and his personal cult were symbolically strengthened in 1997 by moving the capital from the cosmopolitan city of Almaty to the more remote city of Akmola, renamed Astana the following year and largely remodelled in extravagant fashion since. It was widely expected that one of Nazarbayev's children would be groomed to eventually succeed him, but the assumed dynasty came under some strain over a scandal that erupted in May 2007 involving Nazarbayev's son-in-law Rakhat Aliev, who was then married to Dariga Nazarbayeva and serving as Kazakhstan's ambassador to Austria. Aliev was accused of being behind the kidnapping of senior bank executives earlier that year, and connected charges of extortion. Aliev was stripped of his positions, divorced by his wife and subjected to two failed extradition attempts, while he himself maintained his innocence and claimed to have been persecuted as a result of his intention to stand against Nazarbayev in the presidential elections scheduled for 2013.[11] Whatever the truth, the case highlights the intertwining of business and politics and the high levels of official corruption not only in Kazakhstan, but also in other energy-rich post-Soviet countries.

In Uzbekistan, Islam Karimov followed a career path that was similar to Nazarbayev's, rising to the post of First Secretary in 1989 and becoming president in 1990, confirmed by an overwhelming popular vote the following year. Karimov won dubious subsequent elections with overwhelming shares of the vote, took vigorous measures to prevent opposition parties from organising and

---

[11] Farkad Sharip, 'Kazakhstan President's Son-in-Law Faces Criminal Charges', *Jamestown Foundation*, vol. 4, issue 106, 31 May 2007.

suppressed media freedoms shortly after Uzbekistan became independent. Critics of Uzbekistan's human rights record claim torture
and summary executions are regular features. Although Uzbekistan
initially co-operated with the USA over the war in Afghanistan
from 2001, its international isolation deepened following events in
the eastern city of Andijan in May 2005. After days of protests
against the government in the city, troops opened fire on demonstrators. The demonstrations were triggered by the trials of a
number of local businessmen, and the regime also maintained that
Islamic fundamentalism was to blame for the unrest, but general
discontent with Karimov's rule and the inspiration of 'colour revolutions' elsewhere seem to have been what fuelled the demonstrations. In spite of government claims that only terrorists were
targeted and that 187 were killed in total, it is most likely that the
number of dead ran into several hundreds, who were mostly
unarmed civilians. The Andijan massacre led to the diplomatic
isolation of Uzbekistan for a while, but ultimately did little to
undermine the rule of Karimov, who had already stood for election
beyond the prescribed constitutional limits and who, like
Nazarbayev, seemed ready to prolong the rule of himself and his
family indefinitely. Having risen from relative obscurity to power
on the back of Tajikistan's civil war, Emomali Rakhmonov also
developed a mild personality cult. In March 2007 he changed his
name to the less Russian-sounding Rahmon, and has adopted many
of the trappings of a monarchy.[12]

The personality cults that in part characterised not just the ruling
regime but also the whole national character of Azerbaijan, Belarus,
Kazakhstan and Uzbekistan reached unprecedented and ridiculous

---

[12] Akram Qahhorov, 'A Personality Cult Grows in Tajikistan', RFE/RL broadcast,
18 November 2011.

levels in Turkmenistan. The country is second only to Russia as the region's largest gas exporter, and the regular discovery of new fields suggest that Turkmenistan may have one of the world's largest natural gas reserves.[13] With a population of only a little over 5 million, Turkmenistan exports most of its gas to Russia, where it forms a crucial part of Russian export strategy. As a result huge amounts of wealth have been available to the country's rulers, a circumstance which underpinned a rigidly authoritarian regime and one of the most extraordinary personal cults in modern history. Saparmurat Niyazov, better known by his self-proclaimed title of Turkmenbashi ('Leader of the Turkmen') led the Communist Party of Turkmenistan from 1985 to 1991 and rapidly established his personal rule after independence. Dispensing with even the formalities of democracy that were observed in other post-Soviet countries, Niyazov used oil and gas revenues to rebuild the capital city, Ashkhabad, into a space-age metropolis built entirely of marble and to promote his own extravagant personality cult. As well as erecting gold statues of himself, the most famous of which turned continually to face the sun, Niyazov created a shrine to his long-dead brother that visiting dignitaries were obliged to visit and honour, named the months of the year after members of his family and promoted his own book as the fundamental cornerstone of Turkmen identity. All media, including the internet, were tightly controlled and no political opposition at all was tolerated.

The all-powerful nature of Niyazov's rule was reflected in eccentric and often costly projects such as building a huge lake and a cypress forest in the desert and an ice palace and ski slope outside

---

[13] [Simon Pirani], 'Turkmenistan: An Exporter in Transition', in Simon Pirani (ed.), *Russian and CIS Gas Markets and Their Impact on Europe* (Oxford University Press, 2009), 271.

Ashkhabad.[14] Niyazov's death in December 2006 was followed by a period of uncertainty as far as the outside world was concerned, given the impenetrability of Turkmen politics. When Gurbanguly Berdymukhamedov emerged as the new president, confirmed by a sham election in February 2007, and began to gradually dismantle the Turkmenbashi cult, for a while it seemed that a more open era was dawning in Turkmenistan. But not only did Berdymukhamedov not relax political and informational control, but it also soon became clear that his own personality cult was emerging, as portraits and statues of the new leader replaced those of the old one, his own writings were promoted as essential reading for citizens of Turkmenistan, and the figure of the president dominated news and other broadcasts. Although the cult of Berdymukhamedov did not reach the extravagant levels of that of his predecessor, under his rule Turkmenistan remained a highly regimented, eccentric state combining ostentatious displays of national wealth with low standards of education and other signs of backwardness.

NATION-BUILDING AND MINORITIES

The shared Soviet experience and the similar progress of national cultural and political development across the republics in the late Soviet years were not sufficient to ensure that national development proceeded in similar directions after the country's collapse. The full embrace of economic and political liberalism, democracy and a European identity in the Baltic states could hardly contrast more sharply with the sham elections, neglect of human rights and personality cults that characterised some of the Central Asian states and even neighbouring Belarus. In part, these were different

---

[14] 'The Personality Cult of Turkmenbashi', *The Guardian*, 21 December 2006.

responses to the need to promote an independent national identity, which could draw on the cultural and institutional arrangements of the Soviet period but which also needed to be differentiated from the shared past. As most Soviet intellectuals had been educated with a primordial view of nationality, the premise that there were clear divides in character and attitude between members of different nationalities was generally held to be true. This had important consequences in countries where the population was mixed, most obviously where territories were also disputed along ethnic lines in the South Caucasus. But immediately following independence the governments of all fifteen of the former Soviet republics had decisions to make regarding citizenship and language policy. In the first year, only Ukraine stipulated a straightforward requirement that residence on Ukrainian territory at the moment of independence would be sufficient grounds for claiming Ukrainian citizenship.

Elsewhere, criteria were hotly disputed both domestically and internationally. Estonia and Latvia, with their large ethnic Russian populations, not only refused any official status to the Russian language, but also set difficult conditions under which Russians whose families had immigrated during the previous fifty years could claim citizenship. The justification given for this policy was that the Soviet occupation of the Baltic states since 1940 had been illegal, and therefore only those who could trace their citizenship back to the pre-1940 period could have an automatic right to citizenship in the newly independent states. In practice, however, it justified discrimination against ethnic Russians, most of whom chose to stay where they were rather than take up the offer of citizenship in Russia, as the leaders of Estonia and Latvia sought to make more homogeneous populations. In Estonia, an amended version of the 1938 citizenship law was introduced in 1992, which immediately disenfranchised post-1940 settlers and prevented them voting on the new constitution. Over a third of the population of Estonia were now non-citizens, and they could acquire citizenship from 1993 onwards only through a process of naturalisation, the biggest obstacle to which was the requirement to pass a tough test in the Estonian language. International pressure led to some changes in citizenship requirement, so that, for example, in 1998 children under fifteen who were born in Estonia of stateless parents could apply for citizenship, while in 2002 certain categories of disabled people were exempted from the examination requirements. Between 1992 and 2005, 138,246 people acquired Estonian citizenship through naturalisation, compared to an estimated number of just under half a million who had found themselves stateless after 1991. Rules were relaxed under pressure from the EU as a condition of Estonia's joining in 2004 but, after an initial surge in naturalisation, rules and procedures were again tightened up, and the EU had lost the leverage it had previously enjoyed by threatening to deny Estonia membership unless its citizenship rules were reformed.[15]

In Latvia a similar approach was adopted, with initial rules based on 1919 laws effectively restricting citizenship to individuals who had lived in Latvia in 1940 or their descendants. Naturalisation required sixteen years of residence, thus eliminating far more immigrants from this path to citizenship than was the case in Estonia. Amended laws in 1995 eased the process of naturalisation but restricted the number of applicants to an annual quota until 2003. When it was discovered, however, that fewer non-citizens were applying than these quotas allowed, a review of the reasons for the low application rate was carried out. As a result, and under

---

[15] Priit Järve, 'Estonian Citizenship: Between Ethnic Preferences and Democratic Obligations', in Rainer Bauböck, Bernhard Perchinig and Wiebke Sievers (eds.), *Citizenship Policies in the New Europe*, expanded and updated edn (Amsterdam University Press, 2009), 45–66.

international pressure, the quota system was dropped, certain categories were exempted from tests, and measures were put in place to aid learning the language and history needed in order to pass citizenship exams. All the same, in the middle of 2008 there were 365,164 non-citizens in Latvia, still about half the number there were in 1995. Only 128,825 individuals had been granted citizenship through naturalisation, fewer than the number of non-citizens who emigrated between 1995 and 2008.[16]

As a result of deliberate policies, therefore, Latvia and Estonia were left with large numbers of non-citizens, who were unable to participate in national elections (ensuring they were not represented in parliament) and with limited language rights. Non-citizens were barred from certain public offices and professions such as the judiciary. All the same, many ethnic Russians did not acquire citizenship, either because they were unable or unwilling to take the tests, or because non-citizens still enjoy most of the privileges of citizens (such as protection of rights under international conventions) as well as certain advantages over citizens, notably the ability to travel to Russia and within the EU without a visa. But the restrictive citizenship laws underlined the ethnic division of the population, which remained geographically concentrated so that certain cities and regions in Latvia and Estonia stayed predominantly Russian in population. Relations between Latvians and Estonians on the one hand and Russians on the other remained frosty at many levels, although on the whole ethnic violence has been absent in spite of many of the classic ingredients for conflict being present.[17] Perceived

---

[16] Kristīne Krūma, 'Checks and Balances in Latvian Nationality Policies: National Agendas and International Frameworks', in Bauböck, Perchinig and Sievers (eds.) *Citizenship Policies*, 67–96.

[17] Pål Kolstø (eds.), *National Integration and Violent Conflict in Post-Soviet Societies: The Cases of Estonia and Moldova* (Lanham, MD, and Oxford: Rowman & Littlefield, 2002).

discrimination and underlying tensions boiled over, however, in April 2007 in Estonia, when a bronze statue of a Soviet soldier erected as a war memorial in 1947 was removed from its place in Tallinn by the authorities. Ethnic Russians protested against the move, culminating in violent clashes and one death, and the move was also condemned by Russia and opposed by international bodies. As a direct result, Estonian online systems were bombarded in a 'cyberwar' apparently orchestrated from within Russia.

In addition to the ethnic element in the disputed territories of the South Caucasus and Moldova, ethnic tensions have caused difficulties in Central Asia, especially in Kyrgyzstan, where violence between ethnic Kyrgyz and Uzbeks erupted again in the cities of Osh and Jalalabad in June 2010. Tajikistan and Uzbekistan have also been affected, but on a lesser scale. In most regions of the former Soviet Union, Russians remain the largest minority, and they often provide an important source of skilled labour essential to the local economy. While many Russians left Central Asia in the 1990s, substantial numbers remained and were well integrated with the larger community. Kazakhstan in particular pursued a semi-official bilingual policy, allowing the large Russian population in the industrial north of the country to continue enjoying full language and cultural rights. According to a 2001 census, over 17 per cent of the population of Ukraine was ethnic Russian, although considerably more spoke Russian as their first language. Russians and Russian speakers tended to be more concentrated in the east of the country, contributing to an east–west division as well as urban–rural differentiation according to ethnicity.

EAST, WEST OR IN BETWEEN?

The east–west divide in Ukraine, while it should not be exaggerated, has been the clearest illustration of one of the key questions posed to the new governments of each of the post-Soviet states after 1991: in which direction should the country be oriented, not just in foreign policy, but also culturally and economically? After the break-up of the USSR, Russian president Boris Yeltsin joined with other leaders in an effort to give substance to the Commonwealth of Independent States (CIS) that replaced it. The CIS acted for a few years as the successor to the Soviet Union in sporting competitions and played an important part in dismantling the administrative infrastructure of the USSR, distributing state assets and regulating trade. Although even Russia was not fully focussed on the CIS, and its significance waned, the CIS continued to play a role in co-ordinating certain policy areas such as transport infrastructure and cross-border welfare payments, as well as providing a regular forum for summits of the leaders of most of the former Soviet states.[18]

Towards the end of the 1990s Russian political leaders began to take a keener interest in re-establishing Russian regional dominance, beginning with the 'Primakov doctrine' – named after Yevgeni Primakov, who served as Russia's foreign minister from 1996 to 1998 – which promoted the peaceful assertion of Russian influence over the former Soviet space. In addition to the CIS a number of regional organisations grew up, most, but not all, of them dominated by Russia – the Collective Security Treaty Organisation; the Shanghai Cooperation Organisation; the GUAM group involving Georgia, Ukraine, Azerbaijan, Moldova and, for a while, Uzbekistan; and a Customs Union of Russia, Belarus and Kazakhstan which in 2012 looked to be growing in importance with Kyrgyzstan and Tajikistan set to join as well. The

---

[18] Richard Sakwa, 'The CIS: Conflicts of Place and Time', in David Dusseault (ed.), *The CIS: Form or Substance?*, Aleksanteri Papers 2/2007, (Helsinki: Kikimora Publications, 2007), 298–317.

former Soviet countries mostly also took part in pan-European organisations such as the OSCE and the Council of Europe.

For the most part, however, these attempts to establish some kind of security and trade co-ordination had little impact. Natural smaller regional groupings failed to materialise at all – in the South Caucasus, protracted conflict between Armenia and Azerbaijan ensured that regional co-operation could not be achieved, while in Central Asia personal rivalries between the presidents of the five countries blocked co-operation even in areas where it was desperately needed, such as the management of water resources. In practice governments made individual choices about their global orientation according to political preferences, cultural and historical links, and practical issues of trade and security. In some cases this choice was straightforward, while in others it was highly contested or no choice at all was made. Turkmenistan declared itself officially neutral and in practice remained politically isolated while engaging in high levels of energy trade with a number of partners, but mostly with Russia. The other Central Asian countries eschewed regional or religious identities and for demographic and trading reasons maintained strong ties with Russia, although Kyrgyzstan has enjoyed a closer relationship with the west than any of its neighbours. Towards the end of the first decade of the twenty-first century, China also entered on the scene and became an increasingly influential economic actor in Central Asia, forcing Russia to up the tempo of its efforts to retain regional influence.

Belarus under Lukashenko remained steadfastly in the Russian camp, pushing for further reintegration of the two countries even when Russia was unwilling to go that far. Even Russian disillusionment with Lukashenko did not do much to promote any western orientation for Belarus. Armenia, isolated internationally because of its involvement in the Karabakh conflict, with hostile neighbours to the east and the south, and with few economic resources of its own, remained strongly linked with its historical partner, Russia, in spite of the absence of any shared border between the two. At the other extreme, Estonia, Latvia and Lithuania deliberately reduced their links with Russia as far as possible and pushed ahead with developing relations exclusively with Europe, culminating in their admittance as full members of the European Union in 2004.

Elsewhere there was not so clear cut a choice. Azerbaijan was even more successful than Kazakhstan in maintaining generally good relations with both Russia and the west, a task made much easier by international interest in its energy reserves. In the remaining states of Georgia, Ukraine and Moldova, the issue of whether to orient politically and economically towards Russia or towards the west was one of the greatest causes of political conflict, overlapping as it did with divisions between liberal reformers and conservatives. Moldova's east–west divide was sharpened by the close historical and linguistic ties of the west of the country with Romania, while Transdniester – the region to the east of the river Dniestr – had closer ties with Russia and Ukraine. There was also a geographical element to Ukraine's split dual orientation, but in Georgia the divide between those with a purely European orientation and those supporting closer ties with Russia was more of a generational and political one.

AUTONOMY IN RUSSIA

The fall of the Soviet Union in 1991 led to the creation of fifteen independent states, but many smaller nationalities remained within the territory of the bigger states. Some of these will be discussed in Chapter 13, but of the others the most significant could be found inside the Russian Federation – the republics and regions of the

North Caucasus, the Tatars and Bashkirs along with a number of Turkic and Finnic peoples in the Volga region, the Buriats and Yakuts in the Far East, and the numerous small peoples of Siberia and the Russian North, some of whom happened to exist on land that turned out to be of great value for oil, gas and mineral deposits.

At first, it was feared that Yeltsin's exhortations in the last years of Soviet rule for such nationalities to 'gobble up as much autonomy as you can', coupled with the example of Chechnya's declaration of independence, would lead to a series of further secession bids. The key territory for Russian nationality policy in the early 1990s was Tatarstan, the largest (in population) and wealthiest of the autonomous republics of the former RSFSR. Tatarstan had the resources, the sense of identity and nationhood, and the size to exist as an independent state, as well as an ambitious and resourceful leader in the person of Mintimer Shaimiev, who won election as Tatarstan's president on the same day in 1991 as Boris Yeltsin won in Russia. Shaimiev was careful to appeal to all of the nationalities of Tatarstan, emphasising the economic benefits of increasing self-rule rather than any national agenda. Having tried to get separate union republic status for Tatarstan as long as the USSR existed, after its collapse Shaimiev shifted to securing as much self-rule and as great a share of the resources at the disposal of the republic as possible. But the threat of secession, which a weakened Russian state could ill afford, remained.

There followed a game of brinkmanship between Kazan and Moscow, which finally resulted in a bilateral treaty between Tatarstan and Russia signed in February 1994 on very favourable terms towards Tatarstan. Having secured his position, Shaimiev proceeded to promote the Tatar language and culture, notably through a July 1994 law that established Tatar as the leading language in education and academia and that offered bonuses to certain categories of state employee who could master Tatar. Other elements of 'ethnic revivalism' followed, with the backing of the government. This pattern was followed by the other autonomous republics and regions of the Russian Federation, where the norm was for Russian and the titular language to be the official state languages (often at the expense of other minorities). Variations in the extent to which exclusivist language, cultural and promotion policies were pursued were considerable, but overall there were few signs in post-Soviet Russia of severe ethnic tensions outside the North Caucasus.[19] The Soviet attachment to national rights grew in the initial post-Soviet period, when smaller peoples were able to engage in cultural and linguistic revivals and take measures to preserve or reawaken traditional ways of life.

Essentially, the system of autonomy developed in the Soviet Union was maintained and deepened, and given real legal significance. In areas of complex ethnic mix such as Dagestan, Soviet practices of assigning ethnic quotas in parliament and government were maintained and continued to provide some stability. The pursuit of ethnic preference within this framework encouraged the persistence of nationalism including calls for greater independence, but such attitudes were becoming less pronounced among younger people who had undergone education in Russian and who saw progress through a Russian-language higher education system as their main opportunity for advancement.[20]

There was little will and no practical way to avoid the strengthening of the status of the autonomous republics and regions in the chaotic circumstances of Yeltsin's Russia. But once a new president,

---

[19] Dmitry Gorenburg, 'Regional Separatism in Russia: Ethnic Mobilisation or Power Grab?', *Europe-Asia Studies*, 51, 2 (1999), 245–74.
[20] Dmitry Gorenburg, 'Nationalism for the Masses: Popular Support for Nationalism in Russia's Ethnic Republics', *Europe-Asia Studies*, 53, 1 (2001), 73–104.

Vladimir Putin, came to power in 2000, he made it a priority not just to solve the Chechen problem, but also to regularise central authority over the rest of Russia. The creation of seven new 'super-regions' for Russia in May 2000, overseen by envoys directly appointed by Putin, covered the whole of Russia's vast territory, not just the national republics and regions, and did not proclaim any national element. But it was clear that one of the key targets was reining in the growing power of national leaders such as Shaimiev. Also in Putin's first year in office, the upper house of the Russian Parliament, the Federal Council, was reformed so as to meet more regularly but to be less closely tied to regional authorities. More significantly, Putin acquired the right to dismiss elected governors and regional assemblies. Meanwhile the Russian Constitutional Court began to vigorously pursue republics whose laws were deemed to be unconstitutional, provoking conflicts with Bashkiria, Tatarstan, Sakha and Buriatia.[21]

Most leaders in the autonomous republics remained in place and served Putin and his successor as president, Dmitri Medvedev, without much friction. Shaimiev stood down at the end of his fourth term as president of Tatarstan in 2010, having nominated his prime minister as successor. In the same year, Kirsan Ilyumzhinov's eccentric seventeen-year rule of the Kalmyk Republic came to an end. This moving on of the old guard and Putin's determination to strengthen central control have not, to date, greatly affected the situation of most of Russia's autonomous republics and regions, where a cautiously balanced ethnic policy, based on the main nationality but avoiding any offence to Russians, continues to

---

[21] Cameron Ross, 'Putin's Federal Reforms', in Cameron Ross (ed.), *Russian Politics under Putin* (Manchester University Press, 2004), 155–75.

prevail. But the leaders of these republics had considerably less room to manoeuvre than had been the case under Yeltsin.[22]

COLOUR REVOLUTIONS

It was no coincidence that those countries that experienced revolutionary upheavals in the early 2000s – Georgia, Ukraine and Kyrgyzstan – were those that stood in an undecided position between the rigid authoritarianism of the other Central Asian states, Azerbaijan and Belarus on the one hand, and the more or less fully fledged European democracies of the Baltic region on the other. The remaining intermediate states – Armenia and Moldova – were perhaps too involved in territorial conflicts to be drawn into governmental upheaval. What Ukraine, Georgia and Kyrgyzstan had in common was a popular regime turned sour, with corruption flourishing and leaders anxious to hang on to power by any means while enriching themselves and their entourages. Georgia's Eduard Shevardnadze was the first post-Soviet leader since the early 1990s to be overthrown by popular protest. In the second half of the 1990s he oversaw impressive economic growth rates for Georgia, but the general population saw little of the benefit of this, while businessmen and former criminal leaders and warlords were able to make small fortunes through both legal and illicit means. In the last few years of Shevardnadze's rule, corruption became increasingly rife, while relations with Russia deteriorated mostly as a result of Georgia's failure to support the war with Chechnya.

The economic and other successes of Shevardnadze's government owed much to younger reformers in the government, led by the speaker of parliament Zurab Zhvania and joined in 2000 by the

---

[22] Thomas F. Remington, *Politics in Russia*, 7th edn (London: Longman, 2011).

young minister for justice who had a Dutch wife and a degree from New York's Columbia University, Mikhail Saakashvili. Zhvania and Saakashvili both resigned separately in the course of 2001 and began to systematically attack the government for corruption and incompetence. In June 2003 they were joined in opposition by the then popular speaker of parliament Nino Burjanadze, while a new youth movement, Kmara, was steadily growing in size, organisation and visibility. In parliamentary elections on 2 November 2003, independent exit polls showed Saakashvili's National Movement ahead of the pro-government 'For a New Georgia' party, but the official results released later in the day put For a New Georgia ahead. By allowing international observers to conduct an exit poll and by failing to muzzle the Georgian media, Shevardnadze had exposed his own manipulation of parliamentary elections.

Demonstrations in central Tbilisi rolled out from 5 November onwards. As the falsification of election results became ever more manifest, the crowds grew in size and in support of the triumvirate of Saakashvili, Burjanadze and Zhvania, and adopted the red rose as their symbol. On 22 November, as Shevardnadze was convening the new parliament, Saakashvili led a crowd of protestors into the parliament building, forcing Shevardnadze to withdraw in the middle of his speech. The next day, to everyone's surprise, Shevardnadze declared his immediate resignation. The Rose Revolution had dismissed a stale and corrupt regime without a drop of blood being shed, in circumstances where the president had altogether lost the support of his own government, the police and army, and his foreign backers. Saakashvili was duly elected president with massive popular support, and appointed Zhvania and Burjanadze as prime minister and speaker of the parliament respectively. The new government tackled corruption energetically and renewed economic growth successfully, while orienting firmly towards Europe and the USA in its foreign policy. But Saakashvili also assumed a nationalist rhetoric and uncompromising stance over Abkhazia and South Ossetia, which was eventually to lead to splits in the leadership and war with Russia.[23]

A year later Ukraine's Orange Revolution followed a similar course in some ways, but did not succeed in uniting the nation in quite the same way as the Rose Revolution had. In presidential elections on 21 November 2004, exit polls gave the reformist challenger Viktor Yushchenko 53% of the vote ahead of the prime minister and chosen successor to Leonid Kuchma, Viktor Yanukovich, who scored 43%. But officially announced results put Yanukovich 2.5 percentage points ahead. Inconsistencies in official announcements about voter turn-out and share further fuelled the conviction that the results had been falsified. Yushchenko's election campaign had already been severely hampered by negative comment from the state-controlled media and by official harassment, and on 6 September he had to withdraw from campaigning for a while after falling ill from dioxin poisoning, which left him permanently disfigured. The day after the election result was announced, tens of thousands of Yushchenko supporters converged on the centre of Kiev sporting his campaign colour, orange. Yushchenko declared himself president, calling for a general strike and for the security forces not to intervene. The fact that they did not was due to many key officials in the regime, including at the top of the police and army, having grown disillusioned with Kuchma, while a confident civil society and youth movement could easily be tapped into by Yushchenko supporters who had built up grass-roots networks during the election campaign. As demonstrations continued, government supporters in the parliament also

---

[23] Thomas de Waal, *The Caucasus: An Introduction* (Oxford University Press, 2010), 188–94.

began to defect to the Orange camp, and on 27 November the parliament declared the election results invalid, a position that was confirmed by the Supreme Court six days later. A new presidential election was held on 26 December and duly won by Yushchenko.[24]

Ukraine's Orange Revolution was achieved with the help of massive popular mobilization on the streets of Kiev, but support was not as unanimous as it had been in Georgia. In particular, Yanukovich had strong backing in the east of the country and among Russian speakers. Unlike in Georgia, where Russia's leadership had initially been happy to see the back of Shevardnadze, the Orange Revolution was an embarrassment for Russian president Vladimir Putin, who had unequivocally backed Yanukovich. Deteriorating relations with Moscow after the Orange Revolution hit the Ukrainian economy, including through cutting off the supply of gas. The European Union, which had just expanded to include the Baltic states and other former communist countries, while supportive of Ukraine's new leadership, refused to countenance EU membership for Ukraine, something on which Yushchenko had staked much.

With Ukraine divided and hitting economic difficulties, the euphoria with which the Orange Revolution had been greeted died after little more than a year. The new constitution which was approved in the wake of the Orange Revolution weakened the powers of the president, Yushchenko had several run-ins with the parliament, and in 2008 fell out with the popular prime minister Yulia Timoshenko. In January 2010 both Yanukovich and Timoshenko ran for president against Yushchenko, forcing him into third place and leaving Yanukovich to win the run-off vote against Timoshenko. The eventual victory of the man whose false

[24] Adrian Karatnycky, 'Ukraine's Orange Revolution', *Foreign Affairs*, March/April 2005.

victory in 2004 had been annulled by the street protests was a remarkable turnaround for Ukraine, but reflects a country that does not have a clear sense of its own identity or direction as well as some clever political manoeuvring on Yanukovich's part. In spite of predictions that Yanukovich would take Ukraine decisively away from the EU and towards Moscow, in the early part of his presidency he took care to maintain good relations with the EU and proved able to stand up to Russia. Ukraine's reputation for political freedom and human rights was, however, blemished by the persecution and eventual imprisonment, coupled with allegations of torture, of Yanukovich's former rival Yulia Timoshenko.

The third of the post-Soviet 'colour revolutions' took place in Kyrgyzstan in March 2005. Again, clearly fraudulent election results were the trigger for mass protests that forced President Askar Akaev to resign. On this occasion Russia, disillusioned with Akaev's policies and his allowing a US military base in the country, may have actively supported the revolution. Regional divisions played a part here as well, with mass protests breaking out in the south of the country several days before spreading to the capital Bishkek. Although Akaev sought to appease demonstrators by ordering an enquiry into electoral irregularities, protests continued. Once they had swelled in size to the point that demonstrators were able to storm government buildings, Akaev and his family fled first by helicopter to Kazakhstan and then to Russia.

The opposition movement behind Kyrgyzstan's Tulip Revolution was led by Roza Otunbaeva and former prime minister Kurmanbek Bakiev, who was appointed acting president following Akaev's resignation and was duly elected by a landslide majority in new presidential elections in July 2005. Bakiev did not live up to expectations, however, and already faced mass protests in 2006 and 2007. Finally, further protests in April 2010 turned into a second

Kyrgyz revolution which forced Bakiev to flee first to the south of the country and then abroad, and was followed by ethnic violence between Kyrgyz and Uzbeks in Osh and Jalalabad two months later.

All three colour revolutions were greeted with enthusiasm in the west,[25] but the notion that they somehow represented the culmination of a transition from communism to liberal democracy was soon disappointed, as in some ways the revolutions turned full circle. But the premise of a unilinear transition process was always flawed, and the revolutions not only represented significant regime changes but also brought out political activism from mostly a young generation who were to continue developing civil society and keeping pressure on politicians. Largely as a result, the Yanukovich who won the Ukrainian presidential election of 2010 was very different in tone and attitude to the one who had effectively been ousted by the Orange Revolution in 2004. Georgian politics was completely transformed by the Rose Revolution, although the replacement of a stagnant and corrupt elite by one steeped in nationalism brought with it dangers as well as advantages. Kyrgyzstan, meanwhile, remained one of the most unstable countries of the region, riven by ethnic and regional divisions which were ruthlessly exploited by profiteers while the largely rural economy went into further decline. The revolutions were transformational, but did not bring any of these countries to some kind of end point. Revolutionary change in the future cannot be ruled out in any of the post-Soviet states, but if it does occur it is likely to remain within the broad political and

---

[25] Russian politicians and media made much of the support given by the United States and other countries to NGOs, particularly those active in the Orange Revolution. While such support undoubtedly existed and assisted in the material provision of protestors who often camped out in city centres for weeks on end, this in itself is insufficient to back the claim that the colour revolutions were engineered from abroad.

cultural parameters which have already become clear for each of the states, which differ from each other in character and development, for all of their common features and shared Soviet past.

During the first year after the Rose Revolution, relations between Georgia and Russia remained cordial and even constructive, with progress being made in discussions over Russian military bases in Georgia and the co-operation of Russia's foreign minister in settling the troublesome region of Ajaria, in spite of Saakashvili's clear preference for a westward-looking orientation for Georgia. But the Orange Revolution instilled a deep suspicion in the Kremlin of the political instability that appeared to be sweeping across the former Soviet world at the same time as Saakashvili was ratcheting up his nationalist rhetoric. With the initial successes of his reform programme running out of steam and the alliance of oppositionists in the Rose Revolution falling apart (Zhvania died suddenly in February 2005, while Burjanadze resigned as speaker in protest at the president's forceful response to street demonstrations in 2007), Saakashvili placed more and more emphasis on the need to restore the territorial integrity of Georgia by reintegrating South Ossetia and Abkhazia, whose ability to continue to operate as *de facto* independent states was blamed largely on Russian support.[26] Georgia's close relations with Washington and aspiration to join NATO further strained relations with Russia. The governments of the two countries engaged in spiteful action against each other in a spiralling conflict – in March 2006, Russia banned all imports of Georgian wine and mineral water, and half a year later Georgia

[26] This is covered further in Chapter 13.

claimed to have uncovered a Russian spy ring and publicly humiliated the four Russian officials who were arrested before sending them back to Russia.

But it was the status of Abkhazia and South Ossetia that was the real source of conflict. In 2007, Saakashvili took (unsuccessful) measures to engineer a change of political leadership in South Ossetia, while Russia stepped up its military presence in the North Caucasus. Skirmishes between Georgian and South Ossetian forces took place throughout the summer of 2008 and yet, with war becoming a more likely possibility by the week, everybody seemed powerless to prevent it. On the night of 7 August, shortly after Saakashvili announced a further ceasefire, Georgian artillery began to bombard the South Ossetian capital Tskhinvali in an apparent attempt to rapidly gain control over the city before Russian forces could respond. Victims of the shelling included members of the Russian peacekeeping contingent based in Tskhinvali, twelve of whom were killed. The following morning, Georgian forces began a ground assault and almost succeeded in taking control of the city, but by 4 pm on 8 August, Russian tanks reached Tskhinvali and pushed back the Georgian troops after two days of fighting. The small Georgian army was then overwhelmed by the far more numerous Russian forces, supported by a virtually unopposed air force, and took over much of the northern part of the country. The invasion stopped short of assaulting Tbilisi, but destroyed Georgia's army and deliberately damaged much of the transport infrastructure, including major rail lines and the port of Poti. Russian president Medvedev announced an end to military operations on 12 August, just five days after they had begun, and agreed to a six-point peace plan proposed by French president Nicolas Sarkozy, although it took another two months for the Russian withdrawal to be completed. On 26 August Russia unexpectedly granted recognition to both breakaway regions of South Ossetia and Abkhazia, bringing further international condemnation.

At the time of writing, the Russian–Georgia war of 2008 was the first and only occasion on which Russian armed forces had engaged in action against one of the other former Soviet states. Predictions at the time that the war would lead to a more aggressive Russian policy in the region proved largely unfounded, although establishing Russia's leading role regionally was an important aim for Vladimir Putin. In the 1990s, Russia had become embroiled in the Abkhaz and Ossetian questions largely by default, and Georgia, as it had been for much of the twentieth century, proved a particular thorn in Russia's side. Given the Russian leadership's constant references to Russia's great power status, it was little surprise that it should respond to the small nation's provocations with force. Elsewhere, the main weapon through which Russia sought to assert dominance regionally was an economic one, the control of gas resources for many of the former Soviet states. The most significant attempt by Russia to re-exert its regional influence in the twenty-first century came in the form of a Customs Union, based on trade and designed largely to counter growing Chinese influence. Initially comprising Russia, Belarus and Kazakhstan, by 2012 the Union looked set to expand to include Kyrgyzstan and Tajikistan, and was gaining some legal teeth as well as settling a common customs zone. But the extent to which the Customs Union, or Eurasian Union, would expand its powers and with them Russian political dominance remained unclear as President Putin began his third presidency in May 2012.

With the exception of the three Baltic countries, which had joined the European Union, most of the post-Soviet states had developed their distinct orientations which generally stood somewhere in between Russia, the West and China. Attempts by academics and others to characterise the entire Soviet space as Eurasia or under some other label, or to create sub-regional groupings, have proved of little value. Each country has developed its own individual character, which in many ways reflects differentiations which existed already in late Soviet times. In their efforts to distance themselves from the Soviet past, political and intellectual elites have built up images of the nation deploying, in varying degrees, leadership personalities, territorial claims and historical motifs and heroes. All of the post-Soviet states, with the exception of Belarus, have political independence at the core of their national values, and in many respects the winning of independence in 1991 stands as a national myth, often linked to the post-Soviet presidents as fathers of the nation. On a global scale most of the post-Soviet states can be considered small, although some have importance beyond the size of their populations or territories as a result of important gas and oil reserves. But only Russia, which inherited most of the Soviet Union's military capacity including its nuclear arsenal, is capable of being a significant actor on the world stage. While Russia's regional influence remained strong, for economic if no other reason, equally it was impossible that it could fully recreate anything like the Soviet Union given that the appetite for independent nationhood only grew stronger with the progress of time among the other fourteen former Soviet republics.

CHAPTER THIRTEEN

The orphans of the Soviet Union: Chechnya, Nagorno Karabakh, Abkhazia, South Ossetia and Transdniester

In the years after the collapse of the Soviet Union, a majority or significant part of the population in five territories refused to accept the status determined for them by the governments of the new states and recognised by the international community – Chechnya in the Russian Federation, Nagorno Karabakh in Azerbaijan, South Ossetia and Abkhazia in Georgia and Transdniester in Moldova. The demand for outright independence (or union with Russia) has been the bottom line in all five cases, while the newly independent states have appealed to the principle of territorial integrity in insisting that the territories remain within their borders. No amount of negotiation over the precise status of each region has been successful in finding a compromise between two positions which are essentially incompatible. The apparent impossibility of breaking out of a situation where each territory (apart, eventually, from Chechnya) is ungovernable by the state in which international recognition locates it has earned the disputes the label of 'frozen conflicts', while the regions themselves are often described as 'breakaway'.

Supporters of both sides have frequently appealed to ancient history to support their case.[1] The esoteric nature of these disputes

---

[1] See Chapter 10, and Yo'av Karny, *Highlanders: A Journey to the Caucasus in Quest of Memory* (New York: Farrar, Straus and Giroux, 2000), 371–404, and, for example, Lakoba, *Abkhaziya posle dvukh imperii*, 9–13.

contrasts with the actual origin of the conditions of conflicts which in most cases first broke out in 1905. Rather more apt is the sarcastic characterisation by two American historians of the origins of the Nagorno Karabakh conflict as 'shrouded in the mists of the twentieth century'.[2] Soviet nationality policies combined with alternating tolerance of and suppression of chauvinistic nationalism preserved, for the most part, ethnic peace in the Caucasus and elsewhere until the late 1980s. But the same policies that prevented conflict also preserved underlying tensions and, crucially, once the structures of the USSR crumbled, the status of a number of territories was thrown into limbo. While the particular actions of local, Soviet and Russian leaders (and, indeed, the international community) led to crises in each case, and the origins of each conflict was different, what the territories had in common was a peculiar status whose continuation could be guaranteed only by the structures and institutions of the Soviet Union. Hence, Nagorno Karabakh, South Ossetia, Abkhazia and Transdniester are the true 'orphans' of the USSR.[3]

Before dealing with the individual cases it is important to establish a sense of perspective as to the extent of such problems. We have seen in Chapter 4 that, in the aftermath of the break-up of the Russian Empire and the Civil War, dozens of territories of mixed population were disputed by the leaders of the new republics. Borders were especially problematic in the Caucasus, and in Central Asia after the delimitation of 1925. Special commissions dealt with these disputed regions, while some areas were brutally

[2] David D. Laitin and Ronald Grigor Suny, 'Armenia and Azerbaijan: Thinking a Way out of Karabakh', *Middle East Policy*, 7, 1 (October 1999), 146.
[3] The term is used by Irina Kobrinskaya, 'The CIS in Russian Foreign Policy: Causes and Effects', in Hanna Smith (ed.), *Russia and Its Foreign Policy* (Helsinki: Kikimora Publications, 2005), 84.

dealt with by the enforced movement of population, either during the Civil War or later, until as late as the 1950s. In the case of Nakhichevan, the rather untidy solution was adopted of including it as an autonomous part of the Soviet Socialist Republic of Azerbaijan, even if the two territories were not physically linked. But of the many other sources of tension at the time of the Russian Civil War, only Nagorno Karabakh, the central, mountainous part of the Karabakh region, emerged as an issue of serious concern at the time of Gorbachev's *perestroika* and afterwards. In the ethnically complex Caucasus, then, the disputes and conflicts which did erupt were the exception rather than the rule.

In addition to violence between Armenians and Azerbaijanis over Nagorno Karabakh, ethnic conflict erupted around the time of the break-up of the Soviet Union between Ossetians and Ingush in the North Caucasus and between Kyrgyz and Uzbeks in the Osh region of Kyrgyzstan. However, given the mixed population of many regions, the absence of established historical borders in most cases, and the complete breakdown of established central authority, it is perhaps surprising that there have not been more such cases. Social scientists who have modelled the behaviour of competing national or ethnic groups in circumstances of rapid regime change or new state creation generally predict far higher levels of violence and internal secession movements: for example, the 'stateness problem', which focuses on ethnicity, institutions and borders, predicts problems in *all* cases where these do not coincide in new states,[4] while the 'commitment problem' looks at what motivates individuals to join a bid for secession or engage in ethnic conflict, and also predicts a high level of such behaviour in the case of regime

[4] Juan J. Linz and Alfred Stepan, *Problems of Democratic Transition and Consolidation* (Baltimore: Johns Hopkins University Press, 1996).

breakdown and reconstruction.[5] Such models were developed mostly in the light of events accompanying the break-up of the other major communist federal state, Yugoslavia, at around the same time as the Soviet Union, and indeed the proportionately much higher levels of bloodshed witnessed there underline the relative peacefulness of the passing into history of the USSR.

The virtually unchallenged decisions by the leaders of all fifteen union republics, including Russia, to quit the USSR undoubtedly helped to minimise outright conflict in the process. We have seen that independence was followed by a protracted civil war in Tajikistan, and shorter civil wars in Azerbaijan and Georgia. But the ethnic character of these wars was minor and subordinate to the clashes of individual rivalry, group interests or geographic differentiation. While all of the newly independent regimes embarked on a nation-building programme, which often antagonised national minorities (whether intentionally or unintentionally), as a rule extremes of nationalisation were initially avoided and were tempered to take account of the needs of minorities.

International organisations such as the European Union used their influence to encourage respect for minority rights. But international pressure does not explain everything: important features of the Soviet system may have been designed to keep the federation together and prevent national self-expression, but actually eased the eventual break-up. First, the Soviet practice of establishing Russians (or other Slavs) in leading positions in the republics, although one of the major sources of nationalist discontent, had a moderating influence. In some areas initially there was a backlash against this Slavic presence in the leadership so that, for example, in the first

[5] James D. Fearon, 'Commitment Problems and the Spread of Ethnic Conflict', in David A. Lake and Donald Rothchild (eds.), *The International Spread of Ethnic Conflict: Fear, Diffusion, and Escalation* (Princeton University Press, 1998), 107–26.

post-Soviet government of Moldova there were only two non-Moldovans in twenty positions. This situation was reversed, however, with the appointment of a new government as the crisis over Transdniester escalated in the middle of 1992, and elsewhere Slavs continued to be prominent in leadership positions for some time. This presence served to reassure not just Slavs, but other minorities as well. The fact that, with the major exception of Moldova and the less protracted one of Yakutia, ethnic conflict in the 1980s and 1990s by and large did not involve Russians as either protagonists or victims (in contrast to the time of the Russian Civil War and the 1920s) testifies to the stabilising impact of one of the principal long-term causes of nationalist complaint – large-scale Slavic immigration into the non-Russian republics and their disproportionate influence in republican leaderships.

The former monopoly of power by the CPSU, with its officially internationalist perspective, may also have improved the chances of ethnic harmony. Although many former communist leaders did not hesitate to embrace an overt, and sometimes menacing, nationalism, older personal bonds and outlooks continued to hold some sway. Above all, the old *nomenklatura* system ensured that in most cases personal relationships existed between the leaders of the new states, through which disputes could be negotiated. After all, by the mid 1990s the leaders of independent Georgia, Azerbaijan, Ukraine, Kazakhstan and the Russian Federation had all been members of the CPSU Politburo at some stage. The significance of these relationships was illustrated at a conference in the Hague in the 1990s to discuss post-Soviet border conflicts, at which the ease with which all the leaders of the former Soviet states conversed with each other was remarked on by western observers. However, in other cases the absence of these horizontal lines of communication helped to prolong conflicts.

But the more important legacy of the Soviet Union for the post-Soviet order was the system of national-territorial autonomy, which provided a lasting framework for dealing with the situation of national minorities. Autonomy contained the institutional set-up under which minorities could enjoy linguistic and cultural rights while remaining integrated into the new states. In the Russian Federation, the renegotiation of the basis of autonomy in 1993–1994 resulted in a mostly stable framework for the future of nationality relations. In principle, the same procedure could have been followed elsewhere, as was the case, for example, with Georgia's autonomous republic of Ajaria.[6]

But there are a number of cases where these same institutional structures contributed to border and ethnic conflicts and secession crises, although it is worth underlining once more that these cases were the exceptions rather than the rule: in Chechnya and Abkhazia, the institution of autonomy itself provided the basis for secession bids. In South Ossetia, and for a while in Ajaria, the Georgian state's efforts to undermine autonomy provoked conflict, while in Nagorno Karabakh autonomy proved inadequate as a solution to competing demands. Only in the Transdniestrian crisis in Moldova has a serious secession movement developed which was not based on an existing autonomy.[7] These cases, often referred to as frozen conflicts because of their apparently intractable nature, are discussed individually in the remainder of this chapter.

---

[6] Monica Duffy Toft, 'Multinationality, Regions and State-Building: The Failed Transition in Georgia', in James Hughes and Gwendolyn Sasse (eds.), *Ethnicity and Territory in the Former Soviet Union* (London: Frank Cass, 2002), 134–6.

[7] Some political scientists go further in claiming that Soviet autonomy was the sole and inevitable reason for these post-Soviet conflicts. See Svante E. Cornell, *Small Nations and Great Powers: A Study of Ethnopolitical Conflict in the Caucasus* (London: Curzon Press, 2001).

CHECHNYA

On 11 December 1994, Russian armed forces crossed into the North Caucasian republic of Chechnya. After a failed New Year's Eve tank assault on the capital city of Grozny, Russian bombers completely flattened the city centre and left much of the rest of the city in ruins over the course of January. Estimates of the number of civilians killed in the raid range from 10,000 to 27,000.[8] Over the following eighteen months, as Chechen guerrillas took to the mountains, the number of casualties rose to more than 40,000.

The North Caucasus, and Chechnya in particular, had been a thorn in the side of both the Russian Empire and the Soviet Union ever since the tsarist advance into the region began in the 1830s. The lengthy resistance of Imam Shamil centred on the region, while in the 1920s disturbances among the highland Chechens were a regular occurrence each spring once the snows had melted. Chechen and Ingush resistance to collectivisation in the 1930s contributed to Stalin and Beria's decision to deport them wholesale in 1944.[9] Popular stereotypes of Chechens as 'warlike' may have some basis in reality. According to anthropologists, the egalitarian tribal or *teip* system gave the Chechens an unusual coherence and solidarity, while the isolation of the highland villages from the outside world for much of the year and the difficulties the terrain presented to invading armies furthered the feelings of independence.[10] The experience of deportation and the effort of surviving it as a coherent

[8] Thomas de Waal, 'Chechnya: The Breaking Point', in Richard Sakwa (ed.), *Chechnya: From Past to Future* (London: Anthem Press, 2005), 182.

[9] Robert Seely, *Russo-Chechen Conflict, 1800–2000: A Deadly Embrace* (London and Portland: Frank Cass, 2001), 19–95.

[10] Note the important distinction in this respect between the lowland Chechens, seen as more ready to compromise, and the highland Chechens on whom the warlike stereotype is based.

people only strengthened Chechen identity and solidarity in the long run.

But these characteristics on their own do not go far enough in explaining why the Chechens, alone of the peoples of the former RSFSR, declared independence from the post-Soviet Russian Federation. Unlike the other breakaway regions of the former Soviet Union, the break-up of the USSR did not in itself radically alter the constitutional or actual status of Chechnya. A peculiar series of events, the characters of leading protagonists including Boris Yeltsin and Dzhokar Dudaev, and some serious brinkmanship and miscalculation all contributed to the development of Russia's only serious internal conflict after the fall of communism.

In the late 1980s, when Chechnya and Ingushetia were still united as the Chechen–Ingush Autonomous Republic, a popular movement began to develop first around environmental demands and then around Chechen and Ingush national demands. On the back of this movement, in 1989 Gorbachev replaced a conservative Russian First Secretary for the republic with a Chechen, Doku Zavgaev. In November 1990 Zavgaev sanctioned the formation of a Chechen National Congress, intended to act as a talking shop where the Chechen national movement could let off steam while Zavgaev continued to promote people on the basis of their personal connections and loyalty to himself.[11] At the congress, however, Soviet air force major-general Dzhokar Dudaev, then based in Estonia, was elected chairman of its executive committee and commander of its National Guard, and the Congress passed a resolution declaring Chechen–Ingushetia a 'sovereign republic'. The August 1991 Moscow coup was initially supported by the communist-led

---

[11] Anatol Lieven, *Chechnya: Tombstone of Russian Power* (New Haven and London: Yale University Press, 1999), 58.

Supreme Soviet of the republic, and the failure of the coup provided the opportunity for Dudaev, backed by Yeltsin, to oust Zavgaev and seize power for himself. On 6 September a crowd dissolved the Chechen – Ingush Supreme Soviet and forced Zavgaev to sign his own resignation and flee Grozny. On 14 September, the Chechen speaker of the Russian Parliament, Ruslan Khasbulatov, flew to Grozny to give official backing to the new regime. Immediately after his departure, however, Dudaev broke any agreement he might have made with Yeltsin's team and struck out on his own, beginning with the seizure of the KGB building in Grozny. Yeltsin denounced Dudaev on Russian television on 19 October but the Chechen Congress defied him by going ahead with parliamentary and presidential elections on 27 October, which Dudaev won with 85 per cent of the vote. In his first decree, on 1 November 1991, Dzhokar Dudaev declared Chechnya independent.

For the next three years, Chechnya operated effectively as an independent state, including maintaining high-level diplomatic and trading contacts with European states. The early euphoria was short-lived, however, as economic decay, ethnic violence and political infighting culminated in Dudaev's violent dispersal of the Chechen parliament in June 1993 – four months before Yeltsin took a similar course in Russia. Subsequent approaches for a *rapprochement* by Dudaev were rebuffed by Yeltsin. The black market and arms dealing thrived in the outlaw state, while the oil industry continued to prop up the governmental budget. Dudaev controlled the capital but large swathes of the countryside were already in the hands of rival 'warlords'.[12]

---

[12] Carlotta Gall and Thomas de Waal, *Chechnya: Calamity in the Caucasus* (New York University Press, 1998), 103–36.

There was little Yeltsin could do as long as he was not even in control of his own parliament, and he was wary of antagonising the other autonomous republics of Russia. By late 1994, a year after defeating the parliament and pushing through a new constitution, Yeltsin faced a drastic decline in his own popularity, which may have been one of the factors prompting him to decisive action over Chechnya. In words attributed to the secretary of the Security Council, Oleg Lobov, 'We need a small victorious war to raise the president's ratings.'[13] Connections between Chechnya and organised crime in Moscow, and the hijacking of a bus near the town of Mineralniye Vody in the North Caucasus by Chechens in July 1994 further reinforced the notion that Chechnya was a threat to Russia's internal security. Grozny's continuing defiance raised fears that other republics might again push for further concessions, while the oil facilities, including important pipelines, on Chechen territory provided an economic incentive to bring the republic back under Moscow's control.

Whatever the motive, it is clear that Russia's leaders and military commanders expected that the overthrow of Dudaev would be an easy task. In November 1994 the defence minister, Pavel Grachev, famously boasted that 'we would need one parachute regiment to decide the whole affair in two hours'.[14] But the invasion was a disaster. The ill-equipped and demoralised Russian army, for all its numerical superiority in manpower and weapons, found the stubbornness and guerrilla tactics of the Chechen fighters far more of a handful than they had anticipated. After fierce fighting, Russian forces captured the Chechen capital, Grozny, on 26 January, although street fighting continued for over a month.

[13] Carlotta Gall and Thomas de Waal, *Chechnya: A Small Victorious War* (London: Pan, 1997), 161.
[14] *Ibid.*, 157.

The occupation of Grozny was, from its earliest days, marked by a reign of terror, abuse and torture against its citizens. Women and children, and even Russian civilians, were not safe from the abuses of the Russian troops, but it was above all Chechen males who were targeted. Sent to 'filtration camps', including cramped railway carriages at the notorious Mozdok military base, these Chechens were systematically beaten and tortured, and many died from the ordeal. Thousands of civilians went missing, and throughout the war a catalogue of atrocities was committed, much of it well documented and recorded,[15] but the precise extent remains unknown. Russian journalists critical of the wars in Chechnya were subjected to regular harassment.[16] Concern at the abuse of human rights damaged Russia's dealings with the international community, briefly delaying Russia's entry into the Council of Europe and attracting criticisms from the OSCE, the European Union and other bodies.[17]

The behaviour of the Russian forces in Chechnya only hardened resistance and created a base of support for the rebels – who had finally withdrawn in good order from Grozny in March 1995 – allowing them to hold out in the mountains and villages and prepare to strike back. Faced by a far more powerful enemy, the Chechens turned to guerrilla and terrorist methods. The new tactics were first deployed in June 1995 when the most notorious Chechen field commander (and last to depart from Grozny), Shamil Basaev, led a raid on the south Russian town of Budyonnovsk. His men took control of a hospital with more than a thousand hostages, and an

---

[15] See, for example, Gall and de Waal, *Chechnya: Calamity in the Caucasus*, 228–55.
[16] Two much publicised murders, of journalist Anna Politovskaya and former KGB officer Alexander Litvinenko, have been attributed to their opposition to the wars in Chechnya.
[17] Hanna Smith, 'The Russian Federation and the European Union: The shadow of Chechnya', in Debra Johnson and Paul Robinson (eds.), *Perspectives on EU–Russia Relations* (London: Routledge, 2005), 110–27.

attempt by Russian forces to storm the hospital resulted in more than 100 civilian deaths. A similar raid on a hospital in Kizliar in January 1996 led by Salman Raduev culminated in a Russian bombardment of the village of Pervomaiskoye, to where the rebels had withdrawn with hostages. Civilian casualties were fewer this time – twenty-eight – but the episode was still an embarrassment for the Russian military and government.[18]

The Russian military could, however, boast one major success when tracking the signal from a satellite telephone allowed them to fire a rocket with pinpoint accuracy that killed Dzhokar Dudaev in April 1996. With Dudaev out of the way and a presidential election in Russia due in June, Yeltsin opened negotiations with Chechen vice-president Zelimkhan Yandarbiev, but renewed military operations shortly after his own re-election as president.

The rebels struck back on 6 August 1996, the day of Yeltsin's reinauguration. Against all the odds, 1,500 Chechen fighters dramatically attacked and retook Grozny. General Alexander Lebed, who had been a rival presidential candidate to Yeltsin earlier in the summer, was now sent to Khasavyurt in Dagestan to negotiate with the Chechens and effectively bring an end to the First Chechen War. Under the terms of the agreement, which in practice allowed Chechnya broad independence for a period of five years, Aslan Maskhadov was elected president of Chechnya in mostly fair elections in January 1997.

The Khasavyurt agreement was deliberately vague about what would happen at the end of the five years,[19] but in any case was not allowed to run its course. For almost three years Russia did little to interfere in Chechnya, while on the Chechen side personal rivalries

---

[18] Matthew Evangelista, *The Chechen Wars: Will Russia Go the Way of the Soviet Union?* (Washington, DC: Brookings Institution Press, 2002), 40–1.

[19] James Hughes, 'The Peace Process in Chechnya', in Sakwa (ed.), *Chechnya*, 280.

and disagreements led to splits in the rebel ranks. Although the movement did not exactly turn in on itself, the clear signs of the weakening of Maskhadov's authority could only encourage Moscow to renew its attempts to exert control over the republic. In the summer of 1999, three apartment blocks were destroyed by explosions in Moscow, events which still remain shrouded in mystery but which at the time were blamed on Chechen terrorists. Combined with an incursion by Shamil Basaev's forces into the neighbouring republic of Dagestan, this provided the pretext for a renewed offensive, although there is ample evidence that preparations had been underway since at least the spring of that year. With political leadership now effectively in the hands of Prime Minister (and Yeltsin's anointed successor as president) Vladimir Putin, the initial operations of the Second Chechen War, launched in September 1999, were much more effective than those of the First Chechen War. Within a few months the Russian army had established control over Grozny and most of the Chechen lowlands. Chechen guerrillas continued to record local successes, but the rebels' most notorious actions came in October 2002 when they seized a theatre in Moscow, taking 800 people hostage, 120 of whom were killed when the building was stormed, and in September 2004 when rebels took over a school in the North Ossetian town of Beslan. The siege ended in a bloodbath leaving several hundred dead, mostly children.[20]

As Russian forces extended their control over Chechen territory, Chechen resistance was further weakened by the deaths of the key leaders Maskhadov, Basaev and Abdul-Khalim Sadulaev between March 2005 and July 2006. Already by October 2003 the Putin administration felt confident enough to install a new Chechen

---

[20] Timothy Phillips, *Beslan: The Tragedy of School No. 1* (London: Granta Books, 2007).

administration, in which Akhmed-Hadji Kadyrov was elected president. Although Kadyrov was killed by a bomb in Grozny in May 2004, in practice he was succeeded by his son, Ramzan, who became president three years later. The younger Kadyrov swiftly established his own position of power and his ability to act independently of Moscow. He used his own security forces to stamp out resistance, and has been accused of sanctioning torture and summary execution of civilians in pursuit of rebel sympathisers. Much of the mountainous southern region of the republic remained under rebel control, but under Kadyrov the republic was able to begin the process of rebuilding after the painful experience of two wars and to return to some semblance of normality and stability.[21] Putin had succeeded in bringing relative peace to the region at the expense of relinquishing control over Chechnya and turning a blind eye to Kadyrov's excesses. But with his reputation as a peacemaker and the pacifier of Chechnya at stake, Putin was unwilling to present any challenge to Kadyrov before the end of his own presidency.[22]

The Chechen wars differed from the other frozen conflicts in a number of ways: they took the form of conflicts between states rather than between ethnic groups – although Russians did suffer from discrimination and occasional violence under Dudaev, fighting between Chechens and local Russians was not a salient feature; military operations were sustained for much longer periods than elsewhere, while terrorism and large-scale hostage-taking as a tactic was unique to Chechnya; the Chechens relied mostly on their own resources for the whole of the first and the start of the second war, without enjoying the support of a friendly state and only latterly

[21] Liz Fuller, 'Chechnya: Kadyrov Completes First 100 Days in Office', Radio Free Europe/Radio Liberty, 11 July 2007.
[22] Andrei Babitsky *et al.*, 'Kadyrov Inaugurated as Chechen President', Radio Free Europe/Radio Liberty, 5 April 2007.

adopting Islamic fundamentalism and so attracting the direct support of international fundamentalist groups; and Chechnya was less
of an 'orphan' in the sense that it would have found itself transferred
to the control of an entirely new state after the break-up of the
Soviet Union. The conflict might never have happened had it not
been for the headstrong character of Dzhokar Dudaev and the
miscalculations of Boris Yeltsin, who may have missed opportunities for a lasting settlement in 1991, 1993 and 1996. But the Russian
Federation was not the same as the Soviet Union or the Russian
Empire, both of which – in spite of their global superpower status –
had struggled to maintain control over the region. In terms of their
resistance to Moscow's authority, Chechens had proved time and
time again that they were exceptional, and the weakening of central
authority perhaps made a further attempt at complete separation,
however illogical, inevitable. Chechnya was truly exceptional, and
the argument that a successful secession bid would encourage other
groups to repeat the effort is based on flimsy premises and is
contradicted by available evidence.[23] It is true that had Stalin and
Beria's efforts in the 1940s achieved their intended result, the
Chechen problem would not have existed. As it was, the rehabilitation of the Chechens and a framework which allowed them to
re-establish their territorial nationhood reinforced the rebellious
tendencies that had never disappeared.

NAGORNO KARABAKH

The controversies surrounding the status of Nagorno Karabakh
during the Civil War and the 1920s were discussed in Chapter 4,

---

[23] Paula Garb, 'Ethnicity, Alliance Building, and the Limited Spread of Ethnic Conflict in
the Caucasus', in Lake and Rothschild (eds.), *The International Spread of Ethnic Conflict*,
185–200.

and the outbreak of Armenian–Azerbaijani conflict in the 1980s in Chapter 11. To recap, this territory in the southwest of Azerbaijan was populated mainly by ethnic Armenians – 123,000 compared to 37,000 Azerbaijanis in 1979, but was separated from the territory of the Armenian republic by the 'Lachin strip', inhabited by Azerbaijani and Kurdish Muslims. After several years of controversy, the territory was designated an autonomous republic within the borders of the Azerbaijan Soviet Socialist Republic in 1922. This decision has often been blamed for the subsequent violence in and around the region.

The context here was an increasingly evident breakdown of central authority and a clear sense that the future status of the territories of the Soviet Union was up for grabs. The autonomous status of Nagorno Karabakh may not have accorded Armenians the same privileges and protection that it had done in the 1920s, but it still preserved for the local population a distinct sense of identity and hopes that their situation might improve under the new order. It is notable, however, that the first moves to secure the transfer of Nagorno Karabakh to Armenia were spearheaded not by the inhabitants of Karabakh themselves, but by outsiders led by Igor Muradian, whose family came from the region but who himself had spent most of his life in Baku or Yerevan.[24] Extensive links with the Armenian political and cultural elite prolonged the conflict beyond what may have been its natural lifespan. The demonstrations which began on the streets of Stepanakert on 13 February 1988 might have been forgotten in the turmoil that was beginning to sweep across the Soviet Union at the time, but when they were echoed in the larger marches which started in Yerevan six days later,

---

[24] De Waal, *Black Garden*, 16.

the dispute over Nagorno Karabakh's status took on a far greater dimension.

The involvement of outsiders from the beginning of the Karabakh movement helps to explain why little account was taken of the opinions and interests of the Azerbaijani population of the region. But the structures of Soviet federalism contributed to the lack of negotiation at all stages.[25] The Armenian population in Nagorno Karabakh was unique in being in an autonomous territory enjoying access to a union republic dominated by the same ethnic group. It seems that neither the local Armenians or their supporters in Yerevan and Moscow ever saw fit to address grievances directly to Baku. Instead, appeals and petitions were directed exclusively to Moscow. The violent intervention of the Red Army in Baku in January 1990 underlined both the fact that Moscow, the CPSU and the security forces at its disposal were the only existing points of reference in a dispute of this type, and that these structures were rapidly losing their ability to arbitrate and govern in a normal way.

In spite of the horrific inter-ethnic violence in Sumgait, Baku, Askeran, Kafan, Shusha and Stepanakert, and the outbreak of open armed conflict as early as August 1991, the crisis might have taken a very different direction had it continued to develop within the framework of the USSR. As it was, when Armenia and Azerbaijan declared their independence, the political struggle for control of Karabakh intensified. On 26 November 1991 the parliament of Azerbaijan announced the abolition of Nagorno Karabakh's autonomy, while two weeks later a referendum organised among the region's Armenians voted overwhelmingly for independence.

Initially, neither side had an organised army. The Armenian side had the early advantage in spite of the fact that it was not, officially,

---

[25] *Ibid.*, 21.

the state of Armenia that was at war, but a volunteer army based in Karabakh itself. But the Armenians enjoyed a much greater number of trained fighters and officers who had been serving in the Soviet army, and the readiness of Armenians both within and outside Karabakh to volunteer. The breakdown of order in the Soviet armed forces, which had previously acted as a brutal but stabilising force in the region, further stoked the conflict. Regular troops already stationed in Azerbaijan either left their posts to return home or were among the units that gave support to one side or the other – the 366th Motorised Regiment based in Stepanakert backed the Armenians, while the 23rd Division in Ganja (also part of the Fourth Army) lent support to the Azerbaijani side.[26]

Early in 1992, Armenian forces began to push back the Azerbaijani army. On 25–6 February Armenian troops committed the single worst atrocity of the war at the village of Khojali, where close to 500 people, mostly civilians, were slaughtered. This single event lost the Armenian cause much of the moral high ground it had previously enjoyed. On 9 May the key town of Shusha fell. Although a June Azerbaijani offensive regained almost half the territory of Nagorno Karabakh, by May 1994 Armenians had not only regained control of the region and the Lachin strip that separated it from Armenia, they also occupied a substantial swathe of the surrounding territory on which Armenians had no prior claim.

The vertical structures of the USSR proved impossible to replace and left a vacuum in attempts to resolve the conflict. Armenia was left isolated by the break-up of the USSR and was pressed internationally from two directions: on the one side by a diaspora which was less compromising and more strident in its pursuit of national

---

[26] *Ibid.*, 166–7.

demands, including over Nagorno Karabakh, than moderate politicians represented by Levon Ter-Petrossian; and on the other side
by an increasingly close relationship between Azerbaijan and
Turkey. In these circumstances, Armenia's request in 1992 for
Russian troops to remain in Armenia confirmed the reliance on
the main external broker to maintain stability in the region.[27] Once
the Russian internal political situation had stabilised, the key role of
this regional superpower was demonstrated when it achieved a
long-lasting ceasefire in February 1994, something which the
CSCE Minsk Group[28] had failed to achieve.

The three sides – Nagorno Karabakh, Azerbaijan and Armenia –
appeared close to an interim agreement in 1997, when both Armenia
and Azerbaijan seemed ready to accept the first part of an agreement
proposed by the OSCE Minsk Group. These moves foundered on
the Karabakh leadership's refusal to accept any formal subordination to Azerbaijan. Likewise, the solution proposed by Russian
prime minister Yevgeni Primakov for Karabakh and Azerbaijan to
form a 'common state' was frustrated by Azerbaijani intransigence.
Contingent political factors rather than real security fears or irre-
solvable differences lay behind the failure of these peace efforts.[29]
While the 1994 ceasefire held, and there were occasional signs that a
breakthrough might be achievable, the next eighteen years saw no
genuine progress towards a negotiated solution.

Although it is possible to view the objections to both these
solutions as foundering on the largely symbolic question of status,

---

[27] Laitin and Suny, 'Armenia and Azerbaijan', 155.
[28] Involving France, Russia and the United States. The Conference on Security and
Cooperation in Europe (CSCE), later renamed the Organization for Security and
Cooperation in Europe (OSCE), became the main focus for diplomatic efforts following
the entry of the former Soviet states into the organisation in January 1992. Soon after this,
the CSCE held a peace conference on Karabakh in Minsk.
[29] Laitin and Suny, 'Armenia and Azerbaijan', 157–8, 164–8.

the real problem lay in the fact that whatever status could be agreed on would be subject to different interpretations by the three sides, on none of whom were sufficient restraints in place. The solution of territorial autonomy introduced in the 1920s, although imposed from outside, was largely acceptable and maintained stability precisely because it was ultimately overseen by the structures of the USSR.

SOUTH OSSETIA

The South Ossetian conflict was an even more direct result of the demise of Soviet structures than was Nagorno Karabakh. The unilateral decision of the South Ossetian Supreme Soviet to upgrade its status from autonomous region to autonomous republic in November 1989 was one of a series of similar declarations across the Soviet Union which in most cases went no further than the 'war of laws'. But two factors combined to make the situation more serious here than elsewhere. First, the South Ossetian decision combined with a move to unite with North Ossetia, thus threatening to remove it entirely from Georgian jurisdiction. Secondly, Georgian nationalism came to play an institutional and aggressive role earlier than elsewhere. These two factors together led to violent acts on the part of South Ossetia's Georgian population. The victory of Gamsakhurdia's Round Table–Free Georgia bloc in the October 1990 elections on a platform of strengthening the status of Georgian language and the role of Christian Georgians in their homeland made further confrontation inevitable.[30] Gamsakhurdia further stoked the flames by leading a march of 20,000 people on

---

[30] Toft, 'Multinationality', 133–4.

Tskhinvali in November 1990 and symbolically confronting Soviet troops there.

Armed skirmishes between Georgian paramilitaries and Ossetians ensued over the course of 1991. Following the fall of Gamsakhurdia, Eduard Shevardnadze initially followed a policy of appeasement with South Ossetia and opened direct talks with its leaders. Just as he did so, however, Georgian military units renewed artillery shelling on Tskhinvali in April and May 1992. This deterioration in the situation, and the flood of refugees to North Ossetia that resulted, prompted the Russian government to threaten war with Georgia. In mid June Russian helicopters attacked Georgian armoured vehicles, and a column of Russian tanks moved out to the suburbs of Tskhinvali. With Georgia and Russia on the brink of all-out war, direct contact between Yeltsin and Shevardnadze managed to defuse the situation and led to a ceasefire agreement which came into effect on 28 June 1992. Following the Rose Revolution, Georgian forces again advanced on Tskhinvali in the summer of 2004 but stopped short in the face of fierce resistance. While the ceasefire held until August 2008, and there were even signs of a settlement being reached at various points, tensions remained high and there were frequent armed clashes, increasing through 2007 and 2008 simultaneously with the deterioration of Georgian–Russian relations.[31]

The issue here became whether the structures which had been created in the Soviet Union could be replicated in independent Georgia. Georgia had already abolished autonomy for South Ossetia altogether in December 1990, just as South Ossetia sought to strengthen it. Russia's interests in the region and its regard for the rights of South Ossetians made a Georgian military solution impossible

[31] Cheterian, *War and Peace*, 182–5.

and protracted the conflict. What distinguishes South Ossetia from similar conflicts is that the structures of autonomy implemented under the Soviet Union might have provided an early solution, or the basis for later negotiations along the same lines as those that were successfully conducted with Ajaria. The South Ossetian leaders were entirely dependent on the support of Russian peacekeepers throughout this period, and the intransigence of both sides ultimately proved the spark for the 2008 Russian–Georgian conflict.

ABKHAZIA

Abkhazia had enjoyed a special, if at times ambiguous and confusing, status in the Soviet Union at certain times. In 1921 Abkhazia was accorded equal status with Georgia and the other republics which made up the Transcaucasian Federation, but was initially linked to Georgia by a 'special agreement of Union'. Abkhazia's status as a full republic was confirmed in 1925, until the Transcaucasian Federation was abolished in 1936. During this period Abkhazia, under the leadership of Stalin's protégé Nestor Lakoba, flourished economically and culturally. Abkhazia's Black Sea coast provided a favoured holiday location for Stalin and other top leaders – throughout the 1920s and 1930s Stalin spent almost every summer at one of his two holiday homes in Abkhazia or at nearby Sochi. Abkhazia benefitted from favourable investment policies, and it was an anomaly for the time that Abkhazia existed as a national territory at all, let alone one with full republic status – the Abkhaz were clearly a separate nationality from the Georgians, with their own language, but according to the 1926 census constituted only 27.8% of the population of Abkhazia, falling to 18% by 1939.[32]

---

[32] Kaiser, *Geography of Nationalism*, 116.

There was a more Machiavellian reason for this privileging of the region than its status as a favoured elite tourist destination. In the 1920s, Georgia had proved the most troublesome of all the areas under Soviet power. It had been the last republic to be sovietised, requiring the naked use of force by the Red Army in 1921. A year and a half later, in 1922, differences over how to deal with Georgian nationalism led to a split in the republic's communist leadership and threatened the entire Soviet nationalities policy. And nationalists staged a short-lived rising there in 1924. Abkhazia, with its economically and strategically important port of Sukhumi, was seen as a useful counterweight to Georgia, and the favouring of the minority population there was one of the few clear cases of a deliberate divide-and-rule policy. In the 1930s, this status came under challenge as Lavrenti Beria established his power in Georgia, and in Transcaucasia generally. The abolition of the Transcaucasian Federation in 1936 led to the subordination of Abkhazia to Georgia as an autonomous republic. Lakoba was reportedly offered the post of head of the Soviet secret police, the NKVD, but his refusal to move to Moscow underlined his determination to preserve Abkhazia's special status. Shortly after he declined this offer, on 27 December 1936, Lakoba died, apparently poisoned by Beria.[33]

This was followed by the 'georgianisation' of the republic, including forcing the Georgian script to replace the Latin in the written form of the Abkhaz language and the wide-scale repression of Abkhaz intellectuals, a blow from which the Abkhaz language and culture never fully recovered.[34] Its status as the official language of the autonomous republic was restored by Khrushchev after 1953, and in the 1960s and 1970s the deliberate policy of promoting

[33] Simon Sebag Montefiore, *Stalin: The Court of the Red Tsar* (London: Phoenix, 2004), 205–6.
[34] Lakoba, *Abkhaziya posle dvukh imperii*, 14; Toft, 'Multinationality', 130.

Abkhazia's status in order to undermine Georgia was again pursued. The demonstrations in Tbilisi in 1978 that forced the leadership to drop plans to eliminate out the exclusive status of Georgian as the sole official language of the Georgian republic were interpreted in Abkhazia as a renewed undermining of the Abkhaz language.[35] These fears inspired Abkhaz elites to appeal to Moscow, as they had previously done in 1956, 1967 and 1977, requesting greater rights and even a transfer to the jurisdiction of the RSFSR.[36] Overall, the history of Georgian–Abkhaz relations was one of outright competition, often directly encouraged by Moscow. Thus, while elsewhere autonomous status served to enhance the position of national minorities within a larger republic, in the case of Abkhazia it came closer to a zero-sum game, where any advantages enjoyed by the Abkhaz minority were regarded as weakening Georgia, and vice versa.

Towards the end of the Soviet period, the Abkhaz were in a clear demographic decline: their population grew by only 9.2% between 1979 and 1989, compared to 13.6% for Georgians in the same period. According to the 1989 census, Abkhaz made up only 18% of the population of the Abkhaz republic (93,000 out of 525,000), only just outnumbering Armenians in the republic and far fewer than the 46% who were Georgians. Abkhaz made up only 2% of the overall population of Georgia.[37] The relative material advantages enjoyed by the whole population regardless of ethnicity meant that, initially, there was going to be strong support for maintaining or reinforcing autonomous status. However, local ties between Abkhaz and Georgians (most of whom were, in fact, Mingrelians,

[35] Toft, 'Multinationality', 132.
[36] Alekesey Zberev, 'Etnicheskiye konflikty na Kavkaze, 1988–1994', in *Spornye granitsy na kavkaze* (Moscow: Ves' Mir izdatel'stvo, 1996), 43.
[37] Toft, 'Multinationality', 129, 140 n. 18.

speaking a specific dialect of Georgian and with a distinct culture) were weaker than elsewhere, with many not sharing a common tongue and so unable to communicate with each other, and also inhabiting geographically distinct areas. It was the ethnic Abkhaz population that had most to fear from a resurgent Georgian national movement under *perestroika* and that was prepared to mobilise over linguistic and cultural rights. Any loyalties the Georgians of Abkhazia felt towards their autonomous republic were quickly undermined by the growing tide of nationalism on both sides, which were becoming increasingly polarised.

The first open clashes between Abkhaz and Georgians took place in Sukhumi and Ochamchira in July 1989, over plans to set up a branch of Tbilisi State University in Sukhumi. There followed a local version of the 'war of laws' as the Abkhaz Supreme Soviet, now boycotted by its Georgian deputies, and the Georgian government both sought to redefine Abkhazia's status. The Georgian declaration of independence, the election of Gamsakhurdia to the Georgian presidency in the summer of 1991, and his subsequent georgianising policies further exacerbated tensions, and the adoption of a new electoral law by the Abkhaz parliament in August led to a parliament divided between Georgians and Abkhaz and unable to conduct any real business.

The legislative stalemate turned to more open conflict with the appearance of Georgian troops in Abkhazia on 14 August 1992. Georgia's new leader, Eduard Shevardnadze, asserted that this was a matter of legal territorial rights, although the more pressing reasons for the Georgian army's incursion was the restoration of railway links to western Georgia and operations against supporters of the deposed Gamsakhurdia. The Abkhaz leadership, however, immediately denounced the action as a planned and deliberate act of aggression, and the chairman of the Abkhaz Supreme Soviet,

V. Ardzinba, accused Georgian forces of 'spreading death and destruction on our land ... they answer our proposals for a peaceful resolution with tanks, airplanes, guns, murder and pillage'.[38] The escalation of the conflict led to the Georgian National Guard taking over Sukhumi and storming the parliament building, while the Abkhaz leadership relocated to the town of Gudauta, to the north of Sukhumi.

From Gudauta, the rapidly mobilised Abkhaz military forces had to fight the more established Georgian army on two fronts – from Sukhumi to the south, and from a new front in the northeast. At this stage, the conflict acquired international dimensions. At first, Russia attempted to mediate a ceasefire, but this did not hold, and Russia was drawn more directly into the conflict when Abkhaz forces, backed by volunteers from the North Caucasus (some of whom would go on to deploy the experience gained in Abkhazia in Chechnya), managed to push the northern Georgian forces across the Russian border. The extent of subsequent Russian military involvement after that has been disputed: although Russia condemned the third, and successful, Abkhaz attempt to recapture Sukhumi in violation of another ceasefire in September 1993, the suspicion remains that local Russian military support (whether officially sanctioned or instigated by opportunist local commanders, as in Nagorno Karabakh) was key to the outcome. Georgia's subsequent entry into the CIS and request for Russian aid in defeating Zviadist (former supporters of Gamsakhurdia) forces and keeping supply routes open legitimised a Russian military presence, and in 1994 Russian troops became stationed indefinitely along the Abkhaz–Georgian border, constituting a CIS peacekeeping force.

---

[38] A. G. Zdravomyslov, *Mezhnatsional'nye konflikty v postsovetskom prostrane* (Moscow: Aspekt Press, 1997), 58–9.

The United Nations had become involved in Abkhazia as early as 1992, and continued to play a mediating role, as did the CSCE (later OSCE) throughout the 1990s. But in practice the efforts of these international organisations came to very little.[39]

The recapture of Sukhumi in September 1993 precipitated the part-voluntary, part-enforced evacuation of most of the Georgian population. Given that Georgians had made up over 40 per cent of the population of Abkhazia, and they were not easily resettled in Georgia, this led to one of the most serious cases of IDPs (internally displaced persons) in the post-Soviet space. With Russian troops ensuring *de facto* independence for Abkhazia, and its *de iure* constitutional status in suspension, the IDP problem became the most pressing question for the region. Between 1995 and 1998, UN-brokered talks foundered as the Georgian side insisted on the return of IDPs before Abkhazia's status could be determined, while the Abkhaz side laid out determination of Abkhazia's political status as a precondition for the return of IDPs. Frustrated at the lack of progress, Georgian IDPs themselves instituted a blockade of humanitarian aid into Abkhazia in May 1998, leading to a renewed flare-up of violence.

Georgia's Rose Revolution in November 2003 made even less difference in Abkhazia than in South Ossetia. Georgian president Mikhail Saakashvili's offer of broad-ranging autonomy for Abkhazia fell on deaf ears. Russian peacekeepers ensured that Georgia avoided reverting to the military option, and the Abkhaz leadership's insistence on full independence meant that there was no common ground between Abkhazia and Georgia on which to negotiate. Some progress was made in 2005 on reopening railway links from Georgia to Russia through Abkhazia and on the return of

---

[39] Cheterian, *War and Peace*, 185–216, 319–54.

Georgian IDPs to the southern Gori region. But even here Abkhaz insistence that returnees had to surrender Georgian citizenship and harrassment of Georgian railway officials by the Abkhaz authorities suggest that it would be difficult to build on this limited progress. Any possibility of a negotiated reincorporation of Abkhazia into Georgia was finally ended by the Russian–Georgian war of 2008.

For most of the Soviet period, with the exception of 1936–1956, Abkhazia either enjoyed an equal formal status to Georgia or benefitted from the informal patronage of Moscow even if it was formally subordinated to Tbilisi. The collapse of the Soviet Union dealt a fatal blow to this arrangement. In an effort to preserve or enhance their status, Abkhaz leaders continued to rely on Russia, but given that Russia was now a foreign power and Georgia was a sovereign state, the formal relationship between Abkhazia and Georgia was impossible to resolve. No possibility of compromise existed between the positions of independence and autonomy, and hence Abkhazia remained the most intractable of the frozen conflicts resulting directly from the demise of the USSR.

TRANSDNIESTER

The Transdniester region of Moldova (Transnistria to Romanian speakers and Pridnestrov'ia to Russian speakers),[40] at the start of the conflict which led to its *de facto* secession, had a population of 55 per cent ethnic Russians and Ukrainians, with most of the rest made up of Russian-speaking Moldovans and others. Like Nagorno Karabakh and South Ossetia, therefore, its population could look to co-nationals across the border, but unlike any of the other cases it had no existing autonomous status around which conflict centred.

[40] King, *The Moldovans*, 178.

The territory of Moldova to the east of the river Dniester was a
distinct geographical region not only because of the ethnic and
linguistic make-up of its population, but because it had always been
a part of the Soviet Union, whereas the rest of Moldova had been
Romanian territory between the wars and therefore had a certain
cultural as well as linguistic affinity with Romania. Russians, and to
a lesser degree Romanians, were over-represented in managerial
and intellectual occupations and were on average better educated.[41]
As long as the Soviet Union existed, the relatively privileged
position of Russians was preserved. But as soon as the prospect of
Moldovan independence loomed, the population of Transdniester
felt threatened.

The situation was exacerbated by the extreme nationalism and
pro-Romanian position of the ethnic Moldovan Popular Front on
the one side, and the support of the Soviet Fourteenth Army on the
other. But it was above all the fact that the Russian and Ukrainian
population were concentrated in a historically and geographically
distinct territory that enabled them to stand for the whole of the
post-Soviet Russian diaspora and become a *cause célèbre* that
attracted Russian nationalists, Cossacks and communist diehards
to the defence of the region.

The crisis began when Popular Front members of the Moldovan
Supreme Soviet pushed through a law making Romanian the sole
state language of the republic in August 1990. This prompted a
meeting of People's Deputies of Transdniester to declare the creation of a separate Transdniester Moldavian Republic (PMP) on
2 September. At this stage, and for most of 1991, Transdniester
leaders maintained their readiness to remain as federal subjects

[41] Igor Munteanu, 'Social Multipolarity and Political Violence', in Kolstø (ed.), *National Integration and Violent Conflict*, 203–8.

(along with the Gagauz regions) of an independent Moldovan republic, but expressed fears at the Popular Front's growing inclination towards unification with Romania.[42] Paramilitary formations were already operating in several Transdniestrian cities, however, and the regional leaders backed the August 1991 coup attempt in Moscow, condemned by the Moldovan leadership. This act attracted hardline communists to the region, including the head of Soviet OMON Special Forces in Riga, Vadim Shevtsov, who became minister of state security and, in December, president of Transdnistria, now a self-proclaimed independent state.[43]

Sporadic fighting along the Transdniester border in the first months of 1992 came to a head over control of the city of Bender, which was occupied by tanks of the Russian Fourteenth Army on the night of 20–1 June. The active involvement of the Fourteenth Army, led from June by the patriotic Russian general Alexander Lebed, convinced the Moldovan leadership that it had no chance of regaining control of Transdniester by force. In July 1992 Moldovan president Mircea Snegur signed a ceasefire with Yeltsin, which established a security zone patrolled by a joint Russian, Moldovan and Transdniestrian force.[44]

While the ceasefire held, the conflict with Transdniester had a dramatic impact on Moldovan politics. Parliamentary elections in February 1994 saw the pro-Romanian Popular Front routed and replaced as the majority party by the more moderate Agrarian Democratic Party (PDA). A referendum in March indicated overwhelming support (95 per cent of voters) for independent statehood for Moldova – that is to say, a rejection of union with Romania.

[42] Zdravomyslov, *Mezhnatsional'nye konflikty*, 29–30.
[43] Steven D. Roper, 'Regionalism in Moldova: The Case of Transnistria and Gagauzia', in Hughes and Sasse (eds.), *Ethnicity*, 107.
[44] For a brief chronology of these events, see King, *The Moldovans*, 190.

A new Moldovan constitution adopted in July gave Transdniester special status as an autonomous region. Had this position been adopted in 1991 it may well have provided the basis for fruitful negotiations, but by now Transdniester's representatives refused to negotiate on any basis other than that of an equal state.

A number of factors led to a hardening of attitudes on both sides. The ceasefire agreement of July 1992, the Odessa agreement of 1998 and the Kiev agreement of 1999 were unable to address meaningfully the fundamental question of Transdniester's status. The gap between the two sides was regularly widened by support coming from Romania for one and Russia for the other side in the conflict, while the international community, including the EU which could exert enormous leverage on Moldova, failed to make any decisive interventions. Comparative studies have shown that it was opportunity and the historical divergence of what became independent Moldova, rather than the extent of ethnic differences, that lay behind the conflict.[45] But it was Russian favouritism towards the left bank of the Dniester both in the Soviet period and since which has made the separation almost inevitable in the period since independence.

GAGAUZIA AND AJARIA

Although the 'orphans' were the principal exceptions to the otherwise largely peaceful transition to ethnically mixed post-Soviet statehood, both Georgia and Moldova faced other internal secession crises which appeared at times to be heading in the same direction, but which were ultimately settled in a peaceful manner. The Gagauz are a group of Orthodox Christian Turks, 153,468 of whom

---

[45] Kolstø (ed.), *National Integration*.

(according to the 1989 census) lived in Moldova, concentrated in the southern region. Ajars are considered distinct from Georgians by virtue of their Islamic faith rather than any ethnic difference. They are mostly located in the southwestern part of Georgia on the Black Sea coast, and enjoyed autonomous republic status within Georgia for most of the Soviet period.

Gamsakhurdia's victory in the October 1990 elections directly threatened the autonomous status of Ajaria. Gamsakhurdia's brand of Georgian nationalism called for an exclusively Christian Georgia, and he openly proposed abolishing the Ajar Autonomous Republic, whose population was only about 40 per cent Ajar. Although Ajar leaders never made a claim to independence, they reacted to Gamsakhurdia's rhetoric with charges of cultural imperialism. The threat to Ajaria receded with Gamsakhurdia's eventual defeat in the civil war.[46] Over the next decade, the Georgian government's preoccupation with the secession crises over Abkhazia and South Ossetia ensured that a conciliatory attitude prevailed and Ajaria was left to its own devices. Ajaria's leader Aslan Abashidze, first elected in 1991, exploited the weakness of Shevardnadze's government to build up his own power base and ruled Ajaria as a personal fiefdom. Following the Rose Revolution, Mikhail Saakashvili sought to bring Abkhazia under the closer control of Tbilisi and, under pressure from Russia, Abashidze resigned in May 2004 and went into exile. Ajaria retained its autonomous status, however, and continued to enjoy a certain degree of local self-rule. Among Georgia's other substantial minorities, including large numbers of Azerbaijanis and Armenians, in spite of tenser moments, peaceful relations have generally prevailed, while the reluctance of Azerbaijan and Armenia to engage in border

---

[46] Toft, 'Multinationality', 127–8, 134–6.

or minority disputes with Georgia extinguished any revanchist tendencies early on.

Unlike the Ajars, the Gagauz had never enjoyed autonomy under Soviet rule, and the Gagauz language was not recognised after the early 1960s. But Gagauz leaders began to call for increased cultural rights under the impact of perestroika and, in September 1989, fearful of the Romanian cultural orientation of the Moldovan Popular Front government, they proclaimed an autonomous republic. Although the Gagauz made common cause with the Transdnistrians for a while, they never claimed independence, and the defeat of Moldovan forces at Bender led the Moldovan government to look to compromise over Gagauzia. The subsequent election of a more moderate government in February 1994 led to further talks and a law, ratified by President Snegur in January 1995, which was unique in the post-Soviet countries. It allowed for the creation of a special 'territorial autonomous unit' whose borders would be determined by popular vote, down to the level of individual villages who could decide by referendum whether to be included in the new territory or not. On this basis the autonomous district of Gagauz Yeri ('the Gagauz land') was created in March 1995, with Gagauz, Moldovan and Russian all as official languages and enjoying broad autonomy in economic and legal as well as cultural matters.[47]

Whereas the Ajars succeeded in preserving the status they had enjoyed in the Soviet Union, the Gagauz were able to appeal to the principles of Soviet minorities policies in order to secure a new autonomous status. In fact, the widespread use of local referenda to determine the borders of Gagauz Yeri came closer to meeting in practice the theoretical positions on national self-determination

[47] King, *The Moldovans*, 215–20.

espoused by Lenin some eighty years earlier. Both groups were able to take advantage of national governments that were too preoccupied with larger-scale secession crises to risk opening another front, and it is clear that decisions promptly taken at the right moments averted more potential 'orphans' appearing. But the successful resolution of these cases only serves to underline the contingent nature of the territorial problems that followed on the break-up of the USSR.

In the post-Soviet world, international institutions were constantly involved in attempts to mediate the conflicts in the Caucasus and Moldova, in the end to little effect. Certain solutions were closed off as a result of a turn in the accepted principles governing international relations since the end of the Cold War. On the previous occasion when empires had faced rapid and uncontrolled disintegration, at the end of the First World War, the central principle accepted both by US president Woodrow Wilson and by the Bolshevik leader V. I. Lenin, albeit in markedly different forms, was that of national self-determination. This was not ideal, since in ethnically complex regions it could be open to a variety of contested applications, while in some areas it was over-ridden by geo-political considerations. But it did at least lay the basis for a period of relative stability over ethnically contested territories between the end of the Russian Civil War and Hitler's remilitarisation of Germany. The principle that later came to dominate was that of the territorial integrity of states. This was agreed to, tacitly if not explicitly, by the leaders of the Soviet republics who engineered the break-up of the USSR. Russia, faced with its own internal secession problems in Chechnya, consistently adhered to this maxim even where further sub-division might have seemed to benefit it, as in Moldova, while the principle became enshrined in successive UN resolutions following Iraq's invasion of Kuwait in 1990. It is clear that there is no practical way to reconcile self-determination and territorial integrity,[48] and equally clear that intransigence on territorial integrity served to preserve frozen conflicts, when a more flexible approach might at least have opened up a greater range of possible solutions.

The cases of Abkhazia, Nagorno Karabakh and South Ossetia illustrate how, even if the institution of regional autonomy was an effective way of managing ethnic relations in the Soviet Union, this effectiveness was contingent on the existence of the Soviet state. First, the demise of the one sufficiently powerful and interested guarantor of the status of minorities led to a huge exaggeration of the 'commitment problem'. Secondly, the vertical structure of the USSR and CPSU meant that, in most cases, under the new order there were no pre-existing channels of communication and that the new relationships that had to be built between individuals and groups were infected from the beginning with deep mistrust and antagonism. Thirdly, preferential treatment given to certain groups under the Soviet Union were bound to provoke conflict once that country disappeared, as in Abkhazia and, in a different form, Transdniester. Fourthly, the presence of co-nationals across the border provided both real (Nagorno Karabakh, Transdniester) and moral (South Ossetia) ammunition to secessionist regions. Finally, while any threat to the existing status of autonomy could provoke crisis (South Ossetia), in other cases it could still provide an institutional solution (Ajaria, Gagauzia).

Twenty years after the break-up of the Soviet Union, the resulting major state formations had developed their own institutions, identities and global position. A handful of smaller territories

[48] Laitin and Suny, 'Armenia and Azerbaijan'.

missed out on this process in a number of ways. While Abkhazia, Nagorno Karabakh and Transdniester did develop their own state institutions, held elections regularly and returned to a normal economy, they remained unrecognised by all but a handful of countries and yet outside any control by the states in which they were recognised as belonging. Politics locally, actual power relations in the late Soviet years, and the activities and brinkmanship of nationalists on both sides, coupled with unpredictable actions by Russia and ill-judged stances taken by the international community, did as much as the Soviet institutions of autonomy to lead to this intractable situation, which appeared to be leading nowhere until war erupted between Georgia and Russia in 2008.

Conclusion

The late Russian academic and moderate dissident Dmitri Likhachev was fond of making a distinction between two types of national feeling: 'patriotism is the love of one's country, while nationalism is the hatred of other peoples'. The distinction is not as straightforward as Likhachev supposed but he, perhaps unwittingly, had hit on a major paradox of nationalism. Most people in the industrialised world today, and this has been the case for a long time, see nationalism as motivating and providing coherence to the state communities they live in – or at least that is how they see their own nationalisms. But nationalism is also a source of discord and conflict, something which is whipped up in the course of verbal or military conflicts between nation-states, and which in many cases contributes to the emergence of those conflicts. Nationalism also provokes conflict within states, between the dominant nation and minorities, or between different minorities.

In the Soviet Union, conflict was never far away from the nationalities experience, but the focus of conflict shifted over time. With the breakdown of central authority in 1917–1920, the national question merged with the contest between town and country, and the three-way contest between representatives of the old imperial centre, the new revolutionary centre and the peripheries. Mostly, however, these conflicts were local, between Russians and non-Russians or Reds and Whites in particular areas, not between

Russia and the borderlands, at least until the Civil War was settled. Where the contest involved scarce resources such as land, or territorial claims between new states, it took an especially violent form.

In spite of their initial hostility to Bolshevism, most nationalists and their followers were exhausted by the turmoil of the Civil War, and came to recognise that in a world still dominated by empires and emerging great powers, independence was either impossible or came at a great cost. Seduced by the prospect of autonomy or federal status and the promise of cultural self-rule and ethnic preference, many of them made their peace with the Bolsheviks and the contest shifted to the centre itself. Here, the conflict took the form of debate between those like Pyatakov and Bukharin who rejected what they saw as concessions to nationalism and those who took a more practical short-term view, or else understood Lenin's more sophisticated long-term view. This rested on the premise that in order to bring non-Russians closer to Soviet power it was necessary to build up their national identities and promote a Russian–non-Russian *smychka* (alliance) which was analogous to the worker–peasant *smychka* that underpinned the New Economic Policy. Although neither *smychka* really proved effective, the latter was abandoned amid the violence and upheaval of Stalin's collectivisation drive, but the fundamentals of Lenin's national policy remained in place. Under Stalin's despotic rule, the state engaged in open conflict with most segments of society, including ultimately the Communist Party of the Soviet Union itself. Non-Russian political and cultural elites felt the full force of Stalin's terror several times over, and Ukraine's peasants and Kazakhstan's nomads suffered far more than most the consequences of Stalin's drive against the peasantry in the early 1930s. In the maelstrom of the 1930s and the Second World War, and the cultural ossification of the late Stalin years, nationalities were told to reconceptualise their histories and current status but were in no more of a position to resist than anyone else. With the exception of the deported nationalities and post-war anti-Semitism, national conflict as such was hard to distinguish from other forms of conflict.

After Stalin's death, conflict took a new direction in the form of a contest between the centre and the republics. This competition raged over language status, the position of Russians in the republics and the amount of control republican communist parties had over their own economic and cultural affairs. In the last six years of his rule, Khrushchev sought to bring the non-Russian regions and their leaders under his control. Inside the RSFSR he largely succeeded, but with the union republics he failed. The Brezhnev leadership accepted this situation in most spheres, but continued to attempt to influence the character of the republics. A whole series of laws, decrees and exhortations aimed at devoting more attention to the Russian language were simply ignored in the republics, and in almost all cases defiance of the centre did not impair the ability of republican leaders not only to remain in office but also to enrich themselves and their families, to pursue the interests of the nations they led, to erect national cultural monuments and edifices and to develop many of the characteristics of European nation-states.

On the surface the break-up of the USSR resulted from a growing conflict between the centre and the republics, but why should the republics have adopted the extreme measure of secession if this was a conflict they had been winning for the past forty years? In the short term, the break-up of the USSR was provoked by a series of accidental factors: the meltdown of the Soviet economy, the rivalry between Gorbachev and Yeltsin and the inept actions of the August 1991 conspirators. But there is also a sense in which it was perhaps inevitable, and it is difficult to see the major nationalities accepting forever their place within the Soviet Union. In the first place, could it fully satisfy the aspirations of the republics' leaders? Within their own republics, they could, to some extent, rule as they liked, could build their palaces and promote their friends and relatives, could develop their personal cults and adopt all the trappings of a supreme ruler. But there were important restrictions placed on them. Most obviously, they were always subject to sudden removal by an outside force, as happened with Shelest in 1972 and Kunaev in 1986. More subtly, they were constantly reminded that their position was a subordinate one. Valery Tishkov, who knew many of the Soviet and post-Soviet national leaders personally, has provided valuable insights into the way they saw the situation: if he had wanted to prevent the dissolution of the USSR, Gorbachev should have provided senior figures in the republics with private jets and abolished the system whereby they had to apply for permission to travel abroad. However mighty they may have been in their own fiefdoms, on visits to Moscow they were ritually humiliated and constantly reminded of their subservient status.[1] While they enjoyed most of the trappings of power at home, they could have no foreign policy, no army, no currency with their portrait on it.

Similar considerations apply to the populations of the non-Russian republics. However much they might have benefitted in terms of standards of living, access to education and welfare services, and being part of a great power on the world stage within a reformed Soviet Union, and however much they could enjoy their own national cultures and languages and take advantage of policies of ethnic preference, for many non-Russians this was never enough. This was certainly true of the Estonians, Latvians and Lithuanians, for whom the notion of being occupied by a foreign power was not

[1] Tishkov, *Ethnicity, Nationalism and Conflict*, 44–5.

an invention of *perestroika*-era popular fronts or of post-Soviet architects of Museums of the Occupation. Slogans about Russian occupation, colonialism, throwing out Russians and national freedom had figured in graffiti on public buildings and comments scrawled on spoiled ballot papers throughout the post-Stalin years. After 1956 many Georgians felt much the same, and it is no surprise that it was these four republics that were prominent in the path to the break-up.

Emotions, not rational calculation, drove this process forward, as is usually the case with nationalism. Economic collapse certainly shattered some illusions about the advantages of staying within the Soviet system, but for most of the republics there was little prospect of material gain from leaving it. In some cases, notably the three Baltic states, economic prosperity did follow after a few years of transition, at least until they felt the full brunt of the global financial crisis of 2008. For the rest of the former republics, apart from those blessed with large oil and gas reserves, economic recovery has been slower than Russia's.

The culmination of the national contest in the break-up of the Soviet Union led to some of the features of the national republics being developed to extreme forms. Latvian leaders had pushed discrimination against Russians and insistence on the leading place of the Latvian languages so far in the 1950s that they were purged by Khrushchev, but their successors and fellow republican leaders behaved in a more moderate manner only by comparison to them. With the shackles finally thrown off, these policies were pursued to an ever sharper degree in the independent Baltic states. Elsewhere, the personal cults that had been a feature of the late Soviet republics were carried to absurd lengths in Turkmenistan, with Azerbaijan, Kazakhstan and Uzbekistan not far behind.

Separation from the USSR led to a disorientation in the world which has dominated politics in many of the ex-Soviet states. While the Baltic states were immediately comfortable with an exclusive orientation towards the EU, elsewhere the question of whether states should align towards Europe or Moscow or somewhere else has dominated politics. Turkmenistan has effectively cut itself off from the rest of the world politically and has relied on its gas and oil wealth and engaged with Russia only as a necessary trading partner. The other energy-rich states, Azerbaijan and Kazakhstan, have succeeded in keeping open to both Russia and the west. Ukraine and Moldova, by contrast, have been internally divided geographically and politically over which direction they should face. Even Belarus's exclusive orientation towards Russia has come under strain in the Putin–Medvedev years. Armenia, isolated because of its involvement in the Karabakh conflict has, by default, maintained close ties with Russia. Georgia under Mikhail Saakashvili has made no secret of its rejection of Russia and embrace of Europe, but has suffered as a result and continues to pay the price for Georgia's insistence on territorial demands.

This tension lay behind the colour revolutions in Ukraine and Georgia, but was still not fully resolved. As the 2010 elections in Ukraine showed, an orientation in one direction can still be reversed. Georgia paid the price for its westward stance with war and a closed border to the north. Armenia's place in the world is uncertain as long as the Karabakh dispute festers. The future for Central Asia remains uncertain: Kyrgyzstan and Tajikistan remain unstable and, while Turkmenistan has coped with the loss of its supreme leader Turkmenbashi, the possibility of a succession crisis in Uzbekistan and Kazakhstan remains.

The Soviet Union drew up the borders between these countries, and bequeathed some of the internal structures, institutions and political practices that still inform life in the post-Soviet states. But, as this book has shown, beneath the apparent monolith of the USSR, there were always forces at work which, through competition with the Soviet centre, with communism and with competing national forces, shaped the nations that have emerged and been recognised since 1991.

Bibliography

ARCHIVES

APL   Archive of the Communist Party of Latvia, Riga

RGASPI Rossiiskii gosudarstvennyi arkhiv sotsial'no-politicheskoi istorii –
Russian State Archive of Social and Political History, Moscow

RGANI   Rossiiskii gosudarstvennyi arkhiv noveishei istorii – Russian
State Archive of Contemporary History, Moscow

COLLECTIONS OF DOCUMENTS, TRANSCRIPTS OF CONFERENCES, NEWSPAPERS, MEMOIRS AND COLLECTED WORKS

Arkhivy Kremlya: Prezidium TsK KPSS 1954–1964, vol. I, *Chernovye proto-kol'nye zapisi zasedanii Stenogrammy* (Moscow: Rosspen, 2003).

Desiatyi s'ezd RKP (b), mart 1921 goda: stenograficheskyi otchet (Moscow: Gosizdat, 1963).

Dimanshtein, Simeon (ed.), *Natsional'naia politika VKP(b)* (Moscow, 1930).

Dvenadtsatyi s'ezd RKP (b), 17–25 aprelya goda 1923: stenograficheskii otchet (Moscow: Institut Marksizma-Leninizma, 1968).

Gorbachev, Mikhail, *Memoirs* (London: Doubleday, 1995).

Goryachev, Yu. V., *Tsentral'nyi komitet KPSS, VKP(b), RKP(b), RSDRP (b): istoriko-biograficheskiy spravochnik* (Moscow: Parad, 2005).

KPSS v rezoliutsiiakh (Moscow: Gosizdat, 1963).

Lenin, V. I., *Polnoe sobranie sochinenii*, 55 vols. 5th edn (Moscow: Gosudarstvennoe izdatel'stvo politicheskol literatury, 1964).

Libaridian, Gerard J., (ed.), *The Karabagh File* (Cambridge, MA: Zoryan Institute, 1988).

Lur'e, Lev and Irina Malyarova (eds.), *1956 god: seredina veka* (St Petersburg: Neva, 2007).

Natsional'naiā politika VKP(b) v tsifrakh (Moscow: Kommunisticheskaia Akademiia, 1930).

Sakwa, Richard (ed.), *The Rise and Fall of the Soviet Union, 1917–1991* (London: Routledge, 1999).

Sevost'yanov, G. N. (ed.), *'Sovershenno sekretno': Lubianka – Stalinu o polozhenii v stranye*, 12 vols. (Moscow: Institut Rossiiskoi istorii RAN, 2001–8).

Stalin, J. V., *Works*, 18 vols. (London: Red Star Press, 1986).

Sultanbekov, B. F. (ed.), *Tainy natsional'noi politiki TsK RKP: stenograficheskii otchet sekretnogo IV soveshchaniia TsK RKP, 1923 g.* (Moscow: INSAN, 1992).

Tak eto bylo: natsional'nye repressii v SSSR 1919–1952 gody (Moscow: INSAN, 1993).

Vos'moi s'ezd RKP (b) (Moscow: Gosizdat, 1959).

Yakovlev, A. N. (ed.), *Lubianka: Stalin i NKVD-NKGB-GUKR 'Smersh'. 1939–mart 1946* (Moscow: Materik, 2006).

SECONDARY SOURCES: BOOKS AND ARTICLES

Adams, Arthur E., *Bolsheviks in the Ukraine: The Second Campaign, 1918–1919* (New Haven: Yale University Press, 1963).

'The Great Ukrainian Jacquerie', in Taras Hunczak (ed.), *The Ukraine, 1917–1921: A Study in Revolution* (Cambridge, MA: Harvard University Press, 1977), 247–70.

Akiner, Shirin [Shiriin], *The Formation of Kazakh Identity from Tribe to Nation-State* (London: Royal Institute of International Affairs, 1995).

'Uzbekistan: Republic of Many Tongues', in Kirkwood (ed.), *Language Planning in the Soviet Union*, 100–21.

Alexeyeva, Ludmilla, *Soviet Dissent: Contemporary Movements for National, Religious, and Human Rights* (Middletown, CT: Wesleyan University Press, 1985).

Alexiev, Alexander R., 'Soviet Nationalities in German Wartime Strategy, 1941–1945', in Alexander R. Alexiev and S. Enders Wimbush (eds.), *Ethnic Minorities in the Red Army: Asset or Liability?* (Boulder, CO: Westview, 1988).

Allworth, Edward A., *The Modern Uzbeks: From the Fourteenth Century to the Present* (Stanford: Hoover Institution Press, 1990).

(ed.), *The Tatars of Crimea: Return to the Homeland*, 2nd edn (Durham, NC: Duke University Press, 1998).

Alpatov, V., *150 iazykov i politika 1917–1997* (Moscow: Institut Vostokovedeniia RAN, 1997).

Altstadt, Audrey L., *The Azerbaijani Turks: Power and Identity under Russian Rule* (Stanford: Hoover Institution Press, 1992).

Anderson, Truman, 'Incident at Baranivka: German Reprisals and the Soviet Partisan Movement in Ukraine, October–December 1941', *Journal of Modern History*, 71, 3 (September 1999) 585–623.

Arad, Yitzhak, *The Holocaust in the Soviet Union* (Lincoln: University of Nebraska Press, 2009).

Austin, Paul M., 'Soviet Karelian: The Language That Failed', *Slavic Review*, 51, 1 (1992), 16–35.

Avtorkhanov, Abdurahman, 'The Chechens and Ingush during the Soviet Period and Its Antecedents', in Marie Broxup (ed.), *The North Caucasus Barrier: The Russian Advance towards the Muslim World* (London: Hurst & Co., 1992), 146–94.

Babitsky, Andrei, *et al.*, 'Kadyrov Inaugurated as Chechen President', *Radio Free Europe/Radio Liberty*, 5 April 2007.

Balzer, Marjorie Mandelstam and Uliana Alekseevna Vinokurova, 'Nationalism, Interethnic Relations and Federalism: The Case of the Sakha Republic (Yakutia)', *Europe-Asia Studies*, 48, 1 (1996), 101–20.

Bassin, Mark, 'Nurture *Is* Nature: Lev Gumilev and the Ecology of Ethnicity', *Slavic Review*, 68, 4 (2009), 872–97.

Batirov, Sh. B., *et al.*, *Pobeda sovetskoi vlasti v Srednei Azii i Kazakhstane* (Tashkent: FAN, 1966).

Batsell, W. R., *Soviet Rule in Russia* (New York: Macmillan, 1929).

Bauer, Birgit, 'Chechens and the Survival of Their Cultural Identity in Exile', *Journal of Genocide Research*, 4, 3 (2002), 387–400.

Beissinger, Mark R., *Nationalist Mobilization and the Collapse of the Soviet State* (Cambridge University Press, 2002).

Bennigsen, Alexandre A. and S. Enders Wimbush, *Muslim National Communism in the Soviet Union* (University of Chicago Press, 1980).

Bilinsky, Yaroslav, 'Was the Ukrainian Famine of 1932–1933 Genocide?', *Journal of Genocide Research*, 1, 2 (1999), 147–56.

Blank, Stephen, *The Sorcerer as Apprentice: Stalin as Commissar of Nationalities, 1917–1924* (Westport, CT: Westview Press, 1994).

Blauvelt, Timothy, 'Abkhazia: Patronage and Power in the Stalin Era', *Nationalities Papers*, 35, 2 (2007), 203–32.

'Status Shift and Ethnic Mobilisation in the March 1956 Events in Georgia', *Europe-Asia Studies*, 61, 4 (June 2009), 651–68.

Blitstein, Peter A., 'Nation-Building or Russification? Obligatory Russian Instruction in the Soviet Non-Russian School, 1938–1953', in Ronald Grigor Suny and Terry Martin (eds.), *A State of Nations: Empire and Nation-Making in the Age of Lenin and Stalin* (Oxford University Press, 2001), 253–74.

Bourdeaux, Michael, *Land of Crosses* (Chulmleigh: Augustine Publishing Co., 1979).

Brandenberger, David, '"It Is Imperative to Advance Russian Nationalism as the First Priority": Debates within the Stalinist Ideological Establishment, 1941–1945', in Ronald Grigor Suny and Terry Martin (eds.) *A State of Nations: Empire and Nation-Making in the Age of Lenin and Stalin* (Oxford University Press, 2001), 275–99.

National Bolshevism: Stalinist Mass Culture and the Formation of Modern Russian National Identity, 1931–1956 (Cambridge, MA: Harvard University Press, 2002).

Broxup, Marie, 'The Basmachi', *Central Asian Survey*, 2, 1 (1983), 57–82.

Bukshtynovich, Inna, 'BISS Polling Memo: Belarusians Are in between – But No One Is There to Represent Them', *Belarus Headlines*, issue 4, October 2011, 8.

Butkevych, Volodymyr G., 'Who Has A Right to Crimea', 1992, www.infoukes.com/history/crimea/page-12.html.

Buttino, Marco, 'Study of the Economic Crisis and Depopulation in Turkestan, 1917–1920', *Central Asian Survey*, 9, 4 (1990), 59–74.

Carr, E. H., 'Some Notes on Soviet Bashkiria', *Soviet Studies*, 8, 3 (1957), 217–35.

Cadiot, Juliette, *Le laboratoire imperial: Russie–URSS 1860–1940* (Paris: CNRS Éditions, 2007).

Carrère d'Encausse, Hélène, *L'empire éclatè* (Paris: Flammarion, 1978).

The Great Challenge: Nationalities and the Bolshevik State, 1917–1930 (New York: Holmes and Meier, 1992).

Cheterian, Vicken, *War and Peace in the Cacuasus: Ethnic Conflict and the New Geopolitics* (New York: Columbia University Press, 2008).

Chokaev, Mustafa, 'The Basmaji Movement in Turkestan', *Asiatic Review*, 24, 78 (1928), 273–88.

Cohen, Ariel, *Russian Imperialism: Development and Crisis* (Westport, CT: Praeger, 1996).

Comins-Richmond, Walter, 'The deportation of the Karachays', *Journal of Genocide Research*, 4, 3 (2002), 431–9.

Conquest, Robert, *The Harvest of Sorrow: Soviet Collectivization and the Terror-Famine* (Edmonton: University of Alberta Press, 1986).

Cornell, Svante E., *Small Nations and Great Powers: A Study of Ethnopolitical Conflict in the Caucasus* (London: Curzon Press, 2001).

Cosgrove, Simon, *Russian Nationalism and the Politics of Soviet Literature: The Case of* Nash Sovremmenik, *1981–1991* (Basingstoke: Palgrave, 2004).

Counts, George S., *Khrushchev and the Central Committee Speak on Education* (University of Pittsburgh Press, 1959).

Crisp, Simon, 'Soviet Language Planning 1917–1953', in Kirkwood (ed.), *Language Planning in the Soviet Union*, 23–45.

Cummings, Sally N., 'Soviet Rule, Nation and Film: The Kyrgyz "Wonder" Years', *Nations and Nationalism*, 15, 4 (October 2009), 636–57.

Curran, Susan L. and Dmitry Ponomareff, 'Managing the Ethnic Factor in the Russian and Soviet Armed Forces: An Historical Overview', in Alexander R. Alexiev and S. Enders Wimbush (eds.) *Ethnic Minorities in the Red Army: Asset or Liability?* (Boulder, CO: Westview, 1988).

Curtis, Glenn E., 'Kyrgyzstan: A Country Study', in Lydia M. Buyers (ed.), *Central Asia in Focus: Political and Economic Issues* (Hauppauge, NY: Nova Science Publishers, 2003), 117–94.

Dallin, Alexander, *German Rule in Russia 1941–1945: A Study of Occupation Policies*, 2nd edn (Boulder, CO: Westview Press, 1981).

Davies, R. W., M. B. Tauger and S. G. Wheatcroft, 'Stalin, Grain Stocks and the Famine of 1932–1933', *Slavic Review*, 54, 3 (1995), 642–57.

Davies, R. W. and Stephen G. Wheatcroft, 'Stalin and the Soviet Famine of 1932–1933: A Reply to Ellman', *Europe-Asia Studies*, 58, 4 (2006), 625–33. *The Years of Hunger: Soviet Agriculture, 1931–1933* (Basingstoke: Palgrave, 2004).

Dawson, Jane I., *Eco-Nationalism: Anti-Nuclear Activism and National Identity in Russia, Lithuania, and Ukraine* (Durham, NC: Duke University Press, 1996).

de Waal, Thomas, *Black Garden: Armenia and Azerbaijan through Peace and War* (New York University Press, 2004).

The Caucasus: An Introduction (Oxford University Press, 2010).

'Chechnya: The Breaking Point', in Richard Sakwa (ed.), *Chechnya: From Past to Future* (London: Anthem Press, 2005), 181–97.

Dean, Martin, *Collaboration in the Holocaust: Crimes of the Local Police in Belorussia and Ukraine, 1941–1944* (New York: St Martin's Press, 2000).

Deutscher, Isaac, *The Prophet Armed, 1879–1921* (Oxford University Press, 1970).

Ducoli, J., 'The Georgian Purges 1951–1953', *Caucasian Review*, 6 (1958), 54–61.

Edgar, Adrienne Lynn, 'Emancipation of the Unveiled: Turkmen Women under Soviet Rule, 1924–1929', *Russian Review*, vol. 62 (January 2003), 132–49.

Tribal Nation: The Making of Soviet Turkmenistan (Princeton University Press, 2006).

Edmunds, Neil (ed.), *Soviet Music and Society under Lenin and Stalin: The Baton and the Sickle* (London: Routledge, 2004).

Edwards, Robert, *White Death: Russia's War on Finland 1939–1940* (London: Phoenix, 2007).

Etinger, Iakov, 'The Doctors' Plot: Stalin's Solution to the Jewish Question', in Yaacov Ro'i (ed.), *Jews and Jewish Life in Russia and the Soviet Union* (Ilford: Frank Cass, 1995), 103–26.

Evangelista, Matthew, *The Chechen Wars: Will Russia Go the Way of the Soviet Union?* (Washington, DC: Brookings Institution Press, 2002).

Fearon, James D., 'Commitment Problems and the Spread of Ethnic Conflict', in David A. Lake and Donald Rothchild (eds.), *The International Spread of Ethnic Conflict: Fear, Diffusion, and Escalation* (Princeton University Press, 1998), 107–26.

Forsyth, James, *A History of the Peoples of Siberia: Russia's North Asian Colony 1581–1990* (Cambridge University Press, 1992).

Fowkes, Ben, *The Disintegration of the Soviet Union: A Study in the Rise and Triumph of Nationalism* (Basingstoke: Macmillan, 1997).

'The National Question in the Soviet Union under Leonid Brezhnev: Policy and Response', in Edwin Bacon and Mark Sandle (eds.), *Brezhnev Reconsidered* (Basingstoke: Palgrave Macmillan, 2002), 68–89.

Fuller, Liz, 'Chechnya: Kadyrov Completes First 100 Days in Office', *Radio Free Europe/Radio Liberty*, 11 July 2007.

Gall, Carlotta and Thomas de Waal, *Chechnya: A Small Victorious War* (London: Pan, 1997).

Chechnya: Calamity in the Caucasus (New York University Press, 1998).

Garb, Paula, 'Ethnicity, Alliance Building, and the Limited Spread of Ethnic Conflict in the Caucasus', in David A. Lake and Donald Rothchild (eds.), *The International Spread of Ethnic Conflict: Fear, Diffusion, and Escalation* (Princeton University Press, 1998), 185–200.

Getty, J. Arch, and Roberta T. Manning (eds.), *Stalinist Terror: New Perspectives* (Cambridge University Press, 1993).

Gitelman, Zvi Y., *Jewish Nationality and Soviet Politics* (Princeton University Press, 1972).

Gleason, Gregory, *The Central Asian States: Discovering Independence* (Boulder, CO: Westview, 1997).

Golovnev, Andrei and Gail Osherenko, *Siberian Survival: The Nenets and Their Story* (Ithaca: Cornell University Press, 1999).

Gorenburg, Dmitry, 'Nationalism for the Masses: Popular Support for Nationalism in Russia's Ethnic Republics', *Europe-Asia Studies*, 53, 1 (2001), 73–104.

'Regional Separatism in Russia: Ethnic Mobilisation or Power Grab?', *Europe-Asia Studies*, 51, 2 (1999), 245–74.

Gorlizki, Yoram and Oleg Khlevniuk, *Cold Peace: Stalin and the Soviet Ruling Circle, 1945–1953* (Oxford University Press, 2005).

Grant, Bruce, *In the Soviet House of Culture: A Century of Perestroikas* (Princeton University Press, 1995).

Grant, Nigel, 'Linguistic and Ethnic Minorities in the USSR: Educational Policies and Developments', in J. J. Tomiak (ed.), *Soviet Education in the 1980s* (London: Croom Helm, 1983), 24–39.

Hanson, Philip, *The Rise and Fall of the Soviet Economy: An Economic History of the USSR from 1945* (London: Longman, 2003).

Harris, Nigel, *National Liberation* (London: Penguin, 1990).

Henry, J. D., *Baku: An Eventful History*, reprint edn (London: Ayer, 1977).

Hill, Alexander, *The War behind the Eastern Front: The Soviet Partisan Movement in North-West Russia 1941–1944* (London: Routledge, 2005).

Hirsch, Francine, *Empire of Nations: Ethnographic Knowledge and the Making of the Soviet Union* (Ithaca: Cornell University Press, 2005).

'Toward an Empire of Nations: Border-Making and the Formation of Soviet National Identities', *Russian Review*, 59 (April 2000), 201–26.

Hodge, Carl Cavanagh, 'Botching the Balkans: Germany's Recognition of Slovenia and Croatia', *Ethics and International Affairs*, 12 (1998), 1–18.

Hope, Nicholas, 'Interwar Statehood: Symbol and Reality' in Graham Smith (ed.), *The Baltic States*, 41–65.

Hosking, Geoffrey, 'The Beginnings of Independent Political Activity', in Geoffrey Hosking, Jonathan Aves and Peter Duncan (eds.), *The Road to Post-Communism: Independent Political Movements in the Soviet Union 1985–1991* (London: Pinter, 1992), 1–28.

Rulers and Victims: The Russians in the Soviet Union (Cambridge, MA: Harvard University Press, 2006).

Hough, Jerry F., *Democratization and Revolution in the USSR, 1985–1991* (Washington, DC: Brookings Institution Press, 1997).

Hughes, James, 'The Peace Process in Chechnya', in Richard Sakwa (ed.), *Chechnya: From Past to Future* (London: Anthem Press, 2005), 265–87.

Imranli, Kamala, *Sozdanie Armyanskogo gosudarstva na Kavkaze: istoki i posledstviya* (Moscow: Ladomir, 2006).

International Crisis Group, 'Azerbaijan: Vulnerable Stability', International Crisis Group Europe Report no. 207, 3 September 2010.

Iskhakov, Salavat, *Rossiiskie Musul'mane revolyutsiya 1917–1918* (Moscow: Sotsial'no-politicheskaya mysl', 2004).

Ismailov, E., *Azerbaidzhan: 1953–1956: pervye gody 'ottepeli'* (Baku: Adil'ogly, 2006).

Jaimoukha, Amjad, *The Chechens: A Handbook* (London and New York: RoutledgeCurzon, 2005).

Järve, Priit, 'Estonian Citizenship: Between Ethnic Preferences and Democratic Obligations', in Rainer Bauböck, Bernhard Perchinig and Wiebke Sievers (eds.), *Citizenship Policies in the New Europe*, expanded and updated edn (Amsterdam University Press, 2009), 45–66.

Jones, Ellen and Fred W. Grupp, 'Modernisation and Ethnic Equalisation in the USSR', *Soviet Studies*, 36, 2 (April 1984), 159–84.

Jones, Stephen F., 'The Establishment of Soviet Power in Transcaucasia: The Case of Georgia, 1921–1928', *Soviet Studies*, vol. 40, no. 4 (1988), 616–39.

Socialism in Georgian Colors: The European Road to Social Democracy, 1883–1917 (Cambridge, MA: Harvard University Press, 2005).

Kaiser, Robert J., *The Geography of Nationalism in Russia and the USSR* (Princeton University Press, 1994).

Kangaspuro, Markku, 'Russian Patriots and Red Fennomans', in Antti Laine and Mikko Ylikangas (eds.), *The Rise and Fall of Soviet Karelia* (Helsinki: Kikimora Publications, 2002), 24–48.

Kappeler, Andreas, *The Russian Empire: A Multiethnic History* (London: Longman, 2001).

Karatnycky, Adrian, 'Ukraine's Orange Revolution', *Foreign Affairs*, March/April 2005.

Karklins, Rasma, *Ethnic Relations in the USSR* (London: HarperCollins, 1986).

Karny, Yo'av, *Highlanders: A Journey to the Caucasus in Quest of Memory* (New York: Farrar, Straus and Giroux, 2000).

Kautsky, Karl, *Georgia: A Social-Democratic Peasant Republic*, transl. by H. J. Stenning (London: International Bookshops Limited, 1921).

Kibita, Nataliya, 'Moscow–Kiev Relations and the *Sovnarkhoz* Reform', in Jeremy Smith and Ilic (eds.), *Khrushchev in the Kremlin*, 94–111.

King, Charles, *The Ghost of Freedom: A History of the Caucasus* (Oxford University Press, 2008).

    The Moldovans: Romania, Russia, and the Politics of Culture (Stanford: Hoover Institution Press, 1999).

Kirby, David, *The Baltic World, 1772–1993: Europe's Northern Periphery in an Age of Change* (London: Longman, 1995).

    'Incorporation: The Molotov–Ribbentrop Pact', in Graham Smith (ed.), *The Baltic States*, 69–85.

Kirkwood, Michael, '*Glasnost*', "the National Question" and Soviet Language Policy', *Soviet Studies* (1991), 43, 1, 61–81.

    (ed.), *Language Planning in the Soviet Union* (Basingstoke: Macmillan, 1989).

Knight, Amy, *Beria: Stalin's First Lieutenant* (Princeton University Press, 1993).

Kobrinskaya, Irina, 'The CIS in Russian Foreign Policy: Causes and Effects', in Hanna Smith (ed.), *Russia and Its Foreign Policy* (Helsinki: Kikimora Publications, 2005), 77–92.

Kõll, Anu-Mai, 'Tender Wolves: Identification and Persecution of Kulaks in Viljandimaa 1940–1949', in Mertelsmann (ed.), *Sovietization of the Baltic States*, 127–49.

Kolstø, Pål, (eds.), *National Integration and Violent Conflict in Post-Soviet Societies: The Cases of Estonia and Moldova* (London, MD, and Oxford, CO: Rowman & Littlefield, 2002).

Kowalewski, David, 'National Rights Protest in the Brezhnev Era: Some Determinants of Success', *Ethnic and Racial Studies*, 4, 2 (April 1981), 175–88.

Kozlov, Viktor, *Mass Uprisings in the USSR: Protest and Rebellion in the Post-Stalin Years* (New York and London: M. E. Sharpe, 2002).

Kreindler, Isabelle, 'The Changing Status of Russian in the Soviet Union', *International Journal of the Sociology of Language*, 33 (1982), 7–39.

'A Neglected Source of Lenin's Nationality Policy', *Slavic Review* (1977), 1, 86–100.

'The Soviet Deported Nationalities: A Summary and an Update', *Soviet Studies*, 38, 3 (1986), 387–405.

'Soviet Language Planning since 1953', in Kirkwood (ed.), *Language Planning in the Soviet Union*, 43–63.

Krūma, Kristīne, 'Checks and Balances in Latvian Nationality Policies: National Agendas and International Frameworks', in Rainer Bauböck, Bernhard Perchinig and Wiebke Sievers (eds.), *Citizenship Policies in the New Europe*, expanded and updated edn (Amsterdam University Press, 2009), 67–96.

Kurki, Tuulikki, 'The Modern Soviet Man Looks Back: Images and Narratives of Soviet Karelia', in Pekka Suutari and Yury Shikalov (eds.), *Karelia Written and Sung: Representations of Locality in Soviet and Russian Contexts* (Helsinki: Kikimora Publications, 2010), 86–108.

Kuromiya, Hiroaki, *Freedom and Terror in the Donbas: A Ukrainian–Russian Borderland, 1870s–1990s* (Cambridge University Press, 1998).

Laitin, David D. and Ronald Grigor Suny, 'Armenia and Azerbaijan: Thinking a Way out of Karabakh', *Middle East Policy*, 7, 1 (October 1999), 145–176.

Lakoba, Stanislav, *Abkhaziya posle dvukh imperii, XX–XXIvv.* (Moscow: Materik, 2004).

Lane, Thomas, *Lithuania: Stepping Westward* (London: Routledge, 2001).

Levin, Nora, *The Jews in the Soviet Union since 1917: Paradox of Survival*, 2 vols. (London: I. B. Tauris, 1990).

Lewin, Moshe, *Lenin's Last Struggle* (London: Pluto Press, 1975).

Lewis, Robert A., Richard H. Rowland and Ralph S. Clem, *Nationality and Population Change in Russia and the USSR: An Evaluation of Census Data, 1897–1970* (New York: Praeger Publishers, 1976).

Lieven, Anatol, *Chechnya: Tombstone of Russian Power* (New Haven and London: Yale University Press, 1999).

Linz, Juan J. and Alfred Stepan, *Problems of Democratic Transition and Consolidation* (Baltimore: Johns Hopkins University Press, 1996).

Lipset, Harry, 'The Status of National Minority Languages in Soviet Education', *Soviet Studies*, 19, 2 (1967), 181–9.

Lohr, Eric, *Nationalizing the Russian Empire: The Campaign against Enemy Aliens during World War I* (Cambridge, MA: Harvard University Press, 2003).

Mace, James E., *Communism and the Dilemmas of National Liberation: National Communism in Soviet Ukraine* (Cambridge, MA: Harvard University Press, 1983).

'Famine and nationalism in Soviet Ukraine', *Problems of Communism*, 33, 3 (1984), 37–50.

Martin, Terry, *The Affirmative Action Empire: Nations and Nationalism in the Soviet Union, 1923–1939* (Ithaca: Cornell University Press, 2001).

McCauley, Martin, *Gorbachev (Profiles in Power)* (London: Longman, 1998).

Melvin, Neil J., *Uzbekistan: Transition to Authoritarianism on the Silk Road* (Amsterdam: OPA, 2000).

Mertelsmann, Olaf (ed.), *The Sovietization of the Baltic States, 1940–1956* (Tartu: Kleio, 2003).

'Was There a Stalinist Industrialization in the Baltic Republics? Estonia – an Example', in Mertelsmann (ed.), *Sovietization of the Baltic States*, 151–70.

Misiunas, Romuald J. and Rein Taagepera, *The Baltic States: Years of Dependence, 1940–1980* (Berkeley: University of California Press, 1983).

Mitrokhin, Nikolai, 'The Rise of Political Clans in the Era of Nikita Khrushchev: The First Phase, 1953–1959', in Jeremy Smith and Ilic (eds.), *Khrushchev in the Kremlin*, 26–40.

Russkaya partiya: dvizhenie russkikh natsionalistov v SSSR 1953–1985 gody (Moscow: Novoe Literaturnoe Obozrenie, 2003).

Montefiore, Simon Sebag, *Stalin: The Court of the Red Tsar* (London: Phoenix, 2004).

Mote, Victor L., *Siberia: Worlds Apart* (Boulder, CO: Westview Press, 1998).

Mukhina, Irina, 'Germans of the Soviet Union: Ethnic Identity, Tragic Reality' (unpublished Ph.D thesis, Boston College, 2005).

Munteanu, Igor, 'Social Multipolarity and Political Violence', in Pål Kolstø (ed.), *National Integration and Violent Conflict in Post-Soviet Societies: The Cases of Estonia and Moldova* (Lanham, MD, and Oxford: Rowman & Littlefield, 2002).

Nahaylo, Bohdan and Victor Swoboda, *Soviet Disunion: A History of the Nationalities Problem in the USSR* (New York: Free Press, 1990).

Nash, Mark, 'The "Exceptional" Church: Religious Freedom and the Catholic Church in Russia', (unpublished Ph.D dissertation, University of Birmingham, 2007).

Nazarov, S. A., *Rukovodstvo TsK RKP partynim stroitel'stvom v Sredney Aȥii* (Tashkent: Izdatelstvo Uzbekistan, 1972).

Niyazi, Aziz, 'Tajikistan', in Mohiaddin Mesbahi (ed.), *Central Asia and the Caucasus after the Soviet Union* (Gainesville: University Press of Florida, 1994), 164–90.

Northrop, Douglas, 'Languages of Loyalty: Gender, Politics and Party Supervision in Uzbekistan, 1927–1941', *Russian Review*, 59 (April 2000), 179–200.

'Subaltern Dialogues: Subversion and Resistance in Soviet Uzbek Family Law', *Slavic Review*, 60, 1 (Spring, 2001), 115–39.

O' Brien, Matthew, 'Uzeyir Hajibeyov and His Role in the Development of Musical Life in Azerbaijan', in Edmunds (ed.), *Soviet Music*, 209–27.

O'Connor, Kevin, *The History of the Baltic States* (Westport, CT: Greenwood Press, 1967).

Olcott, Martha Brill, 'Kazakhstan: Pushing for Eurasia', in Ian Bremmer and Ray Taras (eds.), *New States, New Politics: Building the Post-Soviet Nations* (Cambridge University Press, 1997), 547–70.

Payaslian, Simon, *The History of Armenia* (Basingstoke and New York: Palgrave Macmillan, 2007).

Pearce, Brian, 'Dunsterforce and the Defence of Baku, August–September 1918', *Revolutionary Russia* (1997), 10, 1, 55–71.

Pennar, Jaan, 'Current Soviet Nationality Policy', *Journal of Baltic Studies*, 12, 1 (1981), 5–15.

'Soviet Nationality Policy and the Estonian Communist Elite', in Tonu Parming and Elmar Jarveson (eds.), *A Case Study of a Soviet*

Republic: The Estonian SSR (Boulder, CO: Westview Press, 1978), 5–15.

Phillips, Timothy, *Beslan: The Tragedy of School No. 1* (London: Granta Books, 2007).

Pikhoya, Rudol'f, *Moskva. Kreml'. Vlast': Sorok let posle voyny 1945–1985* (Moscow: Rus'-Olimp, Astrel'AST, 2007).

Pipes, Richard, 'The First Experiment in Soviet National Policy: The Bashkir Republic, 1917–1920', *Russian Review* (1950), vol. 9, no. 4, 303–19.

The Formation of the Soviet Union: Communism and Nationalism 1917–1923, revised edn (Cambridge, MA: Harvard University Press, 1997).

Pirani, Simon, 'Turkmenistan: An Exporter in Transition', in Simon Pirani (ed.), *Russian and CIS Gas Markets and Their Impact on Europe* (Oxford University Press, 2009), 271–315.

Plakans, Andrejs, *The Latvians: A Short History* (Stanford: Hoover Institution Press, 1995).

Planciola, Niccolò, 'Famine in the Steppe: The Collectivization of Agriculture and the Kazak Herdsmen, 1928–1934', *Cahiers du Monde russe*, 45, 1–2 (2004), 137–68.

Pohl, Michaela, '"It Cannot Be that Our Graves Will Be Here": The Survival of Chechen and Ingush Deportees in Kazakhstan, 1944–1957', *Journal of Genocide Research*, 4, 3 (2002), 401–30.

'The "Planet of One Hundred Languages": Ethnic Relations and Soviet Identity in the Virgin Lands', in Nicholas B. Breyfogle, Abby Schrader and Willard Sunderland (eds.), *Peopling the Russian Periphery: Borderland and Colonization in Eurasian History* (London: Routledge, 2007), 238–61.

Polyan, Pavel, *Ne po svoei vole … Istoriya i geografiya prinuditel'nykh migratsii v SSSR* (Moscow: OGI–Memorial, 2001).

Porat, Dina, 'The Holocaust in Lithuania: Some Unique Aspects', in David Cesarani (ed.), *The Final Solution: Origins and Implementation* (London: Routledge, 2002), 159–74.

Prigge, William, 'The Latvian Purges of 1959: A Revision Study', *Journal of Baltic Studies*, 35, 3 (2004), 211–30.

Qahhorov, Akram, 'A Personality Cult Grows in Tajikistan', RFE/RL broadcast, 18 November 2011.

Radkey, Oliver H., *The Election to the Russian Constitutional Assembly of 1917* (Cambridge, MA: Harvard University Press, 1950).

Raun, Toivo U., *Estonia and the Estonians* (Stanford: Hoover Institution Press, 1987).

Remington, Thomas F., *Politics in Russia*, 7th edn (London: Longman, 2011).

Reshetar, John S., *The Ukrainian Revolution, 1917–1920* (Princeton University Press, 1952).

Roper, Steven D., 'Regionalism in Moldova: The Case of Transnistria and Gagauzia', in James Hughes and Gwendolyn Sasse (eds.), *Ethnicity and Territory in the Former Soviet Union* (London: Frank Cass, 2002), 101–22.

Rorlich, Azade-Ayşe, *The Volga Tatars: A Profile in National Resilience* (Stanford: Hoover Institution Press, 1986).

Ross, Cameron, 'Putin's Federal Reforms', in Cameron Ross (ed.), *Russian Politics under Putin* (Manchester University Press, 2004), 155–75.

Rouland, Michael, 'A Nation on Stage: Music and the 1936 Festival of Kazak Arts', in Edmunds (ed.), *Soviet Music*, 181–208.

Sabol, Steven, 'The Creation of Soviet Central Asia: The 1924 National Delimitation', *Central Asian Survey*, 14, 2 (1995), 225–41.
   Russian Colonization and the Genesis of Kazak National Consciousness (Basingstoke: Palgrave, 2003).

Sahadeo, Jeff, 'Epidemic and Empire: Ethnicity, Class and "Civilization" in the 1892 Tashkent Cholera Riot', *Slavic Review*, 64, 1 (2005), 117–39.
   Russian Colonial Society in Tashkent, 1865–1923 (Bloomington: Indiana University Press, 2007).

Sakwa, Richard, 'The CIS: Conflicts of Place and Time', in David Dusseault (ed.), *The CIS: Form or Substance?*, Aleksanteri Papers 2/2007 (Helsinki: Kikimora Publications, 2007), 298–317.

Sandle, Mark and Igor Casu, 'Rumours and Uncertainty in the Borderlands: Soviet Moldavia and the Secret Speech, 1956–1957', *Europe-Asia Studies*, 65 (2013).

Saparov, Arseny, 'From Conflict to Autonomy: The Making of the South Ossetian Autonomous Region 1918–1922', *Europe-Asia Studies*, 62, 1 (2010), 99–123.

Seely, Robert, *Russo-Chechen Conflict, 1800–2000: A Deadly Embrace* (London and Portland: Frank Cass, 2001).

Senn, Alfred Erich, 'The Polish Ultimatum to Lithuania, March 1938', *Journal of Baltic Studies*, 13, 2 (Summer 1982), 144–56.

Service, Robert, *Lenin: A Political Life*, vol. III, *The Iron Ring* (Basingstoke: Macmillan, 1995).

Seytmuratova, Ayshe, 'The Elders of the New National Movement: Recollections', in Allworth (ed.), *Tatars of Crimea*, 155–79.

Sharip, Farkad, 'Kazakhstan President's Son-in-Law Faces Criminal Charges', *Jamestown Foundation*, vol. 4, issue 106, 31 May 2007.

Sheehy, Ann and Bohdan Nahaylo, *The Crimean Tatars, Volga Germans and Meskhetians: Soviet Treatment of Some National Minorities* (London: Minority Rights Group, 1960).

Shnirelman, Victor A., *The Value of the Past: Myths, Identity and Politics in Transcaucasia* (Osaka: National Museum of Ethnology, 2001). Senri Ethnological Studies no. 57.

  Who Gets the Past? Competition for Ancestors among Non-Russian Intellectuals in Russia (Baltimore: Johns Hopkins University Press, 1996).

Shtroma, Aleksandras, 'The Baltic States as Soviet Republics: Tensions and Contradictions', in Graham Smith (ed.), *The Baltic States*, 86–117.

Simon, Gerhard, *Nationalism and Policy toward the Nationalities in the Soviet Union: From Totalitarian Dictatorship to Post-Stalinist Society* (Boulder, CO: Westview Press, 1991).

Slepyan, Kenneth, 'The People's Avengers: The Partisan Movement', in David R. Stone (ed.), *The Soviet Union at War, 1941–1945* (Barnsley: Pen and Sword, 2010), 154–81.

Slezkine, Yuri, 'The USSR as a Communal Apartment, or How a Socialist State Promoted Ethnic Particularism', *Slavic Review*, 53, 2 (Summer 1994), 414–52.

Smele, Jonathan D., *Civil War in Siberia: The Anti-Bolshevik Government of Admiral Kolchak, 1918–1920* (Cambridge University Press, 1997).

Smith, David J., *Estonia: Independence and European Integration* (London: Routledge, 2001).

Smith, Graham (ed.), *The Baltic States: The National Self-Determination of Estonia, Latvia and Lithuania* (London: Macmillan, 1996).

  'The Resurgence of Nationalism', in Graham Smith (ed.), *The Baltic States*, 121–43.

Smith, Hanna, 'The Russian Federation and the European Union: The Shadow of Chechnya', in Debra Johnson and Paul Robinson (eds.), *Perspectives on EU–Russia Relations* (London: Routledge, 2005), 110–127.

Smith, Jeremy, *The Bolsheviks and the National Question, 1917–1923* (London: Macmillan, 1999).

'The Georgian Affair of 1922: Policy Failure, Personality Clash or Power Struggle?', *Europe-Asia Studies*, 50, 3 (1998), 519–44.

'Leadership and Nationalism in the Soviet Republics, 1951–1959', in Jeremy Smith and Ilic (eds.), *Khrushchev in the Kremlin*, 79–93.

'Nation Building and National Conflict in the USSR in the 1920s', *Ab Imperio*, 3, (2001), 246–60.

'The Origins of Soviet National Autonomy', *Revolutionary Russia* (1997), 10, 2, 62–84.

'Republican Authority and Khrushchev's Education Reform in Latvia and Estonia, 1958–1959', in Mertelsmann (ed.), *Sovietization of the Baltic States*, 237–52.

'Stalin as Commissar for Nationalities', in Sarah Davies and James Harris (eds.), *Stalin: A New History* (Cambridge University Press, 2005), 45–62.

Smith, Jeremy and Melanie Ilic (eds.), *Khrushchev in the Kremlin: Policy and Government in the Soviet Union, 1953–1964* (London: Routledge, 2011).

Spector, Regine A., 'The Transformation of Askar Akaev, President of Kyrgyzstan', Berkeley Program in Soviet and Post-Soviet Studies Working Paper Series (Berkeley: University of California, 2004).

Steinwedel, Charles, 'Resettling People, Unsettling the Empire: Migration and the Challenge of Governance, 1861–1917', in Nicholas B. Breyfogle, Abby Schrader and Willard Sunderland (eds.), *Peopling the Russian Periphery: Borderland and Colonization in Eurasian History* (London: Routledge, 2007), 128–47.

Stojko, Wolodymyr, 'Ukrainian National Aspirations and the Russian Provisional Government', in Taras Hunczak (ed.), *The Ukraine, 1917–1921: A Study in Revolution* (Cambridge, MA: Harvard University Press, 1977), 4–32.

Subtelny, Orest, *Ukraine: A History* (University of Toronto Press, 1989).

Suny, Ronald Grigor, *The Baku Commune, 1917–1918: Class and Nationality in the Russian Revolution* (Princeton University Press, 1972).

Looking toward Ararat: Armenia in Modern History (Hoboken, NJ: John Wiley & Sons, 1993).

The Making of the Georgian Nation, 2nd edn (Bloomington: Indiana University Press, 1994).

The Revenge of the Past: Nationalism, Revolution, and the Collapse of the Soviet Union (Stanford University Press, 1993).

The Soviet Experiment: Russia, the USSR, and the Successor States (Oxford University Press, 1998).

Suraska, Wisła, *How the Soviet Union Disappeared: An Essay on the Causes of Dissolution* (Durham, NC: Duke University Press, 1999).

Suutari, Pekka, 'Going beyond the Border: National Cultural Policy and the Development of Musical Life in Soviet Karelia, 1920–1940', in Edmunds (ed.), *Soviet Music*, 163–80.

Swain, Geoffrey, '"Cleaning up Soviet Latvia": The Bureau for Latvia (Latburo), 1944–1947', in Mertelsmann (ed.), *Sovietization of the Baltic States*, 63–84.

'Divided We Fall: Division within the National Partisans of Vidzeme and Latgale, Fall 1945', *Journal of Baltic Studies*, 38, 2 (June 2007), 195–214.

Swietochowski, Tadeusz, *Russian Azerbaijan, 1905–1920: The Shaping of National Identity in a Muslim Community* (Cambridge University Press, 1985).

Taagepera, Rein, *Estonia: Return to Independence* (Boulder, CO: Westview Press, 1993).

'Inequality Indices for Baltic Farm Size Distribution, 1929–1940', *Journal of Baltic Studies*, 3, 1 (Spring 1972), 26–34.

Tauger, Mark B., 'The 1932 Harvest and the Famine of 1933', *Slavic Review*, 50, 1 (1991), 70–89.

Ter Minassian, Taline, *Erevan: la construction d'une capitale à l'époque soviétique* (Presses Universitaires de Rennes, 2007).

Tishkov, Valery, *Ethnicity, Nationalism and Conflict in and after the Soviet Union: The Mind Aflame* (London: Sage, 1997).

Titov, Alexander, 'The 1961 Party Programme and the Fate of Khrushchev's Reforms', in Melanie Ilic and Jeremy Smith (eds.), *Soviet State and Society under Nikita Khrushchev* (London: Routledge, 2009), 8–25.

Toft, Monica Duffy, 'Multinationality, Regions and State-Building: The Failed Transition in Georgia', in James Hughes and Gwendolyn Sasse (eds.), *Ethnicity and Territory in the Former Soviet Union* (London: Frank Cass, 2002), 123–42.

Tomoff, Kiril, 'Uzbek Music's Separate Path: Interpreting "Anticosmopolitanism" in Stalinist Central Asia, 1949–1952', *Russian Review*, 63 (April 2004), 212–40.

United States Institute of Peace, 'Special Report: The War in Tajikistan Three Years On' (Washington, DC: United States Institute of Peace, November 1995).

van Ree, Erik, 'Stalin and the National Question', *Revolutionary Russia* (1994), 7, 2, 214–38.

Verluise, Pierre, *Armenia in Crisis: The 1988 Earthquake* (Detroit: Wayne State University Press, 1995).

Volkogonov, Dmitri, *The Rise and Fall of the Soviet Empire: Political Leaders from Lenin to Gorbachev* (London: HarperCollins, 1999).

   Stalin: Triumph and Tragedy (Rocklin, CA: Prima Publishing, 1996).

von Hagen, Mark, *War in a European Borderland: Occupations and Occupation Plans in Galicia and Ukraine, 1914–1918* (Seattle: University of Washington Press, 2007).

Williams, Brian Glyn, 'Hidden Ethnocide in the Soviet Muslim Borderlands: the Ethnic Cleansing of the Crimean Tatars', *Journal of Genocide Research*, 4, 3 (2002), 357–73.

Wilson, Andrew, *Ukrainian Nationalism in the 1990s: A Minority Faith* (Cambridge University Press, 1997).

   The Ukrainians: Unexpected Nation (New Haven: Yale University Press, 2002).

Wood, Alan, *Russia's Frozen Frontier: A History of Siberia and the Russian Far East, 1851–1991* (London: Bloomsbury, 2011).

Yemelianova, Galina, *Russia and Islam: A Historical Survey* (Basingstoke: Palgrave, 2002).

Zaprudnik, Jan, *Belarus: At a Crossroads in History* (Boulder, CO: Westview, 1993).

Zberev, Aleksey, 'Etnicheskiye konflikty na Kavkaze, 1988–1994', in *Spornye granitsy na Kavkaze* (Moscow: Ves' Mir izdatel'stvo, 1996).

Zdravomyslov, A. G., *Mezhnatsional'nye konflikty v postsovetskom prostrane* (Moscow: Aspekt Press, 1997).

Index

Index